Essays on Islamic Philosophy and Science

STUDIES IN ISLAMIC PHILOSOPHY AND SCIENCE

Published under the auspices of
the Society for the Study of Islamic Philosophy and Science

ESSAYS ON ISLAMIC PHILOSOPHY AND SCIENCE

Edited by George F. Hourani

State University of New York Press
Albany, 1975

Essays on Islamic Philosophy and Science

First Edition

Published by State University of New York Press,
99 Washington Avenue, Albany, New York 12210

Printed in the United States of America

Library of Congress Cataloging in Publication Data

Hourani, George Fadlo, comp.
Essays on Islamic philosophy and science.

(Studies in Islamic philosophy and science).
A collection of papers originally presented at two conferences sponsored by State University of New York and Society for the Study of Islamic Philosophy and Science; held at S.U.N.Y., Binghamton, Apr. 30-May 1, 1970, and Columbia University, Apr. 23-25, 1971, respectively.

Includes bibliographical references.
1. Philosophy, Islamic—Addresses, essays, lectures.
2. Islam and science—Addresses, essays, lectures.
I. Title. II. Series.
B741.H68 181'.07 74-13493
ISBN 0-87395-224-3
ISBN 0-87395-225-1 (microfiche)

CONTENTS

PREFACE

The collection of articles brought together in this volume grew out of two conferences on Islamic philosophy and science, which took place in the State of New York in 1970 and 1971. The first was organized on a modest scale by faculty members of the State University of New York and held at the University's Center at Binghamton, 30 April–1 May 1970, with financial support from The Research Foundation of the State University of New York. The enthusiasm of the participants led to the creation of the Society for the Study of Islamic Philosophy and Science, an informal association whose original Executive Committee has comprised Muhsin Mahdi, President; George F. Hourani, Vice-President; Parviz Morewedge, Secretary-Treasurer; Nicholas Rescher, and Ehsan Yar-Shater. This Society then sponsored the second conference, held at Columbia University, New York, 23–25 April 1971. Through the efforts of Dr. Morewedge, many of the leading scholars in these fields of study, from North America, Europe, and the Near East, gathered for this event. Financial support was provided by a score of universities in the United States and Canada, as well as the Pahlavi Foundation, the Ben and Abby Grey Foundation, the Islamic Cultural Center of New York, and the University of Tehran. These combined efforts made possible a large and successful conference.

At both conferences a desire was widely expressed to publish the papers, thus making available in a permanent form the wealth of new research and reflection contained in them. Thanks to the cooperation of the authors in offering their papers and revising them, all but three of the formal papers presented at the two conferences are published here. A note of sadness has been added, however, by the death of two contributors since they submitted their articles, our esteemed colleagues Gustave E. von Grunebaum and Martin Levey.

All these articles are devoted to aspects of the thought of medieval Islam, ranging from Māshā'allāh in the eighth century A.D. to Mullā Ṣadra in the seventeenth. No apology is needed for regarding the latter as a medieval philosopher, for we have come to realize the distortion in the older view that medieval Islamic philosophy received its death sentence from Ghazālī, then breathed its last gasp through Ibn Rushd in the twelfth century. The continued vitality of philosophy in Iran is illustrated in several articles, and the two by Fazlur Rahman show in a striking manner how Mullā Ṣadrā refined the main lines of cosmology and metaphysics without breaking from the classical framework of concepts.

Without any design on the part of the program directors of the conferences or this editor, the majority of articles published here are about Persian philosophers and scientists. This preponderance reflects both the facts of intellectual history in medieval Islam and a recent trend in the study of that history, since Henri Corbin, Seyyed Hossein Nasr and others have drawn our attention to the interest of some formerly neglected later Persian thinkers. Still, to attain a balanced view we should not forget that most Persians down to Mullā Ṣadrā and beyond continued to write on philosophy and science in Arabic, as Europeans did in Latin until almost as late a period. Besides, the overwhelming cultural fact was Islam as a religion and a civilization, and the national origin and language of expression of individual scholars were generally considered of minor importance in their own times.

The combination of philosophy and science in the conferences, the present volume, and the scope of the Society's concerns is a natural one in the context of medieval Islam. As in ancient Greece, the boundary between the two fields was not sharply defined; both were included in the learned meaning of the Arabic word *al-ḥikma,* literally "wisdom," a Qur᾿anic term that was used to translate the Greek *sophia* as well as *philosophia*. The major distinction made between branches of knowledge contrasted the traditional or religious sciences, derived from or serving to explain revelation, with the intellectual or philosophical sciences, whose method was the use of reason to explain the data of human experience. The latter were also known as the sciences of the ancients, because of the widespread awareness of their origins in the ancient Near East and Greece.

In editing these articles I have not imposed uniform transcriptions of Arabic, Persian, and other names and words from non-Latin alphabets, but have required only consistency within each article, including its title. The articles are arranged in a roughly chronological order of subject matter, without separation of philosophical from scientific articles. For the convenience of lay readers two appendixes have been added, providing brief biographical and lexical information.

Acknowledgements are due to the editors and publisher of *Agora* for permission to reprint Martin Levey's article, which appeared in that journal in Spring 1970; slight editorial changes have been made in the article as published here. I am grateful to Frank E. Peters and Robert Kunz for many valuable editorial suggestions. Finally, to all those who have contributed in diverse ways to the conferences and the publication of this volume I am truly thankful.

George F. Hourani

RELATIONS OF PHILOSOPHY AND SCIENCE: A GENERAL VIEW

GUSTAVE E. VON GRUNEBAUM

We have come to take it for granted that within any one synchronistic section of history all elements of the economic and social, the artistic and the scientific worlds not only connect but hang together. We can admit the part played by chance; the mutation of moods and concerns is within our ken; primacy may be assigned to politics or to cultural drives; but wherever we may locate starting point or apex, we feel certain that within a delimited political or cultural unit contemporaneity, at the very least, means more than simultaneity, that in fact it implies, if it is not constituted by, actual logical or structural coherence, which itself permits analysis into principles, be they experiential, aspirational, or identifiable as scientific assumptions and metaphors. This iron circle of coherence seems to be firmest, and the interactions of the manifestations of the spirit of the age most immediate and inevitable, at the point where philosophy and science touch and are welded together, or perhaps simply transform and pass one into the other. It has been axiomatic, and it is doubtless borne out by Western intellectual history from the pre-Socratics to our own day, that any change in our outlook on the world as a whole, any change in our view of the capabilities of the human mind (and by no means of reason alone), will directly affect or rather will recondition the sciences as to material considered, methods, and ends. A shift in the concept of the universe, religious or philosophical, brings about without fail a shift in the kind of science that will be cultivated—and the reverse can also be true.

It is not my intention to proclaim any culture, and certainly neither our own nor the kindred one of Islam, as unique in point of coherence or lack of it. It is, however, my purpose to point out that in the case of the Islamic secular sciences, which I view as largely coinciding with what the Arabs themselves would designate as the "foreign" sciences and which include, in our terms, both the natural sciences and philosophy (that is, metaphysics and, by some definitions, logic and epistemology as well), this interconnection and interpenetration of *'ilm* and *falsafa* does not exist to the same extent as in some other cultures. That is, adoption or rejection of an emanationist view of the universe or, again, adoption or rejection of the eternity of the world cannot be shown to have significantly shaped or reconditioned the *descriptio totius mundi*, or the several sciences that investigate the particulars of our universe—be they botany, zoology, anatomy or, even more sensitive to any alteration of the world view, astronomy.

This is by no means to deny that astrology, for example, drew for its justification, in a spiritual setting in which it was essentially a foreign body, on concepts of Aristotelian and Stoic philosophical and scientific thought, nor am I unaware of the fact that the greatest scientific encyclopedias were composed by men outstanding in philosophy. Yet it is hard to see the link that joins precisely this and no other method of exploration with any given philosophical preconceptions—unless this link be found in psychology, or more exactly in the adaptations made by different thinkers to a doctrinal heritage essentially Aristotelian.

In the occidental tradition epistemology or, if you prefer, the search for the forms and limits of the human mind in its discovery and verification of the internal and external universe, has from an early age played an important role in the endeavors of the philosopher, and this role has tended to grow, perhaps beyond its due stature, as we approach modern times. At any rate, it has been this concern with *Erkenntniskritik* that has formed a regulative link between philosophy proper and the individual natural and other sciences, and in turn it has been in *Erkenntniskritik* that scientific progress has had one dependable lever through which to make itself felt in the philosophical interpretation of the world. Not that this was the only link. The perspectives and changes in philosophical outlook have often gravely affected the aspirations and realizations of the sciences.

In the world of classical Islam, which in time coincides with the early and high Middle Ages of the West, this concern for epistemology, this peculiar type of self-interpretation, was undoubtedly less compelling, or compulsive, than among the Greeks and their occidental successors. The categorization and classification of knowledge were to reach considerable subtlety, above all in the service of law and ethics and, beyond them, of theology; yet an approach that would lead to a typology of *'ilm*, and consequently of the several *'ulūm*, as an expression of the intellectual equipment of man, its structure and inherent limitation, from which Revelation might conceivably offer escape when required, was not within the horizon of concerns. Islam as revealed, the world as unveiled, were perhaps too deliberately tailored to the measure of man to motivate an untiring search for the extreme circumference of possible human outreach, in which introspection, hubris, and despair might at times project the borders of the transcendental—the inaccessible but for divine grace—into infinity, only to be reined in again in moody surrender. More even-tempered, classical Islam was spared such passionate efforts to find religious and philosophical certainty through endless assessment of the carrying power of the human mind, except for the tempting crisis of total escape when *'aql* gave itself to the quest of *fanā'*.

But if we compare and contrast classical Islam with kindred cultures, there was, or so it appears to this observer, less inclination to coordinate epistemology with metaphysics on the one hand and empirical science on the other. In law the *uṣūl al-fiqh* did directly affect the *furū'*; and from the *furū'*, and indirectly from the socio-political universe that they circumscribed in legal-substantive and deontological terms, there were repercussions upon the *uṣūl*. But in science and philosophy nothing comparable was attained or even aimed at. Was Ibn an-Nafīs guided by a particular and novel view of man in his pioneering discovery? And if he was—and there is no evidence of this—was this concept coordinated, or at least ought it to have been coordinated in his view and that of his contemporaries, with an epistemology, and this epistemology again with a comprehensive world view whose presence would stimulate, whose absence inhibit anatomical study? His intellectual experiment of having an isolated, spontaneously generated human being discover, through his own *'aql* by means of *naẓar* and the technique of *istidlāl*, general and particular facts determining the structure of the material and the spiritual universe, of having a human intellect, stimulated by observation and experience, deduce an all-inclusive theologico-political system and thus arrive by rational necessity at the perfection of Islam—this experiment does not lose a moment over the definition of man's cognitive powers, the relation of judgement and external world (or reality), in short, over those *Erkenntnisvermögen* to which Kant as a matter of course will devote the first section of his *Anthropology*. And what is true for Ibn an-Nafīs' "self-taught theologian," is true with barely a qualification for the "self-taught philosopher" of his predecessor, Ibn Ṭufail. Certainly, the general tendency of the declining Middle Ages to concentrate all intellectual effort on consolidation of the community, by means of an ever more exclusive dedication to law and theology, did affect and finally paralyze independent research in areas of secondary importance or of doubtful usefulness to what the community had decided were its primary needs. But within the circles of the *falāsifa* and among the devotees of the *'ulūm al-'ajam*, the pursuit of philosophy and the pursuit of natural science were only loosely connected by similar mental attitudes, the tradition of a distinctive kind of training, and, above all, by habituation to the authoritative Greek tradition that imposed, if not a measure of universality, at any rate a predisposition to deal with both branches of knowledge, the theoretical and the (subservient) empirical.

It seems doubtful that this coordination of the three manifestations of the "secular" scientific spirit (philosophy, epistemology, empirical natural sciences) would have been so inadequate had the secular *'ulūm al-'ajam* actually been indigenous or, more precisely, Muslim sciences; in other words, had their cultivation been indispensable for the maintenance and growth of Islam as a doctrine, an order, a way of life. The "Arab" sciences are closely bound together. From prosody to the *furūʿ al-fiqh* it is possible to trace a chain of connections consciously established, the unity of the sciences being based on their service to religion, and specifically to the Holy Book and the Sacred Tradition, whose understanding and whose utilization for the structuring of Muslim society and a Muslim life required studies of various kinds, precisely those which the Muslim scholars classified together as those of the Arabs, as their own. In this sphere, the *uṣūl al-fiqh,* the theory of *tafsīr,* the critique of the *ḥadith,* do provide the epistemological link between theology (which takes the place of philosophy) and the individual sciences. In this sphere, the functional interdependence is every whit as tight as among the Greeks of the great period, at the height of Latin scholasticism and in the post-Kantian (I should prefer to say, post-Cartesian) era of occidental thought.

To the "silent majority" of classical Islam (including Jews and Christians integrated into its civilization) philosophy was suspect and certainly not a need, while the natural sciences were an objectionable or unobjectionable luxury. The community might enjoy their pursuit, it might, in a manner hard to define, profit by it, but their assiduous cultivation was not essential for the community's survival as the community of true believers. There were sciences of an intermediate sphere—geography, for instance, descriptive, political, astronomical—where changing concepts of need and changing views of purpose and method significantly modified the structure of the science in question, in this particular instance to the detriment of mathematical knowledge and the advantage of descriptive and ethnographic knowledge. This was a victory of concern for the earth and especially the *mamlakat al-islām* over speculation about the universe, and perhaps also a victory of the Iranian over the Hellenizing tradition. To the extent that such sciences could be expected to yield results of which the community stood in direct need, the interrelations among scope, method, and world view were firmly embedded in their intellectual structures and remained functionally operative. That such should have been less the case in geography than in law is but an indication of the relative indispensability of the "Arab" sciences to what the community considered its primary raison d'être.

Lacking support as they did in the fundamental aspirations and institutional needs of the *umma,* indeed more often than not being considered an actual or potential menace to the existence of the community as defined and determined by divine ruling, the extraordinary vitality over some five centuries of philosophy and, perhaps for an even longer period, of the secular sciences is an irresistible and justified cause of that *ʿajab,* that thrilled wonderment of what God has wrought, which is the sentiment that the Muslim writer and artist aspires to evoke.

MĀSHĀ'ALLĀH: SOME SASANIAN AND SYRIAC SOURCES

David Pingree

Māshāʾallāh ibn Atharī,[1] a Jew (and perhaps a Persian Jew) from Baṣra, first appears as an authority on astrology as a member of the commission which determined for al-Manṣūr that the propitious moment for the founding of Baghdād fell on 30 July 762. He continued to have an influential position at the ʿAbbāsid court throughout the reigns of the succeeding caliphs, and is said to have lived on into that of al-Maʾmūn, which began in 813, though the latest secure date that we have for him is 809. He wrote prolifically on the various branches of the art of astrology; and, though only a half dozen of his works (together with numerous citations of varying authenticity) survive in Arabic, many others are preserved in Latin translations. His dependence on Sasanian sources for his astrological history and for many of his computations of planetary positions used in casting horoscopes has been discussed elsewhere in detail;[2] these studies have established his knowledge of Pahlavī. This paper is intended to clarify the tradition of one of the Pahlavī sources he had available when he wrote about genethlialogy (natal astrology), and to reveal the possibility of his having used two Syriac texts in composing what appears to be the first detailed discussion in Arabic of the principles of Aristotelian physics and meteorology, and a virtually unique description of a non-Ptolemaic Greek model of planetary motion. Before embarking on this project, however, it may be useful briefly to review something of what we know about Sasanian genethlialogy.

It is affirmed by Zoroastrian tradition that the Sasanian monarchs of the third century sponsored the translation of scientific texts both from Greece and from India into Pahlavī,[3] and that these translations were revised in the sixth century under Khusrau Anūshirwān.[4] These affirmations have been amply confirmed in the case of astronomy;[5] they will shortly be shown to be true of astrology as well.

Unfortunately, little of an astrological nature survives in Pahlavī itself; scientific texts in general were not preserved by those Zoroastrians who survived the Muslim invasions and resisted conversion in Iran or who fled to the west coast of India. The principal extant passage that is relevant is found in the fifth and sixth chapters of the *Bundahišn* in which the nativity of Gayomart is discussed.[6] In this horoscope the ascendent was in Cancer

19° with Tīshtar or Sirius,[7] in the Khūrta (lunar constellation) Azarag, which corresponds to the Indian nakṣatra Āśleṣā (Cancer 16;40°–30°). Each of the planets was in its bālist or exaltation save for Mercury, whose exaltation, Virgo, is removed from the Sun's, Aries, by more than its maximum elongation; this planet, therefore, was placed with Venus in the latter's exaltation and its own dejection, Pisces. The position of the ascendent is undoubtedly a reflection of an attempt to arrive at a noon-epoch for the creation with the Sun in its Greek exaltation, Aries 19° (the Sun's Indian exaltation is 9° before this). The editors' restoration of Padispar or Aśvinī for the Sun's khūrta is, therefore, an error; one needs rather the second khūrta, Pēsh-parvīz or Bharaṇī (Aries 13;20°–26;40°).

This Sasanian horoscope is quite different from the normal Greek thema mundi, with which it has been compared. The Hermetic thema is based on the doctrine of the planetary domiciles:[8] the Sun, Jupiter, Mars, and Venus are at 15° of their masculine domiciles, the Moon, Saturn, and Mercury at 15° of their feminine domiciles, and the ascendent at Cancer 15°. Rather, it is the Indian horoscope of a mahāpurusa (great man) in which all the planets are at their exaltations. The earliest occurrence of this mahāpuruṣayoga in India is in the *Yavanajātaka* composed by Sphujidhvaja in 269/70;[9] elements of this text are independently known to have been familiar to Sasanian astrologers.[10] But it has already been noted that the Greek exaltation of the Sun has been used rather than the Indian; this is also true of the exaltations of the lunar nodes, and a Byzantine version of this Zoroastrian horoscope, more complete than the *Bundahišn's*, indicates that all of the exaltations were taken from a Greek rather than from an Indian source.[11]

The other astrological elements in the *Bundahišn* are equally a mixture of Indian and Greek materials. The spheres of influence of the twelve astrological places do not allow us to distinguish between the two traditions. The specifically Indian navāṃśas (ninths of zodiacal signs) are not mentioned, but one further Indian concept is apparent—that of the chords by which the planets are bound to the chariot of the Sun and which help to regulate their velocity; these are certainly derived from the chords of wind manipulated by demons standing at the planets' mandoccas (apogees of the manda-epicycles) and śīghroccas (apogees of the śīghra-epicycles) according to the *Sūryasiddhānta*.[12] The *Bundahišn* correctly gives the length of the superior planets' chords as 180°, and the length of Venus'—2831' or 47;11°—is quite reasonable. But the figure for Mercury's, 1850' or 30;50°, is surely wrong; one must emend it to 1350' or 22;30°. It should be noted that in the *Zīk i Shahriyārān* of Yazdijird III the maximum equation of the anomaly for Venus was 47;11°, that for Mercury 21;30°.[13]

Though little else of astrology survives in Pahlavī, we do have from the early 'Abbāsid period a number of Arabic translations of Sasanian works on this subject. Of these the earliest appears to be the *Kitāb al-mawālīd wa aḥkāmihā* ascribed to Zaradusht[14]. The long introduction indicates that it was supposed to have been translated from Zoroaster's language (perhaps Avestan is meant) into the familiar Persian language (presumably Pahlavī) by Māhānkard ibn Mihrziyār for the marzbān Māhūyah ibn Māhānāhīdh; this latter individual is evidently identical with the marzbān of Marw, Māhôê the son of Māhpanāh, who betrayed Yazdijird III about 642. Māhānkard's version was in turn translated into Arabic by Saʿid ibn Khurāsānkhurrah for the iṣbahbad Sinbād in the time of Abū Muslim; Sinbād is the magus of Nīshāpūr who set out to avenge Abū Muslim after his murder by al-Manṣūr on 12 February 755, and who was himself killed shortly thereafter. Assuming that this story is essentially correct, our present Arabic manuscripts make available to us a translation made in about 750 in Khurāsān of a Pahlavī recension of about 650 of an older Sasanian handbook of genethlialogy. This conclusion is strengthened by the inclusion in the work of a horoscope which can be dated astronomically 7 October 549[15] (i.e., during the reign of Khusrau Anūshirwān, who is mentioned in the introduction) and by the general character of the astrology taught.

Though the investigation of this text is still in a preliminary stage, it seems safe to conclude that the genethlialogy Zaradusht prescribes is basically Hellenistic, and in particular is heavily dependent on the work of Dorotheus of Sidon, a Greek astrological poet of the second half of the first century A.D.[16] Zaradusht misrepresents Dorotheus as the King of Egypt as the Pahlavî version of the Sidonian also did, and the contents of some Dorothean passages in Zaradusht and of the Arabic translation of Dorotheus agree while their wording does not. From this it is clear that Zaradusht, or rather Māhānkard in whose comments Dorotheus is cited, had independent access to the Pahlavī Dorotheus. This circumstance also tends to validate the historical account in the introduction to Zaradusht.

The text of Dorotheus himself must next be examined as it is one the most fascinating and instructive examples of the transmission of science, appearing, as it does, in whole or in part during the Middle Ages in seven or eight languages and in places as far apart as England and India. Originally composed in hexameters between A.D. 50 and 75, the Greek text is now lost save for some hundreds of quoted lines; but its influence on later astrologers was such that long prose summaries of its teachings can be recovered from the works of such late classical astrologers as Firmicus Maternus, Hephaestio of Thebes, Rhetorius of Egypt, and pseudo-Hermes Trismegistus.[17] According to Ibn Nawbakht, one of Hārūn al-Rashīd's astrologers, it was translated into Persian (i.e., Pahlavī) in the time of Ardashīr I (224–40) and Shāpūr I (240–72)[18]; the fact that in Book III there is placed a horoscope which can be dated 24 September or 20 October 281[19] might support a somewhat later date, though this insertion might as well be a result of the activities of the redactor who revised the text in about 400. This later editor's work is evident in Book III on the haylaj (ἀφέτης, prorogator) and the kadkhudāh (κύριος τῆς γενέσως, lord of the nativity), in Book IV on the revolution of the years of nativities, and in Book V on catarchic astrology (relating to commencements). In the first of these three books he inserts a horoscope whose date he gives as 2 Mihr 96 Darīnūs (i.e. era of Diocletian), and which can be dated astronomically 26 February 381;[20] in the next, a citation from Vettius Valens, whose 'Ανθολογίαι composed in the last half of the second century, were translated into Pahlavī as the *Bizīdajāt* in the middle of the third[21]; and in the last, references to the Indian theory of the nuh baḥrs or navāmsas (ninths of a zodiacal sign). Thus, as the original Zaradusht text, having a Hellenistic origin, was revised in Sasanian Iran in about 550 and then expanded with material from the Pahlavī Dorotheus in about 650, so the latter was revised in about 400, when it was expanded with material both from the Pahlavī Valens and from a Pahlavī translation of a Sanskrit text.

This revised Sasanian version of Dorotheus was translated into Arabic, apparently by ʿUmar ibn al-Farrukhān al-Ṭabarī, in about 800.[22] Already it had been influential in the earliest stages of Islamic genethlialogy, not only through Zaradusht, but also through a pseudo-Dorothean treatise which contains eleven horoscopes datable for the years 765 to 768.[23] But its main influence at this time was through its being the primary source for Māshāʾallāh's *Kitāb al-mawālīd*, from which it also passed into the more widespread treatise of Māshāʾallāh's pupil, Abū ʿAlī Yaḥyā al-Khayyāṭ.[24] Not only did Māshāʾallāh derive much of his methodology from Dorotheus; he even lifted Dorothous' examples recording personal observations and presented them as if from his own files.[25]

After its translation into Arabic Dorotheus' work became the source of much of the genethlialogy of the ninth century, strongly influencing the translator, ʿUmar ibn al-Farrukhān, and such other authorities as Sahl ibn Bishr, al-Ṣaymarī, Abū Maʿshar, and al-Qaṣrānī. Subsequently the Dorothean tradition had an enormous impact not only on later Islamic astrology, but also on that of Byzantium, the Latin West, the Jews, and the Indians. The history of this tradition will be treated in detail in my forthcoming edition of the genuine and spurious opera of Dorotheus of Sidon; here I shall attempt only a brief characterization of two doctrines in the Dorothean tradition of genethlialogy which the Sasanians developed in new ways and which Māshāʾallāh adopted.

Dorotheus is an extremely practical author, totally uninterested in the theoretical foundations of astrology. Basically, of course, he relies on the same union of Hellenistic mathematical astronomy and physics with the Pythagorean doctrine of opposites and Mesopotamian astral omina that all other astrologers had used since the creation of astrology in Ptolemaic Egypt. He emphasizes more than others, however, the various κλῆροι or lots, and vastly expands the practice of catarchic astrology. His most innovative contribution, however, was in the development of methods of continuous horoscopy that allowed the astrologer to advise and collect fees from his clients throughout their lives. There are two basic methods that he employed. One is the assumption of the revolution through the zodiac at a given velocity of a point whose changing positions in relation to the fixed points of the native's geniture determine the varying circumstances of his life; this moving point is clearly derived from the prorogator or ἀφέτης. Dorotheus calls it the χρονοκράτωρ and has it travel at the rate of one zodiacal sign a year; the Sasanians developed from this elaborate systems of qismas and intihā's each divided into four varieties and applied to historical astrology as well as, in part, to genethlialogy. The second method is that of the ἀντιγένεσις in which a new horoscope is cast for each anniversary of the native's birth and compared with his geniture; as the planets transit the various τόποι in the base-nativity they decide the events of each year. This theory is the origin of the Indian doctrine of the aṣṭakavarga, and also of the Sasanian method of casting the horoscopes of vernal equinoxes, which became the fundamental technique of historical astrology. Māshāʾallāh's works demonstrate his adherence both to the original Dorothean forms of these methods as applied to genethlialogy, and also to their Sasanian derivatives applied to the astrological interpretation of history.

In the various works of Māshāʾallāh that have hitherto been studied no interest in theoretical explanations of phenomena has been evident, only an assiduous devotion to application. But in the corpus of his surviving works there is one that is unique in going counter to this general impression of the intellectual limitations of the man, while at the same time possessing some characteristics which indicate that it belongs to the earliest phase of Islamic science. The correctness of its attribution to Māshāʾallāh cannot now be absolutely affirmed, though there is, on the other hand, no definite reason for questioning it.

This treatise in Arabic is lost, but survives in a Latin translation probably made by Gerard of Cremona in the twelfth century. The Latin was twice printed at Nuremberg in 1504 and in 1549;[26] I have used the later edition. It might be of interest here briefly to summarize the contents of its 27 chapters as an indication of what was known of physics and planetary theory in late eighth century Baghdād.

The work falls into three sections: chapters 1–7 are on Aristotelian physics modified to allow for a Creator, and with them go chapters 25–27 on meteorology; the remaining chapters, 8–24, constitute a separate treatise on astronomy. Māshāʾallāh begins in chapter 1 by defining the eighth sphere and emphasizing the regularity and consequent predictability of its circular motion. This sphere, however, though incorruptible and unchanging, was preconceived by God and then realized in time through creation; it is not eternal in Aristotle's sense. The seven planetary spheres were similarly preconceived by the Creator before the creation together with all their various motions. The celestial spheres, then, are bereft of free will, as is also the world of the four elements. This makes possible predictions concerning terrestrial events as the two luminaries, which are efficient causes, travel through the zodiac.

For Māshā'allāh the Creator must know his creation before it is made manifest; otherwise celestial motions would not be periodic. He attacks a doctrine that he specifically ascribes to the Indians according to which, although God (i.e., Brahma) is the cause of things, He does not know His own creation.[27] Therefore, Māshā'allāh believes that the variety of the creation is deliberate on God's part; so that, while we may in a general sense know the future through the predictability of the periodic motions of the planets, we cannot know all of the future as we cannot conceive of all of the variety conceived of by God. Specifically, we remain ignorant of the process and operation of God's creativity, and of its quantity, duration, and time.

The succeeding chapters, 2–7, expound orthodox Aristotelian physics with internested spheres of earth, water, air, and fire, each possessing its standard attributes. The two varieties of linear motion appropriate to the four sublunar elements and their mixtures explain the physical and chemical processes of this world, while the circular motions of the celestial spheres exempt them from such instability. The immutability of the celestial spheres and the changeability of the sublunar region lead Māshā'allāh to regard the motion of the former as being, as it were, the sowing of the seeds of the latter. Clearly this is Peripateticism tailored for the astrologer.

Following this elementary exposition is the treatise on astronomy, beginning with a proof of the Sun's having a greater magnitude than the earth, derived, according to Māshā'allāh, from a work by Theon on the composition of the celestial spheres.[28] Next our author demonstrates that the Sun is self-luminous while the Moon is a reflector; he does not note that this introduces a differentiation into the quality of celestial matter that had in the earlier, Aristotelian section been denied. He then describes a celestial coordinate-system consisting of three great circles (the equator, the local meridian, and the local horizon), three diameters (one connecting the intersections of the equator and the horizon, one connecting the poles of the horizon, and the last connecting the poles of the equator), and seven points (the end points of the three diameters together with the center of the earth).

Māshā'allāh proceeds to discuss the absence of self-luminosity in the planets, the apparent variations in their magnitudes and in the intensities of their brightness, and the variability of eclipse-observations depending on the terrestrial station. Several further chapters are devoted to describing the effect on observation of changing one's station and then he comes to his most interesting section, the description of geometric models of planetary motion. Though these are surely Greek in origin and though Māshāʾallāh refers to Ptolemy, they lack the latter's refinements of simple eccentric-epicyclic models, the equants and the crank-mechanisms, as do also Indian adaptations of similar Hellenistic models.

The section begins with a generalized eccentric-epicyclic model which Māshāʾallāh erroneously ascribes to the Moon, thus giving that planet both an eccentric deferent revolving from west to east and an epicycle revolving in the same direction and producing retrogression. Māshāʾallāh would surely be unique in the annals of astronomy in teaching lunar retrogression except that he does deny this phenomenon by asserting that the velocity of the eccentric deferent is greater than that of the epicycle. His model is equivalent to the standard Indian lunar model with the Moon at the center of the epicycle and its ucca on the circumference. For the Sun Māshāʾallāh proposes an eccentric, and for the star-planets a simple combination of eccentric deferent and epicycle. There is no equant and no crank-mechanism for the Moon and Mercury, and there are no parameters in our text. These planetary models are identical with those known to Āryabhaṭa in 499 from a Greek source translated into Sanskrit.[29]

Another theory similar to the Indians', though one that goes back to Aristotle, is Māshāʾallāh's assumption that all the mean planets travel equal spatial distances in equal times, so that the radii of their orbits are inversely proportionate to their sidereal periods.[30] However, he also cites Ptolemy's opinion regarding the existence of ten spheres (in the earlier, Aristotelian part of his treatise only eight were mentioned); beyond the seven planetary spheres he claims that Ptolemy places the sphere of the fixed stars, the sphere of the zodiac, and a stationary reference-sphere. Ptolemy indeed, in the *Planetary Hypotheses,* does posit ten spheres, but he places the sphere of the zodiac below that of the fixed stars.[31] In this discussion of the order and number of the celestial spheres Māshāʾallāh calls Mercury "the scribe" and Mars "the red one," names which indicate a non-Indian source though, unfortunately, not possessing any greater specificity.[32] But perhaps there is a probability in favor of Syria as the place of origin of the text upon which Māshāʾallāh primarily depended, because of the occurrence, though in corrupt forms, of the Syriac names of the months; this would fit in with the knowledge the author displays of Ptolemy, whose works existed in Syriac.[33]

The true nature of Māshāʾallāh's treatment of his source, however, is indicated by his statement that at the time of the Flood the fixed stars Cor Leonis, Cor Scorpionis, Vultur, and Piscis were in certain degrees of the zodiac, but that now their longitudes have increased; the basis for correcting stellar longitudes is said to be the value of procession ascribed to Cor Leonis in the tables (i.e., in the Ptolemaic *Handy Tables*).[34] This statement represents that union of Greek and Sasanian elements that is characteristic of early ᶜAbbāsid astronomy; the identification of the beginning of a cosmic period with the Flood is Sasanian.[35]

The conclusion of Māshāʾallāh's treatise is a brief explanation of the origination of meteorological phenomena and the growth of plants in terms of the Aristotelian physics expounded at the beginning. The text, then, as indicated above, consists of a tract on Peripatetic cosmology in which, though the universe is regarded as created, the five elements retain their Aristotelian characteristics and in which the motions of the celestial orbs are regarded as the efficient causes of the phenomena of the sublunar region. This treatise probably had a Syriac source and might be connected with Ḥarrān. Into it Māshāʾallāh has inserted a discussion of astronomy based largely, it seems, upon another Syriac original which in turn was aware of Theon and Ptolemy, but whose planetary models represent a non-Ptolemaic Greek tradition which is similar to one that can be recognized in Sanskrit texts of the late fifth and later centuries. Moreover, into both parts Māshāʾallāh has introduced extraneous material; into the first the argument against the Indian theory of Brahma, and into the second the apparently Sasanian identification of the beginning of a cosmic period with the Flood. It is not a profound piece of work, but it is not without some interest.

NOTES

1 See my forthcoming article in the *Dictionary of Scientific Biography*, *s.v.* Māshāʾ allāh.

2 E. S. Kennedy and D. Pingree, *The Astrological History of Māshāʾ allāh* (Cambridge, Mass., 1971).

3 The *Dēnkart* and Ibn Nawbakht cited in D. Pingree, *The Thousands of Abū Maᶜshar* (London, 1968), pp. 7–10.

4 The same two sources plus Māshāʾallāh cited in *The Thousands*, pp. 12–13.

5 D. Pingree, "The Greek Influence on Early Islamic Mathematical Astronomy," *Journal of the American Oriental Society* 93 (1973): 32–43.

6 D.N. Mackenzie, "Zoroastrian Astrology in the *Bundahišn*," *Bulletin of the School of Oriental and African Studies* 27 (1964): 511–29. The same horoscope is quoted by Ḥamza al-Iṣfahānī as from the *Khudai Nāmah* (I, 5; pp. 64–65 ed. Gottwaldt), and appears in a text attributed to the second Hermes (cf. *The Thousands*, p. 17) in Paris BN Arabe 2487 ff. 32v–33r, and in a Byzantine version (*Catalogus Codicum Astrologorum Graecorun* 5, 2, pp. 133–34 [hereafter cited as *CCAG*]).

7 Sirius was almost 30° ahead of tropical Cancer 19° during the Sasanian period. The text must refer to a simultaneous rising of Sirius and the point Cancer 19° on either a sidereal or tropical zodiac, but is clearly of more theological than astronomical significance.

8 See Vettius Valens I 2; Firmicus Maternus III 1; and Rhetorius I and in *CCAG* 7, p. 192.

[9] IX 1 and the commentary on VIII 3–5 in D. Pingree, *The Yavanajātaka of Sphujidhvaja*, forthcoming in the *Harvard Oriental Series*.

[10] D. Pingree, "The Indian Iconography of the Decans and Horās," *Journal of the Warburg and Courtauld Institutes* 26 (1963): 223–54.

[11] *Yavanajātaka*, commentary on I.

[12] *Sūryasiddhānta*, II, 2.

[13] *The Thousands*, p. 49.

[14] I have used Nuruosmaniye 2800; see also S. M. Afnan, *Philosophical Terminology in Arabic and Persian* (Leiden, 1964), pp. 77–78.

[15] The horoscope is:

	Text	*Computation* (7 Oct. 549)
Saturn	Capricorn	Capricorn 25°
Jupiter	Sagittarius	Sagittarius 26
Mars	Capricorn	Capricorn 1
Sun	Libra	Libra 16
Venus	-----	Virgo 0
Mercury	Libra	Libra 8
Moon	Libra	Libra 27
Ascendent	Taurus	*ca.* 7/8 P.M.

There are several other partial horoscopes in the text, at least one of which can be dated in the fifth century.

[16] See the horoscopes taken from Dorotheus by Māshāʾallāh in *The Astrological History*, pp. 166–68.

[17] See V. Stegemann, *Die Fragmente des Dorotheos von Sidon*, 2 parts. (Heidelberg, 1939–43), and my edition of the Arabic translation now in preparation.

[18] Cited in *The Thousands*, p. 10.

[19] This horoscope is:

	Text	*Computation*	
		(24 Sept., 281)	(20 Oct., 281)
Saturn	Sagittarius 12°	Sagittarius 19°	Sagittarius 21°
Jupiter	Gemini 28	Gemini 19	Gemini 19
Mars	Virgo 7	Virgo 2	Virgo 17
Sun	Libra 22	Libra 1	Libra 26
Venus	Leo 28	Virgo 25	Libra 27
Mercury	Libra 29	Libra 6	Scorpio 15
Moon	Cancer 6	Cancer 29	Cancer 16
Ascendent	Scorpio 6	*ca.* 8/9 A.M.	*ca.* 6/7 A.M.

[20] "The Greek Influence," fn. 24.

[21] C. A. Nallino, "Tracce di opere greche giunte agli Arabi per trafila pehlevica," *A Volume of Oriental Studies Presented to Professor E. G. Browne* (Cambridge, 1922), pp. 345–63, reprinted in his *Raccolta di scritti editi e inediti*, vol. 6 (Rome, 1948), pp. 285–303; for a possible reference to this work by Māshāʾallāh see *The Astrological History*, p. 131.

[22] ʿUmar is said to have "commented" on Dorotheus by Ibn al-Nadīm (p. 268 ed. Flügel).

[23] The *Kitāb fī bayān al-ifrādāt* in Leiden Or. 891.

[24] *The Astrological History*, pp. 145–74.

[25] Ibid., p. 166.

[26] *De scientia motus orbis* or *De elementis et orbibus coelestibus* ed. I. Stabius (Nuremberg, 1504); and ed I. Heller (Nuremberg, 1549); see also M. Power, *An Irish Astronomical Text*

(London, 1914). This work is cited several times as the *De sphaera mota* of Meseelach by Albertus Magnus in his *De caelo et mundo*, ed. p. Hossfeld (Monasterii Westfalorum, 1971), written at Cologne in ca. 1251–54; see, e.g., II, 3, 4 (p.148) and II, 3, 11 (p.167).

[27] Cap. 1 on B ii r: Indi qui primi fuerunt philosophiam tractantes, dixerunt Deum causam esse rerum, sicut sol est causa caloris, absque hoc quod sciat se esse causam rerum, a qua Deus omnino sit alienus.

[28] Cap. 8 on D i r-v: Et dico, quod sol apparet parvus, sicut quantitas palmi in palmo, et apparet terra magna, et nos nescimus quantitatem eius ex quantitate solis... et hoc quidem capitulum iam dixit Theon in libro compositionis orbium. Māshāʾallāh's proof that the Sun is larger than the earth seems to come from Theon of Smyrna's proof (pp. 195–97 ed. Hiller) that the earth's shadow is a cone.

[29] Cap. 16–18 and 22–23; *Aryabhaṭīya*, Kālakriyā 17–20, and D. Pingree, "On the Greek Origin of the Indian Planetary Model Employing a Double Epicycle," *Journal for the History of Astronomy* 2 (1971): 80–85; for the Moon see, e.g., O. Neugebauer and D. Pingree, *The Pañcasiddhāntikā of Varāhamihira* (Kϕbenhavn, 1970) IX, 1–4 and 7–8.

[30] Cap. 18 on H i r-v: Dico ergo quod motus harum stellarum omnium ab occidente est motus unus, neque oportet, quod sit ex eis stella velocior, vel tardior stella alia. . . . Si ergo luna esset loco Saturni, perambularet illum circulum in triginta annis. Et si Saturnus esset in orbe lunae, perambularet orbem lunae in viginti octo diebus; see "On the Greek Origin," fns. 31 and 29.

[31] Cap. 18 on H i r-v: Dico ergo quod numerus orbium est X. . . . propinquior eorum ad terram est orbis lunae. Deinde orbis Scriptoris. Postea orbis Veneris. Deinde orbis Solis. Postea orbis Rubei. Deinde orbis Iovis. Postea orbis Saturni. Deinde orbis Stellarum fixarum... est nonus orbis signorum. Deinde orbis magnus, et est orbis rectus. Ptolemy, *Hypotheses* I 3; p. 74 ed. Heiberg.

[32] According to Nallino in his edition of al-Battānī, 3 vols. (Milan, 1899–1907), 1: 291 the name al-Kātib (=Scriptor) is applied to Mercury only in the Maghrib; but, though the common term for this planet in Syriac is a simple transliteration of the Greek, Harmīs, al-Bīrūnī (*Chronology*, p. 192 ed. Sachau) says that the Syriac name is Nafū—i.e., Nabū, the Babylonian scribe-god and planet Mercury. In any case, despite Nallino, it should not surprise us that Mercury was called al-Kātib in late eighth century Baghdād.

[33] Cap. 20 on H iii v: Nizar (=Nīsān), Aiar (=Iyyār), Haziran (=Ḥzīrān), Zammer (=Tāmūz), Rab (=Āb), Elul (=Elūl), Tisrim primus (=Tešrīn qdīm), Tisrim postremus (=Tešrīn ḥrāy), Kemitz primus (=Kānūn qdīm), Kemitz postremus (=Kānūn ḥrāy), Subar (=Sbāṭ), and Adar (=Ādār). The Arabic pronunciation, which would have been represented in Māshāʾallāh's text, is sometimes marginally closer to the Latin than the Syriac (e.g., Ayyār, Ḥazīrān, Tammūz, Tishrīn, and Shubāṭ). For Ptolemy in Syriac see "The Greek Influence," fns. 15–18.

[34] Cap. 20 on H iiir: non completur aequatio alicuius illarum stellarum in canonibus, nisi per aequationem cordis leonis; Ptolemy, *Introduction to the Handy Tables* I; p. 160 ed. Heiberg.

[35] Cap. 20 on H iiir: cor Leonis, et Scorpionis, et Vultur, et Piscis fuerunt in temporibus diluvii in tali, et in tali gradu orbis signorum, et sunt hodie in pluribus gradibus; *The Astrological History*, p. 74.

AL-KINDĪ'S *ON FIRST PHILOSOPHY* AND ARISTOTLE'S *METAPHYSICS*

ALFRED L. IVRY

Yaᶜqūb ibn Isḥāq al-Kindī, who died in Baghdad about A.D. 870, is particularly significant as the first philosopher in Islam, the first Muslim to work with the newly translated Greek texts, the first to "do" philosophy, however imperfectly. The full impact of the Greek heritage—or that part which was retained by late Hellenistic writers—may be first discerned, in Islamic culture, with al-Kindī; and by heritage I mean perspectives and attitudes, as well as textual influences.[1]

All this is apparent in a critical reading of al-Kindī's magnum opus, *Fī al-Falsafah al-ūlā, On First Philosophy*.[2] The treatise analyzes causation, perception, substance, and the categories and predicables of being; presents elementary principles of logic; and defines the concepts of eternity and of body, motion and time, all three of which are deemed finite. Unity and plurality are examined separately and shown to require each other in the existence of every object; which object is then seen as possessing unity only in a nonessential way. This leads to the assumption of an essential cause for all such "accidental" unity, which essential unity must be totally unlike any other kind of unity conceivable: not one by number, form, genus, or even analogy. This unique True One, however, as responsible for the unity of all else, is considered the ultimate cause of the becoming of all substances and of the creation of the world from nothing; achieved apparently by a process of emanation which is just barely mentioned at the end of the treatise.

This reference to emanation, and the emphasis upon the existence of an ultimate One above all of creation, indicates a strong Neoplatonic element in al-Kindī's thought, though he does not attempt to construct an ontological scheme of universal hypostases between the One and man. (He is similarly vague, in *On First Philosophy* and elsewhere, on the status of the individual intellect and its entire relation to a possible universal Agent Intellect.) In distinguishing between the transcendent One and all else, al-Kindī probably goes further than even his Plotinian source.

It is Aristotle, however, rather than Plotinus, who serves as al-Kindī's main source of inspiration in *On First Philosophy*. He works with Aristotle's remarks on the general nature of all substance and being, supplementing sources from the *Metaphysics*, which he follows quite closely, with material that ultimately goes back to the *Categories, Posterior Analytics, Physics,* and

De Anima. He does not, however, refer at all to Aristotle's unmoved mover; rejecting, with his denial of potential infinity as a philosophically significant concept, the notion of an eternal universe and of an infinite extension of time and movement.[3] Instead, he offers proofs for the finiteness of all body, and concomitants of body, which follow arguments originally presented by John Philoponus, and which also appear in a number of al-Kindī's contemporaries (though he does not follow John Philoponus in other, related areas);[4] and he has arguments for the absurdity of predicating unity or plurality exclusively of anything, which are derived ultimately from Plato's *Parmenides,* though they probably reached al-Kindī through a paraphrase contained in some Middle or Neoplatonic work, or a doxography of the sort he uses elsewhere.[5]

These and other sources which are reflected in *On First Philosophy* make it a fascinating example of the great receptivity which al-Kindī had to Greek philosophy; a receptivity which, however eclectic, was anything but naive or undiscriminating.[6] His task was, moreover, complicated by the fact that he lived at the beginning of the Arabic translation movement, and, not knowing Syriac or Greek, could have had only indirect and imperfect knowledge of many of his sources.[7] Thus, of the works just mentioned, only the *Physics* and *Metaphysics*, as well as the pseudepigraphical *Theology of Aristotle* (the abridgement of Plotinus' *Enneads*), were definitely in Arabic at the time of the composition of *On First Philosophy;* and al-Kindī probably had to rely upon written, or more probably oral reports and summaries of various kinds, for knowledge of the other works.[8]

As a major philosophical influence upon al-Kindī in *On First Philosophy* is Aristotle's *Metaphysics,* a closer look at his use of that text should provide a good illustration of the process whereby Greek philosophy was introduced into the Islamic world. Particularly rewarding, in terms of textual analysis, is the first chapter of al-Kindī's work. I have therefore compared five excerpts from Abū Rīdah's edition with W.D. Ross' edition of the *Metaphysics,* and with the Arabic translation of the *Metaphysics* done "for" al-Kindī by one "Asṭāt," and edited by M. Bouyges, S.J., in his edition of Averroes' *Long Commentary on the Metaphysics*.[9] In translation, the first set of comparisons is as follows:

On First Philosophy (ed. M. Abū Rīdah, p. 97, lines 8–14; trans. A. Ivry)

> Indeed, the human art which is highest in degree and most noble in rank is the art of philosophy, the definition of which is knowledge of the true nature of things (*ʿilm al-ashyāʾ bi-ḥaqāʾiqihā)*, insofar as is possible for man.
>
> The aim of the philosopher is, as regards his knowledge, to attain the truth, and as regards his action, to act truthfully; not that the activity is endless, for we abstain and the activity ceases, once we have reached the truth.

We do not find the truth we are seeking without (finding) a cause (*ʿillah*); the cause of the existence and continuance of everything is the True One *(al-ḥaqq)* in that each thing which has being has truth *(li-anna kulla mā lahu annīyah lahu ḥaqīqah)*.

Metaphysics II. 1, 993b 19–31: (Ross' translation):

It is right also that philosophy should be called knowledge of the truth *(epistēmēn tēs alētheias)*. For the end of theoretical knowledge is truth, while that of practical knowledge is action (for even if they consider how things are, practical men do not study the eternal, but what is relative and in the present).

Now we do not know a truth without its cause *(aitias)*; and a thing has a quality in a higher degree than other things if in virtue of it the similar quality belongs to the other things as well (e.g., fire is the hottest of things; for it is the cause of the heat of all other things); so that that which causes derivative truths to be true is most true. Hence the principles of eternal things must be always most true (for they are not merely sometimes true, nor is there any cause of their being, but they themselves are the cause of the being of other things), so that as each thing is in respect of being *(einai)*, so is it in respect of truth.

Asṭāt's Arabic translation of the above *Metaphysics* passage (ed. Bouyges, I:11-13; trans. A. Ivry):

Truly, philosophy is called knowledge of the truth *(ʿilm al-ḥaqq)*, since the end of knowledge is to attain the truth, and the end of action is to act truthfully. If we wished to describe the aim of the view of those who are attracted to the actions of philosophy, then (we would say) that their aim is not (to study) activity *per se*, nor is the duration of the activity endless; rather, their aim is to act for another reason, (namely, for that which is) relative and timely.

We do not know the truth without (knowing) a cause *(ʿillah)*, in that every principle is a cause for subsequent things. . . for example, we say that fire is hot, as it is the cause of the heat of other things. It is known that the first truth is the cause for the truth of subsequent things. Hence the principles of the cause of beings must necessarily be true and eternal, and should not be necessarily so on one occasion and not necessarily so on another; nor should something else be a cause for their being, but rather are they the cause of (the being of) other things. Thus it is necessary that the truth of each thing be like its being *(ḥaqiqat kulli wāḥidin min al-ashyāʾi mithla aysīyatihi)*.[10]

As a glance at these texts shows, al-Kindī's passage, as those which follow, is mostly based upon some lines in *alpha elatton* of the *Metaphysics*, as read through Asṭāt's translation. Having treated this particular extract at length elsewhere,[11] I shall only mention here the obvious parallels of al-Kindī's remarks with those of Aristotle: philosophy is understood by both as knowledge of the truth, and truth is identified with causality and being. Al-Kindī deviates from Aristotle in a number of ways, the most significant being his qualification of philosophy as a "human" art, probably to distinguish it from the "Divine" art of prophecy; and his positing of a "True One" for Aristotle's "true principles." Of course, al-Kindī and his audience would have immediately associated the term *al-ḥaqq*, the "True One" (or "The Truth") with Allāh, as it is so used in the Qur'an (cf., e.g., xx:114, xviii:44), and was—and is—considered by Muslims to be one of the Divine names.

This association with Islamic terms, and his relative ignorance of Greek cultural norms and references, may be held responsible for al-Kindī's deviations from Aristotle even where Asṭāt's translation is quite literal and accurate. Where Asṭāt was himself equivocal, as often happens—and his translation was almost immediately superseded in clarity and probably in popularity by that of Isḥāq ibn Ḥunayn—al-Kindī was more free to interpret Aristotle as he wished. This is evident in our second excerpt, which reads in translation as follows:

On First Philosophy, p. 102, lines 1–4, 10–12.

The truth requires that we do not reproach anyone who is even one of the causes of even small and meagre benefits to us; how then shall we treat those who are (responsible for) many causes, of large, real and serious benefits to us? Though deficient in some of the truth, they have been our kindred and associates *(ansāb wa-shurakā')* in that they benefited us *(afādūnā)* by the fruits of their thought, which have become our approaches and instruments, leading to much knowledge of that, the real nature of which they fell short of obtaining.

It is proper that our gratitude *(shukrunā)* be great to those who have contributed even a little of the truth *(yasīr al-ḥaqq)*, let alone to those who have contributed much truth, since they have shared with us the fruits of their thought and facilitated for us the real, hidden inquiries, in that they benefited us by those premises which facilitated our approaches to the truth.

Metaphysics 993b 11–14, 16–19.

It is just that we should be grateful *(kharin ekhein)*, not only to those with whose views we may agree *(koinōsaito)*, but also to those who have expressed more superficial *(epipolaioteron)* views; for these also contributed something, by developing before us the powers of thought.

The same holds good of those who have expressed views about the truth; for from some thinkers we have inherited certain opinions *(tinas doxas)*, while the others have been responsible for the appearance of the former.

Asṭāt's translation *(Metaphysics,* pp. 8, 9):

> It is not right for us to thank *(nashkur)* only one who has uttered an important remark, of those with whose views we may be associated *(yumkinunā mushārikatuhum)*, rather is it also right for us to thank those who have uttered a small, insignificant remark *(qawl yasīr nazr)*, inasmuch as they have helped us by their prior progress in inquiry?
>
> In the same way do we speak of those who say anything at all about the truth; for we have benefited *(istafadnā)* from the limited *(yasīrah)* views of some of them, while others have been the cause for the being of these?

Al-Kindī has introduced a subtle variation into this text, indicating a historical perspective different from Aristotle's. Aristotle stresses that one should be grateful even to superficial thinkers with whom one does not agree, since their views at least helped train the mind. To al-Kindī it is the major benefactors of the truth (as well as the minor) who have performed this service. Aristotle appears to be saying that, while knowledge of the truth is a collective effort, certain views have some philosophical validity and should be accepted, while others have a kind of historical validity only. Al-Kindī ignores this distinction, choosing to assert, as he does elsewhere, that in general all previous philosophy is equally valid historically, though philosophically incomplete.[12]

We note in passing the verbose, repetitive nature of al-Kindī's writing. This characteristic of his may be explained by his missionary desire to convince his fellow Muslims of the validity of philosophy as practiced by non-Muslims, and, what is even worse, by pagans; it is also due simply to his own rather heavy literary style. There is, however, the additional possibility that al-Kindī's treatises are oral lecture notes compiled by his students; which would account for the uneven quality of much of the material, at times elementary, and at yet other times quite advanced.

The particular section of *On First Philosophy* with which we are dealing, however, appears to be a deliberate literary construction, for between the lines just quoted is a short passage, which is taken from the beginning of *alpha elatton;* moreover, al-Kindī apparently follows Asṭāt's translation here rather closely.

On First Philosophy, p. 102, lines 5–9:

> (We should be grateful) particularly since it has been clear to us and to the distinguished philosophers before us who are not our co-linguists *(ahl lisāninā)*, that no man by the diligence of his quest has attained the truth, i.e., that which the truth deserves, nor have the (philosophers as a) whole comprehended it. Rather, each of them either has not attained any truth or has attained something small *(shayʾ yasīr)* in relation to what the truth deserves. When, though, the bits possessed by each one of them who has

> acquired the truth are collected, something of great worth *(qadr)* is assembled from this.

Metaphysics 993a 30–b 4:

> The investigation of the truth is in one way hard, in another easy. An indication of this is found in the fact that no one is able to attain the truth adequately, while, on the other hand, we do not collectively fail, but every one says something true (as Ross: literally *ti*, "something") about the nature of things, and while individually we contribute little *(mikron)* or nothing to the truth, by the union of all a considerable amount *(ti megethos)* is amassed.

Asṭāt's translation *(Metaphysics,* p.3), clear despite the bad condition of the ms.

> The . . . that the examination of the truth is in one way hard and in another easy, is that no man has been able. . . (either) has not grasped anything of the truth or has grasped something small *(yasīr)* of it. When, though, the bits of it . . . . . . are collected, it becomes something of worth *(qadr)*.

Similarly deliberate would appear to be al-Kindī's remarks, on p. 103, lines 1–3 of *On First Philosophy,* which are introduced as a quotation from Aristotle.

> Aristotle, the most distinguished of the Greeks in philosophy, said: "We ought to be grateful to the fathers of those who have contributed any truth, since they were the cause of their existence: let alone (being grateful) to the sons; for the fathers are their cause, while they are the cause of our attaining the truth."

Al-Kindī then comments *(ibid.,* lines 3–7) on this "Aristotelian" statement with a moving appeal for the acceptance of philosophy and of pagan philosophers.

> How beautiful is that which he said in this matter! We ought not to be ashamed of appreciating the truth and of acquiring it wherever it comes from, even if it comes from races distant and nations different from us. For the seeker of truth nothing takes precedence over the truth; and there is no disparagement of the truth, nor belittling either of him who utters it or of him who conveys it. (The status of) no one is diminished by the truth; rather does the truth ennoble all.

This concern for philosophy is not diminished by the liberty which al-Kindī has taken above in presenting a paraphrase of Aristotle as a direct quotation; even as his previous remarks, at p. 102, lines 7–9 (page 19 above) which *are* essentially a quotation from Aristotle, are not attributed to him, and thus give the impression of being al-Kindī's. This adapting and adopting of sources, which is quite common for al-Kindī, is of course by no means unique to him among Islamic or medieval writers in general. Aristotle actually says the following in *Metaphysics* 993b, 15, 16:

> It is true that if there had been no Timotheus we should have been without much of our lyric poetry *(melopoiian)*; but if there had been no Phrynis there would have been no *(ouk an egeneto)* Timotheus.

Asṭāt translates this (*Metaphysics*, p. 9) quite literally, so that we may be sure al-Kindī's remarks are an interpretation of the text.

> If there had been no Timāʾūs, we would not have had knowledge of the composition. . . of melodies *(taʾlīf. . . al-luḥūn)*; and if there had been no Ufrūnīs, there would have been no *(lam yakun)* Timāʾūs.

Al-Kindī was, in all probability, ignorant of Greek lyric poetry, and of the identities of Phrynis and Timotheus, whom he apparently regards as father and son (understanding Asṭāt's use of *kāna* for *gignomai* in the sense of "to be born"). More importantly, al-Kindī knew that his audience would be completely bewildered by this reference.[13] He therefore paraphrases Aristotle, quoting what he takes to be his essential point and, in the process, intimates that Aristotle had a religious if not Islamic sense of filial piety.

This absorption of Greek sources into an Islamic matrix is evident in *On First Philosophy* elsewhere as well. Thus, in chapter 2 (p. 110, lines 17–19) we read the following:

> Instruction is easy only in customary things *(al-muᶜtādāt)*, the proof of this being the speed of those who learn from sermons and epistles, or from poetry or stories—i.e., whatever is a narrative *(ḥadīth)*—as they are used to the narrative and legends *(al-khurāfāt)* from the beginning of their development.

Again at p. 112, lines 8–12, al-Kindī writes:

> Similarly, every distinctive inquiry has a particular perception different from the perception of another. Therefore many of those inquiring into distinctive things err—some proceeding in accord with a pursuit of probability *(al-iqnāᶜ)*, some proceeding in accord with parables *(al-amthāl)*, some proceeding in accord with historical witness *(shahādāt al-akhbār)*, some proceeding in accord with sensation, and some proceeding in accord with demonstration *(al-burhān)*—when they are unable to distinguish between the pursuits.

These passages are based upon *Metaphysics* II. 3, 994b 32 and 995a 6–8, which Ross translates as follows:

> The effect which lectures produce on a hearer depends on his habits *(ta ethē)*;. . . Thus, some people do not listen to a speaker unless he speaks mathematically, others unless he gives instances *(paradeigmatikōs)*, while

others expect him to cite a poet *(poiētēn)* as a witness.

Asṭāt's translation (*Metaphysics,* pp. 42, 44, 45) is again quite good:

> Lectures proceed by way of what we are accustomed to *(ʿalā mā iʿtadnā)* . . . Some people are not satisfied *(lā yaqnaʿ)* with the speech of a speaker if his speech did not have a clear and evident mathematical demonstration *(burhān taʿlīmī)*; others are not satisfied if the speech did not have examples *(amthāl)*; and others wish the speaker to adduce the witness of a poet *(shāʿir)* for what is said.

Al-Kindī has deviated from this Aristotelian passage by mentioning only traditional Islamic forms of instruction, not mathematics, for example, which he mentions subsequently as a separate subject. The very terms he chooses represent literary forms with which his Muslim audience would have been familiar. Thus Aristotle's "instances," i.e., "examples" taken from everyday life,[14] is probably read by al-Kindī as denoting "parables" or possibly "proverbs," genres of literature and instruction common in Islam. As *amthāl* in Arabic can mean either "example," "proverb" or "parable," it is a particularly fortunate translation for the Greek *paradeigma,* and we cannot be sure what Asṭāt meant by it. We may assume, however, that al-Kindī and his peers, who were probably unfamiliar with the Platonic dialogues or other examples of "paradigmatic discussion," would have understood the term within the sphere of Islamic literature.[15]

This Islamicization of the text is even more evident in al-Kindī's use of the term "historical witness," *shahādāt al-akhbār* (literally, "witnesses of events" or of the "stories" of these events), for Aristotle's "poetic witness." Al-Kindī's audience would have understood the phrase as alluding to reports of individual events, rendered as stories or anecdotes *(akhbār)*; and to the chain of transmitters which precedes the story and testifies to its accuracy. In this form, well delineated by al-Kindī's time, the story or *akhbār* genre of literature resembles that of the *ḥadīth,* and like the latter often dealt with stories of the Prophet or of battles fought.[16] It was common, too, to include poetic insertions in the prose story, and this element—in which the authority of the poet is in effect subordinated to that of other, more pious witnesses—may have served al-Kindī as the bridge for his transformation of a Greek cultural norm into an Islamic one.

Acculturation is, however, a two-way street, and in the process of introducing Greek philosophy into Islam, Islamic thought was itself altered; or rather, its rational and universal elements emphasized. Thus al-Kindī, towards the end of the introductory chapter of *On First Philosophy* (p. 104, lines 8–13), equates the philosophical with the religious approach in the following manner:

> The knowledge of the true nature of things includes knowledge of divinity

(al-rubūbīyah), unity *(al-waḥdānīyah)* and virtue *(al-faḍīlah)*, and a complete knowledge of everything useful, and of the way to it; and a distance from anything harmful, with precautions against it. It is the acquisition of all this which the true messengers *(al-rusul al-ṣādiqah)* brought from God *(Allāh)*, great be his praise. For the true messengers, may God's blessings be upon them, brought but an affirmation of the Divinity of God alone, and an adherence to virtues, which are pleasing to Him; and the relinquishment of vices *(tark al-radhā'il)*, which are contrary to virtues both in themselves and in their effects.

In summarizing the revelation of the "true messengers" of God, viz., Muḥammad and such of his predecessors as Moses and Jesus, as solely or at least mainly concerned with the monotheistic idea and ethical behavior in general, al-Kindī is deliberately minimizing the dogmatic peculiarities of each religion. He has, in effect, accepted a philosophical distinction between essence and accidents, which he now employs as an undeclared criterion in presenting what he regards as the essentials of religion. There is no immediate place, in such a view, for such Islamic "principles of faith" as fasting, pilgrimage, or prayer; though al-Kindī would, no doubt, have subsumed such injunctions under the category of "virtuous acts," if pressed. Little wonder that Muslim traditionalists viewed him, and philosophers in general, with suspicion and anger.[17]

Yet there is no question that, at least insofar as al-Kindī is concerned, his attempt to reconcile religion with philosophy was genuine. Nor is there much doubt that, in this approach, he saw Aristotle, even where he disagreed with him, as his philosophical model.

NOTES

[1] The realization of al-Kindī's significance has led in recent years to increased scholarly interest in his person and writings. For works up to the past decade, cf. N. Rescher, *Al-Kindī: an Annotated Bibliography* (Pittsburgh, 1964).

[2] Cf. M. Abū Rīdah, *Rasā'il al-Kindī al-Falsafīya* (Cairo, 1950), pp. 97–162. I have prepared an annotated translation of this work: *Al-Kindi's Metaphysics* (Albany, 1974).

[3] The use al-Kindī makes of Aristotle and Plotinus has been discussed in my article, "Al-Kindī as Philosopher: the Aristotelian and Neoplatonic Dimensions," *Islamic Philosophy and the Classical Tradition*, ed. S. M. Stern *et al.* (Oxford, 1972), pp. 117–39.

[4] Cf. H. Davidson, "John Philoponus as a Source of Medieval Islamic and Jewish Proofs of Crestion," *Journal of the American Oriental Society*, 89 (1969): 357–91.

[5] Cf. M. Marmura and J. Rist, "Al-Kindī's Discussion of Divine Existence and Oneness," *Mediaeval Studies* 25 (1963): 338–54.

[6] Porphyry, Alexander of Aphrodisias, and Nicomachus of Gerasa are some of the other authors whose writings have apparently influenced this treatise.

[7] That al-Kindī was not a translator from other languages but dependent on others for translations has been shown by M. Moosa, "Al-Kindī's Role in the transmission of Greek

Knowledge to the Arabs," *Journal of the Pakistan Historical Society* 15 (1967): 1–18.

8 For this early period in the translation movement, and the various genres of philosophical literature then available, cf. F. Peters, *Aristotle and the Arabs* (New York/London, 1968), pp. 59–60, 79–87, 96–103, 120–24; and see Peters' bibliographical study, *Aristoteles Arabus* (Leiden, 1968), *passim.*

9 The *Tafsīr Ma Baʿd aṭ-Ṭabīʿat, Notice*, 3 vol. (Cairo, 1938, 1942, 1948 and 1952); and cf., regarding this early translation and its author, the *Notice*, pp. LVI and CXVIII ff.

10 Bouyges reads *aysīyatihi* though the ms. is corrupt for this last word. In view of al-Kindī's above paraphrase of this passage, however, and Asṭāt's use of *annīyah* for *einai* elsewhere in the *Metaphysics*, *annīyatihi* may well have been Asṭāt's choice here.

11 Cf. the article mentioned in note 3 above. As pointed out there, pp. 124ff., this extract is also indebted to a tradition which goes back to the Alexandrian commentaries on Porphyry's *Isagoge.*

12 Al-Kindī's interpretation may well have been influenced by Asṭāt's translation of Aristotle's "certain opinions," *tinas doxas*, as "limited (literally, 'small') views," *ārāʾ yasīrah*; a translation which al-Kindī could take as implying a mild criticism of even the best of previous ideas.

13 Phrynis and Timotheus are fifth century Athenians associated with the development of the *nome* form of Greek poetry; cf. Pauly-Wissowa, *Real-Encyclopädie der Classischen Altertumswissenschaft*², VI: 1331, no. 9; XX:1, p. 925.

14 Cf. Ross's note to 995a7.

15 Similarly, the normally careful Isḥāq ibn Ḥunayn translates Aristotle's *paradeigmatikōs* as "collective witness," *shahādat al-jamāʿah* (Bouyges, *op. cit.*, p. 44); a term which a Muslim reader would associate with teachings based upon the legal sanction of *ijmāʿ*, the "agreement" of the community of believers.

16 Cf. F. Rosenthal, *A History of Muslim Historiography* (Leiden, 1952), pp. 10–11, 59–63.

17 Cf. al-Sīrāfī's parody of al-Kindī, as reported by Yāqūt on the authority of Abū Ḥayyān al-Tawḥīdī and edited by D.S. Margoliouth, "Abū Bishr Mattā and Abū Saʿīd al-Sīrāfī on the Merits of Logic and Grammar," *Journal of the Royal Asiatic Society* (1905): 108–09, 127–28.

RĀZĪ'S MYTH OF THE FALL OF SOUL: ITS FUNCTION IN HIS PHILOSOPHY

Lenn E. Goodman

Among the most puzzling statements attributed to Rāzī by his adversary Abū Ḥātim is the assertion that Rāzī's unusual version of the myth of the fall of the Soul constitutes an argument *(ḥujja)*, indeed the only ultimately cogent argument, against eternalism *(ad-dahriyya)* in support of the creation of the world.[1] My purpose in this paper is to delineate the roles assigned by Rāzī to each principal of his myth, God, Soul, matter, time and space, the end in view being to show that Rāzī's myth is intended to provide a model for a conception of creation which would fall within the parameters of very definite limitations; i.e., it is a response directed to a specific set of difficulties, intended as the unique solution to a dilemma of metaphysics without which creationist theism would, in Rāzī's view, become impossible. Once this has been made clear it will be evident in what sense Rāzī's myth can be construed as representing an argument (the only satisfying argument) for creation, and it will be possible to reconstruct the argument itself, in abstraction from the myth which affords its model, in order to assess its boasted cogency.

The myth which Rāzī relates is this: In the beginning were God, Soul, Time, Space, and Matter.[2] God and Soul were beyond time and space; but matter was extended in them, although not throughout them;[3] it was subject to change, but not yet changing.[4] Soul, because of a passionate and irrational[5] desire for union with matter, confounded herself in the material world, setting the cosmos reeling in a confused and disordered turmoil[6] which only God, the Creator, could prevent from turning into a complete cataclysm. Divine intervention[7] put right the chaos which Soul had set in motion,[8] placing limits and controls to the processes which Soul had been unable to master.[9] Knowledge then became available to Soul,[10] a form of divine inspiration[11] whereby she was enabled to recognize "what was good for her" and what was not, in the long run as well as the short;[12] i.e., she was enabled to recognize that the world which had been the object of her infatuation and into which she had fallen was not her true home,[13] and to seek (and seeking, find)[14] the avenue of her return[15] to the immaterial, transtemporal world.

I call Rāzī's account a myth because it lacks none of what I take to be the three necessary and sufficient conditions of all mythopoeic activity: *(1)* It treats natural and metaphysical principles historically rather than discursively, thematically, analytically, reductively, or in any other fashion. *(2)* It reifies abstractions (time, space, matter) and personifies natural and metaphysical or transcendent principles (God, Soul), assigning them human gender, motives, passions, and desires, thoughts, knowledge, and ignorance, using language which *in the context of the story* cannot be treated wholly as symbolic since it contains the springs by which the fiction itself proceeds and hangs together. *(3)* The fiction itself in turn explains what is "observed" in fact to be the case: In this instance, that the world exists at all, that nature is subject to process which seems to have the character of disorder upon which order has been imposed, that man as a moral and intellectual being is phenomenologically confronted by intimations of his being an alien in this world and belonging perhaps to some other—i.e. the (not unrelated) feelings of existential anomie and mystical awareness.

But Rāzī's is a self-conscious myth; it is far from being the spontaneous outpouring of the untutored intellect; thus it cannot be intended, as naive myth, perhaps, may be, to satisfy *in itself* the problems which it confronts.

Thus if Rāzī has afforded what he takes to be a satisfying[16] account of some of the primary issues of metaphysics, natural philosophy, and psychology, and laid the grounds for an epistemology, an ethic, and a philosophy of religion, he has done so in language somewhat different in its literal meaning from its intension. He has not yet, as he claims, presented an argument. It is not the purpose of this paper to to situate Rāzī's myth within the setting provided by the Gnostic or Plotinian accounts of the fall of the Soul or even to contrast Razı's particular cosmogony with the magnificent and changeless panorama provided by the account of *Genesis* or that of the *Timaeus*, or, for that matter, their fusion in the thought of Philo. Our purpose here is solely to investigate in what sense it is possible for Rāzī to claim that his myth is tantamount to an argument which is the necessary and sufficient condition of any creationist theism.[17]

For Rāzī's myth to be transformed into an argument will require clarification of the relation between the story he tells and the events it describes. Specifically it will require the determination of the ontological, theological, even psychological standing of its principals. And most importantly (if it is to be raised from the level of fictive plausibility to that of apodictic cogency which is claimed for it), the hypotheses from which it derives its explanatory force—that unless things had gone more or less as Rāzī's myth suggests, the world as we know it would not have come into being—must not remain mere plausible suggestions but must be shown to exhaust the realm of possibility.

The requisite transformations can be performed for Rāzī[18] provided that we enter somewhat more deeply into his premises and his problem than perhaps his polemical antagonist was prepared to do. This I believe would be necessary to an understanding of Rāzī as a philosopher even if he had given us his argument in literal terms; it is still more necessary when it is a myth. For as Collingwood was so right to stress,[19] we cannot understand an answer before we understand the question to which it was addressed.

The dilemma which Rāzī, as a creationist, was forced to confront is the old conundrum of the motive and the means, posed long before by Parmenides, restated by Aristotle, and given systematic formulation and rigor by Proclus: If the world has come into being out of nothing then *(a)* there is no possible pattern of process according to which the change from nothingness into being can have taken place, and *(b)* there seems to be no rational way of accounting for the timing of the change or, for that matter, for any other of its modes of determination.

Nāsir-i-Khusraw, who wrote with Rāzī's words on this subject before him, comes, I believe, closest to summarizing[20] the difficulty as it expressed itself to Rāzī: If the world first did not exist and then did exist, a change has taken place; otherwise there would be no difference between the prior and the latter state. But all changes must have causes of one of two possible kinds: natural or voluntary. In either case there are specific conditions which a process must satisfy in order to exemplify its appropriate mode of causation. Thus, with natural causation, a temporal effect requires a temporal cause; with voluntary causation, a primary, i.e., new or original motive, is required to produce an intention which did not previously exist. In either case the results seem to be fatal to the assertion of the world's creation by God. For causation on the natural model will (so it seems) make of God a temporal being,[21] inject him into the natural world, to which the Aristotelian theory *assumes* all causation by "constraint" to be confined. Voluntary causation, on the other hand, will require the Deity to have "changed his mind"—and thus require the postulation either of some outside influence and some inadequacy in God's "prior" knowledge, or some element of whimsy in the divine intention.[22] But all of these conclusions are radically at variance with fundamental tenets of theistic creationism.

Moreover the dilemma which Rāzī was compelled to confront did not confine itself to the mere disjunction of types of change. It extended, as Fakhr ad-Dīn ar-Rāzī makes very clear, beyond the dichotomy of physics and psychology to the even more sensitive realm of theodicy. From the outset, after all, the very question of the world's beginning, for Aristotle and the Aristotelian Platonists, was a matter of theodicy. For, whether creation was construed according to the natural or the voluntary pattern, it was accounted by these thinkers either an unseemly breach of the cosmic order and rhythm or an arbitrary irruption of desire into a realm whose divinity was assured only by its pure intellectuality. No creationist could overcome the weight of Aristotle as self-appointed spokesman for Greek judgment on this matter without somehow reconciling the event not merely with the nature of the material order but also with the impassivity and excellence of the divine. Thus in deciding the issue of the natural means or psychological motive for the creation of the world, Rāzī would be bound not only by his notions as to what sort of process was possible but also by his conceptions as to what sort of process was *seemly* and what sort of product *ought* to have been produced.

But, in Rāzī's view, as we learn from Maimonides,[23] the world was not merely a very mixed and morally problematic sort of creation, it was indeed a realm in which evil outweighed good. Thus Rāzī was forced by his own evaluation of the worth of being to face the problem of evil vis-à-vis creation in an even more radical form than would have been required by the Aristotelian objections. The question of motivation did not confine itself to the rather academic difficulty of a divine change of intention, but extended to the most central (and indeed essential) attributes of the Godhead, moral benevolence and omnipotence. The God who had created such a world as Rāzī's, so it would seem, must have been either impotent, malevolent, or—some combination of the two—unwise.[24]

The avenue of Rāzī's solution to this knotty set of problems was clearly to break the force of the dichotomies upon which the dilemmas rested, to find a middle between, or a third term beyond, the disjunctions which the difficulties presupposed. Thus his first step, logically speaking, was to reject the dichotomy of natural versus voluntary action,[25] for only so could the process which linked the divine realm with the natural be understood. Again in terms of theodicy, the solution was to be achieved by cutting the knot, by rejecting the assumption that if God was responsible for creation he was necessarily responsible for the (admitted) preponderance of evil in creation, or for any whimsy or taint of the arbitrary which might accompany the determination of being's finitude.[26]

But to reject dichotomies is not (as some suppose) to transcend them. What Rāzī required to make his philosophical insights and desires apodictic was a *model* which would demonstrate to doubtful and prejudiced hearers the possibility (i.e. conceivability) of a creationist alternative: an alternative to unmediated natural or voluntary causation. What Rāzī needed was a model of responsibility (i.e., causality in the moral sphere) which would separate good from evil consequences and allow for the determination of the world's finitude without allowing the taint of the arbitrary to attach to God. This model was provided by Rāzī's myth. Thus, Rāzī's argument does not provide the intellectual articulation and rigor of his myth. Rather, his myth provides the intellectual articulation and rigor of his argument.

What I mean by a model here is not greatly different from the mathematical use of the term, and is this: a system which corresponds, element for element and relation for relation, with the system of which it is the image, but which allows (because our knowledge of the model is fuller, surer, or more immediate than that of the subject) the determination of relationships and resolution of difficulties which otherwise might have remained obscure. Descartes thus made algebra the model of his geometry, as geometry for the early Greeks had been the model of their arithmetic. What Newton (pace Leibniz) achieved by his invention of the calculus was the extension of the regions in which mathematical calculations might serve as models of spatial (and numerous other natural) relationships. And so forth.

It is in this sense that a myth such as Rāzī's may have a serious role to play in apodictic reasoning. For each figure of the myth corresponds with an element of Rāzī's universe; and the effect accomplished by his narration of the myth is, as he tells us, to support creationism by showing the theoretical possibility of a resolution of the dilemmas with which that position had been beset.

It is here, I believe, that Rāzī's interpreters, both medieval and modern, sometimes tend to go astray: for they sometimes fail to see how Rāzī's myth is meant to take advantage of the narrow gap of possibility inadvertently left for creation by the proponents of eternalism; and thus they sometimes show a tendency, whether for polemical or merely "pedagogical" reasons, to treat Rāzı's doctrine of the "five eternals" reductionistically, as though to associate absolute time and space etc. with various figures of the Persian pantheon were somehow to explain their function in his philosophy. To succumb to this temptation is fundamentally to misjudge the differences between myth and philosophy.

In speaking of myth, intentional myth, in Rāzī's philosophy, I mean that Rāzī relates myths in the way that Plato does, not in the way that Homer or Hesiod or the "Orphics" do, still less in the way that Ovid does. For philosophy seeks the satisfaction that comes from argument, while myth (in the naive sense) is content with the satisfaction that comes from poetry.[27] Rāzī's philosophy, like all philosophy, is heterogeneous in its origins, but despite the varied origins of its several parts (and to be sure an idea, unlike a person, may have more than one ancestry) all those parts are integrated into an organic whole. To understand Rāzī's philosophy (as distinct from understanding its history) is in the first instance to understand the functions and relations of all its parts.

Each figure in Rāzī's myth has an explanatory function. Thus God is necessary in Rāzī's Universe as the cause of creation (i.e., of all the good that is in creation).[28] Matter, time and space are conjointly necessary as the basis of nature and change.[29] Soul bears the burden of responsibility for whatever is spontaneous, arbitrary, inadequate or "ill-advised"—whatever deficiencies remained, as Rāzī puts it.[30] Thus the myth performs the primitive mythic function of graphic representation and poetic explanation.

But, beyond that function, it has, as Rāzī claims, a higher, apodictic function. For the system of the figures of the myth, with the characteristics they are assumed by the myth to have, functions as a model to demonstrate the conceivability of Razian creation and the inapplicability of the standard dilemmas to it.

For Rāzī to propose roles for his five principles in keeping with the requirements of his creationism is already for him to have shown the possibility of that approach and to have overcome the attendant dilemmas. For him to demonstrate the necessary (and hence eternal) existence of the five with the characteristics he assigns them is for him to establish the main positive tenets of his cosmological metaphysics.

The Aristotelian analysis of change had made it clear to Rāzī (regardless of what it had failed to make clear to him) that without time change was inconceivable. Thus time was for Rāzī a necessary precondition of creation.[31] Likewise the Aristotelian analysis of change had demonstrated to Rāzī's satisfaction (as it had to that of most of the Greeks upon whom Rāzī drew) the necessity of matter as the substrate of all natural change, providing the "from which," the springboard of potentiality whence all processes of becoming must take their start. Thus matter too was a necessary presupposition of Rāzī's system.[32] And so was space if nature was to take on extension—for while Rāzī was certainly unprepared to assert that the process by which creation had been undertaken was merely natural, he recognized that the end product of that process would be nature, and he was even more unprepared to claim that any less went into the making of the world than had emerged in the final product.[33]

Nonetheless, as Rāzī recognized, it was not necessary, in asserting the preeternity of time, space, and matter to assume their interdependence and thus presume the preeternity of the cosmos as well. Aristotle's arguments on that score were not compelling: The necessary preeternity of time did not imply necessarily the preeternity of motion. The necessary preeternity of space did not imply necessarily the preeternity of bodies. The necessary preeternity of matter did not imply necessarily the preeternity of change. No contradiction was involved in the assumption of an absolute time, space, and matter, predating the integration of the three (by creation) into the system we call nature. Thus Aristotle's arguments for the necessary and hence eternal existence of the principal constituents of nature might be accepted without necessitating the acceptance of his conclusion: the necessary and hence eternal existence of the natural world. Exploiting this narrow fissure in the argumentative armor of Aristotelian thinking, Rāzī's creationist model proposes time, space, and matter, the principal constituents of nature, each in an "absolute" form, as yet unmingled and undetermined by one another, as necessary ingredients to the process by which creation (the integration of the three in a world system—cosmos) can have taken place.

By his "concessions" to Aristotle Rāzī opened the door to the solution of the physical problems regarding creation. Not that true Aristotelians would have accepted the quasi-Platonic, quasi-Epicurean notion of *formatio mundi*[34] by which Rāzī was to construct his world—as it were out of "ready to mix" ingredients. On the contrary it was here that Rāzī had to part company with Aristotelian physics and metaphysics by asserting the possibility, indeed the necessity of the absolute, eternal preexistence of the unmixed constituents of his universe—time without change, space without body, matter without form. But this he did willingly, having escaped the Aristotelian dilemmas, upon which, in his view, all doctrines of creation other than his own would necessarily run aground.

The problem of theodicy remained a problem which for Rāzī, as we have seen, expressed itself as a difficulty not over the means but over the very motive of the mingling of the "absolutes." It was primarily in the resolution of this difficulty that Rāzī was forced to add his famous "fifth" principle, Soul, to his already crowded universe of preexistents, God, matter, time, and and space, as the catalyst to that most irreversible of all reactions and the explanation of the obvious deficiencies of the end product.

Indeed the role of Soul in Rāzī's myth is the key to the operation of his model. For eternal matter, time, and space were no more than familiar members of the Aristotelian eternal universe. To introduce them in their absolute forms might aid in the dissolution of Aristotle's difficulties regarding "a time before time," a "place" with nothing in it, and a change which "proceeded from" nothing, but it could not establish how it might have occurred that at a particular (apparently arbitrary) time and in a particular (apparently whimsical) way a world was brought into being with all the general characteristics and particularly the limitations which we observe our world to have. For this an active[35] principle was needed, as Rāzī realized; and, as the problem of theodicy made crystal clear, an active principle distinguishable from God. Traditionally, of course, philosophers of the Greek school had made matter the scapegoat of theodicy, and this, to be sure, Rāzī is quite prepared to do, even contributing the Epicurean void as a further principle of evil, so it seems, to substantiate the Platonic claim that pure evil was pure nonbeing. But matter, and even the void were not enough, if a prime, active cause was needed to precipitate the world into being from the amorphous (and hence only quasi-real) reagents out of which it was to have been formed in time. It was here that Rāzī fell back upon the Gnostic-Platonic expedient of Soul. Given appropriate characteristics there was no dilemma in all the eternalist arsenal which the universal Soul—already a familiar expedient in resolving Gnostic and Platonic dilemmas analogous to those besetting creationism—could not overcome.

Soul, as we have observed, is a personification. It is not a necessary presupposition of Rāzī's philosophy that Soul is a person or even that she be as like as possible to the human beings of our everyday world. It is necessary to Rāzī's philosophy, i.e., specifically to his cosmogony and theodicy, that certain quasi-human characteristics (which Rāzī, with his misogyny, was tempted to think of as feminine—or as immature)[36] be predicated of Soul: viz., she must be characterizable as innately ignorant and oblivious, but susceptible of knowledge and awareness.[37] Again it is not necessary to Rāzī's philosophy that Soul be strictly speaking a voluntary being. But it is necessary that she be subject to a kind of irrational desire (corrigible by reproof) which fits neither the model of Aristotelian natural causation nor that of Aristotelian volition, but seems to have more affinity with the Epicurean theory of desire.[38] Thus it is not possible to conclude that Rāzī treated Soul as human, but only that he borrowed certain human attributes to make clear the nature of her role. For all of these elements, Soul's initial, natural ignorance, irrational desire, awakening, and corrigibility through experience are necessary if Soul is to become the agent of creation without implicating God in the capriciousness and irresponsibility which (the dilemmas assume) would characterize whatever undertook to produce a world in time.

The relationship between God and Soul thus becomes (as it had been for the Gnostics and the Platonists) the crucial link upon which falls the burden of all the difficulties regarding the nexus of the one to the many, the perfect to the inadequate, the transtemporal to the temporal. Rāzī's task, if he is to show the possibility of such a nexus in the creationist account and resolve the dilemmas lodged against creationism, is to describe a relationship such that God retains responsibility for the order of the cosmos, while Soul bears the onus of the arbitrary determination of times and of modes and all the residue of inadequacy attendant upon the mingling of Soul-substance with matter.

Rāzī's parable,[39] then, of the forbearing father, the headstrong son and the tempting but dangerous garden becomes critical to the working of his model. For his parable explicates the motivations, intentions, and spheres of action of the figures of Rāzī's myth, which it is introduced to illuminate. Rāzī asks his disputant to imagine a father whose inexperienced son is attracted by a lovely but somewhat dangerous garden. The father knows that there are scorpions in the garden and is capable of restraining his son, but realizes that only firsthand experience will educate his boy as to the dangers of the garden and calm once and for all the boy's natural desire to play there. Rāzī's point is that it is perfectly conceivable that an all-wise, all-powerful God *would* allow the involvement of Soul in a world which contained no real good for her; perfectly conceivable again that the fruition of such a desire might come spontaneously,[40] unpredictably—and that its achievement *in itself* might not be the most desirable of all possible outcomes—although *overall* and *in the long run* it might be better that the experiment had been attempted, even unsuccessfully, because of what was learned as a result.

Rāzī does not ask his hearers to conceive of God as a father, Soul as a headstrong son, and the world as a worm-ridden garden of earthly delights. His parable, like his myth, is no more than a model. Its apodictic force lies in its power to demonstrate that it is possible to conceive a God omnipotent, omnibenevolent, and all-wise, refraining from interfering with the perpetration of (what in Rāzī's view was) a mistake of cosmic proportions—on the assumption that only so was something to be learned. God's forbearance, the act of creation itself, derive their meaning from the possibility of Soul's learning (through experience, as she must)[41] the locus of her true abode and true focus of her loyalties. Anthropomorphism is necessary in the parable of the garden, as in the myth of creation itself, only to the extent that it aids in the conception of the relations necessary to break the force of the eternalist dilemmas.

In freely postulating the presence and timely operation in Soul of just the right combination of qualities and attitudes Rāzī could neither be wholly guilty nor wholly escape the charges[42] that here—as indeed with all of his five eternals—his was an arbitrary and ad hoc hypothesis. For on the one hand the characteristics of Soul (to wit, an Epicurean soul) are readily accessible to view by introspection and (sc. Epicurean) observation among our fellow humans; on the other, the characteristics which we observe, even if they do somewhat lend truth to their quasi-Epicurean representation, would not guarantee precisely the outcome for which Rāzī relies on them. But this, to Rāzī, is a matter of little importance, for his purpose with his myth, as we have seen, is not to prove that Soul did necessarily create heaven and earth, but rather to prove necessarily that it is not impossible that she did. He offers, as he expressly tells us, a refutation of atheist eternalism *(ḥujja ʿalā ad-dahriyya)*.[43] And in this task he seems to have succeeded handily. For it is not (as all Aristotelians including Plotinians presupposed) inconceivable that the world be brought into being in time by the free act of a divine agency without imputation of malfeasance or caprice to God. The figures of Rāzī's myth provide one model for how this might be done. These figures can be interpreted only as intentionally mythic figures, since the characters and functions which they exhibit in the myth exhaust their significance in the model. But the model itself is the keystone of an argument which goes beyond the level of the myth.

The structure of the argument latent in Rāzī's myth should now be clear: It is asserted (by Aristotle and the Aristotelian Platonists) that creation by God of the world in time is inconceivable, not only because any theory of the means of creation would require (self-contradictory) breaching of the Aristotelian philosophy of nature, but also because any account of the motive for creation would involve assumptions repugnant to the very essence of theism. Rāzī's myth demonstrates the falsity of these assertions by providing a model for the motive and the means of creation which exemplifies the conceivability of the means of creation (without self-contradiction) *outside* the framework of Aristotelian physical theory and proves the acceptability (using assumptions borrowed from the very heart of Neoplatonism) of the motive of creation *within* the framework of theistic assumptions.

It may yet be wondered why Rāzī undertook this argument. Was his intention to prove the existence of God? Yet his model *assumes* the existence of God. The answer I believe is a bit more subtle, but not entirely dissociated from Rāzī's theism.

First, it is necessary to dispel the impression that Rāzī assumes the existence of God in order to establish creationism, by which he will argue the existence of God. What Rāzī's model (through his myth) assumes, it assumes only by way of demonstrating the compatibility of the hypotheses of theism with those of creationism. *Neither* doctrine is established by the model, but the model is necessary, in Rāzī's view, to the establishment of either.

For only if it can be shown that creation is indeed conceivable and the Greek dilemmas reduced once more to corollaries of the world view from which they are sprung, can creation once again become a viable hypothesis toward the explanation of the facts of being as we know it. If creation is possible (and Rāzī's model proves it is), then a creation argument for the existence of God is possible as well; for if creation is possible, then divine creation is likely, and the Creator God of the monotheist tradition need not be in Epicurean fashion deprived entirely of his role in the world or reduced to the mere ontic spring which Platonism seemed to make of him.

True, Rāzī had numerous ways of establishing the bare existence of God,[44] but only a creation argument would in his view open the way to an active role for God in the world—as source of form, intellect, and all true good and being. Creationism, from the Muslim point of view, as from the point of view of Jews and Christians, was the king's highway of monotheism; and Rāzī, like Kindī, Philoponus, Augustine, and Philo before him, and unlike Fārābī and Avicenna after him, was unwilling to experiment too deeply with emanation *as an alternative* to creation. Rāzī's independence of mind is very much his ally here. Since he does not feel bound by the more strictly monotheistic *ex nihilo* view of creation, he readily absorbs and overcomes the Aristotelian objections. Here too his argument acquires its rigor; for the "exhaustion" of the realm of creationist possibilities had been accomplished by Aristotle: Rāzī could assert with confidence that only *such* a model as his would stand the test of eternalist objections.

In recognizing the importance of creationism to theism, then, despite the "heretical" independence of his thought, indeed perhaps because of it, Rāzī anticipates Ghazālī's reinstatement of creationism as the basis of theism,[45] although Rāzī's task, of course, is simplified by the fact that he does not have to deal with a battery of sophisticated *philosophers* of emanation *within* the Islamic fold.

Now Rāzī's "quinquinity," which so shocked his contemporaries and dumbfounded his later readers,[46] was a response to an Aristotelian dilemma, so it is hardly to be expected that the character of his five absolutes will be Aristotelian. One does not break the horns of a dilemma by accepting it on its own terms. Each of the principles in Rāzī's model was meant to perform a function which by Aristotelian standards was inconceivable; conjointly they were to carry out a process (sc. creation) which Aristotle, and indeed most Greek philosophers, regarded as the height of impossibility. For them to effect their roles *even in the mind* would give the lie to all the old claims against creation, but of course these could not be performed on Aristotelian premises.

Thus Rāzī's time is not the time of Aristotle, but an absolute time *(dahr)* predating (as a precondition) all motion.[47] Likewise Rāzī's space is not Aristotelian place *(makān)* but void *(khalā')*, capable of harboring matter or not harboring it, and capable of serving as a metaphysical naught in discussions of ontology.[48] His matter is not Aristotelian matter but atomic, indivisible particles, capable like time and space of being treated as absolute, indeterminate, eternal—and at the same time usable in a contingency argument for the existence of God.[49] Rāzī's Soul is far from being an Aristotelian soul, for it contains an element of irrationality and passion capable of becoming the model of a process which is neither natural nor voluntary in the Aristotelian senses of those terms.[50] And of course Rāzī's forbearing, father-like God is not the God of Aristotle.[51] For Rāzī's nature is not Aristotle's nature—not a continuous rhythmic process, but a sequence (like the Epicurean world) in which chance and whimsy are at work as well as the reason of a thought which thinks itself; and thus radical change, creation of a sort, is possible.

Rāzī's myth, then, does indeed constitute an argument against eternalism. For it demonstrates beyond doubt the falsity of the general eternalist claim that creation is inconceivable. And it provides a model for creation (presumed to be unique in its efficacy) such that, by postulating preeternal matter, time, and space, a quasi-irrational eternal and universal Soul, and a forbearing, teacher-like God, the principal eternalist dilemmas regarding the difficulties of creation for physics and for theodicy are overcome.

But of course for Rāzī to prove the possibility of creation on his own (specially constructed) premises is no great achievement unless the truth of those premises can be shown. It was because Rāzī was aware of this, I believe, that he spent so large a portion of his philosophical energies in the effort to establish the truth of those premises, i.e., to demonstrate the eternal existence of the five principles, with the appropriate characteristics to allow the application of his model to reality:[52] i.e., to prove the doctrine of the "five eternals" —and thereby prove the creation (by God) of the world as we know it.

The arguments which Rāzī offers to defend the eternal existence of five principles with the characteristics required by the figures of his myth (or the members of his model) are many. But none perhaps is more apposite in the present context than the set of arguments, which Rāzī seems never to have far from his mind, based upon the very absoluteness of the five eternals themselves. For the "eternals" of the Aristotelian physical universe, time, space, and matter gain their eternity, as Aristotle's arguments in the *Physics* and *De Caelo* make clear, by their relativity, their interdependence, their conjointly forming a system (nature) in which all parts are necessary to the whole and the whole itself cannot not exist. Rāzī's natural eternals, on the other hand, gain their eternity from their *unmixed* character: only a time beyond motion, a space prior to body, a matter not yet endowed with form could predate the natural world. But such eternal, absolute existence is necessary existence. The atoms cannot not exist since they are simple; nothing could create or destroy them. Thus they must exist at all times, under all conditions as the fundamental building blocks of all actual or potential worlds and the final elements into which all such worlds can be resolved.[53] Likewise with absolute time and space: the flow of time, the extension of space, since they depend (for Rāzī) on nothing else, must always exist. Their nonexistence is inconceivable.[54]

Again the Soul, in Neoplatonism, depends ontically upon the prior divinity. And the Neoplatonic God himself would seem (from a monotheist point of view) to be as dependent upon being as being is upon God. For was it not argued, after all, by no less authoritative a figure than Proclus, that God and the world are correlative? In Rāzī's thought, on the other hand, the divine existence and that of Soul are absolutes, unconditioned by whatever else may chance to be true of the universe. For Soul, it must always be remembered, is the principle of life and consciousness—self-existentiating principles, as Plato long ago had proved; and God *a fortiori* is self-subsistent.

Thus no one of the five eternals but *must* exist. The non-existence of each, for Rāzī, involves a contradiction, the existence of each being established by an analogue of the ontological argument. By an ontological argument here I mean just that, not a pseudo-analytic strictly logical argument—for few medieval philosophers suppose that existential conclusions can be derived from mere tautologies—but rather an a priori examination of being itself and the various candidates for being (in all the categories) in an effort to determine what is dispensable and what cannot not exist. Necessary being for Rāzī is that without which existence itself (for he takes it for granted that *something* exists) is inconceivable. Thus his "proofs" of the necessary existence of the five eternals correspond in ontology rather closely to the transcendental deductions which Kant found it necessary to perform after Hume had transferred the bse of metaphysics from ontology to epistemology—they are deductions of the categories necessary to *being* in just the way that Kant's are the deductions of the categories necessary to experience. This explains, perhaps, why Rāzī attributes *existence* to time and space for example, but does not (despite the anxieties of his critics on this point) assign them substantiality.[55] Rather he avoids the issue of their ontic status: he is concerned with (necessary) being in *all* the categories, i.e., with what is absolute, the non-existence of which cannot be conceived—regardless of the specific mode of its existence.

It may seem strange, at first, that Rāzī should argue ontologically for the necessary, eternal, self-subsistent existence of his five eternals. For they are after all necessary to all the rest of being and therefore numerous other arguments were possible in their defense.[56] But this feeling of strangeness, I believe, may be mitigated to some extent by recognition of the fact that the direction of Rāzī's approach to creationist metaphysics left him little alternative to an ontological argument for the existence of the five (which were, after all, to be absolute and eternal, and therefore all quite susceptible of such an argument). For consider the alternative: had Rāzī, in the context of his creationism, argued solely a posteriori for the existence and necessarily absolute character of the five, inevitably he would have bound himself into a chain of circular reasoning. For that existence and character were to be used in defending the possibility of creation, whence creationism was to be restored as a vital option in religious philosophy. Was it possible in the same breath to argue from the effects of Soul, or God, or even from the character of time, space, or matter to their eternal existence? Of course it was not. To argue only *causally* for the existence of God and Soul or only empirically for the absolute character of unmixed time, space, and matter, would be to beg the question regarding the possibility of creation. Thus while Rāzī allows himself such arguments he cannot rest his case on them. The only order which Rāzī's overall argument could take if it was to allow a restoration of creationist theism was to proceed from the eternal existence of God, Soul, matter, time, and space to the possibility of creation and thence to the reintroduction of these figures as responsible for creation. But if so, the necessary existence of the five could only be established by an a priori examination of the nature of being.

NOTES

[1] *Munāẓarāt*, ed. P. Kraus in *Rhazes Opera Philosophica Fragmentaque quae Supersunt* (Cairo, 1936), p. 308, lines 5 ff. Unless otherwise noted, all references below are to this edition. Only the name of the authority will be cited, followed by the page in Kraus, thus for the present claim: cf. Fakhr ad-Dīn ar-Rāzī, p. 207, Ibn Ḥazm, p. 170. In relating Rāzī's myth, Abū Ḥātim plainly has suppressed the argument, either for want of sympathy or for want of comprehension; cf. note 18 below.

[2] *Munāẓarāt*, p. 307 lines 8 ff.; cf. Ibn Ḥazm, p. 170, Bīrūnī, p. 195, Ibn Taymiyya, p. 196, Isfahānī, pp. 196 ff., Fakhr ad-Dīn ar-Rāzī, pp. 203 ff., etc.

[3] Ibn Ḥazm, p. 171, Nāṣir-i-Khusraw, p. 172, etc.

[4] Ibn Taymiyya, p. 196, Marzūqī, pp. 198, line 10–200, etc.

[5] Marzūqī, p. 197, *Munāẓarāt*, p. 311, line 6.

[6] *Munāẓarāt*, p. 308, lines 10 ff.

[7] *Munāẓarāt*, p. 308, lines 11 ff.

[8] *Munāẓarāt*, p. 308, line 12.

[9] *Munāẓarāt*, p. 308, line 11.

[10] *Munāẓarāt*, p. 308, line 13 ff., cf. Nāṣir-i-Khusraw, p. 284: Rāzī seems faithfully to identify the processes by which matter and soul were to be "en-formed."

[11] *Munāẓarāt*, p. 295; cf. Nāṣir-i-Khusraw, p. 285.

[12] *Munāẓarāt*, p. 295.

[13] *Munāẓarāt*, p. 308, lines 13–14; cf. Fakhr ad-Dīn ar-Rāzī, pp. 206 ff.

[14] For the soul to seek *in the intellectual* was already in a way for her, in Rāzī's view, to have discovered her true object.

[15] *Munāẓarāt*, p. 308.

[16] *Munāẓarāt*, p. 308, lines 5 ff.

[17] *Munāẓarāt*, p. 308.

[18] And we can hardly blame Rāzī for the imperfect state in which we find his argument, since its preservation was left by history to the tender mercies of his critics; and it is Rāzī's opponent, Abū Ḥātim, who presents to our scrutiny only the rhetorical flesh, without the logical bone, of Rāzī's discussion.

[19] "...you cannot find out what a man means by simply studying his spoken or written statements, even though he has spoken or written with perfect command of language and perfectly truthful intention. In order to find out his meaning you must also know what the question was (a question in his own mind, and presumed by him to be in yours) to which the thing he has said or written was meant as an answer." R.G. Collingwood, *An Autobiography* (Oxford, 1939), p. 31.

[20] Nāṣir-i-Khusraw, pp. 282 ff.; cf. Fakhr ad-Dīn ar-Rāzī, pp. 206 ff.

[21] Nāṣir-i-Khusraw, pp. 282–83.

[22] Nāṣir-i-Khusraw, pp. 283–84.

[23] *Dalālatu ʾl-Ḥāʾirīn*, III 12, 16.

[24] *Munāẓarāt*, pp. 309 ff., cf. pp. 295 ff., with Fakhr ad-Dīn ar-Rāzī, pp. 207 ff.

[25] *Munāẓarāt*, p. 311.

[26] Cf. Nāṣir-i-Khusraw, pp. 284 ff.

[27] *Munāẓarāt*, p. 303 with p. 308. For the reductionistic approach to Rāzī's myth, see Ibn Ḥazm, p. 183, Bīrūnī, p. 185, Majrīṭī, p. 186, Masʿūdī, p. 186, Jurjānī, p. 189, Fakhr ad-Dīn ar-Rāzī, p. 203, etc.

[28] Nāṣir-i-Khusraw, pp. 284 ff.; cf. *Munāẓarāt*, p. 308, and especially Fakhr ad-Dīn ar-Rāzī, p. 208.

[29] Marzūqī, pp. 196 ff., Fakhr ad-Dīn ar-Rāzī, p. 205, Nāṣir-i-Khusraw, pp. 224 ff.

30 Qazwīnī, p. 205; cf. p. 209, Fakhr ad-Dīn ar-Rāzī, p. 208.

31 See note 29 above.

32 See note 29 above.

33 See note 29 above.

34 See note 29 above.

35 Jurjānī, p. 189, Isfahānī, p. 196, Fakhr ad-Dīn ar-Rāzī, p. 213, etc. Regarding the void especially see the passages of the *Shuqūq ʿalā Jālīnus* reported by Pines in his "Rāzī Critique de Galien," *Actes du Septième Congrès International d'Histoire des Sciences*, p. 484.

36 Rāzī seems to emphasize the feminine gender in referring to *nafs* somewhat more than the exigencies of subject-verb agreement might have required; his language regarding her infatuation with the world is intentionally evocative of parallels with feminine passion, seen through the Epicurean's misogynistic eye. For the immaturity of Soul, see *Munāẓarāt*, pp. 309 ff.

37 Fakhr ad-Dīn ar-Rāzī, pp. 205-6, Nāṣir-i-Khusraw, pp. 284-85.

38 Sc. through the introduction of the non-Aristotelian, Epicurean conception of chance and spontaneity.

39 *Munāẓarāt*, pp. 309 ff.

40 *Munāẓarāt*, pp. 311 ff.; cf. Fakhr ad-Dīn ar-Rāzī p. 212, Qazwīnī *ad loc.*

41 *Munāẓarāt*, p. 308, line 13; cf. Fakhr ad-Dīn ar-Rāzī, pp. 211 ff., Qazwīnī, *ad loc.*, Nāṣir-i-Khusraw p. 285, etc.

42 So often levelled at thinkers in the Epicurean tradition—cf. Cicero, *De Natura Deorum*, I, 69 ff.

43 *Munāẓarāt*, p. 308.

44 Bīrūnī, p. 195, Qazwīnī p. 204.

45 See my article "Ghazālī's Argument from Creation," *International Journal of Middle Eastern Studies*, II, 1 and 2, January and April, 1971.

46 Isfahānī, p. 202.

47 Bīrūnī, p. 195, Isfahānī, p. 196, etc.

48 Ibn Ḥazm, pp. 171 ff., Marzūqī, pp. 198 ff., etc.

49 Nāṣir-i-Khusraw, pp. 218 ff.

50 Marzūqī, p. 197, *Munāẓarāt* pp. 311 ff., etc.

51 Rather, the Qurʾānic attribute of mercy is predicated of Him: *Munāẓarāt* pp. 295 ff., 308, etc.

52 See particularly Bīrūnī, pp. 195 ff.

53 Cf. Nāṣir-i-Khusraw, p. 221.

54 Cf. Jurjānī, pp. 189 ff., Isfahānī, p. 196, Marzūqī, pp. 198 ff.

55 Rāzī does, according to the direct citation of Marzūqī, pp. 198 ff., refer to time and space as substances (*jawharayn*). But it is doubtful indeed that he can have meant the term in anything like the Aristotelian sense of first substance. The passage is as follows: "Thus it becomes clear that time and space are not accidents but substances. For space does not subsist in body, for if it did it would be destroyed with the destruction of body as growth is destroyed with the destruction of what grows" etc. The emphasis here (cf. Isfahānī, p. 196) is on the self-sufficiency of time and space, not their "thinghood." Each of the five eternals, being an absolute and irreducible facet of reality, was a category in its own right; each had a distinctive mode of being. For Rāzī to have treated them all as substances in Aristotle's sense (i.e., not merely using his formal definition but accepting his conception of the formation of the class) would be for him to defeat the intention of his metaphysics, which is to breathe new life into the program of the *Timaeus*—a task which Platonists had long recognized could not be accomplished in the glaring light of the Aristotelian categories. Rāzī's sole interest in time and space is to establish their absolute and objective character. If he used the language of substantiality, it will have been solely to this end. We have no evidence that the

pseudo-philosophical red herring of the ontic status of the nonsubstantial categories interested him in the least.

[56] Cf. Fəkhr ad-Dīn ar-Rāzī, pp. 213 ff.

THE MEDICAL BIBLIOGRAPHY OF AL-RĀZĪ

ALBERT Z. ISKANDAR

For some time I have been compiling material for a bibliography of Abū Bakr Muḥammad Ibn Zakariyyā al-Rāzī's (Rhazes') medical and scientific works based on existing (Rhazes') Arabic manuscripts, followed by a list of his books mentioned by medieval bibliographers but so far considered lost. Before such a comprehensive bibliography could be assembled, I found it necessary to clarify uncertainties regarding three works: *al-Ḥāwī*, *al-Jāmiᶜ al-kabīr*, and *al-Fākhir*, and I have therefore studied the texts catalogued under these titles in order to solve the questions of their authorship.

Al-Ḥāwī and *al-Jāmiᶜ* have always been wrongly considered identical because of the similarity between the meaning of these two Arabic words. The common roots *ḥawā* and *jamaᶜa*, from which the titles are derived, both mean "collect" or "gather together."

Evidence from manuscripts and printed sources of *al-Ḥāwī (Continens)* shows that it was merely a commonplace book, an *aide-mémoire*, and a private record of the author's comments and reflections on case histories of his patients and on medical books written from the time of Hippocrates down to his own time. In the tenth century, *al-Ḥāwī* would probably have been considered the private library of a well-read physician.

A brief comment on the Hyderabad Arabic edition of *al-Ḥāwī*, of which twenty-two volumes have already been printed, may be appropriate here. This edition relies mainly on sixteen Escurial manuscripts, but it is also based on manuscripts preserved in Lytton Library (now Maulānā Āzād Library) of the Aligarh Muslim University, as well as on manuscripts in New Delhi's National Museum Library, and a few belonging to Ashufta and Phulwari Sharīf which are held in the Dāʾirat al-Maᶜārif al-ᶜUthmāniyya. The publication of *al-Ḥāwī* is a great event. It helps us to see more clearly one of the most illustrious periods in Arabic medicine, and our debt to the editors, therefore, ought to be freely acknowledged. It is unfortunate, however, that this Hyderabad edition gives no descriptions of the manuscripts which have been used, and that the editor's remarks about the manuscript sources are sometimes misleading and confusing. Neither the manuscripts of *al-Ḥāwī* which have been previously studied and judged important nor about fifty manuscripts extant in other libraries have been examined. The Bodleian Library MS Marsh 156 (sections of whose texts are also preserved in the Wellcome Historical Medical Library, WMS Or. 160) ought to have been used in editing parts 14–19. Indeed, MS Marsh 156 contains much material on *taqdimat al-maᶜrifa* (prognosis) and on *al-ḥummayāt* (fevers), which is altogether missing from the Hyderabad edition of *al-Ḥāwī*. This lacuna at the beginning of part 14 should have been filled with the text of the first sixty-five folios in MS Marsh 156. Further, each of the three manuscripts, Marsh 156; Jāmiᶜ al-Pā<u>sh</u>a, Mosul, 143; and Millī Malik, Tehran, 4492, has al-Rāzī's well-known *qiṣaṣ wa ḥikāyāt al-marḍā* (case histories and clinical observations), and should have been used to produce a critical edition of the text printed in part 16 of *al-Ḥāwī*. The same applies to sections which appear in both MS Marsh 156 and in the Hyderabed edition on fevers, smallpox and measles, the pulse, nails and whitlow, and many other topics. The readings in MS Marsh 156 are sometimes more intelligible than those of the Hyderabad edition.

Three titles should be carefully identified here: *al-Ḥāwī (Continens)*, by which I mean the medical diary which was published posthumously by al-Rāzī's medical students; *Kitāb al-Ḥāwī*, the four books written by al-Rāzī himself and published shortly before his death (preserved in WMS Or. 123); and *K. al-Jāmiᶜ al-kabīr*, a medical encyclopedia in twelve books on which he worked for fifteen years, and to which he had hoped to add at least two more books.

AL-ḤĀWĪ

Many of al-Rāzī's published works have been traced to their original rough drafts in *al-Ḥāwī*. Certain private notes in it provide conclusive evidence that he had the intention and the subject matter to write three more books: *On Urine*, *On Crisis and Critical Days*, and *On Fevers*. The subject matter of each of these three unfinished books is still preserved in its entirety in the form of rough notes in manuscripts almost ready for publication. These titles, however; have never been mentioned by any of al-Rāzī's bibliographers, and his premature death prevented their publication. His three unfinished books deserve careful study because they throw much light on his method as an author.

The arrangement of the subject matter in *al-Ḥāwī* gives the impression that the author probably had several study-files, each containing quires *(kurrāsāt)* for copying notes from reference books. He did not neglect to record even those opinions which seemed false to him, invariably adding his private comments and personal experiences and identifying them as his own with the possessive *lī* (mine). Sometimes he corrected statements which he quoted from reference books, and wrote remarks under such titles as: "mine, with amendments." Each of al-Rāzī's medical study-files was reserved for notes on a certain topic: one was specifically for diseases of the head, another for diseases of the chest, and so forth. These medical files might have been arranged in a certain systematic order, in accordance with the accepted method of writing medical books, beginning with the head and working downwards to the toes *(min al-qarn ilā al-qadam)*. From these private notes al-Rāzī selected subject matter for his other written works, such as *al-Qūlanj (Colitics)*; *al-Manṣūrī*; *al-Jadarī wa* al-ḥaṣba *(Smallpox and Measles)*; and *al-Adwiya al-mufrada (Materia Medica)*. Clinical observations concerning illnesses which affected al-Rāzī himself are recorded in *al-Ḥāwī*. In one remark, he writes on an effective treatment he used for inflammation of his uvula, by gargling with astringent and acid vinegar. Again, learning by personal experience from a fever which attacked him, he writes a short private note: "...mine: During my sojourn in Baghdad, I was smitten by a fever accompanied by rigor. The pulse was increased and then I became feverish. No sweats came upon me. The fever then departed and did not recur. Accordingly, we should learn that when fever is accompanied by rigor it is not necessarily nonephemeral; as the contrary is also true..." In another note, written strictly for private use, he writes on his swollen right testicle (a matter which did not worry him in the least because it was not painful) and adds that he used emetics continuously until his testicle became as it originally was.

AL-JĀMIᶜ AL-KABĪR

It is understandable that al-Rāzī should have neglected to mention *al-Ḥāwī* and *Kitāb al-Ḥāwī* by name in any of his other books, since authors do not cite the titles of their private notebooks, nor do they refer to the few published parts of their last work. Al-Rāzī refers several times to his book *al-Jāmiᶜ al-kabīr* and describes the lengthy years of hard work he had spent on writing it. In his book *al-Sīra al-falsafiyya (Philosophic Conduct)*, he writes that he labored hard for fifteen years, working night and day on the production of *K. al-Jāmiᶜ al-kabīr*, until his sight failed and the muscles of his hand were painfully strained (probably writer's cramp). In another place in the same book he mentions the titles of some of his medical writings as samples of his achievements as an author, and concludes with the statement: "...none of my countrymen has ever produced any work to rival *K. al-Jāmiᶜ al-kabīr*, nor has my example been followed..."

Al-Rāzī also refers four times to *K. al-Jāmiᶜ al-kabīr* in his book *al-Fuṣūl (Aphorisms)*, which was written to serve as an introduction to medicine and to guide prospective physicians in choosing books from a reading list, and again he refers to *al-Jāmiᶜ al-kabīr* in his *al-Aqrābādhīn al-mukhtaṣar (Abridged Formulary)* of which I have been able to trace only one manuscript, in the Wellcome Historical Medical Library (WMS Or. 9). In *K. al-Shukūk ᶜalā Jālīnūs (Dubitationes in Galenum)*, one of al-Rāzī's works written in his later life, he consolidates his criticism of some thirty Galenic works in the fields of medicine and philosophy. One of his criticisms concerns Galen's *K. al-Burhān (De demonstratione)*, a work supposedly lost in the original Greek; fortunately some extracts from it are preserved in *K. al-Shukūk*. His intention to write a book *On Fevers* is mentioned in a criticism of Galen's book *Aṣnāf al-ḥummayāt (The Types of Fever)* which he describes as "...abounding in uncertainties, all of which shall mention in a book I intend to write on fevers..." And in his private notes, *al-Ḥāwī*, he writes that he hopes to publish his book *On Fevers* as a part of *K. al-Jāmiᶜ al-kabīr*. In *K. al-Shukūk* he accuses Galen of intentional repetitions (which would convince only inexperienced physicians) and adds that Galen's prolonged discussions in his books *Taᶜarruf ᶜilal al-aᶜḍāᵓ al-bāṭina (Diagnosis of Diseases of Internal Organs)* and *Ḥīlat al-burᵓ (Method of Healing)* are intended to cover up his failure to give actual causes of certain diseases. He then refers the readers of *K. al-Shukūk* to better accounts in his own book, *al-Jāmiᶜ al-kabīr*.

In *K. al-Shukūk* he criticizes Galen also for failing to explain the causes of accumulation of fluids beneath the peritoneum in dropsical patients, for failing to outline the courses these fluids would take to reach special localities, and for neglecting to mention why such abundant fluids would not leave the body as excretions through the urinary tract. Further, al-Rāzī finds unacceptable Galen's interpretations as to why in ascites *(istisqāᵓ ziqqī)* fluids are restricted to the abdomen, but in anasarca *(istisqāᵓ laḥmī)* they are widespread; as to the causes of hydrothorax *(istisqāᵓ ṭablī)*, Galen according to al-Rāzī did not utter one single word! Al-Rāzī writes: "...We mentioned these points in *al-Jāmiᶜ al-kabīr* where we wrote on dropsy, endeavoring to the best of our ability to elucidate its causes..."

In one section in *al-Ḥāwī*, on diseases of the eye, there is further evidence that al-Rāzī had intended to add another part on ophthalmology to the twelve parts of *K. al-Jāmiᶜ al-kabīr*, and in another section, on the diagnosis of a composite attack of tertian and hectic fevers, he jots down a remark that he would make a thorough study of this subject and then would write down the results of his research in *al-Jāmiᶜ al-kabīr*.

Taken together the above mentioned sources, which include five of al-Rāzī's books, provide conclusive evidence that he wrote a medical encyclopedia which he called *al-Jāmiᶜ al-kabīr*, and that he had hoped to increase the number of its parts by two, one entitled *al-Jāmiᶜ fī al-ᶜayn* and the second *al-Jāmiᶜ fī al-ḥummayāt*. Since he refers to *K. al-Jāmiᶜ al-kabīr* in *al-Ḥāwī*, these two works are evidently different.

So far I have been able to identify three out of the twelve parts of *K. al-Jāmiᶜ al-kabīr* (mentioned with the wrong title, *al-Ḥāwī*, by Ibn al-Nadīm and Ibn Abī Uṣaybiᶜa), namely: *Abdāl al-adwiya*, *Ṣaydalat al-ṭibb* and *Istinbāṭ al-asmāᵓ*..., but I shall limit my remarks to the last two.

In *K. Ṣaydalat al-ṭibb*, al-Rāzī states that pharmacy is a subsidiary branch of medicine. Nevertheless, studying this subject during leisure, he says, is a sign that a physician has great interest in his work. This subsidiary art and other similar arts should come second to a good grasp of the basic subjects or, at least, not before a good grounding in the minimum essentials in the basic subjects. Al-Rāzī was also aware that some gifted physicians are naturally equipped with the ability to study an art like pharmacy without any fear of being unable to master the theory and practice of medicine.

This book emphasizes an early date of specialization in Arabic pharmacology, and furnishes Arabists and orientalists with new and original pharmaceutical literature. A study of its text, together with a later text by al-Bīrūnī, *K. al-Ṣaydala fī al-ṭibb*, should help to establish in a new dimension the history of Arabic pharmacy in relation to medicine. Galen distinguished between physicians and pharmacists. Al-Rāzī favored this distinction and, according to him, books on pharmacy should contain among other things accounts of origins and descriptions of pure and adulterated forms of drugs, good and bad specimens, and virtues of drugs. These works are written for *ṣayādila* (pharmacists), whom al-Rāzī considers to be specialists in a branch closely associated with medicine and contributing to it, but far from being physicians. Pharmacists should be mainly concerned with purchasing pure species of drugs, storing them safely, and ensuring nonadulteration of drugs.

On the other hand, *Aqrābādhīnāt* (Formularies) are written by physicians, and for the use of practitioners. They contain recipes and instructions on the compounding of drugs both for physicians who dispense their own drugs and for pharmacists who serve them.

The earliest known *Aqrābādhīn*, that of Sābūr b. Sahl (d. 869) is so far considered a lost work. Its text is vaguely known through an abridged version by an unknown author. It has no introduction and contains interpolations by later physicians. One manuscript, however, dated 734/1333–34 (Millī Malik, n. 4234) is indexed as *Aqrābādhīn* Sābūr b. Sahl. Al-Kindī (c. 800–870) wrote an *Aqrābādhīn* containing drugs selected amongst those which he had compounded, tested and actually used. Al-Rāzī wrote an *Aqrābādhīn*, called *al-Adwiya al-murakkaba* (Compound Drugs), preserved in a few known manuscripts, one in the Bodleian Library, another in Millī Malik Library. Further, al-Rāzī wrote an *Aqrābādhīn mukhtaṣar* (Abridged Formulary), existing in one manuscript. So far, these two works of al-Rāzī have not been published.

Medical education in the time of al-Rāzī was based mainly on reading translations of foreign books. So that physicians and prospective physicians might benefit more from translations, al-Rāzī thought that it would be necessary to define the names of drugs, diseases and organs which, though transliterated, were not translated into Arabic. It was equally essential, in his opinion, to have a knowledge of foreign units of weight and measures for writing recipes, together with their equivalents in the Arab world, if foreign formularies were to be used at all by practicing physicians. On one occasion, in his book *Smallpox and Measles,* he states that he consulted physicians whose mother tongue was Greek and Syriac to learn whether or not Galen wrote on the disease *Jadarī* (smallpox) anything of particular importance which might have escaped Arabic translators. This statement, however, should not be interpreted as an indication that he read only Arabic, his mother tongue. From the introduction to *Kitāb Istinbāṭ al-asmāʾ wa al-awzān wa al-makāyīl,* it appears that he had a command of Greek, Syriac, Persian, and some Indian language, sufficient to enable him to compile a medical lexicon in which he could verify, if he wished, each term according to its original language.

Although he wrote in his introduction that he would mark the linguistic origin of each unfamiliar term, by writing next to it a certain letter of the alphabet, these key letters are very frequently missing from the texts. Prospective editors of this particular part of *K. al-Jāmiʿ al-kabīr* are likely to meet a wide range of etymological difficulties, in five different languages. A Bodleian manuscript copyist, who probably knew very little about the text he was transcribing (MS Bod. Or. 561), says in a marginal remark, ". . . these terms seem to be in different tongues; their obscure meanings are intelligible only to able linguists of sound judgment. . ."[2] More difficulties are added by the absence of diacritical points and vowels. Further, al-Rāzī mentions a great number of terms in *Hindī* ("Indian"), without specifying the language or dialect. He also adds that he intentionally included exotic words with corrupt forms of Arabic spelling because these were frequently found written thus in the recipes in many medical books.

A short note may be given here with regard to *K. al-Fākhir*, which was a popular book in its time and survived in many manuscripts as well as in Latin translation. It is not mentioned in al-Rāzī's own bibliography, and it should be related to him rather than considered as his own book. It was summarized by his former students from other works of his, mainly *al-Ḥāwī, al-Manṣūrī,* and *Smallpox and Measles,* but, contrary to Ibn Abī Uṣaybiʿa's claim, not extensively from al-Rāzī's *K. al-Taqsīm wa al-tashjīr (Classification and Tabulation of Diseases).*

NOTES

[1] This paper is an abstract of a book entitled *New Light on al-Rāzī's Medical Bibliography* which has been prepared for publication. For this reason I have excluded all references and other scholarly apparatus.

[2] *hādhih al-alfāẓ kaʾannahā lughāt mukhtalifa, lā yaʿrifu maʿnāhā illā al-jahābidha al-ʿārifūn bi al-alsun.*

REMARKS ON ALFARABI'S *ATTAINMENT OF HAPPINESS*

MUHSIN MAHDI

I

The *Attainment of Happiness* does not begin with an explanation of what happiness is or a description of the way to it. Instead, it enumerates four *human* things (theoretical virtues, deliberative virtues, moral virtues, and practical arts) whose presence in political communities (nations or cities) indicates that happiness is present in these political communities and that their citizens are already in possession of it (1.2–5).[1] The presence of these four human things seems to be the condition whose fulfillment will produce two kinds of happiness: the worldly happiness of this present life and the supreme or ultimate happiness of the life beyond. The opening sentence declares all this abruptly, without justifying it or promising to do so in the sequel; apart from the sequence in which these four human things are enumerated, and naming the first three "virtues" and the last "arts," it offers no clue as to their order of rank or how they are related. It is followed immediately by an exposition of the first class of virtues, the theoretical. The reader is thus led to expect four consecutive expositions, treating the four human things in the order in which they have just been enumerated. He will pursue the discussion with the hope of learning what these four human things are in order to judge whether the political communities he sees around him possess them.

The distinction between the happiness of this life and the happiness of the life to come may not be the exclusive property of religious communities or revealed religions. Yet the Arabic expressions employed by Alfarabi are standard Islamic—even Quranic—terms. It is possible that he means to give them a meaning or a content that is different from their generally accepted meaning or content. But he does not do so explicitly, here or in what follows. Indeed, he does not mention "worldly happiness" or "this present life" anywhere else in the trilogy.[2] One can explain this by suggesting that Alfarabi's main interest lies in the attainment of the highest happiness, the happiness of the world to come; as a true Muslim, he was entitled to consider worldly happiness unimportant, secondary, or instrumental. But this makes all the more urgent the question whether the possession of the four human things is a sufficient condition for the attainment of this happiness, and whether man can hope to attain it by his unaided effort. The "philosopher of the Muslims" (as Alfarabi was called) could not simply have overlooked what most Muslims believed to be the primary condition for attaining ultimate happiness—the presence in nations of certain divine favors: knowledge of divine things, divine providence, divine moral virtues, and divine arts—which condition is realized not by human, but by divine choice—divine revelation, the legislation of divine laws, and the example of a prophet.

Alfarabi, however, begins with a discussion of theoretical virtues and a recapitulation of the elements of Aristotle's theory of scientific knowledge: its ultimate purpose; its division into the preexistent and acquired; the division of the acquired into what is acquired through investigation, inference, instruction, and study; the distinction between problems and conclusions; and the description of the latter as conviction that may constitute either opinion or science. Concern with nations and cities and with men as citizens is set aside; knowledge of the things that are is spoken of as preexisting in, and pursued or acquired by man as an individual.

The distinction between opinion and science raises the question of the different ways or methods leading to knowledge; and although Alfarabi's immediate purpose is to describe knowledge that is certain, the description of the method that leads to certainty requires that it be differentiated from methods that do not lead to certainty and, consequently, a description of the kinds and arrangements of premises characteristic of each one of these methods. Like the knowledge of which Alfarabi has spoken, these methods are not the special property of any nation or city. They are the methods through which man as man arrives at different sorts of convictions.

Yet Alfarabi does not proceed to describe the method that leads to certainty, but diverges to what appears to be a plea for the need to understand the *differences* among these methods, for the necessity of knowing with certainty the characteristic features of each, and for the view that such knowledge is a prerequisite for the investigation of the things that are and for distinguishing conclusions that are certain from those that are not (3.3–4.15). Throughout this passage—that is, until he resumes the description of the method that leads to certainty (4. 16 ff.)—Alfarabi speaks exclusively of *us*[3] rather than of man in general. The topic as such does not indicate that Alfarabi means by *us* anything more than "human beings": for lack clarity about the specific differences among the methods is a general human predicament. It is only when Alfarabi refers to the investigators and speculative thinkers "whom we observe" (3.16) that the reader is compelled to consider the possibility that he may be in the presence of something more than stylistic variation.

II

The interlude in question is divided into two sections, each of which can be subdivided into two parts. The first section begins with the assertion (in the passive voice) that what is sought in every question is "the certain truth"; yet Alfarabi proceeds immediately to assert also that *we* do not attain certainty in most cases. What actually happens in such cases is *(1)* we attain certainty about part of the question and "belief" in the rest; or *(2)* we "imagine" something about it; or *(3)* we stray from it, and still "believe" that we have grasped it; or *(4)* we are perplexed about it. In the second part of this section Alfarabi offers to explain the cause of this state of affairs. We must be following a variety of methods; and since we seem to consider these conclusions satisfactory and in one case *(3)*, at least, we are satisfied with a belief that is not true, we must be unaware that these methods are different or where the differences among them lie; indeed we must believe that there is only one method and that it is the one we happen to follow. Alfarabi repeats this through an example in which he indicates that we may have to follow different methods in different questions: in one problem, e.g., a method that leads to certainty, and in another a method that leads to an image of the truth or a method that leads to belief about it. Here again, being unaware of the differences among these three methods, we hold that there is only a single method. Now, since according to Alfarabi what is sought is certain truth, the fact that we believe that there is only one method implies that we believe this single method to be the method that leads to the certain truth; and the fact that we are unaware of the varieties of methods implies that we are unaware of the varieties of conviction or of the different states of the soul that correspond to them. We are unaware of the difference between truth, belief, and image; and we are unaware of the difference between certainty, persuasion, imagination, straying away or being lost, and perplexity. Alfarabi's example does not deal with the last two states of the soul. He is more particularly interested in the fact that we are unaware of the difference between imagination–representation and persuasion-belief on the one hand, and certainty-truth on the other. He concludes this section by emphasizing again that this is how we find the matter to stand *with us* in most cases and specifying that this is how the matter stands with the overwhelming majority of those who investigate speculative matters whom *we* observe around us. Who are *we*? Although all the terms which Alfarabi employs and the methods he mentions in this section have their technical meanings in the art of logic, the need for a technical knowledge of these matters, or even of the fact that they are the object of a special art, is not presupposed in this section; on the contrary, we only become aware of the need for such technical knowledge when we consider the consequences of its absence. We may therefore call Alfarabi's use of these terms pretechnical.

All the terms used by him, whether referring to the methods or their conclusions, are also Quranic terms. The most notable among them are "the certain truth" *(al-ḥaqq al-yaqīn)* and "going astray" or "being lost" *(ḍalāl)*, which describe the Islamic revelation and ignorance of it respectively. Yet Alfarabi does not draw the distinction between those of *us* who are Muslims and those of *us* who are not, but rather between those of *us* who are Muslims and those of *us* Muslims who have observed the condition prevalent among us. Also, the awareness of the cause of the prevalent confusion (the variety of methods) does not result from possessing a non-Islamic or foreign science, but rather from observing the existence of various kinds of convictions among us. Alfarabi speaks here as a Muslim; he merely identifies himself with those Muslims who, observing the prevalence of confusion among their coreligionists, are concerned with its cause and remedy.[4]

The second section begins with a request to the party to whom the work is addressed. It is not the nations and the cities, or man in general, or *you* in the plural. The addressee is referred to in the second person singular, asked in the imperative form to consider the condition prevalent among *us* and its cause and to reach the evident conclusion that—unlike the rest of *us* who are investigating questions and arriving at hybrid convictions—*we* cannot escape the need to abandon their ways and to realize three things which they do not realize: *(1)* that all these methods are technical, that is, not natural to us or revealed and established by authority; *(2)* that we need a science by means of which to discern the specific differences among these methods; and *(3)* that our natural aptitude for science is not sufficient for discerning these differences. Therefore, in addition to natural aptitude, we need a special art to develop this aptitude and give us an account of the differences in question. Through this art "we become certain" about those premises and their arrangements which lead to certainty-truth, being lost-perplexity, belief-persuasion, and imagination-representation. In the second part of this section, Alfarabi repeats that only after acquiring this knowledge should we take further steps. In the repetition, he substitutes the "science of beings" for the "investigation of problems" mentioned at the beginning of the section. Also, both there and in the entire preceding section he was entirely silent about instruction and study, about "what *we* had learned from others" and "what *we* ourselves teach others." But now we are ready to look for the "science of beings" in all these ways. For now we know what manner of thing each of them is; we possess the power to distinguish the various sorts of conclusions we reach and the various sorts of convictions we achieve. Finally, we can now *test* what we have learned from others and what we ourselves teach others.

Only on rare occasions does Alfarabi identify his addressee or direct our attention to him. But once he is introduced, we have to learn all we can about him and keep him in view. For it is to him that Alfarabi speaks directly and not to us: we are only the audience of the dialogue. When Alfarabi speaks of *us*, he is speaking of himself and of his addressee; he means *I* and *thou* or a larger group to which *I* and *thou* belong, but which is still delimited: *we; we* Muslims; *we* who have observed the condition prevalent among *us* Muslims regarding the methods; *we* who cannot escape realizing that these methods are technical or the product of art, who need a science by means of which to designate their specific differences, and who possess natural aptitude for science and need to develop it through an art which makes it possible to ascertain the character of the premises and the arrangement proper to each method; *we* who set out to seek the science of the things that are only *after* acquiring this prerequisite knowledge; *we* who claim to know how to investigate and teach and learn only *after* proficiency in logic; *we* who have the power to test the truth of what we discover, of what others teach us, and of what we teach others, and who can distinguish between truth, beliefs, and representations. There is, of course, a difference between the *I* and the *thou* of these *we's*. On the very rare occasions when Alfarabi speaks of himself in the first person singular, he says *I mean*: that is, he proceeds to explain a statement whose meaning is clear to himself but not to the addressee. And whenever he speaks directly to his addressee, he commands him to do something or indicates the way in which the addressee can reach a certain conclusion. The addressee does not yet belong to the more restricted *we* to which Alfarabi belongs; he is being led by the arm. At this stage, for instance, he is required to train himself in the art of logic so as to qualify for stepping up from membership in *us*, the Muslims who are observing the methodological confusion we are in, to membership in *us*, the logicians who have overcome that confusion and who possess the proper equipment to acquire knowledge of the things that are.

If the reader now follows the discussion of logic and the sciences of the things that are (mathematics, physics, divine science, and human or political science) with this last distinction in mind, he will notice that in every instance where Alfarabi interrupts the progress of the anonymous "investigator" (8.16 ff.) to speak of *us*, the topic is the same: the distinction between things as they are known to us and things as they are known by nature. Alfarabi develops the logical implications of this distinction (the classical statement about it occurs in the opening chapter of Aristotle's *Physics*) immediately after concluding the passage just analyzed. From this discussion it becomes clear that *certain truth* and the *way* to it are equivocal terms, and that to begin with primary cognitions is the necessary but not sufficient condition for achieving the ultimate aim of theoretical science. This is brought out by the distinction between the "principles of instruction" and the "principles of being," a distinction that goes beyond the formal differentiation of the various logical methods.[5] Thus *our* scientific method is distinguished by our recognition that the principles of instruction we employ may be different from the principles of being. (In the case of one being, the ultimate principle or God, we possess only the principles of *our* knowledge of it.) We persist in progressing through the effects known to us toward the causes or the principles that we do not know; only when we come to know these principles on the basis of what is clear to us do we proceed to explain the effects of these principles which are hidden from us. In mathematics, these problems do not arise. The principles of instruction are identical with the principles of being, and mathematical proofs (as Alfarabi emphasizes through the interjection *I mean* [9.19]) are purely formal. It is in this sense that the inquiry into numbers and magnitudes is "easier" and least susceptible to "perplexity and confusion," and hence less likely to give rise to differences of opinion regarding the character of its method and the certainty of its proof. Alfarabi does not speak of *us* anywhere in connection with the mathematical sciences. In natural science, in contrast, the principles of instruction are for the most part different from and subordinate to the principles of being; here Alfarabi refers again to those of *us* who ascend from the principles of instruction to the principles of being, and then descend to explain the things that originate from the principles of being which originally were unknown to us.

It is curious, however, that when Alfarabi proceeds to describe the progress of the investigator through the part of natural science that deals with man, his perfection, and sociability, through divine science, and through human or political science, he does not refer to *us* again; the "investigator" is now mentioned more frequently; and, instead of being given "demonstrations," we are told that the conclusions of these matters "become evident *to him*." For the time being, we restrict ourselves to the following observations. Alfarabi's last reference to *us* occurs at the end of the science of nature in the strict sense—that is, the investigation of bodies and things corporeal. The investigation of the principles of being of the heavenly bodies and of the human intellect leads to the recognition that these principles "are not natures or natural things..., nor bodies nor in bodies" (12.16–17). The investigation of metaphysical or divine beings begins with principles of instruction, then the investigator recognizes that none of these beings possesses a material cause, and his investigation of their other three causes leads him finally to a Being that has no cause or principle of being at all. Hence the ultimate aim of divine science, which is the knowledge of this Being, is confined to the knowledge *that* this Being exists, and does not include any knowledge of the principles of its being. As for the investigation of man, it too leads to the recognition that "natural principles" are insufficient. As it considers soul and intellect, it recognizes that their principles consist of certain "ends" and of the "last perfection" of man which, again, do not act as natural causes, but are objectives for which man has to work by making use of certain rational principles that are in him. Having learned about this perfection, the investigator now knows the end of human deliberation, moral acts, and practical arts, and this knowledge enables him to distinguish those of them that serve man's perfection from the ones that do not, or that obstruct man's perfection. Unlike the investigation of bodies or corporeal things, the theoretical investigation of man does not lead to knowledge of the causes or the grounds of an existing thing, but only of the "perfection which [man] should achieve." Whereas in things that are strictly natural the investigation starting from the principles of instruction can lead to certainty regarding their existence and all the grounds of their existence, in divine science the principles of instruction make it evident "to the investigator" merely *that* an ultimate principle exists and *that* it must be perfect without qualification, and in human or political science the principles of instruction lead him to see *what* and *how* is man's perfection or end—that is, the *that* of such a perfection remains a problem.

At the end of his description of theoretical science, Alfarabi turns once again to the addressee and speaks to him as follows: "This, then, is theoretical perfection. *As you see*, it comprises knowledge of the four kinds of things through which the citizens of cities and nations attain the utmost happiness" (16.15–27). "To see" *(raʾā)* is the verb from which the technical term "opinion" *(raʾy)* is derived and in turn gives its signification back to the verb, which thus means also "to opine" or "to form an opinion." Alfarabi does not expect his interlocutor, who not long ago had to be asked to reflect on the confusion of methods among *us*, to have had an opportunity to attain "the certain truth" or "knowledge" about theoretical perfection. But he does expect him to be able now to form a likely view or opinion about what is comprised by theoretical perfection or about the kind of knowledge it is. His ability to form such an opinion presupposes the ability to see the necessity of discerning the character of the various methods, learning the method that leads to the certain truth, and joining those of *us* who are logicians. But it presupposes also that he had an opportunity to observe how *we logicians* proceed in attaining knowledge of the things that are in the way they really are, and especially how *our* method ascertains the *that* and *why* of natural beings. This means that our associate has had an opportunity to observe how *we physicists* apply the method that leads to certainty first and foremost in the study of nature and natural beings, including man; how we refuse to discourse about things that do not form part of the natural world in which we live until the investigation of the principles of the things we know *forces* us to inquire into things that are "not nature or natural"; and how we proceed then to investigate divine things on the basis provided by the knowledge of nature and natural beings, admit only what becomes evident through this investigation, and refuse to accept as certain that which we have not been able to ascertain. Alfarabi is not instructing the addressee in the theoretical sciences; he leads him through them to show how they operate and helps him form a conviction that theoretical perfection consists of what can be known in and through these theoretical sciences alone. Since we have no way of measuring the addressee's reaction apart from Alfarabi's speech, we can only express our amazement at the implications of the question that follows; for, the mere fact that it is asked indicates the measure to which Alfarabi's enterprise has been successful: "Are you, then, of the opinion [do you suppose, is it possible] that these theoretical sciences have also supplied what can make these four [bases of happiness] actually exist in nations and cities?" (16.19–17.1.) The addressee does not seem to object to the definition of theoretical perfection or the claim that it is knowledge of all the things required for the attainment of happiness. On the contrary, he is ready to be asked the question—and the two interlocutors are ready to consider the problem—whether theoretical perfection by itself comprises everything needed for the attainment of happiness; whether it supplies, in addition to knowledge, whatever is needed to bring everything that leads to the attainment of happiness into actual existence among citizens and in political communities.

Before undertaking to describe the method of certainty and the different theoretical sciences, Alfarabi chose to draw the addressee's attention to *us* Muslims and the confusion of methods prevalent among *us*. Now, with more important issues at stake—what constitutes perfection and ultimate happiness, and how they are realized—he is oblivious to what *we* Muslims believe them to be or how *we* believe they should be realized. It is possible to explain Alfarabi's silence in part as follows. Because *we* do not differentiate the methods from each other, *we* cannot distinguish certainty from persuasion or imagination and cannot judge which is knowledge of the truth and which is an opinion about it or an image of it. Therefore, only *we* Muslims who are also logicians and physicists know what science is and can determine what "theoretical perfection" consists of. Since the theoretical knowledge that concerns man includes knowledge of his perfection and happiness, *we* alone are competent to judge what these, too, consist of. Yet even *we* do not know, at least not prior to examination, whether theoretical perfection is sufficient for the attainment of happiness or whether something else is needed. Before exploring Alfarabi's understanding of religion, it would be premature to question the implicit claim made here for *us* logicians and physicists. Those of *us* who are Muslims without being logicians or physicists would certainly dispute that claim and suggest that the best knowledge of man's happiness, especially his "ultimate" happiness, is that which is presented in the divine law, and that it is the divine law also which shows the way to achieve this happiness. We shall see that Alfarabi does not dispute this suggestion but acknowledges everything it claims. However, since even *we* logicians and physicists are willing to consider the question whether theoretical perfection is sufficient for the attainment of happiness, a superficial examination does not make clear why Alfarabi does not indicate how this question appears to *us* Muslims. Furthermore, by asserting that knowledge of man's perfection and happiness can be acquired through unaided reason, Alfarabi the logician and physicist does not cease to belong to *us* Muslims; otherwise, the Quranic injunction that *we* ought to investigate the heavens and all existing things would have been in vain. The question is thus relevant to *us* Muslims; yet, to be relevant to *us* it has to be formulated as follows: does this theoretical perfection supply everything needed for the attainment of ultimate happiness?

Should the answer to this question be in the affirmative, it will inevitably lead one to wonder about the use of religion and the divine law, apart, that is, from urging us to acquire this theoretical perfection. If, on the other hand, theoretical perfection supplies only knowledge of ultimate happiness and what leads to it, there will be still need for something else that brings what is known theoretically into actual existence, and this can be the function of religion and the divine law. This latter position, which implies that the function of religion and the divine law is to bring into actual existence what man's unaided reason comes to know in theoretical science, is said by some to have been taken by Muslim philosophers, including Alfarabi. It is therefore all the more surprising that in this context Alfarabi refuses to take a stand on the issue of religion and that his interlocutor, too, finds no difficulty in accepting Alfarabi's answer, which is this. Theoretical perfection is not sufficient for actualizing happiness in cities and nations; what is needed additionally, however, is not religion and the divine law but something like prudence. The interlocutor seems to show an unexpected readiness in accepting this answer. Yet it is possible that we had underestimated him from the outset. Alfarabi hints at this possibility by reminding his interlocutor of the opening sentence, which asserted that every kind of happiness can be attained by citizens of cities and by nations, provided they come to possess the four human things enumerated there, and that he, the interlocutor, had already accepted that assertion. The question now is whether knowledge of what these four things are is the same as their possession by, or realization among the citizens and political communities. To answer this question negatively is to affirm Alfarabi's original statement—that is, that the attainment of happiness presupposes the possession of all the four accomplishments, not theoretical virtue alone; and the present discussion proceeds to show why, besides theoretical virtue, we need the deliberative virtue or the virtue of prudence. The problem which is of immediate interest to the interlocutor is not whether we need divine assistance in addition to the four human accomplishments, but whether we need any other human virtue and art besides theoretical virtue and its perfection; and the fact that Alfarabi devotes almost half of the *Attainment of Happiness* to convince him that such a need exists is indicative of the importance of this problem as well as of the interlocutor's defective knowledge of practical matters.

III

In contrast to sections 1 and 4,[6] in each of which Alfarabi speaks twice directly to his addressee, sections 2 and 3 (which attempt to find a solution to the problem just mentioned) contain no direct reference to the addressee. Moreover, we find only two cursory references to *us* in section 2 and none in section 3. The reason Alfarabi could refer to *us* on numerous occasions in section 1 (at the end of which he was also able to say with confidence that the addressee could form his own opinion about the presentation that had preceded and that this opinion agreed with his own) no longer seems valid. This change corresponds to a change in the main theme. The theme of section 1 was theoretical virtue; its hero was the "investigator" whose aim is to make intelligible with certainty the things that are; logic and the investigation of nature held the central position. The theme of sections 2 and 3 is the realization of the four human things in cities and nations. Section 2 attempts to show that this requires, not only theoretical perfection, but also the highest deliberative virtue, the highest moral virtue, and the highest practical art; and that all four should be acquired by a human being equipped for them by nature. Its hero is not the "investigator" of the theoretical sciences as such, but someone who possesses the will and decides to bring the four human things required for the attainment of happiness into actual existence in cities and nations. Therefore, he needs another faculty besides the theoretical and should acquire the political virtue and all the other qualifications of the "prince."

Alfarabi's arguments are still directed to the addressee, to the logician and physicist. Nevertheless, at the beginning of section 2, Alfarabi indicates that the matters under discussion do not fall within the domain of physics; they emerge only when one sees the distinctions between them and natural beings. Particular natural beings are actualized and given their attributes by nature, while it is by the activity of the will that virtues and arts are realized. Alfarabi uses natural beings to explain and make evident to his addressee some of the problems involved in realizing things that depend on the will, and to explain that the latter fall in a class by themselves. Alfarabi's difficulty in guiding his addressee in the direction which he intends can perhaps be seen best from the particular manner in which he formulates the two phrases in which he refers to *us* in this section. Temperance and wealth, like man, are intelligible notions, but unlike the notion man they are not natural but voluntary. Therefore, "*if we decide* to bring them into actual existence," we have to know how their attributes vary in time, place, and so forth (19.5 ff.). Again, the most authoritative or the highest art is that which precedes all other arts; "*if we decide* to perform its functions," we will have to make use of the functions of all the other arts. In the case of natural beings, it is sufficient to know the intelligible notions, for nature itself brings the particular natural beings into existence and supplies them with the required attributes. But in the case of voluntary notions, the knower himself performs this function, and knowledge alone does not enable him to perform it well. Further, there is no necessary connection between knowledge of the intelligible notions temperance and wealth, and the activity of bringing these notions into actual existence. The activity depends on a further condition, the desire and the decision to perform it. The conjunction "if" *(idhā)*, which Alfarabi employs in both instances, implies a condition which is not necessarily present in the possessor of theoretical science. Beyond this Alfarabi ceased to speak of *us* in divine science and human or political science in section 1, and thus we begin to suspect that the absence of the desire and decision which he specifies here affects the theoretical study of divine and human things, as distinguished from logic and physics where the common ground hinted at by the frequent reference to *us* was most apparent. Absence of the will in the addressee to actualize voluntary intelligible notions in cities and nations somehow affects his theoretical understanding of them, or it produces a lack of enthusiasm for divine and human things as distinguished from logic and physics.

Be this as it may, the addressee is excluded from section 3. The theme of this section is no longer the argument that the possessor of theoretical virtue must also possess the highest deliberative and moral virtues and the highest practical art—that is, that he must become a true prince. Rather it describes what a prince who has achieved these virtues must learn and do. Since he ought to be able to actualize the specialized virtues and arts in cities and nations, Alfarabi proceeds to explain how he ought to teach and form the character of his subjects, persuade and conquer, legislate, order the classes of his subordinates, and lead cities and nations and every group and every individual to the ultimate happiness for which they are equipped by nature. The implication of this material with reference to the addressee seems to be clear. It is up to him to decide whether he wishes to become a prince. If he decides to become one, and succeeds, this will be his reward. If not, he will be excluded from this great power and glory, and Alfarabi excludes him from it now in a symbolic way by not addressing him and not including him among the "supreme rulers" who, among other things, will have the power to control the teaching and investigation of the theoretical sciences.

IV

With the termination of section 3 the treatment of the subject matter of the *Attainment of Happiness*, strictly speaking, is completed. The four human things whose possession leads to happiness have been dealt with, both in themselves and in respect to the ways whereby they are realized in nations and cities. A cursory glance at the opening and concluding remarks of each one of the first three sections suffices to show that Alfarabi supplies a rigid framework to remind the reader of the steps of his argument and that within this framework the concluding remarks of section 3 announce that the subject matter upon which the author had embarked is now definitely terminated. Section 4 seems to be a kind of epilogue which is extraneous to the theme formulated in the opening sentence of the *Attainment of Happiness*. Were the latter indeed the true theme of the work, it would be difficult to justify the presence of this last section. Moreover, section 4 introduces a number of new topics, all of which are treated with relative haste. It begins with a praise of theoretical science and traces its origins. It explains the meaning of "philosophy" and "religion" and the relation between them "according to the Greeks." It explains the ideas as well as the *names* of "prince," "philosopher," "legislator," and "*imām*" (religious ruler). It explains how the same human being can be a philosopher and a religious lawgiver. It distinguishes between the false and true philosopher, and asserts the latter's claim to rule. Finally, it traces *this* kind of philosophy to the Greeks in general and to Plato and Aristotle in particular, and this serves as a transition to the remaining two parts of the trilogy. The swiftness with which these topics are treated is compensated for, however, by relatively frequent direct references to authorities, a practice which Alfarabi had avoided up to this point with a single exception: the reference to Plato with respect to the education of the prince in section 3 (30.7).

Once we consider these references, we begin to discern the general theme of this section and the relationship between it and the theme of section 1. We remember that section 1 concluded with the assertion that *theoretical* science encompasses knowledge of the four human things whereby cities and nations attain ultimate happiness and that Alfarabi took it for granted that the addressee understood what this assertion meant. But consideration of the problem whether theoretical science is sufficient for realizing these four things led to the conclusion that, not one, but *four* kinds of science are required: *(1)* theoretical sciences that make intelligible the things that are by certain demonstrations; *(2)* rhetorical sciences that present these same intelligibles by way of persuasion; *(3)* poetic sciences that supply representations of these intelligibles by way of persuasion; and *(4)* sciences extracted from the first three for each nation (35.2–8). Alfarabi does not tire of repeating in this section that the first kind is the highest. But his intention is to convince the addressee that he should accept the other three sciences as necessary and useful, and that these sciences should be employed to fulfill the purpose of theoretical science which is man's ultimate happiness (38.9–13; cf. 34.1). The addressee does not need to be convinced of the superiority of theoretical science. Alfarabi tried to prove in section 2 that, by themselves, the theoretical sciences are not sufficient for the realization of ultimate happiness, and he proceeded in section 3 (apparently without noticing whether the addressee was able or willing to follow this discussion) to elaborate the activities of the "prince" who teaches the citizens and forms their character by their consent and by compulsion. Originally, the addressee was asked to admit that other things are needed in addition to theoretical science. Now he is being asked to admit that three other kinds of science are needed besides the theoretical.

Alfarabi does not call these three kinds "rhetorical," "poetic," and "national"; but these names are appropriate if we consider their definitions. If we place ourselves in the position of the addressee, the first question that comes to mind is whether Alfarabi is justified in calling the nontheoretical disciplines "sciences" or whether the usage is arbitrary. Through frequent repetition of the name "science," by itself and in conjunction with the demonsstratives "*this* science," "*these* sciences," and "*those* sciences," Alfarabi forces the addressee to wonder about this question, distracts him from other objections he might have had, and almost reduces the whole issue to one of *names*. Then he proceeds to show his own competence as an authority on names and their meaning, that his manner of using names is based on solid authority and understanding, and that the addressee should learn this from him.

The problematic character of names emerges in this section as follows. Alfarabi justifies the existence of the other sciences on the ground that they are necessary for the instruction of the vulgar. He sets forth the distinction between the vulgar and the elect on the basis of the distinction between common opinion and knowledge. But the names, "vulgar" and "elect", are not applied in general usage to those who accept common opinions and those who seek to know, respectively; they are not employed strictly on the basis of knowledge but on the basis of belief: people who are skilled in a certain art say that they themselves belong to the elect and that others are vulgar, because they believe that they themselves possess knowledge and that others follow generally accepted opinions (37.3–14). Alfarabi does not introduce this common and imprecise usage to cast doubt on the true distinction between the vulgar and the elect, but to support it. The common usage, based on what people think or believe, reflects the true meanings of these names. The distinction between the vulgar and the elect is known best, not by the practitioners of the arts who are confined to their own belief about what they know, but by the practitioners of the sciences, especially those of them who possess the highest science which is not based on generally accepted opinion.

Alfarabi turns from the practitioners of the arts to the practitioners of this science, attempts to determine which was the first or earliest group to possess it, and tries to find out what the name "science" meant according to "them." But here he meets with the following problem. Tradition relates ("it is said") that the first to possess this science were the Chaldeans, and that it passed from them to the Egyptians, the Greeks, the Syrians, and finally the Arabs. Alfarabi did not have the literature of the Chaldeans or the Egyptians on the subject, or he did not trust what went under that name in his time. (He did not know, for instance, whether what was reported to be the wisdom of the Chaldeans and of the Egyptians meant "this [theoretical] science" or "the other sciences.") The only literatures he knew embodying the expression of this science were in the Greek, the Syriac, and the Arabic tongues. In order to find out the earliest uses of the name, science, he had to go back to the Greeks ("among whom it remained for some time"). They are Alfarabi's best authority, both because they possessed this science and because we have the "names" they applied to it and know what they "meant" by these names. In section 3 Alfarabi broadened the meaning of science to include the other three kinds of sciences besides the theoretical, and broadened the function of "science" to include a political, besides the cognitive role. Now he defends all this as the original meaning and function of science "among the Greeks who possessed *this* science." The first name they had for it was "absolute wisdom" and the "highest *wisdom*"; they gave the name "science" to the acquisition of that wisdom. They had a specifically Greek name, "philosophy," for the scientific state of mind; but what they *meant* by philosophy was the *love* of that highest wisdom. The one who acquires this wisdom is not named "scientist" by them but "philosopher," by which name they meant the *lover* of the highest wisdom. Alfarabi's account of these names thus shifts away from "science" to "wisdom" and love of wisdom—to philosophy and the philosopher. Finally, he reports the view or opinion of the Greek philosophers about the object of their love, the highest wisdom (that potentially it encompasses *all* the virtues), reports the names they gave to it ("the science of sciences" and so forth), and explains what they meant by such names.

The conclusion is this. Alfarabi is not an innovator. The innovators are those who restrict the meaning of science to theoretical science only. Whatever the advantages of this restriction, it departs from the original meaning of wisdom and philosophy. Seen in that original and wider perspective, the investigations of theoretical science alone do not constitute the search for the highest wisdom, and the philosophy which obtains theoretical science without the power to instruct and form the character of the multitude is incomplete philosophy. Alfarabi's notion of science, wisdom, and philosophy, is the original notion, which is also the perfect and most complete notion. In comparison, the concept of science as merely theoretical is an innovation and a partial or incomplete concept. Seen in this partial perspective the philosopher need not be the supreme ruler; but were one to recover the original, unrestricted concept of the philosopher (the notion of the absolute philosopher), then "philosopher" and "supreme ruler" would mean the same thing. Moreover, by returning to the original use of names, we recover, concomitantly with the older, more authoritative, and unrestricted meaning of philosophy, the meaning of "religion" according to the ancients and the relationship between philosophy and religion, which finds its highest expression in the activity of the philosopher-lawgiver. Finally, the recovery of the original Greek names "wisdom," "science," and "philosophy," teaches us, not only the original meanings of these names and the relationship among them, but also how different names can indicate different aspects of the same thing. It enables us to see how these names indicate separate things when we think only of the restricted signification of the names, and that to find out their true meaning is to recover their unconditional or unrestricted signification. For instance, "lawgiver" signifies the discovery of the particular conditions under which happiness can be sought by a particular political community. But this presupposes that the lawgiver knows what happiness is, or that he has acquired philosophy. The name "philosophy" has acquired the restricted significance of theoretical virtue. But the existence of the theoretical virtue in its last perfection requires the presence of the other, nontheoretical virtues as well. The name "prince" signifies complete power. But to possess complete power without restriction means to possess also the inner power of thought, virtue, and art. The name "*imām*" (cf. 29.18, *passim*) in Arabic means being followed and accepted as a guide. But in order to be followed and accepted without condition or restriction, a guide should have the highest purpose, science, virtue, and art. Alfarabi does not return to the original meaning of science merely to justify his own manner of using this name or to recover the original meaning of wisdom and philosophy, but to recover the way Greek philosophers (the ancients) thought about names (such as *imām*) which were not known to the Greeks but whose meaning has to be sought out "according to the Arabic language."

This, then, seems to be the immediate object of section 4: to train the addressee in the method of transcending the restricted signification of names. In the third of the four instances in which Alfarabi speaks directly to the addressee, and in the second of the three instances in which he employs the formula "make it evident to yourself" he commands him to learn that the logical, abstract, or unrestricted meaning (*maʿnā*) of the expressions (*alfāẓ*), "philosopher," "supreme ruler," "prince," "lawgiver," and "*imām*," is one and the same (43.18–19). He also alludes to the way he, the addressee, can learn the unity underlying this diversity of expressions. "Whichever one of these expressions you take, proceeding then to consider what each one of them signifies according to the majority of those who speak *our language* you will find that in the end they all agree by signifying one and the same meaning" (43.19–44.2). Thus the addressee cannot learn what Alfarabi asks him to learn merely by taking the expressions themselves, but only by going further and finding out what they signify among those who speak *our* language. Had we not become aware of the problem of language and the central place it occupies in the present section, and also of the fact that (apart from the colophon) this is the sole instance in it in which Alfarabi refers to *us*, we might have been satisfied with the apparent linguistic meaning of *our* language—Arabic, the language spoken by Alfarabi and his addressee. But immediately prior to this command Alfarabi explained the *meaning* of *imām* "in the language of the Arabs" and said that "it signifies merely the one whose example is followed and who is well received." Then he proceeded to explain how one must understand this definition: when the implied restriction of the signification of the name is lifted, then *imām* will come to mean the same as "philosopher." The latter signification is surely not "according to the language of the Arabs." Further, the name "philosopher" is Greek and not Arabic, and Alfarabi, who had labored so much to point out the importance of recovering the original Greek meaning of names such as "science" and "wisdom," could not be asking the addressee to accept, as his final authority on what the name "philosopher" signifies, its signification among the majority of those who do not speak Greek and who could not, for instance, surmise by looking at the word *faylasūf* that it means "the one who loves and is in quest of the highest wisdom," which, according to Alfarabi's report, is the authoritative meaning given to the Greek name by those among the Greeks who possessed the highest science. By the same token, *our* language could not mean Greek, for *imām* is not a Greek name. And although Alfarabi mentions the fact that the highest science was expressed "in the Greek tongue," he never explains the meaning of any name according to the Greek tongue, but only according to "those among the Greeks who possessed this science." These two are not necessarily identical. For instance, in the Greek tongue, "philosopher" means the one who loves or is in quest of wisdom; while those among the Greeks who possessed this science "meant by philosopher the one who loves and is in quest of the *highest* wisdom." In his explanation of the meaning of *imām*, which goes beyond the meaning of the name "in the language of the Arabs," Alfarabi does not follow the signification of the name according to the Greek tongue but follows the practice of "those among the Greeks who possessed this science" and who gave Greek names meanings that go beyond the common meaning of the expressions in question. *Our* language is, therefore, neither Greek nor Arabic; it is the language of "those who possess this science," whether Greeks or Arabs. It is also not the language common to Alfarabi and his addressee. The addressee, we found out, is a neophyte in *this* language: he is commanded to learn it. The estrangement between Alfarabi and his addressee, which reached its climax in section 3, is not resolved here through a common denominator (the Arabic language). Alfarabi only holds forth the promise that the addressee can join a new community to which he does not yet belong, provided he learns its language. Only by learning this new language can he know what "philosophy," "legislation," and "religion" truly mean, and that mere knowledge of theoretical science is the sign of the counterfeit, vain, and false philosopher.

Although Alfarabi does not specify further who the Greeks or the ancients who spoke his language were, there is a figure who plays a significant role in this section and, as it were, embodies the authority on which Alfarabi bases his reinterpretation of the meaning of "science." Plato enjoys the distinction of being the only philosopher whose name is mentioned in the text of the *Attainment of Happiness*. He is mentioned for the first time in section 3 where, in connection with the education of *imāms* and princes and their political role, Alfarabi refers the reader to Plato's account (in the *Republic*) of the steps which they should follow in learning the sciences and acquiring the habits of character from their childhood until they become the supreme rulers of the city (30.7). Although it is evident that he is the primary authority for that entire section, it is only in section 4, after Alfarabi's reference to the ancients and their view of the relation between philosophy and religion, that Plato emerges as the key figure in the *Attainment of Happiness*. Alfarabi refers to what Plato does in the *Timaeus* as the model for the production of sensible images of intelligible things (41.5). This imagemaking activity is said to be characteristic of religion in contrast to philosophy, which presents a demonstrative account of the things themselves. (There is a mysterious figure [41.6] who is said to have represented matter by abyss or darkness or water, and nothingness by darkness. Alfarabi does not mention the name of this anonymous prophet, but the suggestion that he imitated Plato is strengthened by the hint that "philosophy precedes religion in time" [41.12].) Then, in the concluding discussion concerning the distinction between the true and the false philosopher, Alfarabi refers again to Plato's account in the *Republic* of the necessary equipment that the student of theoretical science should possess in order not to end being a counterfeit, vain, or false philosopher (45.17). In the same connection, he refers again to the "fire (sun) of Heraclitus" mentioned by Plato (in the *Republic*) to illustrate how the light of theoretical science learned by the false philosopher who lacks natural equipment, and by the vain philosopher who lacks proper habits, is quenched as they grow old (46.2).

If we now consider these four references to Plato, we see that they are concerned exclusively with the proper education of future philosophers and the relationship between philosophy and religion. They refer to two of Plato's works, the *Republic* and the *Timaeus*, which are also the only writings mentioned in the *Attainment of Happiness*. What Plato does in the *Timaeus* is presented as a model for the imitative activity which resulted in what the ancients called "religion." What he mentions in the *Republic* is presented as the normative account of the upbringing and education of the true philosopher.

According to Alfarabi, Plato specifies in the *Republic* that, in order to avoid becoming a false philosopher, the student of theoretical science "should have sound convictions about the opinions of the religion in which he is reared, hold fast to the virtuous acts in his religion, and not forsake all or most of them" (45.6–7). This statement is patently ambiguous. Nevertheless, on the basis of it no student of theoretical science can be considered a true philosopher if he turns his back on the opinions and actions of his religion or pursues theoretical science in utter disregard of the religious community in which he lives. If we remember that Alfarabi's references to Plato appeared after Alfarabi abandoned the common ground on the basis of which he could refer to himself and the addressee of the *Attainment of Happiness* as *we*, and that Plato is the only one among those who speak *our* language who is mentioned by name and whose works are cited by Alfarabi, we begin to perceive the apparent implication of this change of attitude toward the addressee. Plato is the authority to whom Alfarabi refers the addressee to support his reevaluation of the status of theoretical science. If the addressee is to become a true philosopher and not a mere student of theoretical science or a false philosopher, he should learn the language of Plato or what Plato does and says in the *Timaeus* and the *Republic*.

The argument of section 4, especially the emphasis on the education of the future philosopher-prince and the relation between philosophy and religion, prepares us for the dominant theme of the concluding remarks, which is the distinction between philosophy itself, the ways leading to philosophy, and the ways through which philosophy is to be reconstructed or reestablished when it has become defective or extinct (47.4–5). But it does not prepare us for the assertion that the philosophy described by Alfarabi in section 4 (the only section in which the name "philosophy" appears) "has come down to us through the Greeks from Plato *and* Aristotle" (47.3–4). Aristotle is not mentioned anywhere else in the *Attainment of Happiness*. He is undoubtedly the main authority for the logical methods and the natural science described in section 1; yet, even there, Alfarabi avoids mentioning him by name. Subsequently Alfarabi leads the addressee to a view of science which seems to be characteristically Platonic and postpones the mention of philosophy until after he mentions Plato and until he can equate philosophy with the new view of science emerging from the wider meaning of philosophy. The argument of the work as a whole deliberately culminates in the education of the future philosopher-prince according to the program offered in Plato's *Republic* on the one hand, and in indicating the philosophic importance of the question of religion which finds its solution in Plato's *Timaeus*, on the other. Yet after having led us to this conclusion, Alfarabi now affirms unequivocally that we can learn *this* philosophy from *Aristotle* as well: Still, Plato and Aristotle gave us two separate accounts of philosophy and of the ways to it and to reestablishing it. Alfarabi calls them "Plato's philosophy" and "Aristotle's philosophy," respectively, and announces his intention to present a separate account of each. (Alfarabi's trilogy, the *Philosophy of Plato and Aristotle*, was also known under the title the *Two Philosophies*.)

Without indicating the manner in which these two philosophies have become *the* philosophy described by him in the *Attainment of Happiness*, Alfarabi turns to his addressee with a final request. He asks him to learn "from this" (from the preceding account, from the following two separate accounts, or from both) that Plato and Aristotle had a single purpose and that they aimed at giving an account of a single philosophy. The addressee is asked next to go beyond what Alfarabi is offering him in this trilogy, to seek for the evidence regarding the unity of the purpose and aim of Plato and Aristotle. Alfarabi leads the addressee to the two philosophies and ends by pointing toward their purpose and aim, but he does not show them to him. This is something which the addressee has to find for himself. The only aid the addressee receives from Alfarabi in this respect is a number. The *Attainment of Happiness* begins with the number 4, leads the addressee by the arm to the number 2, and requests him to look by himself for the number 1.[7]

All this seems rather enigmatic. It certainly does not offer a direct answer to the difficulties encountered in Alfarabi's concluding remarks, when they are considered not as a transition to the two parts of the trilogy yet to come, but as a conclusion of the *Attainment of Happiness*. Yet if we are concerned with Alfarabi's purpose and aim, we must proceed to study parts 2 and 3, in which Alfarabi hides behind Plato and Aristotle, to see if they shed further light on part 1 where he is presenting his own account of the way to their philosophy. Although the concluding remarks raise more questions than they answer, they are helpful in one decisive respect. They vitiate the conclusion to which every step in the *Attainment of Happiness* seemed to be leading, and for which the surface movement of the argument seemed to offer massive support, that is, that Alfarabi is leading his addressee away from the philosophy of Aristotle and to the philosophy of Plato. We now know that the work is designed to lead the addressee to the philosophy of Aristotle as well as of Plato; that he needs an account of the philosophy of Aristotle just as much as of that of Plato; and that the work aims at training the addressee to understand, not only Alfarabi's account of Plato's philosophy, but his account of Aristotle's philosophy also. Why, then, did Alfarabi preserve complete silence about Aristotle until the last moment? The Aristotle who was not mentioned earlier in the *Attainment of Happiness* is an Aristotle who leads up to Plato. But there is another Aristotle who will be engendered by Plato and who "sees the perfection of man as Plato sees it and more."

NOTES

1 All references in the text are to the pages and lines of the Hyderabad edition (1345 A.H.); cf. "Notes to the Arabic text of the *Attainment of Happiness*," in *Alfarabi's Philosophy of Plato and Aristotle*, translated with an introduction by Muhsin Mahdi (Ithaca, New York: Cornell University Press, 1969). The translation includes the *Attainment of Happiness*, the *Philosophy of Plato*, and the *Philosophy of Aristotle*, whi make up a trilogy.

2 Ibid.

3 Alfarabi usually takes advantage of the construction of the Arabic verbal sentence to leave the subject or the actor implied or hidden in the verb. (This gives rise to serious problems when an editor or translator is forced to specify the implied noun or pronoun in question. The manuscripts differ in the extent to which they supply the necessary diacritical points and are not reliable in the vowel signs they provide. To supply these means to decide upon the gender, number, person, and tense of the verb; not infrequently, all this may have to be decided on the basis of what might be called circumstantial evidence.) But in the passages to which we refer, Alfarabi makes certain that no ambiguity remains regarding the fact that he is now speaking in the first person plural or in the second person singular. These passages are not evenly distributed. The longest occurs near the beginning (3.4–4. 15). They become less frequent and shorter as one advances toward the center (25.11–12). Thereafter, they disappear completely, except for a single sentence that occurs toward the end (43.19–44.2). The last passage is the author's colophon (47.3–10).

4 In this respect, the *Attainment of Happiness* is an exoteric work.

5 In his short commentary on the *Posterior Analytics* (MS, Hamīdiyyah, 812, fol. 67r) Alfarabi explains this distinction by the following example. We observe a gradual increase in the light of the moon as it turns from crescent to full moon. From this we infer that the moon is spherical. The increase in the light of the moon is the cause of our knowledge that the moon is spherical. Yet it is the spherical shape of the moon that is the cause of gradual increase in its light. This is what Alfarabi means by saying that the principles of instruction are the causes of our knowledge of the principles of being, and yet the principles of being are the causes of the existence of whatever we happen to employ as principles of instruction.

6 The division of the text into four sections is the one made in the translation cited above, n.1.

7 The trilogy begins with the *Attainment of Happiness* as Part I, followed by the "two" philosophies in Parts II and III. But there is an unwritten "fourth" Part in which the addressee is asked to look for the common purpose and aim of the two philosophies. This "fourth" Part is hinted at again at the beginning of Part III, where a new set of four things is introduced (and recalled in the remarks that conclude the trilogy).

THE SIGNIFICANCE OF PERSIAN PHILOSOPHICAL WORKS IN THE TRADITION OF ISLAMIC PHILOSOPHY

Seyyed Hossein Nasr

Without doubt Arabic is the most important language of Islamic philosophy and even the Persians, who have had the largest number of Islamic philosophers, have written mostly in Arabic and produced some of the best known classics of Islamic philosophy in the Arabic language, such as the *Shifāʾ* and the *Maqāṣid al-falāsifah*. But it is equally true that Islamic philosophical texts in Persian constitute an important corpus without whose study the understanding of later Islamic philosophy as it developed in Persia and the Indo-Pakistani subcontinent would be impossible. Moreover, even in the case of some of the earlier figures who wrote in both Arabic and Persian, men like Ibn Sīnā and Ghazzālī, the totality of their message cannot be understood without taking into consideration their Persian writings. There are even figures in both the earlier and the later centuries of Islamic history who wrote mostly or completely in Persian, such as Nāṣir-i Khusraw and Afḍal al-Dīn Kāshānī, and who are usually left out of consideration in most of the general histories of Islamic philosophy precisely because of the language in which they expressed their ideas. Of course Turkish and Urdu are also of some importance for certain philosophical texts written during the past two or three centuries, but the use of Persian goes back over a thousand years and the Persian language must be considered along with Arabic as a main language in which the Islamic intellectual sciences were expressed in Persia itself as well as in the subcontinent and even to a certain extent in the Turkish world.

Because the modern Western approach to Islamic philosophy developed within a scholastic tradition in which knowledge of Islamic philosophy was limited to Arabic texts, the tendency has continued in the Occident to ignore the considerable corpus of Islamic philosophy written in Persian.[1] Only during the past few years has attention been paid to this body of writing, and gradually important philosophical works in Persian by such men as Ibn Sīnā, Nāṣir-i Khusraw, Suhrawardī, Afḍal al-Dīn Kāshānī, Naṣīr al-Dīn Ṭūsī and others are beginning to see the light of day. The field is, however, still a virgin one. Much remains to be done even to discover the titles of all the Persian philosophical texts, and much more to edit and publish them.[2]

The fact that Persian was destined to become an important intellectual language in Islam is difficult to explain in terms of purely historical factors.

The "asymmetry" in the matter of language which one sees in early Islamic history, namely both Muslimization and complete Arabization of the lands of *dār al-islām* west of Arabia, and Muslimization but only partial Arabization east of Iraq, left room for the rise of modern Persian as an Islamic language. Once Islam developed a unified civilization with two centers of culture, one Arabic and one Iranic, Persian was bound to develop as a language of intellectual discourse especially since the Persians were themselves so active in the intellectual sciences (*al-ᶜulūm al-ᶜaqliyyah*) and contributed so much even to the development of Arabic prose in science and philosophy. As Persia gradually became independent of the caliphate from the fourth/tenth century onward, the Persian language began to develop rapidly in both poetry and prose, and from that early period scientific and philosophical works appeared in Persian which laid the foundation for the more lucid and successful Persian philosophical texts of subsequent centuries.

THE EARLIEST PROSE works of the Persian language, which belong to the fourth/tenth century, deal with either religious subjects, especially commentaries upon the Qurᵓan and Sufism, or with those branches of the intellectual sciences which are only partly related to Islamic philosophy. Such early prose works in Persian as *Kitāb al-muᶜālajāt al-buqrāṭiyyah* of Aḥmad ibn Muḥammad Ṭabarī, the physician of Rukn al-Dawlah the Dailamite, and the *Hidāyat al-mutaᶜallimīn fi'l-ṭibb* of Abū Bakr Ajwīnī Bukhārī, one of the students of Muḥammad ibn Zakariyyāᶜ Rāzī[3] deal with medicine but contain sections that belong also to natural philosophy. From another angle, some Sufi works of the same period, such as the *Nūr al-ᶜilm* of Abu'l-Ḥasan Kharraqānī, are also concerned with certain metaphysical themes closely related to *falsafah*.[4]

At the end of the fourth/tenth and the beginning of the fifth/eleventh century Persian philosophical works properly speaking began to appear. The Ismāᶜīlīs, whose intellectual center continued to be Persia even when the focus of their political activity became Egypt, produced some of the earliest philosophical works of the Persian language. The commentary of Abū Saᶜd Muḥammad ibn Surkh Nayshāpūrī upon the philosophical poem (*qaṣīdah*) of Abu'l-Haytham[5] and the Persian version of the *Kashf al-maḥjūb* of Abū Yaᶜqūb Isḥāq Sijistānī[6] belong to these early years. Shortly after this period Nāṣir-i Khusraw, that most neglected theologian and philosopher, wrote all of his philosophical works in Persian. His *Jāmiᶜ al-ḥikmatayn*, *Zād al-musāfirīn*, *Wajh-i dīn*, *Safar-nāmah*, *al-Ikhwān* and *Gushāyish wa rahāyish* represent, along with Ḥamīd al-Dīn Kirmānī's masterpiece in Arabic *Rāḥat al-ᶜaql*, the peak of development of Ismāᶜīlī philosophy of the Fāṭimid school.[7]

During this same period there also appeared the first Persian works of the Peripatetic school, initiated by Ibn Sīnā's epoch-making *Dānishnāma-yi*

ʿalāʾī, which is the first systematic work of Peripatetic philosophy in Persian.[8] Although it did not succeed in establishing the Persian language immediately as an instrument for the expression of *mashshāʾī* philosophy, because some of its technical expressions remained somewhat forced, this work marks the beginning of a process which reached its peak two centuries later with Suhrawardī and Ṭūsī. The *Dānishnāmah* is important not only as a document in the history of the Persian language but also as revealing certain aspects of Ibn Sīnā's thought not to be discovered so easily in his Arabic Peripatetic works. Chief among these is the very manner of discussing the question of being, since in Arabic there is no copula between the subject and the predicate while in Persian such a copula does exist. Moreover, the very possibility of using the word for being in Persian (*hastī*), in addition to the Arabic *wujūd* and *mawjūd*, made it possible for Ibn Sīnā to be fully aware of the important distinction between being as a state and being as an act. Later Persian philosophers were also to draw advantage from this possibility; for example we observe Mullā Ṣadrā referring to *hastī* even in the middle of an Arabic work to make fully clear the basic difference between the state and the act of being.[9] This important development in ontology in Islamic philosophy and its relation to problems of semantics must be traced back to a large extent to the *Dānishnāmah* and the attempt made by Ibn Sīnā to discuss ontology in two languages which possess a completely different grammatical structure.

A series of Persian works appeared during Ibn Sīnā's lifetime or shortly thereafter which are attributed to him but which most probably are translations of his Arabic works by his immediate disciples and the followers of his school. This collection includes such treatises as the *Ẓafar-nāmah*, *Ḥikmat al-mawt*, *Risāla-yi nafs*, *al-Mabdaʾ wa'l-maʿād*, *al-Maʿād*, *Ithbāt al-nubuwwah*, *Risālah dar aqsām-i nufūs*, *Risāla-yi iksīr*, *Qurāḍa-yi ṭabīʿiyyāt*, *Risālah dar ḥaqīqat wa kayfiyyat-i silsila-yi mawjūdāt wa tasalsul-i asbāb wa musabbabāt*, *ʿIlm-i pīshīn wa barīn*, *Risāla-yi ʿishq*, *Risālah dar manṭiq*,[10] the Persian translation of *al-Ishārāt wa'l-tanbīhāt*[11] and the Persian translation and commentary upon *Ḥayy ibn Yaqẓān*.[12] The sudden appearance of all these works belonging to the school of Ibn Sīnā in Persian was certainly instrumental in spreading the influence of the master of Muslim Peripatetic philosophy in Persia beyond the circle of traditional philosophers, who also knew Arabic, to a wider audience embracing nearly all classes of men interested in learning and at the same time familiar with the Persian language.

The Seljuq era was a golden age for Persian prose. During the period there appeared the great Persian prose masterpieces of Sufism such as the *Kashf al-maḥjūb* of Hujwīrī, the *Asrār al-tawḥīd* of Abū Saʿīd, the works of Khwājah ʿAbdallāh Anṣārī, the Persian translation of the *Risālat al-qushayriyyah* and the monumental esoteric and gnostic commentary upon the Qurʾān, the *Kashf al-asrār* of Mībudī, all important indirectly in the later development of theosophy (*ḥikmah*). As for Sufi works of this period which directly influenced later schools of *ḥikmah*, the writings of Ghazzālī and ᶜAyn al-Quḍāt Hamadānī must especially be mentioned. Ghazzālī's Persian works have never received the careful study they deserve. His *Kīmiyā-yi saᶜādat* and *Naṣīḥat al-mulūk*, both in Persian, influenced centuries of Muslims concerned with ethics and politics, while his Persian *Letters* (*Mukātabāt*) contain keys to the solution of many delicate aspects of his thought. Some of his works such as the *Ayyuha'l-walad* are Arabic translations of an original Persian work, in this case the *Farzand-nāmah*. There is even an important Persian work of Ghazzālī on eschatology *(Zād-i ākhirat)* which has remained completely neglected and unedited until now.

As for ᶜAyn al-Quḍāt, his *Tamhīdāt*, *Risāla-yi jamālī* and *Nāmah-hā*, all in Persian,[13] mark an important phase in the development of the intellectual expression of Sufism which found its full perfection in the hands of Ibn ᶜArabī and members of his school. This type of writing naturally influenced later schools of Islamic philosophy in most of which gnosis (*ᶜirfān*) was a major constitutive element.

As for philosophy proper, it suffered an eclipse during the Seljuq period and fewer philosophical works were written in either Arabic or Persian at this time than either before or after. Nevertheless, important philosophical works were composed in mature and lucid Persian during this period. Khayyām not only translated the Arabic *Khuṭbat al-gharrā'* of Ibn Sīnā into Persian but also wrote several independent Persian philosophical treatises of which the *Risāla-yi wujūd* is particularly noteworthy.[14] There also appeared cosmological and cosmographical compendia in Persian of philosophical importance of which *Nuzhat-nāma-yi ᶜalā'ī* of Shāhmardān ibn Abi'l-Khayr and *Gayhān-shinākht* of Qaṭṭān Marwazī may be mentioned.

The most important Persian philosophical corpus of this period belongs not to the Peripatetic school but to the new school of Illumination (*ishrāq*) founded by Suhrawardī.[15] The thirteen Persian treatises by Suhrawardī, the authenticity of two of which had at one time been disputed by some scholars but is now beyond question, are among the most outstanding masterpieces of the Persian language.[16] In a Persian that is at once lucid and extremely rich in symbolic imagery, Suhrawardī wrote works dealing with subjects ranging from logic and natural philosophy to symbolic and mystical recitals. Suhrawardī succeeded not only in opening a new intellectual dimension in Islam but also in developing the possibilities of the Persian language for the expression of a whole range of subjects from the most rigorous debates of logic and metaphysics to the most poetic descriptions of the spiritual transmutation of the human soul. Like *ishrāqī* theosophy itself, which is a bridge between the world of logic and the ecstasy of spiritual union, the Persian language developed by Suhrawardī became a most powerful instrument for the expression of all types of philosophical and theosophical ideas contained in the Islamic intellectual tradition ranging from the logical to the purely esoteric and gnostic.

Suhrawardī's schoolmate in Ispahan, Fakhr al-Dīn Rāzī was, like Ghazzālī, a theologian opposed to *falsafah*, but also like Ghazzālī and perhaps even more than he, he became deeply influential in the later development of Islamic philosophy. Rāzī wrote several treatises in Persian such as the *Jāmiʿ al-ʿulūm*, which is a compendium of the sciences, *Risālah dar uṣūl-i ʿaqāʾid* on the principles of religion and *Risālat al-kamāliyyah* on *Kalām*. His works are typical of a tendency at this time to write not only philosophy but also *Kalām* in Persian, a tendency that was to continue strongly during later centuries when Shiʿite *Kalām* entered the scene and gradually replaced the Ashʿarite school in Persia.

A major corpus of prime importance for Persian philosophical prose that appeared just at the end of the sixth/twelfth and beginning of the seventh/thirteen centuries is the treatises of Afḍal al-Dīn Kāshānī, known popularly as Bābā Afḍal, who was both a *ḥakīm* and a Sufi. He was a relative of Naṣīr al-Dīn and influenced the philosophers who came after the Mongol invasion in more than one way. Afḍal al-Dīn is the author of thirteen treatises along with several letters and answers to various questions, in Persian of a very high quality.[17] The treatises combine views of the Peripatetic school with those of Sufism and Hermeticism and are characteristic of the later development of Islamic philosophy in Persia in which different schools were gradually synthesized. The writings of Bābā Afḍal, along with those of Suhrawardī, represent a summit of philosophical prose in Persian in which intellectual discourse of the highest order is expressed in a language of the greatest clarity and beauty.

With the coming of the Mongols and throughout the Timurid period, a large number of works on philosophy continued to appear in Persian. The central figure in the revival of the intellectual sciences after the Mongol invasion, Khwājah Naṣīr al-Dīn Ṭūsī, wrote numerous philosophical works in Persian such as *Aqsām al-ḥikmah*, *Baqāʾ-i nafs*, *Jabr wa ikhtiyār*, *Rabṭ al-ḥādīth biʾl-qadīm*, *al-ʿIlm al-iktisābī*, as well as two important ethical works, the well-known *Akhlāq-i nāṣirī* and the less well-known *Akhlāq-i muḥtashimī*.[19] His student and collaborator, Quṭb al-Dīn Shīrāzī, is the author of *Durrat al-tāj*, the most voluminous compendium of Peripatetic philosophy in Persian.[20] Of course important works were also written in Arabic by both Naṣīr al-Dīn and Quṭb al-Dīn as well as other members of their school such as Dabīrān Kātibī Qazwīnī, author of *Ḥikmat al-ʿayn*, and Athīr al-Dīn Abharī, who wrote the famous classic *Kitāb al-hidāyah* which became a standard text for the study of philosophy for many centuries. But Persian texts of high literary and doctrinal quality appeared parallel with the Arabic texts and are characteristic of the school of Naṣīr al-Dīn.

From the seventh/thirteenth to the tenth/sixteenth centuries, during the least known period of the development of Islamic philosophy in Persia, important works continued to appear in Persian, only a small part of which has been studied so far. A significant landmark of this period is the treatises of Ṣāʾin al-Dīn ibn Turkah who lived in the eighth/fourteenth century and who wrote nearly forty treatises in Persian which foreshadow the final synthesis between the *mashshāʾī*, *ishrāqī* and *ʿirfānī* schools achieved by Ṣadr al-Dīn Shīrāzī in the tenth/sixteenth century.[21] These treatises have been neglected until now even in Persia itself and only after their edition and publication, which is under way, will they gain the popularity they deserve among an audience that is more extensive than the few who are acquainted with manuscript material in this field.

A second important corpus of works of this period in Persian is the writings of Jalāl al-Dīn Dawānī who of course like Ibn Turkah, Quṭb al-Dīn, and Suhrawardī also wrote in Arabic. Of his Persian works the *Akhlāq-i jalālī*, modeled upon the *Akhlāq-i nāṣirī*, is well known in the West mostly because of its popularity in India and its translation into English during the past century. But he also wrote a number of works in Persian dealing with *Kalām* and Sufism as well as philosophy.[22] His writings, like those of Ibn Turkah, display the tendency to synthesize the different schools of Islam, in his case mostly *Kalām* and philosophy.

Strangely enough with the advent of the Safavids, which marked the establishment of a national state in Persia, the use of the Persian language in the intellectual sciences diminished rather than increased. Mīr Dāmād, the founder of the "School of Ispahan"[23] wrote only one theosophical work in Persian, the *Jadhawāt*, although he composed some fine Persian poetry. The greatest *ḥakīm* of this age, Ṣadr al-Dīn Shīrāzī, also wrote only one major work in Persian, the *Si aṣl*,[24] the rest of his numerous doctrinal treatises being in Arabic. Only among the later Safavid figures such as Mullā Muḥsin Fayḍ Kāshānī, the author of *Kalimat-i maknūnah*, ʿAbd al-Razzāq Lāhījī, the author of *Gawhar-murād*, and Qāḍī Saʿīd Qummī, the author of *Kalīd-i bihisht* do we find again a greater interest in writing in Persian although even in these cases most of their works were in Arabic. Kāshānī and Lāhījī, however, were also important poets of the Persian language and in fact expressed much of their metaphysical teaching in didactic poetry. Altogether during the Safavid period the Indian subcontinent was perhaps the most active arena for Persian prose in the field of the intellectual sciences, while in Persia itself there was a definite decrease in the usage of philosophical and scientific Persian in comparison with the periods either before or after.

During the Qajar period there was a marked renaissance of Persian prose and a return to writing philosophical works in Persian although Arabic remained the main language of the traditional sciences. During the Qajar period, especially from the time of Nāṣir al-Dīn Shah when Tehran became the center for the study of traditional philosophy, a movement began to translate major works of the Islamic sciences, and particularly philosophy, into Persian. Several works of Mullā Ṣadrā for example were translated from Arabic at this time[25] in a movement that resembles somewhat the work of the fifth/eleventh and sixth/twelfth centuries to translate Ibn Sīnā and other masters into Persian. Parallel with this movement, many of the outstanding *ḥakīms* of the day wrote major works in Persian. Ḥājjī Mullā Hādī Sabziwārī, the best known figure of his day in *ḥikmah*, wrote one of his major works, the *Asrār al-ḥikam* in Persian[26] and also composed several independent treatises on *ḥikmah* in that language.[27] Mullā ʿAbdallāh Zunūzī wrote two major treatises mostly on eschatology entitled *Lamaʿāt-i ilāhiyyah* and *Anwār-i jaliyyah* in Persian,[28] while his son, Mullā ʿAlī Zunuzī, who was perhaps the most original *ḥakīm* of his day, wrote all of his works, of which the *Badāyiʿ al-ḥikam* is the best known, in Persian. This tendency continued into the Pahlavi period among traditional *ḥakīms* as can be observed in the writings of such masters as Sayyid Muḥammad Kāẓim ʿAssār, Sayyid Abu'l-Ḥasan Rafīʿī Qazwīnī and ʿAllāmah Ṭabāṭabāʾī, all of whom write in both Arabic and Persian.

The vast majority of Persian philosophical texts written in Persia itself as well as in the subcontinent and Turkey remain unedited and have been only rarely studied. The few works mentioned here are only the summits of a few mountain peaks. The rest of the range remains hidden beneath clouds which only careful and patient scholarship can gradually disperse until the complete anatomy of the range becomes visible. Practically every library catalogued recently in Persia has revealed important manuscripts in this field that had not been known before. These texts invite the talents of scholars who must perform the often thankless task of editing these works so as to make them available to a larger audience.

The vast body of philosophical and theosophical works in Persian is an integral part of the Islamic intellectual heritage without a knowledge of which many chapters of the history of Islamic philosophy and the sciences will remain completely obscure. Moreover, this body is of the utmost significance for the present-day intellectual life of Persia, Afghanistan, and even Tajikistan and the Muslims of the subcontinent because it is these works—more than those in Arabic read by fewer people in these lands today—that can influence the direction of thought and life of the Muslims of these areas in the future. The rich intellectual heritage of Islam, which alone can provide the necessary weapons to combat the deadly influences of secularism and modernism, is naturally most easily accessible to the Persian-speaking world through works written in its own language. For the general public with a modern education in these lands whose knowledge of classical Arabic has unfortunately become limited, these texts provide the most direct avenue of access to that "paradise of wisdom" which came into being in the bosom of Islam and which is a most precious heritage for all Muslims. As for scholars and specialists in the field of Islamic philosophy, this Persian corpus is a necessary supplement to the basic Arabic works. Without it the vast panorama of the Islamic intellectual sciences cannot be completely seen, a panorama which was destined to be depicted mostly in Arabic but also to a significant degree in Persian, although many ethnic groups contributed to its execution.

NOTES

[1] Even in Persia itself the traditional courses on Islamic philosophy are taught to this day from Arabic texts which are usually read by the master and then commented upon in Persian. That is why the major effort to publish texts of Islamic traditional sciences including philosophy (which we use throughout this paper in its traditional Islamic sense of *ḥikmah* and not in its profane meaning) in lithographed editions during the past century in Persia was concerned for the most part with Arabic texts and only a few Persian texts appeared at that time. Only during the present generation, with the decrease in knowledge of Arabic among people with modern education, has the importance of Persian texts in keeping Islamic philosophy alive for these classes become fully realized and an effort begun during the past few years to edit the Persian texts. See S. H. Nasr, "Islamic Philosophy in Contemporary Persia; A Survey of Activity During the Past Two Decades," Middle East Center, University of Utah, Monograph, 1971.

[2] The systematic catalogues of different Persian libraries that have appeared during the past few years under the care of such men as M. T. Danechpazhuh, A. N. Monzavi, Ibn Yūsuf, ʿA. H. Ḥāʾirī, S. ʿA. Anwār, A. Gulchīn Maʿānī, have brought to light many important manuscripts. See A. Monzavi, *A Catalogue of Persian Manuscripts*, 3 vols (Tehran: Regional Cultural Institute, 1969-70); and the pioneering work of C. A. Storey, *Persian Literature. A Bio-Bibliographical Survey, 1927–58.*

[3] Edited by Jalāl Matīnī, who is a specialist in 4th/10th and 5th/11th century Persian prose, Mashhad, 1344 (A. H. solar).

[4] In his *Tārīkh-i adabiyyāt dar Irān,* 3 vols., Tehran, 1342 on, Dr. Ṣafā has listed many of the philosophical, scientific, theological and Sufi works in Persian up to the Mongol invasion.

[5] H. Corbin, ed., *Commentaire de la Qasida Ismaélienne d'Abuʾl Haitham Jorjani* (Tehran-Paris, 1955).

[6] H. Corbin and M. Moʿin, eds., *Kashf al-Mahjub* (Tehran-Paris, 1949).

[7] For a history of this much too neglected school see S. H. Nasr, "Philosophy," in *Cambridge History of Iran,* vol. 4, ed. R. N. Frye (in press); and H. Corbin (with the collaboration of S. H. Nasr and O. Yahya), *Histoire de la philosophie islamique*, vol., 1, (Paris, 1964), pp. 110 ff.

[8] The metaphysics and natural philosophy of this work were edited by A. Khurāsānī, Tehran, 1315; and S. M. Mishkāt, Tehran, 1331; and M. Moʿīn, Tehran 1331 (A.H. solar).

[9] See the introduction of H. Corbin to Mullā Ṣadrā, *Kitāb al-mashāʿir* (*Le livre des pénétrations métaphysiques*) (Tehran-Paris, 1964).

[10] Most of these works were published by Anjumān-i Athār-i Millī in Tehran on the occasion of Ibn Sīnā's millennary celebrations, the majority edited by Ghulām Ḥusayn Ṣadīqī. See S. H. Nasr, *An Introduction to Islamic Cosmological Doctrines* (Cambridge, 1964), pp. 296–97.

11 Edited by E. Yarshater, Tehran, 1333 (A.H. solar).

12 H. Corbin, ed. and trans, *Avicenne et le récit visionnaire*, vol. 2 (Tehran-Paris, 1954).

13 See ᶜA. ᶜUṣayrān's edition of ᶜAyn al-Quḍāt, *Tamhīdāt*, Tehran, 1341 (A. H. solar); and ᶜA. Monzawī and ᶜA. ᶜUsayrān's edition of his *Nāmah-hā*, Tehran, 1348 (A.H. solar).

14 See the *Rasāʾil* of Khayyām, ed. by M. Awistā, Tehran 1338 (A. H. solar), and *Kulliyyāt-i āthār-i fārsī-yi Ḥakīm ᶜUmar-i Khayyām*, ed. by M. ᶜAbbāsī, Tehran, 1338 (A.H. solar).

15 On the significance of this corpus see S. H. Nasr, "The Persian Works of Shaykh al-Ishrāq Shihāb al-Dīn Suhrawardī," *Islamic Quarterly*, vol. 12, no. 1–2 (1968), pp. 3–8.

16 We have edited this complete corpus as *Les Oeuvres persanes de Sohrawardī* (Tehran-Paris, 1970).

17 Edited by M. Minovi and Y. Mahdavi as *Muṣannafāt*, 2 vols. (Tehran, 1331–37).

18 This best known of Muslim works on philosophical ethics has been a main text in the educational curriculum of generations of Persian and Muslims of the subcontinent. See G M. Wickens, trans. *Nasirean Ethics* (London, 1964).

19 Edited by M. T. Danechpazhuh, Tehran, 1339.

20 Most of this vast work was edited by S. M. Mishkāt, Tehran, 1317-20.

21 These treatises have been edited for the first time by S. ᶜA. Mūsawī Bihbahānī and I. Dībājī and are being printed by the Tehran University Press.

22 Most of these were edited by I. Wāᶜiẓ Jawādī in different numbers of the bulletin *Taḥqīq dar mabdaʾ-i āfarīnish*. He is now planning a complete edition of Dawānī's Persian works in a single volume.

23 See S. H. Nasr, "The School of Ispahan," in *A History of Muslim Philosophy*, ed. M. M. Sharif vol. 2 (Wiesbaden, 1966), pp. 904 ff.

24 Edited by S. H. Nasr, Tehran, 1340.

25 See for example the translation of Mullā Ṣadrā's *Mashāᶜir* by Badīᶜ al-mulk, edited by H. Corbin in *Le livre des pénétrations métaphysiques* (*Kitāb al-mashāᶜir*).

26 Edited by A.Shaᶜrānī, Tehran, 1380 (A.H. lunar).

27 Edited by S.J. Āshtiyānī, *Rasāʾil* (Persian and Arabic), Mashhad, 1970.

28 Currently being edited by S.J. Āshtiyānī.

IBN SĪNĀ SAVANT

IBRAHIM MADKOUR

Nous savons que les recherches scientifiques en terre d'Islam ont commencé d'assez bonne heure. Déjà au premier siècle de l'Hégire, on a semé les premières graines des études juridiques, dogmatiques et linguistiques. Au IIè siècle, le mouvement scientifique musulman proprement dit a été poussé, et durant deux siècles consécutifs il se developpa et finit par atteindre son apogée aux IVè et Vè siècles. On voulait tout apprendre, on puisait à toutes les sources, on s'adressait aux centres culturels voisins, à Alexandrie, à Jundai'sabur et à Ḥarran. On appelait des spécialistes de tous les côtés et on envoyait des missions à la recherche des livres précieux. On traduisait du persan et de l'hindou, du syriaque et du grec[1]. On travaillait chacun de son côté ou en groupe, d'une manière privée ou sous l'égide des autorités. Les premiers Khalifs Abbassides ont joué un rôle très important dans ce mouvement scientifique, en particuier al-Manṣūr (m.A.D.775), al-Rashīd (m.809) et al-Maʾmūn (m.833). Ils construisirent des centres des recherches et prodiguèrent les récompenses aux chercheurs. Ils ont fondé des laboratoires et des observatoires pour faire des expériences propres à eux.[2] Il n'y avait ni racisme ni sectarisme, des Persans et des Arabes collaboraient ensemble, des Juifs et des Chrétiens travaillaient côte à côte avec les Musulmans.

Les Arabes ont commencé par les sciences pratiques, spécialement par la médecine, l'alchimie, et l'astronomie. C'est tout naturel, il faut vivre avant de philosopher; mais ils ont fini par embrasser toutes les sciences physiques et mathématiques connues alors: chimie, biologie, physiologie, médecine, zoologie, botanique, arithmétique, géométrie, astronomie et musique. Dans toutes ces sciences, les Musulmans ont eu recours à l'héritage humain oriental et occidental. Ils ont surtout profité de l'encyclopédie grecque qui a servi de base à leurs recherches scientifiques. Ils ont aussi ajouté à cet héritage leurs propres contributions. On peut bien parler des sciences arabes, comme on parle des sciences grecques.

I. Le IVè siècle de l'Hégire est généralement considéré comme le siècle d'or des études rationnelles et scientifiques musulmanes. En effet, si les Arabes se sont occupés pendant les IIè et IIIè siècles de traduire les sources étrangères et de les assimiler, ils se sont adonnés au IVè siècle à leurs propres recherches. Grâce aux Muᶜtazilites, la théologie musulmane (*al-Kalām*) s'est déjà constituée comme une science complète, et al-Ashᶜarī (m.935) n'a fait que la formuler d'une autre manière. La mystique musulmane (*al-taṣawwuf*) avec al-Junayd (m.970) et al-Ḥallāj (m.922) passait de l'ascétisme à l'extase et à l'union avec Dieu. Al-Fārābī (m.950), lui-aussi, organisait avec pénétration et profondeur les diverses parties de la philosophie. La médecine arabe, à son tour, ne se contentait plus de repéter les données d'un Hippocrate (m.377 av. J.C.) ou d'un Galien (m.A.D.); le grand al-Rāzī (m.932) y ajoutait le fruit de ses propres expériences. La chimie, après Jābir Ibn Ḥayyān (m.776) et son école, est devenue une science très attrayante. Le même al-Rāzī l'a bien developpée et s'en est occupé avec beaucoup de finesse. L'astronomie et les mathématiques ont fait de grands progrès, il suffit de mentionner ici le nom d'al-Bīrunī (m.1048), contemporain d'Ibn Sīnā.

En fait, c'est dans ce siècle qu'al-Sheikh al-Raʾīs fut né (370 h = A.D. 980) et dans cette atmosphère qu'il a été élevé. D'une famille ismaᶜilienne il a eu, dès son enfance, un entourage familier avec la science et la philosophie. Son père veillait bien à lui assurer une vie uniquement consacrée à l'étude. Il faut remarquer que l'ismaᶜilisme a joué un rôle dans la formation et le développement des sciences musulmanes. A l'âge de dix ans, Ibn Sīnā commença à apprendre l'arithmétique et la géométrie. A seize ans, il s'engagea à faire de la médecine.[3] Pendant les vingt premières années de sa vie, il s'est adonné entièrement aux études. Il s'appliquait au travail intellectuel avec une ardeur infatigable. Il dormait peu et consacrait ses jours et ses nuits à l'étude.[4] Il ne laissait jamais un livre qu'il avait commencé sans le terminer.[5] L'acquisition des livres à cette époque n'était pas difficile. Sa famille d'abord avait une bonne bibliothèque mise à sa disposition.[6] Il ne s'arrêtait d'ailleurs pas là, il eut la fortune d'utiliser une des plus riches bibliothèques de l'époque, celle de Nūḥ Ibn Manṣūr le Samanide (m.997), où il put consulter des documents rares et très précieux.[7] De cette vaste et pénétrante lecture, Ibn Sīnā est arrivé à une connaissance encyclopédique. A vingt ans, il devient une autorité dans les sciences physiques et mathématiques contemporaines qu'il a su plus tard exposer dans son grand *Shifāʾ*.

II. Faute de lieu, nous mettons de côté sa médecine et ses recherches mathématiques et astronomiques. Nous nous contentons de dire quelques mots de ses études chimiques et physiques. Là, nous nous reférons surtout à son *Shifāʾ* qui est une grande source des connaissances scientifiques.

A l'exception de la médecine, il n'y a peut-être pas d'étude scientifique qui eut, en terre d'Islam, un essor égal à la chimie pendant les IIè, IIIè et IVè siècles de l'Hégire. Elle fut, d'assez bonne heure, un sujet de recherche et d'expérimentation.[8] Malgré les controverses concernant l'existence de Jābir Ibn Ḥayyān et l'authenticité de ses oeuvres, il n'en demeure pas moins qu'il y eut déjà au second siècle de l'Hégire des études chimiques arabes.[9] Ces études portent sur diverses expériences, décrivent certains éléments et se servent de quelques appareils scientifiques.[10] Nous avons déjà remarqué qu'au IVè siècle de l'Hégire, la chimie arabe devient une science ayant sa méthode, ses lois et ses problèmes. Abū Bakr al-Rāzī est considéré, à juste titre, son second fondateur. Il voulait en soumettre les théories à un examen rigoureux et leur accorder un caractère plus positif.[11]

Ibn Sīnā ne pouvait ne pas s'occuper de la chimie; dans son entourage, il y en avait déjà quelques amateurs. Il connaissait aussi la ferveur quʾ al-Rāzī et al-Bīrūnī avaient eu pour elle. Il nous a laissé un petit traité chimique intitulé *al-Ixīr* qui a été traduit en persan et en latin. Ruska se doute à tort de son authenticité.[12] Dans ce traité, Avicenne explique des questions chimiques et réfute la fausse prétention des Alchimistes.[13] Pour lui, le fondement de l'alchimie est faux, car les métaux ne dérivent pas, comme on le dit, d'une même origine. Au contraire, chaque métal est une espèce indépendante et il n'y a pas de moyen de transmuter les espèces.[14] C'est à tort de croire que l'on peut transformer les métaux vils en métaux précieux.

Ibn Sīnā est donc un chimiste qui nie complètement les prétentions des alchimistes. Il est plutôt pour l'expérimentation chimique et n'admet pas la fausse idée de la transmutation des métaux, soutenue par les anciens alchimistes. Il se rapproche par là des chimistes modernes. Il est à remarquer que si Albert le grand (m.1280) et Roger Bacon (m.1294), parmi les scolastiques latins, ont aussi refusé l'idée de la transmutation des métaux, c'est sans doute sous une influence avicennienne.[15] Inutile d'ajouter que l'étude de la chimie avicennienne est encore à faire.

III. Jusqu'à présent, on n'a pas fait assez attention aux études physiques d'Avicenne, on s'est occupé surtout de sa philosophie, de sa mystique et de sa médecine. Nous croyons que son *Shifāʾ*, dans sa nouvelle édition, nous en offre une matière abondante. Là encore, nous ne pouvons que dire quelques mots de certaines disciplines physiques dont il s'est occupé.

Dans son livre: "le Ciel et le Monde" (*al-Samāʾ wal-ʿĀlam*), Ibn Sīnā soutient que la terre est ronde.[16] Il prouve sa rotondité par différentes manières, particulièrement par la fameuse preuve tirée du fait qu'un navire arrivant de loin n'est pas vu tout entier d'un seul coup.[17] Cette idée de la rotondité de la terre passa au moyen-âge chrétien et prépara sans doute la voie à Copernic (m.1543) et à Galilée (m.1642).[18]

Dans son livre: *"Les Actions et les Passions" (al-ʿAfʿāl wal-Infiʿālāt)*,[19] il parle de la salure de l'eau de la mer et de son poids spécifique, montrant qu'elle est plus lourde que l'eau de rivière.[20] L'eau, en elle-même, est normalement douce, sa salure provient de son mélange avec un autre corps. La salure de l'eau des mers est le résultat de son contact avec des couches terrestres.

La preuve en est que l'on peut distiller l'eau de mer et elle devient douce.[21] C'est à tort qu'Empédocle (m.430 av. J.C.) dit d'une manière poétique que la salure de l'eau de mer vient de ce qu'elle est la sueur de la terre.[22] Il y a des lieux, remarque Avicenne, d'où les eaux se sont retirées, comme à Najaf en Iraq. Voilà des données géographiques et géologiques assez interessantes pour leurs temps.

Ibn Sīnā développe encore davantage ses études géographiques et géologiques dans sa "Météorologie" (*al-ʾĀthār al-ʿUlwiyya*).[23] En géographie, il y traite de l'eau, de la terre, de l'équateur, des tropiques du Cancer et du Capricorne, du pôle nord et du pôle sud. Il traite aussi des vents, des nuages, du tonnerre, des éclairs, des tempêtes et des étoiles brillantes.[24] C'est par les vents que la pluie tombe et que la glace et la neige se forment.[25]

En géologie, Ibn Sīnā traite de la formation des montagnes et des rochers, des tremblements de terre et des métaux.[26] Son exposé fournit des remarques précises et des idées dont un grand nombre rappelle les principes de la géologie moderne. Il est à remarquer surtout que sa manière d'expliquer la formation des montagnes est à la base de la théories des volcans donnée au XVIIè siècle A.D.[27]

IV. Dans sa "Botanique" (*al-Nabāt*)[28], Ibn Sinā compare constamment les plantes aux animaux, en essayant de déterminer les différences spécifiques entre le règne végétal et le règne animal.[29] Il explique les principes de la nutrition des plantes et leur génération.[30] Il décrit leurs différentes parties: tiges, branches, feuilles, ainsi que les grains et les fruits.[31] Il résume brièvement leurs variétés.[32] Aussi ce traité peut-il être considéré comme une étude de la botanique générale.

De tout temps, la botanique est liée à la médecine. Hippocrate, parmi les Grecs, avait déjà emprunté aux herboristes antérieurs certains détails concernant les grains et les racines des différentes plantes. Ibn Sīnā ne traite pas les plantes seulement dans sa physique du *Shifāʾ*, il les traite aussi dans son grand livre de médecine, *le Canon*.[33] Là, il décrit encore soigneusement les différentes sortes de plantes, en indiquant leurs tiges, leurs fleurs, leurs feuilles et leurs fruits. Il ne manque pas naturellement de désigner leurs effets dans les médicaments. Ces deux textes se complètent donc l'un l'autre et nous aident à avoir une idée claire de la botanique avicennienne. Cette botanique a été connue dans le monde latin.[34] Elle n'a pas manqué de jouer un rôle chez les botanistes arabes postérieurs, en particulier Ibn al-Bayṭār (m. 1248).

V. Dans son *Ṭabāʾiʿ al-Ḥayawān*[35] "(*Caractères des Animaux*)", Ibn Sīnā, à part ses études zoologiques, s'occupe de la biologie et de la physiologie. Pour lui, la biologie est soumise aux lois de mouvement et de changement; elle dépend de l'idée de forme et de matière, et fait en un mot partie de la physique.[36] Elle est aussi étroitement liée à la psychologie. N'est-ce pas l'âme qui est à la fois principe de vie et de mouvement chez l'homme et chez les animaux? On examine en biologie la sensation et la perception qui sont des éléments psychologiques. La psychologie, elle-même, ne peut se passer d'une base biologique.[37] Il en est de même de la médecine qui ne se détache pas de la biologie. Ibn Sīnā était en même temps médecin et biologiste. Il traite de la biologie aussi bien dans ses écrits de médecine que dans ses écrits de physique. Dans son *Ṭabāʾiʿ al-Ḥayawān*, il s'occupe de l'homme plus que des animaux, il explique en détail ses systèmes digestif, respiratoire et génital.[38]

En tant que biologiste, Ibn Sīnā croit fermement au principe de finalité. Il pense que les parties d'un être vivant s'entraident en vue de réaliser ce qui est le plus utile pour lui. Dans la nature, il y a des finesses et des ingéniosités frappantes; rien n'a été crée en vain. Dans le monde des vivants, il y a des miracles et des prodiges éclatants. "Que Dieu soit béni, il est le Meilleur des Créateurs."[39] Tout vivant, même tout organe, a son utilité qui nous échappe parfois. Nous savons que Ibn Sīnā était un grand optimiste, pour lui, le monde est le meilleur possible.[40]

VI. Il accorde enfin à la physiologie une importance très grande car elle prouve, elle aussi, la Providence divine et nous explique comment les êtres existent et vivent. Il pense qu'il y a trois organes principaux pour conserver l'individu et l'espèce, à savoir le coeur, le cerveau et le foie. Le coeur est le principe de la vie; le cerveau principe du mouvement et de la sensation; le foie principe de la nutrition.[41] Chacun de ces organes a ses serviteurs: les poumons et les artères sont au service du coeur; les organes de nutrition et les nerfs au service du cerveau; l'estomac et les veines au service du foie.[42]

Ibn Sīnā donne une image claire du système digestif. Il indique le rôle qu'y jouent la bouche et les dents. Il considère l'estomac comme la cuisine des aliments.[43] Il connait l'oesophage, le diaphragme, le duodenum, le pylore, le pancréas, l'intestin grêle et le gros intestin.[44] Il explique en quoi les sécretions et la bile en particulier contribuent à parfaire la digestion.[45]

Il a prêté grande attention à la respiration et a parlé clairement de tout le système respiratoire. Il a connu la trachée artère et l'épiglotte. Il a donné l'anatomie des poumons, exposé ses diverses ramifications et indiqués la fonction de cet appareil. C'est lui qui prépare l'air pour nourrir le corps et l'esprit. Et ce n'est pas sans raison que l'homme a deux poumons: si l'un s'arrête, la respiration continue quand même.[46]

On voit ainsi que dans le domaine des sciences naturelles, Ibn Sīnā a fait des études en chimie, en géographie physique, en géologie, en botanique, en zoologie, en biologie et en physiologie, sans parler de la médecine. Certes, il profite des recherches précédentes, mais il les a développées par ses propres moyens. Il mentionne quelquefois les faits qu'il a constatés lui-même[47] et les questionnaires qu'il avait posés.[48] C'est surtout dans ses études scientifiques qu'il se sert de l'observation et de l'experimentation. Il a déjà donné dans son *Canon* quelques règles de l'expérimentation qui nous font penser à la méthode expérimentale d'un Claude Bernard.[49] Ces études avicenniennes ont eu leur influence aussi bien dans le monde latin que dans le monde arabe.

Nous n'avions pas à donner ici un tableau complet de l'oeuvre scientifique d'Avicenne. Nous avons voulu simplement attirer l'attention et jeter un coup d'oeil sur un coin abandonné de sa pensée. En effet, on s'est beaucoup occupé de sa philosophie et de sa mystique. On a aussi dégagé quelques traits de sa médecine. Mais l'Avicenne savant est presqu'inconnu. Il est à remarquer cependant que ce savant et médecin fut traduit d'abord en latin et par sa médecine on a été appelé à sa philosophie. Ayant vécu avec les *Ṭabī*ᶜ*iyyāt* et les *Riyāḍiyyāt* du *Shifā*ᵓ dans les dernières années, j'ai constaté qu'il y a là beaucoup à faire. J'espère que la nouvelle édition de ces deux parties appellera les chercheurs. Au fond, l'histoire des sciences arabes est presque une terre vierge et ses sources sont jusqu'à présent pour la plupart manuscrites.

NOTES

1 I. Madkour, L'*Organon d'Aristote dans le monde arabe*, 2è éd. (Paris, 1969), p. 30.

2 Ibn Abī Osaibiᶜa, ᶜ*Oyūn al-Anbā*ᵓ (Koenigsberg, 1884), t. 2, p. 187.

3 Pour la bibliographie d'Avicenne, voir en particulier les sources arabes principales: al-Qifṭī, *Tārīkh al-ḥokamā*ᵓ (Leipzig, 1903), pp. 413–26, Ibn Abī Osaibiᶜa, ᶜ*Oyūn*, t. II, pp. 2–20; Bayhaqī, *Tārīkh al-ḥokamā*' (Damas, 1946), pp. 52–72; Shahrazūrī, *Rawdat al-afrāḥ*, inédit et que nous sommes en train de publier.

4 Qifṭī, *Tārikh*, p. 412.

5 *Ibid.*, p. 422.

6 *Ibid.*

7 *Ibid.*, p. 416.

8 Ibn al-Nadīm, *Fihrist*, pp. 498–99.

9 Ibn Khaldūn, *Muqaddima* (Beyrouth, 1879), p. 468.

10 I. Madkour, "Avicenne et l'Alchimie," *Revue du Caire* (1951), pp. 120–29.

11 M. Meyerhof, "Science and Medicine," in *Legacy of Islam* (Oxford, 1931), pp. 313–55.

12 J. Ruska, "Die Alchimie des Avicenna," *Isis*, t. XXI, 1934, pp. 14–51.

13 A. Atech, "Risālat al-Ixīr," dans *Millénaire d'Avicenne*, Le Caire, 1952, pp. 60–64.

14 Ibn Sīnā, "Risālat al-Ixīr," dans *Millénaire*, p. 63; *al-Shifā*ᵓ, *la Physique*, t. V. *Météorologie*, Le Caire, 1965, pp. 30–31.

15 Berthelot, *La chimie au moyen-âge*, t. 2, pp. 282, 292.

16 Ibn Sīnā, *al-Shifā*ᵓ, *al-Ṭabī*ᶜ*iyyāt*, II, *al-Samā*ᵓ *wal-*ᶜ*Ālam*, Le Caire, 1969.

17 *Ibid.*, p. 55.

[18] M. T. D'Alverny, "Les traductions latines chez Ibn Sina," dans *Millénaire*, pp. 59–69.
[19] Ibn Sīnā, *Shifāʾ*, *Ṭabīʿiyyāt*, IV, *al-ʾAfʿāl wal-Infiʿālāt*, Le Caire, 1960.
[20] *Ibid.*, p. 206.
[21] Ibid., pp. 207-8.
[22] Ibid., p. 209.
[23] Ibn Sīnā, *Shifāʾ*, *Ṭabīʿiyyāt*, V, *al-ʾĀthār al-ʿUlwiyya*, Le Caire, 1965.
[24] Ibid., p. 43.
[25] Ibid., pp. 65–67.
[26] Ibid., p. 9.
[27] I. Crombie, *Avicenna's Influence on the Medieval Scientific Tradition* (Cambridge, 1951).
[28] Ibn Sīnā, *Shifāʾ*, *Ṭabīʿiyyat*, VII, *Nabāt*, 1965.
[29] Ibid., pp. 9–10.
[30] Ibid., pp. 18–20.
[31] Ibid., pp. 27–31, 33–37.
[32] Ibid., pp. 38–44.
[33] Ibn Sīnā, *le Canon*, Le Caire, 1294 h., IIè livre: *Fil-Adwiya al-mufrada*.
[34] D'Alverny, "les traductions."
[35] Ibn Sīnā, *Shifāʾ*, *Physique*, T. VII, le Caire, 1969.
[36] Ibid., p. 188.
[37] Ibid., p. 210.
[38] Ibid., pp. 242–46, 277–85.
[39] Ibid., pp. 247, 300.
[40] Ibn Sīnā, *Ilāhiyyāt*, le Caire, 1960, T. II, pp. 414–21.
[41] Ibn Sīnā, *Al-Ḥayawān*, p. 15.
[42] Ibid., p. 15.
[43] Ibid., p. 292.
[44] Ibid., pp. 295, 296.
[45] Ibid., p. 320.
[46] Ibid., pp. 277–82.
[47] Ibn Sīnā, *Āthār ʿUlwiyya*, pp. 58, 60, 61.
[48] Ibn Sīnā, *Ḥayawān*, p. 119.
[49] Ibn Sīnā, *Canon*, Rome 1593, pp. 115–16.

AVICENNA'S CHAPTER, "ON THE RELATIVE," IN THE *METAPHYSICS* OF THE *SHIFĀ᾽*

Michael E. Marmura (1)

INTRODUCTION

Avicenna in the *Shifā᾽* (*The Healing*) devotes two discussions to the concept of relation—in the *Categories* of the *Logic* and in the *Metaphysics*.[1] These overlap at points, but differ in approach, aim, and to a good extent in content. The first and more extensive treatment, consisting of three chapters, is essentially an interpretive expansion of Aristotle's doctrine in his *Categories*. Its approach is linguistic and logical and, although it discusses some of the ontological questions treated in the *Metaphysics*, its primary aim is to define the term "relation" and to exhibit its semantic features.[2] By contrast, the discussion in the *Metaphysics* is specifically concerned with ontology, particularly with the question, not discussed in the *Logic*, of whether relations exist in concrete things (*al-aʿyān*) or whether they are merely subjective concepts in the mind.

The chapter in the *Metaphysics* divides naturally into three parts. The first introduces relations as accidents occurring to the categories—here, as the context shows, regarded not so much as terms but as modes of being—and discusses their classification. This classification draws heavily on Aristotle, but exhibits refinements. The second part presents the argument that one and the same relation cannot belong to more than one subject, this holding true of symmetrical as well as asymmetrical relations. The third and longest part is devoted to refuting the argument, encountered in Islamic dogmatic theology (*kalām*), which denies the existence of relations outside the mind.[3] This is the familiar argument that the supposition of such extramental existence leads necessarily to the infinite regress of relations. It is also said to lead—in the version Avicenna reports—to the absurdity of relating an existent to a nonexistent, namely, a state of affairs in the present to a nonexistent one either in the past or the future.

Avicenna, as he tells us in introducing this part, regards the question of the existence of relations as the most important in the chapter. He rejects the argument from infinite regress, affirming quite explicitly that there are relations that exist in concrete things. But the sense in which he holds that they so exist is not altogether clear. Avicenna's language at sensitive points in the argument is ambiguous.

In what follows we offer a translation of the Arabic with a commentary largely on the content, relegating as much as possible discussion of purely linguistic and editorial matters to the footnotes.

TRANSLATION AND COMMENTARY

On the Relative[4]

RELATIVES AND THEIR CLASSIFICATION

> As for discussing the relative and showing how one ought to ascertain the nature and definition of the relative and of relation, what we offered in the *Logic* is sufficient for those who have understood it. Regarding [the supposition] that if relation has existence, then it would be an accident, this is undoubtedly the case since this is something inconceivable in itself, but is always conceived of as something in terms of [another] thing; for there is never a relation which is not an accidental occurrence. (p. 152, lines 4–7)

When Avicenna refers us to the *Logic* for the definition of "the relative (*al-muḍāf*) and relation (*al-iḍāfa*)," he intends a distinction between these terms, a distinction encountered in the *Logic*.[5] "The relative" is the generic term, referring to whatever is related as well as to the category, relation, as such.[6] Avicenna identifies this generic term with Aristotle's first definition in *Categories*, 7, 6a, 35 ff.—in Avicenna's language, that "whose nature is predicated with respect to another."[7] "Relation," on the other hand, is sometimes used as the specific term, referring only to the category, relation. Avicenna identifies this with Aristotle's second definition in *Categories*, 7, 8a, 28 ff., where, to use the language of the Oxford translation, "relation to an external thing is a necessary condition for existence." Avicenna expresses this second definition as follows: "Things belonging to the relative are those for which the existence they have consists in that they are related."[8]

In the above quotation, however, we note that the term, "the relative," is used where one expects the term "relation." Avicenna's terminology shifts and in both the *Logic* and the *Metaphysics* we find him for the most part using these two expressions interchangeably. Still, he uses them in places as distinct terms to convey the difference between the two Aristotelian definitions of relation. In the third part of the chapter, as we shall see, it is the generic, nonrestricted definition that is used to answer the question of whether relations exist in concrete things.

Avicenna also states in this introductory passage that if relations are supposed to exist—that is, to exist objectively in things—then they would have to be accidents. The reason for this is clear in the text. But the statement carries with it something else, namely, that accidents are part of the furniture of the objective world. One must bear this in mind when it comes to ascertaining what Avicenna means when he affirms that relations exist in the concrete.

The above passage is followed by a discussion of the classification of relations, introduced as accidents occurring to the various categories. This analysis is naturally rooted in Aristotle's discussions of relation in *Categories*, 7, and *Metaphysics*, V, 15. (It also repeats some of the things Avicenna states in his *Logic*.)[9] But there is development and refinement, perhaps influenced by the literature of commentary available to Avicenna.

Avicenna begins by discussing two-termed relations, dividing them into those that agree and those that differ in their terms.

> Its first occurrence is either to substance, as for instance, father and son, or to quantity. Some relations differ in their two terms, while some agree. Those that differ[10] are like the half and the double; those that agree are like the equal and the equal, the proximate and the proximate,[11] the corresponding and the corresponding, the touching and the touching.
>
> With some of those that differ, the difference is definite and ascertainable, as for example, the half and the double; with some it is unascertainable but is based on what is ascertainable, as in the case of the excessive and the deficient, the [indeterminable] part and the aggregate. The same obtains when one relative occurs within another, for example, the more excessive and the more deficient; for the excessive is excessive as measured against something also excessive in comparison with a deficient.
>
> Some of the relatives belong to quality. Of those some agree [in their two terms], as for example, the similar; while some disagree, as for example, the fast and the slow in motion, the heavy and light in weights and the sharp and grave in sounds. Again, in all these one relation may occur to another. [Relations also belong] to place, as, for instance, the higher and lower; to time, as for example, the prior and the posterior; and to [matters] of such description. (p. 152, line 8 to p. 153, line 4)

Avicenna now goes on to discuss relations, not only as accidents occurring to the various categories, but also as types in their own right, as it were, listing them under the divisions of equality, excess and deficiency, action and passion, and resemblance. Here, again, Aristotle is very much in evidence.

> It almost seems that relatives are confined to the divisions of equality, excess and deficiency, action and passion, whose source is power, and resemblance. Those pertaining to excess belong either to quantity, as you know, or to power, as in the case of the vanquisher, the conqueror, the repeller and the like. Those pertaining to action and passion are like

father and son, the cutter and [the thing] cut and similar things. Those pertaining to resemblance are like knowledge and the [thing] known, sensation and the [thing] sensed. For between these there is resemblance; knowledge resembling the state of the thing known; sensation, the state of the thing sensed. But the measure and limit of this resemblance is unascertainable. (p. 153, lines 4–11)

The above division of the relatives, however, is not inclusive and leaves out such directional relations as being to the left or to the right of. Avicenna is aware of this and in the concluding section of this part suggests another way of classifying relations.

Relative things, however, may [all] be encompassed in one way. Two relatives may not require any of those things by virtue of which a relation between them would occur. An example of this is that which is to the right of [something] or to the left of [it]. For in that which is to the right of [something] there is neither a quality nor any other state of affairs by virtue of which it acquires the relation of being to the right of. [Nothing makes it so related] other than the very fact of its being to the right of. [On the other hand] it may be required that there should be in each of the two related things something by virtue of which they become related to one another, as in the case of the lover and the loved. Thus, there exists in the lover an apprehending state which is the principle of the relation, while in the loved an apprehended state which renders him loved by the lover. Such a thing may exist in one of the two things, but not the other, as in the case of the knower and the [object] known. The latter became related only because something in the former has occurred, namely, knowledge. (pp. 153, line 12 to p. 154, line 7)

The example of the third type of relation (between knower and object known) has a background in Aristotle (*Metaphysics*, V, 15, 1021a, 30ff.) where we are told, in effect, that the object of knowledge is called relative, not because it itself refers to something else, but because something else refers to it. Aristotle has been understood to be speaking of a unilateral relation and this suggests that Avicenna is doing the same. This is certainly a possible and natural way of reading the Avicennan passage and the Latin text has been so understood.[12] But whether this interpretation accords with Avicenna's intention is not, as we see it, entirely certain.

There is first of all the matter of emphasis. As we read him, Avicenna's primary concern is with a criterion for an inclusive classification of relations, so that, even if in fact he intended to give an example of a unilateral relation, this to him would be of secondary interest. (It should perhaps be observed that the analysis of knowledge as a relation does not assume in Avicenna's writings the significance it assumes in the theology of St. Thomas Aquinas, who, incidentally, refers us directly to Aristotle's *Metaphysics*).[13] Then there is the wording of Avicenna's discussion. Knowledge is that "state of affairs" or "quality" by virtue of which knower and object known become related. The wording reads almost as though knowledge is not the relation between knower and object known, as though it is only that which renders the two related. Finally, there is a lexical consideration. In the *Logic*,[14] Avicenna assigns the term *nisba* to a unilateral relation, a term never used in the metaphysical chapter, and the term *iḍāfa* to a bilateral relation, the term consistently used in the chapter and in association with knowldge.

This first part on the classification of relations sets the stage for the subsequent ontological discussions. The distinction drawn between relations that agree and differ in their terms is of direct relevance to the discussion that immediately follows.

Relation as an Accident Belonging to One Subject Only.

If anything, this second part reveals the total commitment of Avicenna's doctrine of relation to a substance-accident ontology. His main argument is that a relation numerically one and the same does not belong to the related subjects taken together. Thus, if *A* and *B* are related, Avicenna argues in effect, then there are two relations, a relation P belonging to *A* and referring to B and a relation Q belonging to B and referring to A. True enough, in the case of symmetrical relations there is identity. But this is identity "in species," or kind. It is not numerical identity.

The underlying reason for this view is not difficult to discern. For Avicenna, relation is an accident and an accident can belong only to one subject. As J. R. Weinberg points out, the above view of relation as belonging to one subject only, though not explicitly stated by Aristotle, is implied in his doctrine.[15] Avicenna here is very much the Aristotelian. Interestingly, however, in the opening sentences of this second part, Avicenna tells us that the view he is expounding is not held by the majority. There is an indication in Alfarabi's recently published *Book of Letters* that its author belonged to this majority.[16]

This section of the discussion poses no special problems in exegesis. It speaks for itself and we simply present the translation.

What remains for us here concerning the relative is to know whether relation is an idea, one in number and subject matter, found between two things but having two aspects, as some, indeed most have thought, or whether there is for each of the two related things, in being related, a special property. We say:

Each of the two related things has in itself an idea with respect to the other, which is not the idea the other has in itself with respect to [the first].

This is evident in the things whose related terms differ, as in the case of the father. Its relation to fatherhood, which is a description of its existence, is in the father alone. But it belongs to the father with respect to something else [only as something] in the father. Its being with respect to the other does not make it exist in the other. Fatherhood does not exist in the son. Otherwise it would be a description [of the latter] from which a name for it is derivable. Rather, fatherhood belongs to the father. The same applies to the state of the son with respect to the father. There is nothing here at all which is in both of them. Here there is nothing but fatherhood and sonship. As for a state posited for both fatherhood and sonship, this is something unknown to us and has no name.

If [such a state of affairs] consists in the fact that each of the two has a state with respect to the other, this is similar to the case of the swan and snow, each of which is white. Nor is [this state] rendered identical by the fact that [it stands] with respect to the other; for whatever belongs to each individual with respect to the other, belongs to that individual and not the other; but it [possesses it] with respect to the other.

If you have understood this from what we have given you by way of example, then know that the [identical] state of affairs [obtains] in the rest of the relatives that do not disagree [in their two terms]. It is here, however, that most of the confusion occurs. Thus, [for example], since in the case of the two brothers, one has a state relative to the other and the other has a state relative to the first, and since the two states are of the same species, [these states] have been thought to be one individual. But this is not the case. To the first belongs [the state] of being brother to the second, that is, he has the description of being the brother of the second. [Now] this description is his, but [only his] with respect to the second. This is not the [same] description of the second numerically, but only in species, just as the case would be if the second was white and the first was white. Indeed, the second is the brother of the first because he has in himself a state predicable with reference to the first.

The same applies to touchability in two touching things. Each of the two touches the other in that it has [the state] of touching it which exists only with respect to the other if the other is similar [in its relation to it]. You must never think that an accident, one in number, exists in two substrata. Thus there is no need for you to apologize in this connection by making "accident" a problematic name, as some, who have little discernment, have done. (p. 154, line 7 to p. 155, line 16)

The Question of the Existence of Relations in "Concrete Things"

Avicenna begins this section by posing the question of whether "relation in itself exists in concrete things or whether it is something only conceived in the mind." He asks, that is, whether it is one of the things that become universal, particular, essential and so on, only when conceived in the mind, thereby giving expression to his conceptualism.

> But what is more important than this is for us to know whether relation in itself exists in concrete things or whether it is something only conceived in the mind, being like many of the states that adhere to things when conceived, after occurrence in the mind. For, when conceived, there occur to things in the mind circumstances that did not belong to them [externally]. They thus are rendered universal, particular, essential and accidental; they become genus and differentia, subject and predicate and things of this order. (p. 156, lines 1—5)

He first states that some have held that relations exist only as concepts. He then presents the opposing view, the argument for the objective existence of relations, an argument that has antecedents in Plotinus and Simplicius.[17]

> Some people have thus maintained that the reality of relations also occurs only in the soul when it conceives things. Another group has said, "On the contrary, relation is something found in concrete existents," and argued saying: "We know that this is in existence the father of that, and that that is in existence the son of this, regardless of whether this [fact] is conceived or not. We know that plants seek nourishment and that seeking involves relation. Plants do not, in any manner, have intellects, or apprehension. We know [moreover,] that the sky is in itself above the earth and that the earth is below it, regardless of whether or not this is apprehended. Relation is nothing other than these things to which we have alluded and their like, It belongs to things, even when it is not apprehended." (p. 156, lines 6–12)

Avicenna then reports the counterargument from infinite regress and also a shorter argument to the effect that the supposition of real relations leads to the absurdity of relating an existent to a nonexistent. It should be noted that the argument from infinite regress is so formulated that its applicability is not confined to the doctrine that a relation exists only in one subject.

> The other party has argued: "If relation were to exist in things, then from this it would follow that relations become infinite. There would exist, [for example], between father and son a relation. This relation would be either [common] to both, belong [only] to one, or to each [separately]. [Now] inasmuch as fatherhood belongs to the father, occurring accidentally to him, he being subject to its occurrence, it would be related; the same being the case with sonship. Thus we would have a connection between fatherhood and the father and between sonship and the son, external to

the connection between father and son. It would then follow necessarily that for [each] relation there is another relation and that this would lead to infinity. [Moreover, if relations were to exist in things, it would follow] that among relations there would be those which are between an existent and a nonexistent inasmuch as [for example] we are posterior to the centuries that have preceded us and have knowledge of [the future] resurrection." (p. 156, line 13 to p. 157, line 2)

Avicenna responds differently to the two arguments in this passage against the reality of relations. In the lengthier answer to the argument from infinite regress, he simply attempts to refute it. But he does not reject the shorter argument concerning relations between existents and nonexistents. As we shall see, he admits that relations between noncontemporaneous events are always ideal. What he strives to do is to explain how such ideal relations obtain.

In his answer to the main argument, he invokes the generic, "absolute" definition of the relative.[18] In so doing, he seems to be giving unqualified support to the argument of those defending the doctrine that relations exist in the concrete. One notices, however, that the opening words of his reply suggest that what he is offering is a resolution of difficulties in both the objectivist and subjectivist arguments, a point to which we will return.

What resolves for us the perplexity in both ways [of argument] is to turn to the absolute definition of the relative. We say: The relative is that whose nature is only predicated with respect to another. Thus anything in the concrete that happens to be such that its nature is only predicated with respect to another belongs to the relative. But among the concrete existents there are many things of this description. Hence the relative in concrete things exists. (p. 157, lines 3–6)

In the sentences that immediately follow something in the wording seems to be amiss. The translation we offer is based on a variant reading in the *apparatus criticus*. This reading helps solve some but not all questions of meaning.

[Now] should the relative have some other nature, then [from this nature] one must separate the idea conceived with respect to another which [the relative] has; for this idea is in reality the thing conceived with respect to another—a thing being conceived with respect to another because of it.[19] (p. 157, lines 6–8)

What does Avicenna have in mind when he speaks of the "other nature" which a relative might have? We can think of two possible answers. The first is suggested by Avicenna's discussion of the term "knowledge" in the

Logic.[20] Considered in itself, we are told, it is a qualitative term. But it is also a relative term when asserted with respect to the object of knowledge or to the knower. Thus knowledge would have a qualitative nature and a relational one. The second answer is suggested by a distinction implicit in the discussion that follows, namely, between the relational idea in its function, as it were, of relating one specific subject to another and its being considered in its abstractness: for example, the fatherhood relating *this* father to *this* son and the concept, fatherhood, as such.

But the main point in Avicenna's reply to the argument from infinite regress is that whatever relates to another thing relates in itself, not through something else which is relation. Thus, referring to the idea which is conceived with respect to another, he states:

> This idea, however, is not conceived with respect to another for any other cause than itself, but, as you have already learned, is in itself related. Hence, we do not have an essence and something else which is relation, but only that which is related in itself, not by another relation. In this way relations become finite. (p. 157, lines 8–11)

He develops thc argument by stating:

> As for the fact that this idea, which is in itself related, is present in this subject, then inasmuch as it is in this subject, its nature is conceived with respect to this subject. It has, however, another existence, as for example, the existence of fatherhood. But this [latter relation] is not the [former relation]. (p. 157, lines 12–15)

Here, it should be noted, Avicȩnna is not necessarily making a distinction between relations in the concrete and abstract relations, existing in the mind. When he speaks of the relational idea as being in "this subject," the reference is to something specific, but not necessarily to something objective and concrete. The distinction between concrete and abstract relations is central to his analysis and is discussed by him shortly after the above. At this stage, however, the distinction he draws is really between (*a*) the relational idea in its role, as it were, of relating a specific (but not necessarily concrete) subject to which it belongs to something else and (*b*) the relational idea in its abstractness, having, as he puts it, "another existence, as for example, the existence of fatherhood."

Now the relational idea in its abstractness exists only in the mind. When Avicenna, however, refers to its having "another existence," he is not so much speaking about its existence in the mind (which is taken for granted), but about something else. What he means by "another existence" coincides with what he means by "special existence," *al-wujūd al-khāṣṣ*, in *Metaphysics*, I, 5, where we are told that "to everything there is a reality by virtue of which it is what it is. Thus the triangle has a reality in that it is a triangle and whiteness has a reality in that it is whiteness. It is that which we should perhaps call 'special existence,' not intending by this the meaning given to affirmative existence."[21] As we shall see, Avicenna uses the term "special existence" in the concluding sections of the chapter on relation, in line 17, p. 159.

In other words, the distinction is between a relation, *R*, belonging to a specific subject as it relates this subject to something else and *R* in its special existence and abstractness, its "Rness." This "Rness" we are told is also a relational accident occurring to *R*. *R* and "Rness" are both related to each other. But—and this is the thrust of the argument—each is related to the other in itself, not through another relation. Thus, referring to the abstract relation he goes on to say:

> Let then this [latter, i.e., fatherhood] be an accidental occurrence arising from the former relation], existing concomitantly with it, each of the two being related in itself to that to which it is related, without any additional relation. Thus being predicated (*maḥmūl*) is in itself related. For this very [state of] being [such things] is related in itself, not requiring another relation by virtue of which it becomes related. Rather, it is in itself a nature conceived with respect to the subject. In other words, it is such that if its nature is conceived, it would require that something else should be brought to the mind, with respect to which it is conceived. (p. 157, line 15 to p. 158, line 5)

Avicenna now applies this analysis to relations obtaining between concrete things, arguing in effect that the supposition of such relations does not lead to an infinite regress.

> Indeed, if this is [now] taken as a relation in concrete things, it would exist with another thing , [conjoined to it] in itself, not by some other apprehended conjunction, it itself being the very "with" or conjunction specified by the species of that relation. If conceived, its conception requires the presentation of something else with it [to the mind]. This is similar to the nature of fatherhood, inasmuch as it is fatherhood; for it is related in itself, not by some other connecting relation, although it is up to the mind to invent something between [it and that to which it is related] as though this is a conjunction external to both of them. [This, however, is something] which conception itself is not compelled to do, being one of the aspects which attach to things [after conception] enacted by the mind. For the mind may connect things according to the diverse [possible] ways of considering things, not out of necessity. In itself [fatherhood] is [simply] a relation, not [something related] by a relation, because it is in itself a nature, conceived with respect to another.

> There are many relations that adhere in themselves to some essences, not by virtue of some other occurring relation, but only in the manner in which this type of relation adheres to the relation of fatherhood. An example of this is the adherence of relation to the state of knowledge; for it would not be adhering to it through another relation inherent in things themselves,[22] but adheres to it in itself, even though the mind may at this juncture invent some other relation. (p. 158, line 6 to p. 159, line 2)

The main line of argument here is clear: just as with abstract relations where whatever is related is related in itself, not through an additional relation, so it is when the related things are concrete. Any additional relation is something invented or constructed by the mind. But there is no necessity or compulsion for such an added relation. Hence, a regress, to say nothing of an infinite regress, is not a necessary consequence. Furthermore, since such added relations are invented by the mind, they are conceptual or ideal. Hence, if from the supposition of real relations in the concrete an infinite regress of relations were to ensue necessarily, this would be an infinite regress of ideal relations. But, as we have seen, Avicenna denies that such an infinite regress is a necessary consequence. In this he differs from Alfarabi who in *the Book of Letters* argues that such an infinite regress of ideal relations must ensue, but that this kind of infinite is possible and does not render a doctrine of real relations impossible.[23] Hence, although Alfarabi and Avicenna reject the argument from infinite regress for the impossibility of real relations, they do so on somewhat different grounds. The last part of Avicenna's answer to the argument from infinite regress begins as follows:

> Since you have known this, you now know that the relative exists in concrete existence in the sense that it has this definition. This definition only necessitates that the relative should be an accident which, when conceived, would have the above-mentioned description; but it does not necessitate that it should be a self-subsisting thing, one in number, connecting two things. (p. 159, lines 3–6)

When Avicenna speaks here of the relative as having "this definition" or "the above-mentioned description," he is again referring to the generic definition. In this passage he also reiterates his basic concept that relation is not something common to the related things but is an accident belonging to one thing but which points to another. He then goes on to state:

> As for the predication [of the nature of the relative] with respect to [another] (*wa ammā al-qawl bi al-qiyās*), this occurs only in the mind. Hence it pertains to intellectual relation, whereas existential relation is what we have shown, being namely that which is such that if conceived, its nature is conceived with respect to [another]. Its being in the mind, on the other hand, consists

> in its being conceived with respect to another. Thus [relation] in existence has one governing rule (*ḥukm*) and in the mind another, inasmuch as it is [something] in the mind, not insofar as relation is concerned. It is possible to have invented relations in the mind which the mind enacts by reason of the special property it has with respect to them. (p. 159, lines 7–11)

Needless to say, this is a crucial passage. It is also a very perplexing one. We are first told, in effect, that in the case of two concrete things, *X* and *Y*, if *X* is related to *Y*, the predication of *X* with respect to *Y* occurs only in the mind and belongs to intellectual or ideal relation. Existential or concrete relation consists in the fact that *X* is such that *if* conceived, it is conceived with respect to *Y*. The existence of the relation seems to depend on its being conceived by the mind. Such language is suggestive of certain theories that were to become current in the medieval Latin West, for example, the doctrine that relations are ideal but that some have a basis in reality, or even the doctrine that some relations exist potentially in concrete things, but in actuality only in the mind.[24] One is perhaps further encouraged to interpret Avicenna's thought as moving in this direction by his statement immediately following his presentation of the arguments for and against the objective existence of relations. As we have seen, he speaks there of resolving "the perplexity in both ways (of argument)," which may well be an indication that his endorsement of the argument for the objective existence of relations is not total.

But then Avicenna makes another statement which, though certainly not very clear, lends itself to a different interpretation. He states that relation in existence has one governing rule and in the mind another, adding the phrase, "inasmuch as it is something in the mind, not insofar as relation is concerned." What does he mean by "relation" in the phrase, "not in so far as relation is concerned?" A possible answer is that he is in fact referring to relation as an objective state of affairs belonging to one concrete thing and pointing to another and as distinct from the concept of this relation in the mind. As such, in the case of the two concrete things *X* and *Y*, *X*'s relation to *Y* is not dependent on its being conceived by the mind. Rather, *X* is such that if conceived it is conceived with respect to *Y* precisely because *X* stands with respect to *Y* in objective reality. But whether this is what Avicenna means is far from being certain.

There is one consideration which at first sight seems to give support to the second interpretation. This is Avicenna's conception of relation as an accident. His statement in the opening sentences of this chapter to the effect that if relations exist in the concrete they must be accidents indicates there that he regards accidents as part of objective reality. But when we examine this concept further, its support for the second interpretation becomes less than it first appears to be. Relation for Avicenna is a special kind of accident. It is not a sensible accident but an accident whose apprehension requires a conceptual act. Is this requirement a purely epistemological one, as the second interpretation suggests, or is it included as part of the very definition of relation, as suggested by the first interpretation? Avicenna does not give a clear answer to this question and his position, to our mind, remains ambiguous.

In any case, in summing up this part of the discussion, he begins by asserting once more that the relative exists in concrete things:

> Thus the relative in concrete things exists. Moreover, it has become evident that its existence does not necessitate that for [each] relation there should be another [relation] *ad infinitum*. Nor does it follow from this that whatever is conceived as related should have a [corresponding] relation in existence. (p. 159, lines 12–14)

* * *

The final part of the chapter takes up the problem of relating what exists in the present to what has ceased to exist or to what is yet to exist in the future. The problem is discussed by Avicenna in greater detail in the *Logic* in an expansion of Aristotle's statement in *Categories*, 7, 7b, 15–8a, 12, concerning the question of the temporal coexistence of correlatives. A fundamental point Avicenna makes in the *Logic*[25] and repeats in this chapter is that in the case of things or events that do not coexist in time the relation is not between the things themselves but only between the concepts of these things. Thus, for example, the relation is never between what exists in the present and what has existed in the past, but between the concept of what exists in the present and the concept of what has existed in the past. These concepts when related coexist in the mind. As such relations of this sort fulfil the condition of coexistence and are always ideal.

Avicenna begins this section as follows:

> As for [the question] of the temporally prior and posterior, one being nonexistent and so forth, [the answer is that] priority and posteriority are relations obtaining between existence when conceived and the conceived that does not derive from special existence. Know this. (p. 159, lines 15–17)

The wording of this passage leaves something to be desired. But from what comes immediately after, it becomes clear that when Avicenna speaks of "existence when conceived," he means the concept of what presently exists. It also becomes clear that "the conceived that does not derive from special existence" refers in part, but only in part, to what does not exist in the present. In fact a variant reading for the clause, "does not derive from special existence," (*laysa maʾkhūdhan ʿan al-wujūd al-khāṣṣ*), given by three manuscripts is "does not derive from present existence," (*laysa maʾkhūdhan ʿan al-wujūd al-ḥāḍir*). This reading makes very good sense and the temptation to adopt it is very strong. The reading, "special existence," which the editors have adopted, however, should stand, not only because most of the manuscripts give it, but also because the *Logic* supports this reading, as we shall show. Accordingly, the point Avicenna wishes to make in his reference to "special existence" is that the relation is not between the concept of what presently exists and an abstract quiddity or special existence. Rather, it is the relation of a concept that has a counterpart in the concrete at present to a concept that either had a concrete counterpart in the past or will have one in the future. The passage in the *Logic* supporting this has to do with knowledge of such a future event as the resurrection:[26]

> As for knowledge of the resurrection, it belongs to the category (*ḥukm*) of [what] will be. For the knowledge that it will be is [(a)] knowledge of its state existing in the mind together with [(b)] knowledge that it will be—[knowledge, that is], existing in the mind, not when [the resurrection] comes into being, but prior to that, when it is nonexistent in the concrete, existing in the soul. As for the conception of the quiddity of the resurrection in abstraction, this, inasmuch as it is conception, is not related to anything in existence.

To return then to the text of the *Metaphysics*, the concluding part of the chapter on relations is as follows:

> For a thing in itself is only prior in terms of something existing with it. This type of priority and posteriority exists for both terms [of the relation] in the mind; for when the concepts of the prior and the posterior are presented to the mind, the soul conceives this comparison as existing between two existents in it, since such a comparison obtains between two existents in the mind. Before this, a thing in itself cannot be prior; for how could it be prior to nothing existing? Hence, whatever relations are of this order, their relation to each other is in the mind only, having in existence no subsisting idea with respect to this priority and posteriority. Indeed, this priority and posteriority is in reality one of the intellectual ideas, one of the relationships imposed by the mind and one of the aspects that occur to things when the mind compares them and refers to them. (p. 160, lines 1–9)

This passage affirms Avicenna's distinction between what exists in reality and what exists in the mind, a distinction fundamental to his ontology.[27] He invokes it here to resolve the difficulty of relating what exists at present to what does not. In so doing, he concedes to those who maintain that all relations are ideal that in these instances the relations are always ideal. For, as we have seen, he has argued that when, for example, we relate a present existent to one that existed in the past, we are not relating an existent to a nonexistent. What we are really doing is relating the concept of what exists at present to the concept of what had existed in the past.

Avicenna, in other words, is reducing relations between noncontemporaneous events to ideal relations between coexisting concepts. Does not this reduction lead him to a subjectivist theory of time? This is one of the questions posed by this passage. Another, by no means a less important one, pertains to the kind of relations obtaining between an existent and its conceptual counterpart in the mind. Are these ideal or real? Avicenna, however, does not discuss this question at all.

NOTES

1 Ibn Sīnā (Avicenna), *al-Manṭiq (Logic) II: al-Maqūlāt (Categories)*, ed. G. Anawātī, A. F. Ahwānī, M. Khuḍayrī, and S. Zāyid, rev. ed. (Cairo, 1959), pp 143–64; *al-Ilāhiyyāt (Metaphysics)*, ed. G. Anawātī, S. Dunyā, and S. Zāyid, rev. ed., 2 vols. (Cairo, 1960), pp. 152–60. These two works will be referred to in the notes as *Maqūlāt* and *Ilāhiyyāt*, respectively.

2 This is clear from the context. But Avicenna in introducing the discussion makes the following explicit remark: "It is not for the logician to prove the existence of the relative and to show its state in existence and in conception. Whoever undertakes to do this, undertakes, inasmuch as he is a logician, that which is neither his concern nor his special task." *Maqūlāt*, 143, lines 15–16.

There are two main ontological questions discussed in the *Logic* as well as the *Metaphysics*. The first (*Maqūlāt*, 153–55) is the problem of relating noncontemporaneous events (this is discussed more exhaustively in the *Logic* than in the *Metaphysics*). In the *Logic* it is a natural development of Avicenna's expansion on Aristotle's discussion in *Categories*, 7, 7b, 15–8a, 12. The second (*Maqūlāt*, 163–64) is a brief statement of the doctrine that the relative belongs only to one subject.

3 See I. Madkūr's Arabic and French introduction to the *Logic* (*al-Maqūlāt*, 12–13, xvi–xvii) and the references given there; also, J. R. Weinberg, *Abstraction. Relation and Induction* (Madison and Milwaukee, 1965), pp. 78, 90, 91, for parallels between Stoic and *kalām* subjectivist views on relations and the probability that Avicenna had also the Stoics in mind in this third part of the chapter.

4 *Ilāhiyyāt*, Book III, Chap. 10, pp. 152–60. The pages and lines that appear after each translated section refer to the *Ilāhiyyāt*.

5 This distinction, for example, is conveyed by the following statement: "It is easier for the mind to know relatives (*al-muḍāfāt*) than to know pure relations (*al-iḍāfāt*) that constitute the category." *Maqūlāt*, 144, lines 1–2.

6 Ibid., 158, lines 5–15.

7 *Ilāhiyyāt*, 157, line. 4. Avicenna prefaces this statement by referring to it as the absolute definition of the relative. What he means by "absolute definition" is perhaps clarified by the fuller definition in the *Logic* where he states: "Things belonging to the relative are those whose natures are predicated with respect to other [things] either absolutely or through some other mode of connection (*nisba*)." *Maqūlāt*, 144, lines. 2–3. Those predicated absolutely, he goes on to explain, are those whose names denote their full meaning, giving "brother"

as an example. Those predicated through some other mode of relation are terms which in themselves may be relatives but only become so through a linguistic connection. Ibid., 144–45. Those things which in themselves are not relatives, but become so "by some other mode of relation," acquire another nature than the one they originally had. Ibid., 147, lines 16–18.

The definition as it occurs in the *Logic* differs from other medieval Arabic versions only in its use of the term "absolutely," in word order and some of the vocabulary. But the key terminology and sense remain essentially the same. See, for example, Khalil Georr, *Les catégories d'Aristote dans leur versions syro-arabes* (Paris. 1948), pp. 332; Alfarabi, *Kitāb al-Ḥurūf* (*Book of letters*), ed. M. Mahdi (Beirut, 1969), pp. 87, lines. 20–22, and the editor's comment referring to this section on p. 228, giving Ḥunayn Ibn Isḥāq's version). All these versions define the relative as that whose "nature" (*māhiyya*) is "said of" or "predicated" (*tuqāl*) "with respect" (*bi al-qiyās*) to another.

Throughout the translation and commentary we have rendered the Arabic *yuqāl* or *tuqāl* as "predicated," an accepted meaning which is less cumbersome than the more literal, "said of." The more specific term for "predicated" or "predicate," *al-maḥmūl,* is used in this chapter only once (*Ilāhiyyāt*, 158, line. 1) in a context where it is equivalent to *maqūl*, the passive participle of the passive imperfect *yuqāl.*

[8] *Maqūlāt*, 157, line 6. Book v, Chap. iv, of the *Logic* (*Maqūlāt*, 155–64) is devoted to a discussion of the difference between the two Aristotelian definitions, interpreting the second as referring to the category, relation. For Alfarabi's parallel but shorter explanation see Alfarabi, Book of letters, 87–88. For a brief statement of the treatment of this distinction by the Latin scholastics, see J. R. Weinberg, *Abstraction,* 72–73.

[9] *Maqūlāt*, 146–48.

[10] The Cairo edition reads *bi al-mukhtalif*, clearly a printing error. The expression should read *fa al-mukhtalif.*

[11] The text reads, "the proximate and the proximate and the proximate," an editorial slip which we have emended.

[12] J. R. Weinberg, *Abstraction,* 92.

[13] *Summa Contra Gentiles*, II, 12 and *Summa Theologica*, I, q. 13, a. 7.

[14] *Maqūlāt*, 145–46.

[15] J. R. Weinberg, *Abstraction*, 71, 75.

[16] Alfarabi, *Book of letters*, 85, lines. 9–17.

[17] J. R. Weinberg, *Abstraction*, 93.

[18] For a comment on the use of the term "absolute," see n. 7 above.

[19] The clause, "for this idea is in reality the thing conceived with respect to another" is a translation of, *fa dhālika al-maᶜna huwa bi al-ḥaqīqa al-maᶜnā al-maᶜqūl bi al-qiyās ilā ghayrihi*, given by the Tehran printed text and the *Dār al-Kutub al-Miṣriyya* MS. no. 144. This reading with slight variations is also given by the *Dār al-kutub al-Miṣriyya* MSS. nos. 826 and 894 and by the British Museum MS. no. 7500, the first two having the word, *al-ḥaqīqa*, instead of *bi al-ḥaqīqa*, the third adding the word *wa ghayrihi* at the end.

The editors adopted the reading of the *Bakhīt* MS. that omits the clause, giving simply *wa ghayrihi* instead. The *Bakhīt* version of the above passage reads somewhat as follows: "(Now) should the relative have some other nature, then from [this nature] one must separate the idea conceived with respect to another and another which [the relative] has, a thing being conceived with respect to another only because of this idea."

[20] *Maqūlāt*, 144. See above n. 7.

[21] *Ilāhiyyāt*, 31, lines. 5–8. A possible relationship between Avicenna's use of this term in the *Shifāʾ* and his use of the Persian term *hastī,* "being" is in need of inquiry. On *hastī*, see P. Morewedge, "Philosophical Analysis and Ibn Sīnā's 'Essence-Existence' Distinction,"

JAOS, 92 (1972), pp. 425–35. In the *Ilāhiyyāt,* immediately after the passage translated above, Avicenna seems to speak of a thing's "special existence" as its nature. Thus he states: "The expression, 'existence,' is also used to denote many meanings, one of which is the reality a thing happens to have. Thus, [the reality] a thing happens to have is, as it were, its special existence. . . . It is evident that each thing has a reality proper to it, namely, its nature. It is known that the reality proper to a thing is something other than the existence corresponding to what is offered." Ibid. 31, lines 8–11.

[22] *Fi nafs al-umūr*: *al-umūr*, "things," "matters," probably refers to knowledge and its correlatives.

[23] Alfarabi, *Book of Letters,* 92, lines 3–8. Alfarabi refers the reader to an earlier section (pp. 64–66) for a fuller discussion of the possibility of this kind of infinite.

[24] The first of these theories is associated with William of Ockham who distinguishes between rational and real relations. Real relations for him, however, are conceptual, but, unlike mere rational relations, have a basis in reality. The second theory is associated with Petrus Aureoli. Cf. J. R. Weinberg, *Abstraction,* 103–106, 109.

[25] *Maqūlāt,* 153–4.

[26] *Ibid.,* 154, lines. 15–17.

[27] See *Ilāhiyyāt,* Bk. I, Chap. V, 29–36; also for the relevance of this distinction for Avicenna's analysis of causation, ibid., 167–9.

GHAZALI'S ATTITUDE TO THE SECULAR SCIENCES AND LOGIC

MICHAEL E. MARMURA (2)

I

The intellectual and religious career of Ghazali (d. A.D. 1111) represents, among other things, a turning point in the history of the Ashᶜarite school of dogmatic theology *(kalām)*, to which he belonged. This school was founded by Ashᶜarī (d. 935) who started his career as a member of the then leading school of *kalām,* the Muᶜtazilite, but rebelled against it, formulating a theology that reversed its basic tenets. With his successors, Ashᶜarism gradually gained ascendancy to become the dominant school of *kalām*.

Ghazali's attitude toward science and logic[1] can only be understood against the background of the occasionalism and atomism this school endorsed and refined. The Ashᶜarites are noted for their denial of the concept of natural causation, that is, that there are acts that proceed from a thing's very nature or essence. Maintaining that action belongs only to a voluntary agent, they adopted the occasionalist view that causal efficacy resides exclusively with the divine will. They also denied Aristotle's theory of the eternity and potential infinite divisibility of matter, subscribing instead to a theory of contingent atoms and accidents. These, they maintained, are created *ex nihilo,* combined to form bodies, and sustained in temporally finite spans of existence by direct divine action. The orderly flow of these events, which constitutes nature's uniformity, has thus no inherent necessity: it is simply a habit *(ᶜāda)* or custom *(sunna)* arbitrarily decreed by the divine will. Consequently, disruptions of this uniformity, that is, miraculous happenings, are not impossible.

It is not difficult to discern the primary theological motive of this metaphysics, namely, the defense of a concept of divine omnipotence. Here, however, we are not concerned with the particulars of Ashᶜarite theology, the specific doctrines relating to the nature of the divine attributes and to theodicy. To such doctrines Ghazali contributed little that was new, except, perhaps, a certain stylistic lucidity and verve in reexpressing them. His chief contribution to Ashᶜarism lay elsewhere. It lay in the task he undertook of defining the Ashᶜarite position in relation to the metaphysical and the other sciences expounded by the philosophers of medieval Islam.

This defining of position, from the Ashʿarite point of view, was sorely needed. The tenth and eleventh centuries witnessed the rise of two related and imposing philosophical systems, those of Alfarabi (d. 950) and Avicenna (d. 1037). The metaphysics of these two philosophers was necessitarian and emanative, deriving ultimately from Aristotle and Plotinus. In their political philosophy, which was essentially Platonic, they identified the God of their metaphysical systems with the God of the Qurʾān by interpreting the latter's language metaphorically. This posed for the medieval Muslim the question: is this identification valid and legitimate? Moreover, the writings of these two philosophers included comprehensive treatments of logic, mathematics, and physics. Religious zealots were prone to condemn such secular, "foreign" sciences as contrary to Islamic teaching. What if these sciences were demonstrably true? Would not such condemnation result in detriment to religious principle? To what extent, if at all, did each of these sciences have an actual bearing on religion? It is to such questions that Ghazali in his *Tahāfut al-Falāsifa (The Incoherence of the Philosophers)* and other related writings addressed himself.

The criterion Ghazali employed in answering such questions was that of demonstrability. A science whose conclusions are not demonstrably true and which are in conflict with the literal assertions of scripture must be rejected. On the other hand, if what is demonstrably true contradicts the literal sense of scriptural language, then the latter must be interpreted metaphorically. Ghazali shared with the majority of medieval thinkers the rationalist view that God cannot enact what is self-contradictory. The Islamic philosophers' cardinal metaphysical doctrines, he tried to show in detail, failed to satisfy the conditions of demonstrative proof. Some, he argued, in fact were self-contradictory. Moreover, since these doctrines were not consistent with scriptural language, or its intent, as Ghazali understood it, he condemned many of them as heretical innovations *(bidaʿ)*, some as constituting outright Islamic unbelief *(kufr)*.

Unlike metaphysics, Ghazali held mathematics to be demonstrably true. But, he argued, it has no bearing on religious matters, nor, for that matter, is the study of it necessary for understanding metaphysics, contrary to what the philosophers claim.[2]

The two sciences that concern us most are logic and physics. As we shall see, Ghazali insisted that the philosophers' logic is a doctrinally neutral tool of knowledge and can be used to advantage in the defense of religion.[3] To understand his attitude to natural science, one must distinguish psychology, included in the Aristotelian scheme of things among the sciences of nature, from the purely physical sciences. In the *Tahāfut*, Ghazali undertook to refute Avicenna's psychology, condemning his doctrine of the soul's individual immortality that denies bodily resurrection, as constituting *kufr*.[4] (It should be added in passing, however, that in other writings Ghazali betrays less aversion to this doctrine and that in general Avicenna's psychology had considerable influence on him.) Turning to Ghazali's attitude to the physical sciences, it is here that we are at once confronted with what appears to be a glaring inconsistency. He maintained that these are demonstrable and certain, and yet, in the seventeenth discussion of the *Tahāfut,* he criticises and rejects the principle of necessary causal connection, the cornerstone of Aristotelian demonstrative science. As we shall see, Ghazali attempted a resolution of this problem; an accommodation between the then current canons of scientific method and the occasionalism to which he was committed. This attempt is largely included in his logical writings, to which we must now turn. These writings, more than anything else, reveal his attitude to the philosophers' secular sciences.

II

Ghazali wrote a number of logical treatises, some as independent tracts, others as parts of larger works.[5] These consist by and large of expositions of the fundamentals of Avicenna's logic. They are works of popularization of a high order, in which Ghazali strove to render this logic relevant to Islamic religious scholars by informing it with examples of legal and theological reasoning. For Ghazali endorsed Avicenna's logic and wrote these treatises urging his fellow theologicians to accept it. There are also indications that Ghazali wrote some of these works partly for himself, as an exercise in self-instruction while he was mastering the subject. Whatever the theological motives that prompted his acceptance of this logic, he showed genuine interest in it. This preoccupation suggests that logic was the discipline of the philosophers that impressed him most.

These treatises reveal that Ghazali adopted a variety of means to render this logic acceptable and attractive to the Ashᶜarites. Some of these we have discussed elsewhere,[6] but here we are mainly concerned with two fundamental theses that underlie Ghazali's endeavor to promote this logic. Before we turn to them, however, something must be said about a third and most drastic effort of Ghazali's, namely, the argument he adopted in his *al-Qisṭās al-Mustaqīm (The Just Balance)*. This independent tract, written in the form of a lively dialogue between Ghazali and a Shīᶜite *taᶜlīmī*—one who holds that the only source of true knowledge is the infallible *imām*—argues for the divine origin of logic. Here Ghazali maintains that the Qurʾanic "balance" *(al-mīzān)* is the balance of knowledge, the criterion for testing the validity of arguments and identifies it with the three Aristotelian figures of the syllogism and the two Stoic conjunctive and disjunctive syllogisms. In explaining these he analyzes Qurʾanic arguments, and shows that they possess the forms of these syllogisms. In brief, Ghazali sanctifies the philosophers' logic. But this does not mean a rejection of logic's doctrinal neutrality. It remains a mere tool of knowledge, "the balance," and the balance by its very nature must remain impartial. But this impartiality, the accuracy of the balance, is now guaranteed by revelation.[7]

How sincere was Ghazali in all this? There is this much that one can say in his defense. The doctrine that the ultimate principles of all knowledge are first intuited by "the masters of intuition" *(arbāb al-ḥudūs)* and then taught to others is a philosophical view expressed by Avicenna. It is, moreover, expressed in the same context in which Avicenna identifies intellectual prophecy with the direct intuition of all or most of the intelligibles.[8] Thus, while it is true that Ghazali has fundamental disagreements with Avicenna's theory of prophecy,[9] he does not object to this aspect of it, but in fact endorses it.[10] Hence it would be natural for him to seek the principles and basic patterns of logical argument in the revealed word. But whether or not this argument exonerates Ghazali, some of his critics remained unimpressed with the view he expressed in *al-Qisṭās*. Hence the wry remark of the Ḥanbalite lawyer Ibn Taymiyya (d. 1328):[11] "Stranger than this, [Ghazali] wrote a book he called *al-Qiṣṭās al-Mustaqīm*, attributing [in it logic] to the teachings of the prophets. He only learned it from Avicenna who learned it from the books of Aristotle."

We must now turn to the two main theses which Ghazali advocated in his logical writings. The first is that the philosophers' logic only differs from the logic already in use by the theologians in the terms it uses and in details. The second is that the philosophers' logic is simply a tool of knowledge, not committed to any philosophical view or doctrine. Both these views are expressed in the introductions to the *Tahāfut*, and the *Tahāfut* was intended in part to prove the second thesis, since Ghazali intentionally uses the terminology of the philosophers' logic and their patterns of reasoning to refute their own doctrines. But the theses are perhaps best expressed in *al-Munqidh min al-Ḍalāl (The Deliverer from Error)* where Ghazali writes:[12]

> As for their logical sciences, none of these relates to religion either by way of denial or affirmation. They are no more than the study of the methods of proof and standards for reasoning, the conditions of the premises of demonstration and the manner of their ordering, the conditions of correct definition and the manner of its construction.
>
> They simply affirm that knowledge is either conception, arrived at through definition, or assent, arrived at through demonstration. Nothing of this ought to be denied. It is the same kind of thing the theologians and religious speculative thinkers mention in their treatments of proofs. The philosophers differ from them only in their expressions and idioms and their more exhaustive definitions and classifications.

To what extent then was Ghazali justified in maintaining both these theses?

A consideration of the first—the thesis that the differences between the logics of *kalām* and philosophy are not essential—requires a brief review of the Ashᶜarite doctrine of created knowledge of which their logic is an essential a part. For the Ashᶜarites, knowledge is either divine and eternal or human and created. Our concern is with the latter. Created knowledge, in turn, divides into two categories: *(1)* compulsory *(iḍṭirārī)* or necessary *(ḍarūrī)*; *(2)* reflective *(naẓarī)*, also termed "acquired" *(muktasab)*.[13]

The first type of knowledge is created directly in us by God and we are compelled to accept it. It includes (a) self-evident truths, such as the law of excluded middle; (b) knowledge of the world around us attained immediately from the various senses; (c) self-knowledge, that is, knowledge of our own existence and our own physical and psychological states; (d) *tawātur,* "wide transmission," that is, knowledge of particular events or geographical places obtained through numerous mutually corroborative reports.

Reflective, or acquired knowledge, on the other hand, is knowledge inferred from necessary knowledge. It is also created in us by God, but differs from necessary knowledge in that it is created together with the "power" that accompanies the acquisition. Whether this power plays a part in the process of acquiring this type of knowledge or whether it is a mere concomitant of the acquisition is a moot point in the interpretation of the notoriously ambiguous Ashᶜarite doctrine of *kasb,* "acquisition." Whatever the metaphysical interpretation of this activity of *naẓar,* the important thing is that on the ordinary, common-sense level, it represents inferential knowledge. It includes, to begin with, the inference from effect to cause. The Ashᶜarites, it must be remembered, denied the theory that there are natural or essential causes that necessitate their effects, but not the principle, which is quite different, that every temporal event must have a cause. On this principle they based their argument to prove God's existence. There was, however, another sense of cause (*ᶜilla,* sometimes, *sabab)* used in *naẓar* that has a parallel in Islamic legal reasoning, namely, the ground or reason in analogical argument. This form of argument, sometimes termed, "reducing the unobserved to the observed," *radd al-ghāᶜib ilā al-shāhid,* involves transferring a judgment from one particular to another that resembles it in some respect.[14]

But what about Aristotelian and Stoic syllogistic inference? The fact that one may chance in Ashᶜarite writings upon arguments that fit the Aristotelian syllogistic form does not mean much. For the question here is whether they consciously used such forms of inference with full knowledge of the rules and the answer to this is negative. The same seems to be true, although we are less positive about this, with respect to the Stoic hypothetical conjunctive syllogism, corresponding in its two modes to the *modus ponens* and *modus tollens*. Significantly, this is the one form of reasoning that Ghazali in his

Tahāfut goes out of his way to explain.[15] The situation is quite different[15] with the second type of Stoic syllogism, the disjunctive, where the connective "or" was used in the exclusive sense. This is the most common use of argument found in *kalām* literature and the theologians seem to have used it with full awareness of the rules. In fact, they had a technical name for it, *al-sabr wa al-taqsīm*, "probing and dividing."[16]

What is striking about the division of knowledge into compulsory and reflective is that it parallels the philosophers' distinction between the syllogism's "matter," *mādda,* and its "form," *ṣūra.* The matter of the syllogism involves the epistemological status of its premises; the form, the rules for valid inference. To take the formal aspect first, the philosophers' logic is the more comprehensive as it includes, for example, the Aristotelian figures which, prior to Ghazali, were not included in *naẓar.* It also includes a more precise formulation of analogical reasoning which, for example, Alfarabi reduced to the first Aristotelian figure and which, probably following him, Ghazali urged his fellow theologians to adopt.[17] But there is nothing in the philosophers' logic that conflicts with *naẓar,* so that Ghazali is at least justified in maintaining that the differences between the two are not essential.

As to the status of the premises of argument, it appears at first that Ghazali is even more justified in his thesis. For we find that all the types of knowledge included in the Ashᶜarite category of compulsory or necessary, not excluding *tawātur,* are included in Avicenna's category of demonstrative premises.[18] The converse, however, is not the case. This makes all the difference. For Avicenna also includes among demonstrative premises the class of tested propositions, *al-mujarrabāt,* and the related class of intuited propositions, *al-ḥadsiyyāt.* Now, as we shall see, these are the premises in Avicenna's logic whose certainty derives from the theory of natural necessary efficient causation, in other words, from the very theory to which Ashᶜarite occasionalism is totally opposed. Here, not only Ghazali's first thesis becomes questionable, but also his second.

III

Ghazali's second thesis, proclaiming the neutrality of the philosophers' logic, also proclaims, in effect, the neutrality of Aristotelian demonstrative science, because it involves the premises of argument. Can one subscribe to Aristotelian science without subscribing to Aristotelian causal metaphysics? This causal question relates most obviously to the class of tested and intuited premises mentioned above and to which we shall later turn. But it also relates to an epistemologically prior class of empirical premises. These, termed by Avicenna, *al-maḥsūsāt,* "the sensory premises," relate to knowledge of particulars in the world around us attained immediately by our senses.

In Avicenna's Aristotelian demonstrative logic, this class of premises is based on a common sense causal theory of perception. For Avicenna, when the proper conditions obtain, man attains through his senses indubitable knowledge of particulars external to him. In visual perception, for example, these conditions would include the proper functioning of the visual organ, the presence of light, the proximity of the object and the absence of impediments in the intervening medium. A fundamental necessary condition is the natural causal power of the object to influence the sense organ.

The significant point here in comparing Avicenna's logic with that of the Ashᶜarites is that the Ashᶜarites also acknowledge the certainty of knowledge derived from sense perception. How can they do this while denying any natural causal power in the things that are said to affect our senses? If we press the logic of their position, drawing also on some explicit assertions of Ghazali,[19] their account of indubitable knowledge derived from perception would run something as follows: God, being benevolent, not malevolent, and hence not a deceiver, has so ordained the habitual course of nature that when He creates conditions corresponding to those in Avicenna's account, with the exclusion, however, of any causal property in natural things, He creates simultaneously in man indubitable knowledge of the object. In other words, knowledge and its object are two concomitant events with no direct causal connection. They are only indirectly connected in that both are caused by God.

This Ashᶜarite account of perception is really the key to Ghazali's treatment of the tested and intuited premises which he reinterprets on similar occasionalist lines. In Avicenna's logic, this latter class of premises relates to regularly associated events in nature. In the case of the tested premises, the association is fully observable. Thus, for example, we arrive at the certainty of the premise, "whenever fire touches cotton, cotton burns," by having repeatedly observed the contact of fire with cotton and the latter's conflagration. In the case of the intuited premises, the association is not fully observable, although it is dependent on the observation of regularities. Thus, Avicenna argues, from the observation of the regular behavior of the sun and the moon we intuit the fact that the moon derives its light from the sun.[20] This derivation we do not observe directly. In both these premises, however, the observation of regular sequences is a necessary condition for acquiring the certainty that these premises are true. But it is not a sufficient condition. Avicenna, no less than Ghazali, insists that mere observation only proves concomitance, not necessary causal connection. Along with observation, he argues, there is an implicit rational argument, "a hidden syllogism," to the effect that if in the past regularity had been coincidental or accidental it would not always have continued. From this he concludes that the regularity is essential and derives from the inherent causal properties in natural things.[21]

This argument, which represents an epistomological justification of the principle of nature's uniformity, has its genesis in Aristotle's *Physics*.[22] But from Avicenna's writings we can extract a more pervasive metaphysical justification. This we find in his discussion of contingent existents, the existents that in themselves are possible, not necessary.[23] Avicenna argues, in effect, that the existence of these possibles is not sufficiently explained by simply maintaining that they are caused by something else. One must maintain that they are caused necessarily, that is, that they are necessitated by something else. It is on this premise that he builds his proof for God's existence, since it is the chain of necessitated and necessitating existents that must be finite, requiring a first necessitating cause that is not necessitated. For Avicenna, the world proceeds from God as a chain of necessitated and necessitating existents. It is the immutability and eternity of this prime necessitating principle, God, that in the final analysis guarantees the perpetual regularity of the natural order.

Since this concept of a necessitating God is fundamentally opposed to Ashᶜarism, Ghazali does not accept it. On the other hand, he accepts the premises of Avicenna's epistemological argument but draws from them a different metaphysical conclusion. To see this in its proper context, a brief review of Ghazali's critique of natural causation is necessary.

In the *Tahāfut's* seventeenth discussion, Ghazali argued that if any two events, habitually regarded as cause and effect, are two distinct things—a point, incidentally, the philosophers insist on—then the affirmation of the one and the negation of the other would not constitute contradiction. Hence neither the appeal to logic nor the appeal to empirical observation, which only shows concomitance, would prove necessary causal connection. For Ghazali this does not mean that the concomitance itself is not caused. When cotton, for example, is brought in contact with fire and the cotton burns, these events are all caused. But it is not the fire that enacts the burning. It is God who enacts this on the occasion of the contact of fire and cotton.

With this in mind, we turn now to Ghazali's discussion of the tested and intuited premises in his logical treatise, *Miᶜyār al-ᶜIlm (The Standard for Knowledge)*. He repeats the premises of Avicenna's epistemological justification of the principle of nature's uniformity. Since observation of regularity only shows concomitance, it does not suffice to prove universality. There is in addition the hidden argument that the observed invariance could not have been accidental or coincidental. The conclusion Ghazali draws from these premises, however, differs from Avicenna's. The invariance is not due to the natural causal properties in things. For Ghazali, these causal properties do not exist. The invariance, he holds, is due to divine voluntary action.

After discussing the tested premises, he writes:[24]

Someone may say: How do you consider this certain when the theologians have doubted this, maintaining that it is not decapitation that causes death, nor eating, satiation, nor fire, burning, but that it is God, the Exalted, who causes burning, death and satiation at the occurrence of their concomitant events, and not through them?

We answer: We have already directed attention to the depth and true nature of this problem in the book, *Tahāfut al-Falāsifa*. Suffice it here to say that when the theologian informs the questioner that his son has been decapitated, the theologian does not doubt his death—no rational man would doubt this. The theologian admits the fact of death, but inquires about the manner of connection between decapitation and death.

As for the inquiry as to whether this is a necessary consequence of the thing itself, impossible to change, or whether this is in accordance with the passage of the custom *(sunna)* of God, the Exalted, due to the fulfilment of His will that can undergo neither substitution nor change, this is an inquiry into the mode of connection, not into the connection itself.

This passage speaks for itself. One should add, however, that just as in the case of perceptual knowledge of particulars, the knowledge is created in us by God, so too is the knowledge of uniform sequences. God creates both the natural regularities and the knowledge of these regularities. Moreover, God creates in man the knowledge that these regularities are not in themselves necessary, but can be disrupted without contradiction. When a disruption, that is, a miracle, occurs, God removes from our hearts knowledge of the past regularities and the anticipation of their continuity, creating instead knowledge of the miracle.

As we have tried to show in detail elsewhere,[25] Ghazali's occasionalist interpretation of the empirical premises of demonstration is capable in principle of giving a new account of Avicenna's highly sophisticated theory of natural efficient causality. In sum, Ghazali divests the Avicennian concept of efficient causes of the ideas of power and of necessity. He retains, however, the relational aspects of priority and posteriority, whether temporal or ontological, to enable him to maintain the distinction between what we habitually regard as causes and effects. Ghazali does not object to our using causal language with respect to natural inanimate things. He argues that verbs of action are correctly used in connection with inanimate natural things, but, he insists, this is correct metaphorical usage only.[26]

Our main concern here, however, is with Ghazali's attitude towards logic and demonstrative science as embodied in the two theses underlying his logical writings. *(1)* In the light of his occasionalist interpretation of the empirical premises of demonstrative science, can he still maintain that there are no essential differences between the logics of *kalām* and philosophy? *(2)* Moreover, can he still maintain that demonstrative logic is philosophically neutral?

As to the first thesis, what Ghazali has really shown—if we grant his theological presupppositions—is that the differences between the philosophers and the Ashᶜarites need not pertain to the epistomological claims of the empirical premises of demonstration, but that they only pertain to the philosophical justification of these claims. This thesis, then, would have to be modified accordingly. Regarding the second thesis, what Ghazali seems to have shown is not that demonstrative logic is philosophically uncommitted, but only that its philosophical commitment is not necessarily to an Aristotelian causal metaphysics. With such modifications of his theses Ghazali would probably have been satisfied, his chief concern in his logical writings being pragmatic—to induce the theologians to accept Avicennian logic.

The matter cannot rest here, however, for Ghazali's position, if pursued, destroys his second thesis. He holds that the Aristotelian theory of natural efficient causation is false. Needless to say, if the epistemological claims of natural science are true and if the Aristotelian causal theory justifying these claims is false, then natural science cannot be committed to this theory. The corollary to this seems obvious: If Ashᶜarite causal theory is the true one, then it alone can justify the epistemological claims of natural science. Thus demonstrative natural science becomes doctrinally committed and—astounding as this may appear—committed to Ashᶜarite occasionalism.

Ghazali, in effect, has offered a theological justification of the principle of nature's uniformity. This uniformity is not necessary in itself, but is created by God who is powerful and good, who creates in us the assurance that, with the rare exception of miraculous happenings, this uniformity will go on uninterrupted. Ghazali's is ultimately a justification by faith, not Santayana's animal faith, but religious faith buttressed by rational arguments, often ingenious, at points cogent and incisive.

NOTES

1 For general expressions of this attitude, see al-Ghazālī, *Tahāfut al-Falāsifa*, ed. M. Bouyges (Beirut, 1929), pp. 9–13, 14–17, 268–71. This work will be abbreviated in the notes as *TF*.

2 *TF*, pp. 14–15.

3 *TF*, pp. 15–16.

4 *TF*, pp. 297–376.

5 These include: (1) the first part of *Maqāṣid al-Falāsifa*; (2) *Miᶜyār al-ᶜIlm*; (3) *Miḥakk al-Naẓar;* (4) *al-Qisṭās al-Mustaqīm;* (5) the first part of the legal work, *al-Mustaṣfā min ᶜIlm al-Uṣūl*. One should also draw attention to the brief, but telling, discussion of logic in *al-Iqtiṣād*: al-Ghazālī, *al-Iqtiṣād fī al-Iᶜtiqād*, ed. I.A. Çubukçu and H. Atay (Ankara, 1962), pp. 15–20. For the chronology of these works, see G.F. Hourani, "The Chronology of Ghazālī's Writings," *JAOS* 79, no.4 (Oct.–Dec., 1959): 225–33.

6 See the author's, "Ghazali on Ethical Premises," *The Philosophical Forum*, 1, no.3 (1969): 393–403.

[7] Al-Ghazālī, *al-Qisṭās al-Mustaqīm*, ed. V. Chelhot (Beirut, 1959), pp. 45–46.

[8] *Avicenna*'s *De Anima*, ed. F. Rahman (Oxford, 1958), pp. 249.

[9] See the author's "Avicenna's Theory of Prophecy in the Light of Ashᶜarite Theology," *The Seed of Wisdom*, ed. W.S. McCollough (Toronto, 1964), pp. 159–78.

[10] *TF*, pp. 272–76; al-Ghazālī, *Mizān al-ᶜAmal*, ed. S. Dunya (Cairo, 1964), p. 207. W. Montgomery Watt, who in his "The Authenticity of the Works Attributed to al-Ghazālī," *JRAS* (1952): 24–45, has argued that parts of the *Mizān* are spurious, on p. 38 uses Ghazali's statement on prophecy as part of an argument relating to the dating of the work. Admittedly, the *Mizān* is problematic, particularly as Ghazali in it seems to be shifting from an Ashᶜarite to an Aristotelian ethical theory. Nonetheless, to our mind Watt's arguments that parts of this work are not authentic are inconclusive.

[11] Ibn Taymiyya, *al-Radd ᶜalā al-Manṭiqiyyīn*, ed. S. Nadwi (Bombay, 1949), p. 15.

[12] Al-Ghazālī, *al-Munqidh min al-Ḍalāl*, ed. F. Jabre (Beirut, 1959), p. 22.

[13] See al-Bāqillānī, *K. al-Tamhīd*, ed. R.J. McCarthy (Beirut, 1957); W. Montgomery Watt, "The Logical Basis of Early Kalam," *Islamic Quarterly* 6, no. 1-2 (Jan.–April, 1961): 2–10; 7, no. 1-2 (Jan.–June, 1963): 31–39. For the sake of clarity, in what follows we have changed the Ashᶜarite ordering of the classification of necessary knowledge. Bāqillānī, for example, maintains that necessary knowledge is attained in six ways, five in association with the five senses. These we have classified under one category (b) below. Bāqillānī's sixth way includes what we have listed as categories (a), (c), and (d).

[14] Al-Ghazālī, *Miᶜyār al-ᶜIlm*, ed. S. Dunya (Cairo, 1961), pp. 165 ff. This work will be abbreviated as *MI*.

[15] *TF*, pp. 82–83; 304–305.

[16] *MI*, p. 156; al-Ghazālī, *al-Mustasfā min ᶜIlm al-Uṣūl,* 2 vols. (Cairo, 1937), 1: 27.

[17] See note 14 above. For Alfarabi's formulation, see N. Rescher, *Al-Fārābī's Short Commentary on Aristotle's Prior Analytics* (Pittsburgh, 1963), pp. 36–37, 43–44, 93–95.

[18] Ibn Sīnā (Avicenna), *al-Ishārāt wa al-Tanbīhāt: I, Logic*, ed. S. Dunya (Cairo, 1953), pp. 389 ff.

[19] *TF*, 280 ff. See also al-Bāqillānī, *K. al-Tamhīd*, 11, par. 15.

[20] Avicenna defines intuition (*al-ḥads*) as an action of the mind that grasps by itself the middle term of a syllogism. See for example Avicenna's *De Anima*, 249. In the *Logic* he speaks of intuition as "an excellence of movement of this faculty [of mind] for snatching by itself the middle term." He goes on to write: "an example of this would be for a person to observe the moon and that it gives light according to its various shapes only from the side facing the sun. The mind then, seizes a middle term, namely that the cause of its light is from the sun." Ibn Sīnā (Avicenna), *al-Shifāᵓ*; *Logic V*; *Demonstration*, ed. A.E. Afifi (Cairo, 1955), p. 259; see also p. 64 where the mental power for grasping by itself the middle term is referred to as natural intelligence (al-*fiṭra*).

In the *Ishārāt* he writes: Among the [premises] that follow the same course as the tested premises are the intuited premises. These are propositions where the basis of judgment concerning them is a very strong intuition of the soul with which doubt is dispelled and to which the mind acquiesces.... An example of this is our judgment that the moon's light derives from the sun by reason of the varied forms of light in it [the moon]. In these [premises] there is also a syllogistic power and they are very similar to the tested [premises]." Ibn Sīnā (Avicenna), *al-Ishārāt wa al-Tanbīhāt*, vol. 1, *Logic*, ed. S. Dunya (Cairo, 1953), pp. 396–97. Ghazāli's discussion of these premises in *MI*, 191–92, seems to be an expansion on Avicenna's statement in the *Ishārāt*.

[21] *Logic V.*; *Demonstration*, 95, 96, 223.

[22] Aristotle, *Physics*, ii,5,196b, 10–16.

[23] Ibn Sīnā (Avicenna), *al-Shifāᵓ*: *al-Ilāhiyyāt* (*Metaphysics*) ed. G.C. Anawati, S. Dunya, M.Y. Musa, and S. Zayd, 2 vols. (Cairo, 1960), 1: 37 ff.

[24] *MI*, 190–91.

[25] Michael E. Marmura, "Ghazali and Demonstrative Science," *Journal of the History of Philosophy*, 3, no. 2 (Oct., 1965): 183–204.

[26] *TF*, 98–102.

A PROPOS DE *L'ISHRĀQ* DE SUHRAWARDĪ: VALEURS SPECULATIVES ET EXPÉRIENCE VÉCUE

LOUIS GARDET

Grâce aux travaux des Professeurs Henry Corbin et S.H. Naṣr, nous avons maintenant à notre disposition les plus grands textes de Suhrawardī, *shaykh al-ishrāq*[2]. A partir de cet ensemble, je voudrais essayer de dégager aujourd'hui non encore la "philosophie" du *shaykh* synthétiquement prise, mais simplement quelques lignes d'horizon où s'inscrit le dynamisme de sa pensée. Quels sont les thèmes, les "philosophèmes" si l'on veut, qui dominent? Quelle est la raison de leur choix, et leur valeur propre, ou spéculative ou expériencielle?

LES DEUX "SAGESSES"

Une précision de vocabulaire: qu'il s'agisse *d'ishrāq* ou de *mashriq*, ces deux termes, ici, restent pris dans une *aura* symbolique, où "Orient" et "Illumination" ne cessent d'interférer. C'est donc à bon droit, me semble-t-il, que l'on peut parler avec M. Corbin d'une "sagesse orientale-illuminative."

Mais s'agit-il de philosophie ou de mystique? Je dirais volontiers: *l'ishrāq* met expérience mystique et philosophie spéculative dans un rapport étroit et constant, selon une démarche qui lui est propre. Les traités de Suhrawardī débutent volontiers par des considérations philosophiques que l'on peut appeler "classiques", conformes aux traditions du péripatétisme arabo-persan. Non seulement les *Alwāḥ ʿimādī*, mais la *Ḥikmat al-ishrāq* elle-même consacrent leurs premiers chapitres à des questions de logique, de cosmologie, d'anthropologie. On pourrait à leur propos cerner toute une "philosophie" où la toile de fond aristotélicienne est sans cesse corrigée ou agrémentée par des influences stoïciennes, et surtout platoniciennes ou plotiniennes: ces dernières au surplus intégrant plus d'une fois des éléments venus soit du moyen platonisme, soit de Plotin ou Proclus confondus avec Aristote, soit directement de Fārābī et d'Ibn Sīnā, soit enfin d'apocryphes célèbres, les pseudo-Empédocle, Pythagore ou Hermès. Peut-être même certaines critiques du Stagirite ont-elles subi l'influence du *ʿilm al-kalām*[3].

Une recension analytique de ces données de base mettrait en valeur les sources très variées de Suhrawardī, et donc le riche milieu culturel qui fut sien. Mais y voir les axes majeurs de sa pensée serait sans doute un contresens. En effet, après les premiers chapitres consacrés à ces exposés "classiques," chaque grand traité (ou presque) prend comme un second départ. Ce sont bien des thèmes philosophiques qui sont à nouveau présentés, du moins en noétique et en métaphysique, mais selon une tout autre ligne de recherche. Les Maîtres cités le seront cette fois selon un choix préférentiel, qui insiste sur la figure archétypale d'Hermès ou sur les "grands Sages" de l'ancien Iran. Les "péripatéticiens" *(mashshāʾyūn)* de Grèce ou d'Islam sont fortement critiqués.[4] Car ce n'est plus à un effort uniquement abstractif qu'est sollicité le lecteur, mais à une expérience (intellectuelle) qui serait une métamorphose vécue.

C'est ainsi que Suhrawardī distingue et, à première vue, oppose deux "sagesses" qui sont deux modes de procéder: d'une part *al-ḥikma al-baḥthiyya,* qui opère par investigation théorétique, et qui est la voie des *mashshaʾyūn;* d'autre part, *al-ḥikma al-dhawqiyya,* la sagesse qui se "goûte", fruition des saveurs spirituelles, tout enflammée d'un désir d'absolu. Elle est celle des *ishrāqiyyūn*[5]. La première se situe au sommet du discours, mais dans la ligne même du discours. Quand la seconde s'exprime, ce n'est point par enseignement discursif, mais pour inciter à l'expérience celui qui *déjà* en a soif. C'est pourquoi elle se revêt, et doit se revêtir du chatoiement des symboles.

Or, ce n'est qu'en apparence que ces deux sagesses s'opposent. Le véritable *ishrāqī* doit savoir maîtriser "la sagesse d'investigation"; c'est à cette condition seule qu'il pourra pénétrer la sagesse "qui se goûte." La fonction essentielle de la "philosophie" sera donc non la saisie objective et désintéressée de ce qui est, mais de *préparer* à une expérience qui tend à un au-delà du contingent. Dès lors, l'expérience d'absolu recherchée ne se trouvera-t-elle pas comme orientée par tel ou tel philosophème jugé indubitable—et indubitable non point parce que "prouvé," mais dans la mesure où s'y rejoignent l'abstraction du philosophe et le symbole du mystique?

SUHRAWARDĪ ET IBN SĪNĀ

J'essayerai de mieux cerner la question en comparant quelques aperçus suhrawardiens aux données aviceniennes correspondantes.

1. L'Etre Premier, pour lui Lumière sur-essentielle et source de toute lumière, Suhrawardī aime à l'appeler *Khurra,* du Nom sacré dont usaient les "anciens Sages" de la Perse. Mais l'Etre Premier, ici, est bien, comme chez Ibn Sīnā, à la fois suprême Intellection et suprême Amour (et c'est par le même terme *ʿishq* que l'Amour est désigné). La comparaison de certains textes suhrawardiens, telle *l'Epître des Hautes Tours*[6], et de la *Risāla fi l-ʿishq*[7] d'Ibn Sīnā serait éclairante.

Lumineux par soi, le *Khurra* ne peut pas ne pas irradier la lumière, et donc, en se diffusant, diffuser l'être. C'est ainsi qu'il est Créateur de toute éternité. Comme chez les *falāsifa,* et pour des raisons semblables mais différemment exprimées, le monde ne peut pas ne pas être éternel[8].

2. A l'instar d'Ibn Sīnā encore, Suhrawardī revient abondamment sur la distinction entre l'Etre nécessaire par soi, et l'être "contingent," nécessaire par autrui dans l'ordre de l'existence, et qui n'est que potentialité dans l'ordre de l'essence[9]. Mais c'est par le symbole de la lumière et de l'obscurité que s'exprimera ici le rapport entre acte et puissance[10]. Deux remarques:

a) pour Suhrawardī, ce symbole est en fait la seule traduction suffisamment signifiante de la réalité. Pour l'*ishrāqī,* "nécessaire par soi" et "nécessaire par autrui" (qui relèvent de la "sagesse investigatrice") ne sont que des approches, valables sans doute, mais qui n'atteignent cette réalité que du dehors et discursivement. Elles ne reçoivent leur portée exacte qu'en référence à la Lumière absolue, et à sa dégradation dans et par le processus même qui l'irradie;

b) il ne s'agit point en cela d'un "dualisme" écho de l'ancien mazdéisme, ou du plus récent manichéisme. Le contingent n'est pas le lieu de rencontre de deux principes antagonistes, quand bien même le Principe lumineux serait premier par rapport au Principe des ténèbres. Comme chez Fārābī et Ibn Sīnā, la production des êtres s'opère toujours selon l'adage Plotinien que "de l'Un ne peut sortir que l'un." Mais la Lumière est diffusive de soi; à mesure qu'elle s'éloigne de sa Source, c'est sa diffusivité même qui crée l'apparence des ténèbres, le monde du *barzakh*[11], "entre-deux" où les corps obscurs font écran. Elle reste lumière cependant, et une tradition imāmite définit le *barzakh* comme *nūr ẓulāmī,* "lumière obscure."[12]

3. L'âme humaine n'est pas forme substantielle du corps, même au sens large d'Ibn Sīnā (qui fait du corps l'"instrument" de l'âme). Elle est l'image-reflet de la "Lumière régente," Ange-Ame céleste qui la gouverne. Elle appartient de soi au monde intelligible de la *malakūt,* et la relation qui l'unit au corps n'est qu'accidentelle[13]. Au contraire de Fārābī, et tout autant qu'Ibn Sīnā (mais pour d'autres raisons), Suhrawardī affirme ainsi la vie personnelle de l'âme après la mort[14].

La vie future de l'âme purifiée est un "retour" *(maᶜād)* au monde des Intelligibles, diraient les *falāsifa,* aux mondes des Lumières régentes, des Anges Archétypes, des Lumières victoriales, selon Suhrawardī. Elle peut commencer dès ici-bas, quand à la "sagesse d'investigation" succède la sagesse intuitive et unitive de *l'ishrāq.* Image-reflet de la Lumière dont elle émane et qui la gouverne, l'âme humaine, une fois purifiée de son attachment au *barzakh,* devient l'objet même qu'elle connaît, par union d'identité ontologique. C'est l'une des thèses centrales de Suhrawardī que cette affirmation de l'identité ontologique du connaissant et du connu[15] dans l'acte de connaissance purifiée (mystique). Par delà Ibn Sīnā, il rejoint ainsi la noétique fārābienne.

4. On peut se demander si ce n'est pas cette "théorie de la connaissance" qui donne en quelque sorte la clef de la démarche du *shaykh al-ishrāq.* Car l'identité ainsi atteinte n'est autre, à ses yeux, que l'expérience réalisatrice de la Lumière substantielle qui, en dégradés successifs, *est* la "réalité" *(ḥaqīqa)* secrète, le constitutif secret de toute existence.

Bien plus: tous les "philosophèmes" sur lesquels il revient de traité en traité, tous les symboles et "mythes privilégiés" qu'il demande à l'ancien Iran, aux Sages de la Grèce, aux traditions islamiques, ne sont-ils pas pour lui comme la projection dans le monde du discours et de l'imagination transcendantale, de la saisie par voie d'immanence d'un pur exister, dépouillé de toute limite de temps et d'espace? Dans un tout autre climat culturel, sous l'irradiation et le symbole de la Lumière sur lumineuse du *Khurra* iranien, ne rejoindrions-nous pas ici "la trace de l'Un qui est en nous" de Plotin, ou le Soi absolu des grandes *Upanishad*? ......

VERS LE MONDE DES LUMIÈRES

Bien d'autres exemples de "philosophèmes" pourraient être proposés: problème de l'Un et du multiple, les imbrications et le déploiement des hiérarchies angéliques. . . . La pensée du maître de l'*ishrāq* est complexe et riche. Elle est gnose plus que philosophie, c'est-à-dire lecture symbolique et mythique d'une réalité vécue, qui est à elle-même sa propre norme.

Suhrawardī y revient sans cesse:[16] ses écrits ne sont pas un enseignement didactique, mais un "appel" à une expérience vécue, et peut-être déjà un jalonnement sur la route. Les développements—je dirais presque les prosopopées—sur les hiérarchies des Lumières angéliques et le processus de leur émanation, ne se réfutent ni ne se prouvent :ils demandent à être saisis dans une vision intuitive, dont ils sont comme l'image approchée. Pour Suhrawardī, la raison d'être de ses traités, c'est de devenir des repères lumineux, éclairant la voie. Tel est sans doute le sens de l'ésotérisme dont il entoura le texte capital de la *Ḥikmat al-ishrāq*. On sait qu'il prit soin de le transcrire en langage chiffré. Car il le réserve à ceux qui ne se contenteront pas de le lire, ni même de l'étudier, mais qui, en le lisant, "se mettront en route." Il précise que ce traité ne doit être confié qu'au seul mystique qui, après avoir dominé la philosophie des "péripatéticiens," se sent enflammé d'amour pour la Lumière originelle.[17] Et si l'"itinérant" ne peut en saisir par lui-même le vrai message, qu'il s'adresse au "mainteneur du Livre" *(qā'im al-kitāb)* dont il recevra aide et directive.

Suhrawardī n'hésite pas à confier à son lecteur ce que fut sa propre démarche.[18] Tant qu'il resta dans la voie de l'investigation discursive, il fut péripatéticien. Mais un jour vint où il *vit*, en rapt d'extase *(khaṭfa)*, le monde des pures Lumières dont toutes choses existantes ne sont qu'image et reflet. A qui douterait de son témoignage, il conseille de pratiquer les "exercices spirituels" *(riyāḍāt)*, et de se mettre à l'école des "maîtres de la vision" *(aṣḥāb al-mushāhada)*.[19] Peut-être le chercheur sincère verra-t-il alors, dans un ravissement analogue au sien propre, ces Anges-Lumières qui régissent les âmes. Et c'est sous le haut patronage d'Hermès, de Platon, de Zarathustra *(Zarādusht)*, du "roi fidèle Kay Khusraw," et de "tous les Sages de la Perse," qu'il situe cette vision illuminative.

Nous saisissons ici le mode de procéder de Suhrawardī quand il entreprend d'exposer le thème de l'*ishrāq*. Tout est centré sur une expérience personnelle de vision, qui est pour lui l'entrée dans le Monde de la seule vraie Réalité, indûment voilé par la frange obscure du *barzakh*. Expérience personnelle sans doute, mais ouverte à toute âme de l'"espèce humaine." Ce à quoi Suhrawardī veut entraîner son lecteur, c'est à vivre la vision extatique lumineuse que lui-même a vécue. C'est après une retraite de quarante jours, dit-il,[20] que l'on peut entreprendre une lecture savoureuse et méditée de la *Ḥikmat al-ishrāq*, et c'est par deux *wārida*, sorte d'hymnes "inspirées," qu'il soutient et scande l'élan extatique qui traverse les derniers développements de son livre.

Une page très dense décrira la progression de l'expérience.[21] Avec un grand luxe d'analyse, Suhrawardī y distingue quinze venues successives et progressives de la Lumière: selon sa modalité, ses effets, et les phénomènes auditifs ou olfactifs qui l'accompagnent.[22] Nous avons ainsi comme le schéma volontairement non explicite des arcanes où s'inscrit une expérience de déprise du moi contingent—vers les sources de son être et de l'être. Est-ce une expérience du Dieu Un de la foi musulmane, telle que nous la trouvons affirmée chez un Ḥallāj? La question reste posée, et demanderait, pour être résolue, d'autres précisions d'analyse.

Je le répète: la vision suhrawardienne du Monde des Lumières ne se réfute ni ne se prouve. Et pour en mieux pénétrer la portée, un double travail, me semble-t-il, devrait se poursuivre:

1) Etudier de près, en ses sources et sa systématisation, la représentation discursive qui en est proposée: sans oublier cependant que cette vision n'est jamais une recherche de vérité par intuition abstractive (donc judicative), qu'elle se mesure non à ce qui est, à la trame ontologique des choses, mais à l'authenticité de l'expérience subjectivement vécue;

2) Distinguer, autant que possible, l'expérience comme telle de sa représentation; et l'étudier en elle-même. Il est certains élans des *wāridāt*, ou des récits symboliques, et plus encore cette venue progressive des quinze lumières dont nous parlions tout-à-l'heure, qui mériteraient d'être lus et médités de près. Et sans doute conviendrait-il d'y joindre, en schèmes comparatifs, certains apports d'autres climats religieux. Dégager la valeur expériencielle de ces textes, en sa portée, ses limites peut-être, son authenticité sur le plan qui lui est propre, ne serait-ce pas rendre à Suhrawardī, dans l'histoire des idées et de la mystique, l'hommage qui lui est dû?

NOTES

[1] Cette communication est la première approche d'une étude plus exhaustive, destinée au volume qui sera publié au Caire en l'honneur de Suhrawardī par le "Conseil Supérieur des Arts, des Lettres et des Sciences Sociales" de la République Arabe Egyptienne (volume actuellement en cours de composition).

[2] Essentiellement: tome I (*Talwīḥāt*, *Muqāwamāt*, *Muṭāraḥāt*), éd. H. Corbin, Istanbūl, 1945; tome II (*Ḥikmat al-ishrāq*, *Iʿtiqād al-ḥukamāʾ*, *al-Ghurba al-ghurbiyya*), éd. H. Corbin, Téhéran-Paris, 1952; tome III, "*Oeuvres persanes*," éd. H. Corbin et S.H. Naṣr, Téhéran-Paris, 1970.-Nous nous référerons à ces trois ouvrages sous la simple indication: I, II, III.

[3] Cf. *Encyclopédie de l'Islam*, lère éd., art. *Suhrawardī* par S. van den Bergh.

[4] Respectivement III, p. 92 et ss. (éd. arabe courante, Le Caire, 1335 H., p. 20 et ss.); II, p. 106 et ss.

[5] Voir remarques de H. Corbin, III, "Prolégomènes", p. 133.

[6] *Risālat al-abrāj* (encore appelée *Kalimāt dhawqiyya*), texte arabe III, pp. 462–71.

[7] Texte édité (avec trad. franç. glosée) par A.F. Mehren, ap. *Traités Mystiques d'Avicenne*, éd. Brill, Leyde, 1894.

[8] V.g. *Hayākil al-nūr*, III, pp.97-98 (texte arabe pp.29-30); également *Alwāḥ ʿimādī*, III, p. 134 et ss.

[9] V.g. *Hayākil*, III, p. 94.

[10] Principe affirmé et réaffirmé, ainsi *Alwāḥ*, III, p. 148.

[11] Le thème revient souvent; voir spécialement *Ḥikmat al-ishrāq*, II, pp. 129–31, le chapitre sur *Aḥkām al-barzakh*.

[12] Cf. Louis Massignon, *Passion d'al-Ḥallāj*, lère éd., Paris, 1922, p. 482.

[13] Encore que Suhrawardī reconnaisse une possible relation de principe de l'âme au corps, cf. *Hayākil*, texte arabe, p.24 (III° "Temple"), texte persan III, p.94.

[14] Dans le traité persan de la "Connaissance de Dieu" (*Yazdān shanākht*), III, pp. 441–43, il décrit le sort des âmes dans l'Au-delà selon les schèmes mêmes proposés par Ibn Sīnā à la fin du *Shifāʾ* et de la *Najāt*, et en diverses remarques des "Gloses" sur la pseudo-*Théologie d'Aristote*.— L'attribution du *Yazdān shanākht* à Suhrawardī fut parfois mise en doute. A la suite de Sayyed Ḥusayn Naṣr, M. Corbin se prononce pour son authenticité (III, "Prolégomènes", p.14).

[15] Ainsi *Talwīḥāt*, I, pp. 70–74.

[16] Et à sa suite, ses deux grands commentateurs, Dawwānī et Ghiyāṯ al-Dīn Shīrāzī.

[17] *Ḥikmat al-ishrāq*, II, p. 258.

[18] *Ibid.*, pp. 156–58.

[19] *Ibid.*, p.156.— Fréquentes sont ces allusions aux exercices spirituels, oraisons, oratorios, etc. Ainsi à la fin de l'*Iʿtiqād al-ḥukamāʾ*, II, pp. 280–81.

[20] *Ḥikmat al-ishrāq*, II, p.258.

[21] *Ibid.*, pp.252–53.

[22] On songerait, analogiquement, à certains passages d'Ibn 'Aṭā' Allāh d'Alexandrie dans son *Miftāḥ*, décrivant l'emprise progressive du *dhikr* et les phénomènes concomitants.

NEW LIGHT ON THE POLITICAL PHILOSOPHY OF AVERROËS

CHARLES E. BUTTERWORTH

Averroës once spoke very sharply about al-Ghazzālī, even going so far as to accuse him of changing allegiances to suit the occasion or, as we might say, of trying to be all things to all people.[1] However appropriate the accusation may have been in that controversy, it inevitably comes back to haunt its author whenever the secondary literature about his thought is considered. Indeed, were Averroës to be judged solely on the basis of the secondary literature, he would necessarily be found guilty of having completely succeeded in doing that of which he accused al-Ghazzālī. The extent to which the secondary literature accuses Averroës of having tried to be all things to all people is especially evident in the scholarly debates about whether he should be considered more a disciple of Aristotle or of Neoplatonic thought, as well as in the great controversy about his religious standing—i.e., whether he is to be classed among those faithful to the tenets of Islam or among the unfaithful.

Behind these controversies lie questions of major significance to students of Islamic philosophy, but heretofore arguments that Averroës was primarily an Aristotelian have been largely limited to the well-known fact that he commented very extensively on most of Aristotle's works and highly praised the Stagirite for his acute perception. Consequently, little attention has been given to the fact that Averroës saw nothing inconsistent in his attempt to complete his statement about politics by writing a commentary on Plato's *Republic* rather than on Aristotle's *Politics*. Precisely because he considered a kind of harmony to exist between Aristotle's *Nicomachean Ethics* and Plato's *Republic*, a harmony similar to the one existing between Aristotle's *Nicomachean Ethics* and his *Politics*, the claims that Averroës may have been more partial to one of the two Greek philosophers or to a particular school interpretation of them become less important than an investigation of how he thought it possible to harmonize these authors and books.[2] Similarly, now that more is known about the logical writings of Averroës and his concern about speaking in different ways to different people is more thoroughly recognized, the arguments about his standing as a Muslim must give way to deeper questions about his thoughts concerning the relation between religion and politics. In his logical writings Averroës explained that the reason for the distinctions in speech was his awareness of the importance of speech to political community, as well as his awareness that preservation of the political community was an essential requisite for decent human life. Consequently, it is necessary to wonder whether those works heretofore most consulted by scholars to determine his religious orthodoxy (i.e., *The Decisive Treatise* and *The Destruction of the Destruction)* are representative of his deepest thoughts on religion (or, more precisely, on the relation between reason and revelation) or whether they have a more limited and specifically political goal. By his own admission, these works were addressed to a general audience and used arguments appropriate to such an audience. The question of his religious orthodoxy thus depends on a better appreciation of his understanding of the way in which religion is taught to a people and how it affects political life.

It appears, then, that previous scholarly concerns really require a better understanding of why Averroës thought the political community to be essential to decent human life. They also seem to point to the question of what way he thought it should be ordered to bring about such an end, as well as how he thought the philosophy of Aristotle and Plato were in agreement about these issues. His most explicit political writings (the *Commentary on Aristotle's Nicomachean Ethics* and the *Commentary on Plato's Republic)* not only raise these issues; by their very subject matter they promise to clarify them.

According to Averroës, his *Commentary on Aristotle's Nicomachean Ethics* presents his teaching about the first or theoretical part of politics, and his *Commentary on Plato's Republic* presents his teaching about the second or practical part. When introducing the reader to the second, and admittedly more public, part of this teaching, Averroës explained the reason why he divided his political teaching into two parts. Although politics is to be classed among the practical sciences because of the nature of its subject matter and basic principles, as well as because of the nature of its end, there is a somewhat theoretical part of politics. That somewhat theoretical part is concerned with the general issues on which individual political actions are based, just as other practical arts have a somewhat theoretical side in addition to their simply practical function. For Averroës, medicine was the best example of this mixture of theory and practice in explicitly practical arts. Once the general view of the subject matter and basic principle of politics was presented, it was possible to understand how politics might be practiced, i.e., what should be done so that the end discovered in the theoretical part of the science could be brought about in fact.[3] What these general remarks mean for an understanding of the political thought of Averroës can best be determined by taking a closer look at his description of that theoretical part of politics.

Although quite faithful to the order of Aristotle's book, Averroës' *Commentary on Aristotle's Nicomachean Ethics* is much more explicitly political than Aristotle's text. This more explicitly political teaching was presented by subtle changes in the emphasis of Aristotle's argument. For example, when

Aristotle argued that the hierarchy which one can discern in arts, inquiries, practical pursuits, and choices insofar as each aims at some end suggests that all things aim at some end and that the end which would be most able to control other ends would be most desirable, Averroës concurred. Similarly, Averroës agreed with Aristotle's conditional argument about politics being the art which furnishes the end most desirable for its own sake. The argument for both was that if the political art orders all the activities pursued in a city, and if all activities seek some end, the political art must order all the other activities in such a way as to bring about a greater and more desirable end than any one of them might be able to bring about. However, this very agreement provides the grounds for the beginning of a basic disagreement. Whereas Aristotle subsequently remained silent about the political implications of that conditional argument and concentrated his efforts upon the search for the most desirable end, Averroës refused to allow those political implications to remain silently implicit. Thus, he insisted throughout his commentary that the major purpose of the speech about ethics was governance of the city in general and, more specifically, the good to be sought in such governance.[4]

In a similar manner, he followed Aristotle's method in searching for a determination of the most desirable end, or happiness, but was much more explicit than Aristotle when confessing the limits imposed upon this particular quest by the context in which it took place—i.e., a political or practical context. Thus, when Aristotle mentioned the tentativeness of such a study and cautioned the reader against expecting too much in the way of demonstrable answers, Averroës emphasized the limits of the inquiry even more strongly and told the reader where a fuller discussion of the subject could be found. That is, he explained that a fuller discussion of the most desirable end belonged to an inquiry as theoretical as logic or first philosophy, i.e., metaphysics. Unlike Aristotle, Averroës explicitly stated the reasons why the problems connected with ultimate happiness could not be fully examined in this book on moral habits: this book has a practical goal and therefore contains logical premises which are more general and less demonstrable than those used in explicitly theoretical books; any student of the logical arts was expected to recognize the necessary limitations on practical arts and thus to understand the limitations of this book.[5] In general, then, Averroës seized upon the political character of Aristotle's ethical teaching and ordered his comments around that political character. At one point, he even went so far as to insist, despite Aristotle's silence on the matter, that what was under discussion in the treatise was nothing less than the most noble art: that of ruling a city.[6]

Averroës' loquacity about things concerning which Aristotle was silent must be contrasted with his silence about things concerning which Aristotle was loquacious. For instance, despite numerous references by Aristotle to the divine character of happiness, Averroës never seized the opportunity to speak about the happiness peculiar to citizens in a community enlightened by revealed religion, nor did he mention the happiness of the life to come.[7] In fact, when Aristotle spoke about the opinions men held about whether happiness was something which must extend beyond death and treated the subject as something which was a matter of utter speculation, Averroës treated the matter in the very same way. Even more surprising to a reader who might expect Averroës to have been intent on pointing out how Islamic teaching altered Aristotle's ideas is that Averroës made no attempt to go beyond Aristotle's thoughts about whether the actions of the living could affect the happiness of the dead. Instead, he commented on Aristotle's reasons and suggested their correctness solely on the basis of what is known to unassisted human reason.[8] Nowhere in his *Commentary on Aristotle's Nicomachean Ethics* is there evidence that Averroës believed it necessary to modify Aristotle's general statements about happiness in the light of anything peculiar to his time or place. In short, Averroës presented his comments as though addressed to a man who wanted to know about the highest, practical questions he might consider when trying to decide how to rule a city.

Differently stated, for Averroës the theoretical part of politics was supposed to teach that political rule should be directed to the happiness of the citizens, and it contained some general indications of what the elements of that happiness might be. That happiness was apparently a happiness of this life alone. More importantly, as presented in the theoretical part of politics, happiness seemed to be a result of training and to be directed to practice. It was no more a happiness of intellectual development than it was the happiness of another life. Thus, even though it was admitted that intellectual happiness or contemplation might be the highest kind of happiness, the book containing the presentation of the theoretical part of politics limited the presentation of happiness to a discussion of the kind of happiness attainable by most people; the discussion of contemplative happiness was explicitly assigned to another book, just as the discussion of how to bring about the kind of happiness attainable by most people was assigned to another book. If anything, Averroës was much more emphatic about excluding a consideration of contemplative happiness from the theoretical statement of politics than he was about excluding a consideration of the happiness pertinent to the other life. Whereas his ideas about the latter kind of happiness can be gathered only from whatever significance is attached to his silence about the matter, he explicitly relegated the discussion of contemplative happiness to other kinds of discussion.

Similar instances of unexpected loquacity and silence occur in the discussion devoted to Aristotle's views about natural law. Although Averroës followed the basic thread of Aristotle's explanations, even to the extent of agreeing that sacrifices represented conventional aspects of justice, he said nothing to suggest that natural law might have some affinity to divine law. More importantly, Averroës completely overlooked Aristotle's suggestion that the justice of the gods might everywhere be the same even if the justice of man admits of variety.[9] This does not mean that Averroës set out to neglect all of Aristotle's references to divine matters, but it does suggest that he was more concerned about examining the general significance of Aristotle's ideas than he was about applying these ideas to the generally received opinions of a particular community. As a consequence he did not strive to make an explicit correction of Aristotle's explanations which reflected pagan theology or Greek convention, though he often corrected those remarks without alluding to Aristotle's error. For example, when Aristotle spoke about justice as something basically human because it implied having no more than a proper amount of just things, whereas the gods could presumably never have too much of just things, Averroës suggested a different reason for justice being a basically human concept: namely, there is a certain limit to the amount of justice men might achieve since there is a different order of justice typical of divinity which men can never attain. Again, in trying to decide whether a man could treat himself unjustly, Aristotle pointed out that even though suicide was something not expressly permitted by the law, a man who committed suicide would have to be called unjust since whatever the law did not expressly permit, it prohibited. Although Averroës followed Aristotle's general argument closely, he simply ignored the involved reasoning regarding suicide and explained that suicide was unjust because it was prohibited by the law; as a result, he had to put suicide into a category of unjust acts other than the category denoted by Aristotle.[10]

To be sure, part of the reason for Averroës' failure to make explicit his correction of such explanations by Aristotle and for his reluctance to point out the minor differences in interpretation arising from Aristotle's distinct theology must derive from Averroës' concern about his whole philosophical project. In trying to make Greek philosophy better known to fellow Muslims and in his own personal acceptance of Greek philosophy, he always had to be wary of the claim that the ways of the Greeks were so different from those of the Muslims that nothing at all could be learned from them and that no steadfast Muslim should place faith in Greek teachings.[11] Still, such a practical consideration explains at best only a certain terseness in Averroës' style; it does not at all account for any of his attempts to extend Aristotle's remarks. Only Averroës' conviction that the teaching presented in the *Nicomachean Ethics* constituted the theoretical part of the practical art of politics can explain his liberal expansion of Aristotle's remarks.

Throughout the *Nicomachean Ethics*, the goal of Aristotle's inquiry was that end at which all arts and sciences, and especially the most authoritative arts and sciences, aim. Because politics appeared to be the most authoritative art, the art which directed the activities of all the other arts and sciences, its end seemed to be identical with the end to which the inquiry was directed. At least that is the way matters appeared to him at the start. However, as the inquiry progressed, it became increasingly evident that there was a difference between the ultimate end to which some men could aspire and the end which the political art sought to bring about. In part the investigation of the intellectual virtues contributed to this conclusion, for it became clear in that investigation that prudence was subordinate to theoretical wisdom, i.e., that theoretical wisdom was of a higher order than prudence. Since prudence was the intellectual virtue of the political art, the art of politics would have to be considered to be of a lower order than the art whose virtue was theoretical wisdom. Neither Aristotle nor Averroës did more than suggest these consequences until the discussion turned to the consideration of ultimate happiness. Once it became evident that contemplation was more likely to be ultimate happiness because it represented the best kind of activity, the end of politics could no longer be said to be identical with that highest goal—the activity of the political art being quite different from contemplative activity.

Still, properly directed, the activity of the political art could be in accordance with, and foster, excellence. The excellence so fostered also had the advantage of being more readily accessible to most human beings. Aristotle was concerned at the end of his inquiry to indicate how that excellence, moral virtue, could be engendered in others. In order to examine that question, he reflected on the force of law. The conditional argument which provided the grounds for his turn from the investigation of the *Nicomachean Ethics* to that of the *Politics* was: "surely he who wants to make men, whether many or few, better by his care must try to become capable of legislating, if it is through laws that we can become good." Support for acceptance of that condition had been prepared by the immediately preceding consideration of how virtue might best be fostered, a consideration which ended by placing heavy emphasis on the good effect of habituation backed by some kind of necessity or force.[12] So there was a strong implication, but only an implication, that Aristotle intended to study the art of legislation in order to learn how men could be made good, i.e., in order to discover what laws would be most apt to engender in citizens the kind of habits that lead to moral virtue. There was no implication that Aristotle considered the inquiry begun in the *Nicomachean Ethics* to represent the theoretical part of the subsequent investigation; it seemed, rather, that one incidental aspect of the earlier inquiry—how men could be trained in moral virtue—raised questions which could only be answered by looking more carefully at the legislative art.

The difference between Averroës and Aristotle arises in part from the fact that Averroës did not at all think Aristotle's turn from the discussion of the *Nicomachean Ethics* to the *Politics* was based on a conditional syllogism. Because it appeared to him to be so obvious that men could be made good only by laws, he was persuaded that in the *Politics* Aristotle intended to answer the very practical question of which laws would make men good.[13] However, Averroës was of the opinion that Aristotle's pursuit of such a practical question followed directly from the conclusion reached by the theoretical investigation of the *Nicomachean Ethics*. That is, Averroës did not consider the inquiry into the legislative art as a pursuit of problems which arose incidentally. To him, the problem of training men in moral virtue had guided the whole inquiry of the *Nicomachean Ethics*, even though it had become an explicit problem only towards the end of the book. The *Nicomachean Ethics* constituted the theoretical part of the political art because the investigation presented in that book resulted in general ideas about moral virtue and explained how the cultivation of moral virtue was intimately related to the political art. Once these general ideas had been set forth, it was the task of the practical part of the political art to investigate particular instances in which they might be applied.

That Averroës held this opinion about what Aristotle had done in the *Nicomachean Ethics* and intended to do in the *Politics* explains why he was so much more outspoken than Aristotle about the limits of the inquiry and about the necessity of investigating contemplative happiness by other sciences. That is, because he perceived the purpose of the *Nicomachean Ethics* as distinctly political, he was intent upon removing any considerations which would detract from that political purpose.[14] Nonetheless, that Averroës assigned contemplative happiness to a different kind of investigation, does not imply that it had no relation to the happiness attained in political life. To the contrary, he argued that the investigation into the legislative art would be guided by the intellectual virtue of theoretical wisdom rather than by prudence—an opinion virtually without support from Aristotle's *Nicomachean Ethics*, but which is grounded on Averroës' argument that the basic difference between theoretical and practical arts arises from differences in the subject matter and the purposes of the investigation rather than from the intellectual virtue directing the inquiry into these different arts.[15] The significance of his argument that theoretical wisdom would guide the investigation into the legislative art is that the very intellectual virtue which was said to lead to contemplative happiness is also supposed to indicate the substance of political happiness. In other words, the difference between the happiness which most men could ultimately hope to attain by virtuous conduct in a political community and that which a few men could ultimately hope to attain by contemplation need not be construed as a qualitative difference. Thus, while the presentation of Aristotle's teaching about happiness in the *Commentary on Aristotle's Nicomachean Ethics* is very secular, it prepares the more particularly Islamic presentation of happiness of the *Commentary on Plato's Republic*.[16]

Indeed, when Averroës presented what he called the practical part of his political teaching, he did not at all hesitate to remind the reader of the crucial difference separating the author of the commentary and the author of the original text in time and place. Many of the general observations arrived at in the theoretical part of his political teaching were modified in the discussion of the practical part by conventions of which he was acutely aware.[17] In addition to these explicit references to particular circumstances which indicate how general ideas would be modified in their application, Averroës' *Commentary on Plato's Republic* is marked by an emphasis on the educational task of the ruler. That is, Averroës interpreted Plato as having taught that the best ruler was a man with theoretical knowledge of practical matters who sought to instruct the populace by rhetorical and poetical speech. Such an interpretation enabled him to argue that the ruler of an actual political community must be able to speak in different ways to different people and ought to have a knowledge of political matters based on something other than practical wisdom.

However, Aristotle's decision to investigate the legislative art was partly due to doubt about the effectiveness of mere speech for training citizens in moral virtue. As Averroës noted, Plato also saw the need for something more than speech if citizens were to be trained in moral virtue. In all respects, then, Averroës' interpretation of Plato's *Republic* corresponds to the demands of the practical part of politics. It also seems to be a natural sequel to Aristotle's *Nicomachean Ethics,* if Averroës' argument about theoretical wisdom guiding practical wisdom can really be attributed to Aristotle. But since it is generally known that Aristotle did not accept that argument in the *Politics,* Averroës' attempted substitution must be rejected. Such a rejection, while concluding the present discussion, poses an important question for all students of Averroës' political teaching: in what way does it make sense to say that theoretical wisdom can guide practical matters?

NOTES

1 Averroës, *Kitāb Faṣl al-Maqāl (The Decisive Treatise),* ed. George F. Hourani (Leiden: E.J. Brill, 1959), pp. 17:21–18:4 (pages and lines cited according to Mueller's *editio princeps,* as reproduced in the margins of Hourani's edition).

2 Cf. Averroës, *Commentary on Plato's Republic,* ed. and trans. E.I.J. Rosenthal (Cambridge: University Press, 1966), I.i.8 (i.e., First Treatise, Chapter One, Section Eight, according to Rosenthal's divisions):

"The first part of this art [of Politics] is contained in Aristotle's book known as *Nicomachea,* and the second part in his book known as *Politics,* and in Plato's book also upon which we intend to comment. For Aristotle's *Politica* has not yet come into our hands."

It is also important to consider the relation Averroës perceived between the two works before he began to comment on Plato's *Republic*. Cf. Averroës, *in Libros Decem Moralium Nicomachiorum Expositio*, in *Aristotelis Opera cum Averrois Commentariis* (Venice: Apud Junctas, 1562), Vol. 3, folio 160 G-H:

"Et hic explicit sermo in hac parte huius scientiae: et est ea quae habet se in scientia civili habitudine notitiae, quid est sanitas et aegritudo in arte medicinae: et illa, quam promisit, est pars quae habet se in hac scientia habitudine effectivae sanitatis et destructivae aegritudinis in medicina. et est in libro eius, qui nominatur liber de regimine vitae: et nondum pervenit ad nos, qui sumus in hac insula: quemadmodum non pervenerant ad nos primitus de isto libro, nisi primi quatuor tractatus, donec perduxit eum ad nos amicus noster vir nobilis dominus Omar filius Martini, rogatu amicorum suorum, et Deus retribuat ei pro nobis regratiationem completam. Et fortassis erit aliquis amicorum, qui adducat librum, in quo est complementum huius scientiae, si Deus voluerit. Apparet autem ex sermone Abyn arrim Alfarabii [i.e., Abū Naṣr al-Fārābī], quod inventus est in illis villis. Si vero hoc non contingerit, et Deus contulerit inducias vitae, perscrutabimur de hac intentione juxta mensuram nostri posse. Nam ex sermone Philosophi apparet in hoc loco, quod quod est in libro Platonis de regimine vitae, incompletum est, et videtur quod sic se habeat res in seipsa, nam in illo libro perscrutatur Plato duobus modis hominum tantum, et sunt conservatores et sapientes. deinde ostendit, quommodo permutantur civitates simplices ad seinvicem. Sed perscrutatio artificialis exigit ut rememorentur leges, et fori communes civitatibus simplicibus: deinde rememoretur post hoc, quod appropriatur singulis civitatibus ex eis, intendo quod appropriatur aggregationi nobili honorabili, et aliis aggregationibus. Et similiter rememoretur quod impedit universas aggregationes, et quod impedit modos singulos ex ipsis: et inquirantur exempla huius in vita inventa in illo tempore. et hoc est illud, ad quod innuit Aristotelis hic, et est res quae non completur in libris Plato. Qualiter igitur dixit Albubekrim filius aurificis [i.e., Abū Bakr Muḥammad ibn al-Ṣāʾigh or Ibn Bājjah] quod locutio de aggregatione nobili iam expedita erat in libro Platonis, et quod loquetur de eo in quo iam locutum est, dummodo inveniatur, est superfluitas, aut ignorantia, aut malitia. veruntamen non pervenerat ad ipsum complementum istorum tractuum. Et ego quidem explevi determinationem istorum tractatuum quarto die Jovis mensis, qui Arabice dicitur Ducadatim anno Arabum, Dlxxii. Et grates Deo multae de hoc. Dixit translator. Et ego complevi eius translationem ex Arabico in Latinum tertio die jovis mensis Junii, anno ab incarnatione Domini, Mcclx. apud urbem Toletanam, in capella sanctae trinitatis, unde sit benedictum nomen Domini, qui est trinus et unus.

[3] Averroës, *Commentary on Plato's Republic*, I.i.1–7, I.i.9–I.iii.5; also Averroës, *Moral. Nic. Expos.*, 160G.

[4] Cf. Aristotle, *Nicomachean Ethics*, 1094a 1–15, 1094a 27–1094b 11, 1102a 7–26, 1145a 6–12; Averroës, *Moral. Nic. Expos.*, 1H–K, 2C–G, 3F, 8I, 12F, 16M–17C, 93E–F.

[5] Cf. Aristotle, *Nicomachean Ethics*, 1096b 7, 1097a 12, also 1142a 12–19; Averroës, *Moral. Nic. Expos.*, 7B–C, 7E, 7G, 9M–10A, also 87L–M.

[6] Ibid., 8H–I.

[7] Aristotle, *Nicomachean Ethics*, 1099b 11–18, 1177a 12–18, 1177b 27–1178a 8, 1178b 8–32; Averroës, *Moral. Nic. Expos.*, 12D–F, 153 D–E, 153M–154D, 155M–156D, 156G–H.

[8] Aristotle, *Nicomachean Ethics*, 1100a 10–1101a 21, 1101a 23–1101b 8; Averroës, *Moral. Nic. Expos.*, 13H–14I, 15A–E.

[9] Aristotle, *Nicomachean Ethics*, 1134b 18–29; Averroës, *Moral. Nic. Expos.*, 73M–74E.

[10] Aristotle, *Nicomachean Ethics*, 1137a27–31, 1138a 4–13, and cf. also 1139b 10–11, 1140b 8–19; Averroës, *Moral. Nic. Expos.*, 78D, 80C–E, and cf. also 82L, 84K–M.

[11] Cf. Averroes, *Kitāb Faṣl al-Maqāl*, 3:18–4:6.

[12] Aristotle, *Nicomachean Ethics* 1180b 23–25 and 1179b 20–1180b 13. The citation is from the translation of W.D. Ross: *Ethica Nicomachea* in *The Works of Aristotle Translated into English*

(Oxford: University Press, 1949) vol. 9.

[13] Averroës, *Moral. Nic. Expos.* 159 I: "Et ex quo necessarium est ei, qui vult efficere per regimen et gubernationem aliquos meliores, quam sint sive multos, sive paucos, ut sit lator legum: cum per legem quidem bonum faciamus." Cf. also 158L–159G. St. Thomas read Aristotle, *Nicomachean Ethics*, 1180b 23–25 in the same way as Averroës; cf. St. Thomas Aquinas, *In Decem Libros Ethicorum Aristotelis ad Nicomachum Expositio*, ed. R.M. Spiazzi (Turin: Editrice Marietti, 1964), pars. 2179–2180 with 2153–2154 and 2163.

[14] Cf. *supra*, pp. 118–20.

[15] Averroës, *Moral. Nic. Expos.*, 1591 K; *Commentary on Plato's Republic*, I.i.2–4, I.i.10, I.iii.7.

[16] Averroës, *Commentary on Plato's Republic*, I.x.8, I.xi.7, and II.xvi. 10 with I.vii. 1–4, Ix.1, I.x.3–4, and I.xii.6. To Agree with printed text

[17] Ibid., I.vii. 11, I.viii.4, I.xi.3, I.xii. 7-11, I.xiiA.3, I.xiiA.9–10, I.xiv.4–5, and *passim*. Cf. also I.viii.1 with *Moral. Nic. Expos.*, 79C–G.

ETHICS IN MEDIEVAL ISLAM: A CONSPECTUS

George F. Hourani

The aim of this paper is to present a general review of one theme of Islamic ethical thought that should be of significance and interest to modern philosophers: analytical discussions of the meanings of ethical terms, together with some background information on normative ethics which provide the basis for the evolution of analytical ethics. Two other topics of contemporary interest were also discussed extensively by Muslim thinkers, the psychology of moral action and the question of moral freedom, but I shall leave these aside and concentrate on the first topic.

I shall start with a simplified classification of types of ethical writing in medieval Islam, which will provide a frame of reference for the types we are interested in. Two levels of generality in ethical thinking have already been mentioned, which were called "normative" and "analytical." (I should have liked to call the latter "philosophical," but as we shall see there is a theological theory which is consciously antiphilosophical, though just as general. The term "meta-ethics" is currently in use, but I find it nothing but a modish substitute for what used to be simply "ethics.") There are also two traditions of ethical thinking, which we can call secular and religious, according to their conceptions of the proper sources of ethical knowledge. Thus we can derive a fourfold scheme of types of writing on ethics: *(A.)* Normative religious ethics. *(B.)* Normative secular ethics. *(C.)* Ethical analysis in the religious tradition. *(D.)* Ethical analysis by philosophers. I am going to review *A, B,* and *D* rapidly, and to concentrate on *C,* where it seems to me that the most interesting thought is to be found. I shall then discuss whether one school of religiously oriented analytical thought, that of the Muʿtazilites, is not really philosophical in its method, in spite of the usual classification as theological.

A. Normative religious ethics begins in the primary sources of Islam, the Qurʾān and the Traditions, which prescribe many rules of law and morality for man. The Qurʾān also contains suggestions for answers to some more general questions of ethics, but it is not a book of philosophy or even theology, and its suggestions are not without ambiguities. If they had been, there would have been less controversy among Muslim theologians on these questions. The Traditions include the same kind of materials, more extensively but carrying less weight for Muslims. Next, we have the books on *furūʿ*, the details of Islamic law, systematizing and classifying the prescriptions of the Qurʾān and Traditions. Another genre of moral literature in the religious tradition is the books on "noble qualities of character" *(makārim al-akhlāq)*, which are concerned not with detailed law but with religious virtues. Then we have Ṣūfī books for meditation and manuals of instruction in the path to God, which are deeply moral in a practical or normative sense. All these kinds of normative religious books provided materials for analytical ethics, without themselves analyzing ethical terms.

B. Normative secular ethics is represented by "Mirrors for princes" in the Persian tradition, giving advice to sultans and wazirs about government and politics. We may also include here wisdom literature contained in proverbs and poetry. Then there is a Greek tradition of popular Platonism, found in books like the treatises of the Sincere Brethren. The books of Miskawayh and others on character *(akhlāq)*, listing the virtues and vices, should really be put here, as I shall explain when I come back to them in their customary location under philosophical ethics. All these kinds of literature at least provide materials for more philosophical efforts.

Of a more inward character in both lines of normative writing, *A* and *B*, there are abundant works of Sufism and Platonic mysticism. These two traditions, which merged in later centuries, came close to philosophy through presenting total outlooks on life, although often not fully reasoned.

C. The study of ethical principles in the religious tradition starts with the jurists' discussions of the sources of divine law *(sharīʿa)* in the eighth and ninth centuries A.D. In these controversies we have the roots of an analytical treatment of the concepts of justice and obligation, because they take theoretical stands on how the law is known. From about the middle of the eighth century there are, roughly speaking, two parties on this issue. The party of rational opinion *(raʾy)* held that in deciding questions of Islamic law and morals judges and lawyers might make their own rational judgements independently of scripture, in cases or aspects where scripture gives no guidance. The other party, more strictly traditional, held that legal judgements can be based *only* on the divine law, or derived from it in certain approved ways, such as analogy *(qiyās)*. The conflict on this question was focussed by Shāfiʿī in particular, with his systematic critique of legal methods. Shāfiʿī worked out in a very thorough way the theory of a positive law, based entirely on Islamic revelation; and he states his primary principle in his maxim that justice is nothing but obedience to the law.

Theologians' discussions *(kalām)* of the sources of right probably arose out of the jurists' discussions, but they paid more attention to principles. The division of parties follows the same lines: the partisans of reason maintaining that man can know much of what is right and obligatory by independent thought, the traditionalists supporting revelation as the sole source of such knowledge. This debate is part of a wider one on the sources of knowledge in religion.

In surveying the history of this debate, I shall begin with the early Muᶜtazilites. They have some historical relation to Greek philosophy, Christian theology, and the partisans of opinion in law, but the details of influences on them are still rather obscure. Their rationalistic ethical theories are known only in outline from the books on sects by their opponents, Ashᵓarī and others, who give their bare positions with little of the arguments leading to them.

The early reactions of traditionalist theologians against rationalistic ethics were closely connected with traditionalist fears of reason in jurisprudence. Following up the line of thought started by Shāfiᶜī and Ibn Ḥanbal, theologians before Ashᶜarī as well as Ashᶜarī himself formulated these reactions, although still in rather brief statements. The main objection they raised against rationalistic ethics was that independent human reason implies a limit on the power of God; for if man could judge what is right and wrong he could rule on what God could rightly prescribe for man, and this would be presumptuous and blasphemous. They further objected that the judgements of reason were arbitrary, based only on desires; that such judgements in fact always contradicted each other; and lastly that they arrogated the function of revelation and rendered it useless. The doctrine of this school on ethics corresponded with that of Shāfiᶜī on legal justice; in brief, that right action is that which is commanded by God. In fact we can find an even closer relation than one of correspondence, for such a view merges right ethical action with legal justice. I call this view (of both jurists and theologians) "theistic subjectivism." It is subjectivist because it relates values to the view of a judge who *decides* them, denying anything objective in the character of acts themselves, that would make them right or wrong independently of anyone's decision or opinion. And the view is theistic because the decider of values is taken to be God.

Now, going on to the later developments inside *kalām*, I shall return to the rationalistic side and describe its more developed form. This was worked out by the later Muᶜtazilites in defense against traditionalist attacks. By the tenth and still more the eleventh century they have been vigorously criticized. So they are alert to the objections and have to be more sophisticated in answering these and elaborating their theory. Their position is seen in its most detailed form in the later Muᶜtazilite ᶜAbd al-Jabbār (c. 935–1025), whose enormous work the *Mughnī* in about twenty volumes was recovered in the 1950s in a single Arabic manuscript in Sanᶜa, Yemen, and has since been edited in Cairo by I. Madkour, G. Anawati, and others. So we have this vast material available, and it contains the most extensive discussion of ethical principles known in Islamic literature. It is not entirely ʿAbd al-Jabbār's original creation, but develops a school tradition, going back about a century earlier to Abū Hāshim (d. 932) and his father Jubbāʾī (d. 915).

It is indeed an elaborate theory of ethics. Much space is devoted to defensive arguments, showing that the power of God is not limited in any way that matters by the existence of rational human judgements of value, for God is always superior and we never have the slightest ground to criticize Him morally for what He does, thinks or commands. Moreover, our judgements of reason when properly made are not arbitrary but conform to objective principles. What these are is set forth in the detailed system of ʿAbd al-Jabbār. His principles of ethics resemble those of British intuitionism, and they are such as any rational person can know—e.g., the principle that lying is wrong, so long as it does not come into conflict with a more insistent ethical consideration. (Here we enter into a complication, which will be mentioned later.) The rationalism of ʿAbd al-Jabbār and his predecessors allows a place for revelation as an indispensable supplement to reason. It tells us some important truths on value that reason unaided could not have discovered, although reason can recognize and accept them as rational when once they have been revealed—e.g., the value of prayer in building character.

In their offensive efforts against opponents, the later Muʿtazilites argued that the commands of God are not enough to constitute right and do not by themselves, in their character as mere commands, fulfill the requirements of what we normally mean by "right." Moreover, we have the natural ability to know the right independently of any command or revelation, as is shown by the existence of moral judgements outside Islam. They also pointed out what they took to be the immoral consequences of theistic subjectivism, such as that God could then make lying right for men if He wished to do so, simply by commanding men to tell lies. And then if He wished He could punish them for not lying—or again, if He wished, for lying!

The traditionalist reactions against rationalism were sharp, and were formulated by several famous theologians, in particular Ibn Ḥazm, Ghazālī, and Shahrastānī. They renewed the insistence on the omnipotence of God: He must not be limited in any way in His power to command man. They accepted fearlessly consequences such as God's power and right to command things which seem wrong to man, such as lying, and rejected the charge of immorality in God as being meaningless or blasphemous. They attacked the rationalists' principles as inconsistent, discordant with scripture, and not really known by reason since they are not universally accepted. They objected strongly to the suggestion that revelation was supplementary, and reaffirmed that it is the primary source of ethical knowledge and provides everything that is needed. Reason is only an aid to understanding scripture, according to Ibn Ḥazm, but others allowed its use to extend the prescriptions of scripture by certain legitimate methods. To prove these positions, scripture itself was called upon regularly for quotations of texts showing approval of the traditionalist theory.

The general result of this debate in the Muslim world was that rationalism continued to be widespread in Shiᶜite countries such as Iran, where it was incorporated into Shiᶜite Islam, while the traditionalist view prevailed in Sunnite countries until modern times. But with the incursion of western rationalism, that type of view on ethics seems to receive a favorable welcome among modern Muslim intellectuals in all countries, without any commitment to the particular Muᶜtazilite doctrines.

After this review of schools, I want to raise an important historical question of method. Is the *kalām* discussion of ethics theology or philosophy? With regard to subject matter, Islamic ethics in *kalām* is seldom far from God, and in this respect it can be classed as always theological. But with regard to method we distinguish two types of theology: revelational, based entirely on information derived from scripture (after an initial rational apologetic justifying scripture as authentic), and philosophical, based on natural knowledge and not relying on scripture for anything essential. So the question can be reworded, How much of *kalām* ethics is philosophical in method? To answer this question we have to consider the two main schools separately.

Muᶜtazilite theology as a whole starts from a few broad principles learned initially from the Qurʾān, such as the unity and justice of God. I am not sure whether even these principles are not also justified by independent rational arguments. R. M. Frank has done significant work on the methods of *kalām*, and we may hope that he will give us further clarification of this basic question. But certainly when the Muᶜtazilites work on ethical theory it seems to me that their method is philosophical, not revelational. To judge from ᶜAbd al-Jabbār, the negative evidence is clear enough: he does not quote scripture as a decisive argument, but only in passing, if at all. The positive evidence consists in the types of argument that he uses. Two types are prominent, according to the subject matter.

First of all, there are arguments for definitions. These are asserted with reasons, then defended dialectically by answering objections. For example, an act that is *wājib*, "obligatory," is defined in the *Mughnī* as that act whose agent deserves blame for omitting it (without deserving any praise for doing it). Such acts are called "*wājib*" by everyone, as can be confirmed by the authority of lexicographers. The objections which ᶜAbd al-Jabbār thinks he has to answer are those of inconsistency, of discordance with linguistic usage, and of irreligion and immorality, and each one is refuted by an appropriate method. He criticizes his opponents' definitions in the same ways. For example, the definition of *wājib* as commanded by God, or that of which the omission is punished by God, implies that one cannot use "*wājib*" intelligently without knowing that there is a commander. This is false, because pre-Islamic peoples and pagans remote from the Islamic world have known what "obligatory" means.

A second type of discussion concerns the specific content of the obligatory, the good and so on: ethical rules such as "lying is always evil," "wrongdoing is always evil." At this level of ethical thinking, we sometimes have to weigh relevant factors against each other, so this leads to a theory of prima facie goods and evils like that of W.D. Ross. And, again as in Ross, the rules are known by rational intuitions. He answers objections in ways similar to those mentioned before. Opponents assert, for example, that if God commanded lying it would be good. He criticizes such an assertion as immoral, i.e., ultimately discordant with our ordinary conception of what is "moral."

The question of method in Muʿtazilite ethics needs further investigation, as does method in Muʿtazilite theology in general. Provisionally, I have to conclude that it is primarily philosophical, in a modern sense that is not essentially tied to the Greek tradition as is Islamic philosophy in the accepted sense. The Muʿtazilites have usually been classified as theologians because of their origins, their interests and, above all, the absence of explicit influences from Greek philosophy.

The method of the traditionalists accords with their first principle, that the primary source of religious knowledge is revelation. This principle is itself supported by rational apologetic arguments, such as the miracle of the Qurʾān; if it were supported by revelation the argument would be circular, as Ibn Ḥazm and others noted. But, once revelation is established as a source of truth, all knowledge of theology and ethics after that point is based on scripture or traditions or their derivatives. Consequently, the clinching arguments of Ashʿarī, Ibn Ḥazm, and others of their tendency are quotations from the sacred texts, correctly interpreted. Quotations are not used merely to illustrate or support, as we might think at first sight; they are the main evidence, sufficient and final. So the ethics of this school is revelational, not philosophical in its method. This fact does not exclude an extensive use of dialectic to refute opponents.

This difference in primary principles and methods between the two schools often produces arguments at cross purposes. If the Muʿtazilites claim that some kind of act is immoral and therefore cannot have been approved of by a prophet, Ibn Ḥazm answers that a prophet approved of it, therefore it cannot be immoral and the Muʿtazilite criticism of it is irreligious. This ploy follows the rules of gamesmanship in controversy, that you must whenever possible score a point that cannot be answered frankly by your opponents, in the intellectual environment of the times, for fear of ridicule, disapproval, censorship, or worse. Thus in the present instance the Muʿtazilites could not reply that even if a prophet had approved of something, such as stealing, it would still have been wrong, because it was not acceptable in medieval Islam to declare that a prophet was mistaken about anything, and least of all that Muḥammad was. Shahrastānī, too, is often at cross purposes with his opponents and answers arguments of rationalism made on the human level with theological considerations. Thus, when the Muᶜtazilites say that we know truths of ethics by reason, he is apt to change the subject and discuss how God knows such things or to write about the relations of obligation between God and man.

The sustained discussion on ethics in the *kalām* literature is all the more remarkable because it owes little to the Greeks except in an indirect and diffuse way. It is original in Islam, and grew quite naturally out of the early theological and juristic debates among Muslims. It appears to me as chronologically the second major occurrence in history of a profound discussion on the meanings and general content of ethical concepts, the first being that of the ancient Greek sophists and Plato. If this is a sound judgement, it gives an importance to medieval Islamic ethics in the general history of philosophy that has not been realized up to now. It is to be hoped that in the future it will be more appreciated as a result of the recovery of other substantial texts in addition to those of ᶜAbd al-Jabbār.

D. I shall say little about ethics in the mainstream of Islamic philosophy. What is usually known as such is the books on *akhlāq* ("character" rather than "ethics") by Miskawayh, Naṣīr ad-dīn Ṭūsī, and Dawwānī. These works follow a settled tradition of Hellenic philosophy in Arabic, dealing with the perfection and ends of the soul, virtues as means and vices as extremes. They contain much of interest for the social history of medieval Islamic morals, manners, and society. But their philosophical framework is taken from Aristotle, the Peripatetics, and Neoplatonism, and offers little of general philosophical interest that is new. The authors do not enter into the controversy of *kalām* about the concepts of right and wrong, good and evil, so that these *akhlāq* books are not the place to look for ethical philosophy in an analytical style.

In the major philosophers, Fārābī (870–950), Ibn Sīnā (980–1037) and Ibn Rushd (1126–98) we do find significant remarks on these concepts, in the Neoplatonic tradition but with individual developments. But they did not write much on ethics in lengthy passages or separate works, so we have to piece their views together from scattered pages. We find that Ibn Rushd, for instance, has much to say on ethics, but perhaps even in him the main interest comes just where he is reacting against Ashᶜarite *kalām* and its theistic subjectivism. He compares it to the ethics of the sophists, having observed with his usual acuteness the common elements of subjectivism between the two schools, so remote from each other in time and environment. He strongly upholds the objectivism of Plato and Aristotle, with full consciousness of the great tradition he is following.

Later philosophy is predominantly mystical, a blend of Islamic Sufism and Hellenic Neoplatonism. We can look forward to finding ethical ideas of interest in the Persian works of Ṣadr ad-dīn Shīrāzī and others in this tradition, now being studied intensively by S. H. Nasr and F. Rahman.

METHODOLOGY AND THE HISTORY OF SCIENCE

† Martin Levey

The major problems that confront society today involve science and technology. But, because these problems are by no means amenable to purely scientific-technological solutions, they are, of necessity, interdisciplinary with the social sciences and humanities.

NEWER AREAS IN THE SYSTEMATICS OF SCIENCE

The history of science and its close ally, the philosophy of science, are about to come of age. We are beginning to understand them as approaches toward the utilization of the past for the understanding of the present and future. For this purpose, some of the new methodologies, which seem to be of value in a difficult field, are concerned with the techniques of systems analysis, social and technological forecasting, the use of the history of science in validating processes, and other functions. These methodologies, it is hoped, will go a long way to deepen our understanding of the human condition, past, present, and future, theoretically and practically.

So much for the broad framework. A little more concretely, we know that the fundamental roots of modern society, including its philosophical relations with science and technology, developed over thousands of years. It is urgent that students of history of science and philosophy of science relinquish their uncertain, largely extrapolative methods for determining the more substantive indicators of the past. These indicators are important as determinants and validating instruments in helping to set up societal, scientific, and technological scenarios for the future.

Yet more specifically, our philosophical and historical studies, if they are to be more useful to future advances in culture, should be such as to evaluate fully the options available.[1] Within medieval Arabic science and technology, for example, there are discernible components which lend themselves to examination as decisive elements of participating constituent systems. These factors are "indicators" for the understanding of scientific-technological development toward the present and future. It is part of the task of philosophers and historians of science and technology to identify these changing special parameters or indicators.

INDICATORS OF SYSTEMS

Examples of indicators and their applications may come from such areas in the history and philosophy of science as the following, briefly described:

1. The development of the medieval Arabic, Persian, and Hebrew *Fachliteratur*,[2] particularly the vocabulary and etymology of the *termini technici* with reference to earlier and later Sanskrit, Mesopotamian, Egyptian, and Greek literature and the Latin, Chinese, and later vernacular writings. Often this determination is valuable for studies of the paths of transmission of scientific and technological knowledge and thought.

2. The evolution of model construction and simulative thinking as a valuable tool to aid reconstruction of the medieval Arabic scientific and technological panorama. This can lead to the building of better scenarios for the succeeding period of Latin hegemony. The development of laboratory procedures may be subsumed here.

3. Cultural freedom arising from religious, political, and mainly economic forces gives rise to critical parameters. These indicators would partially reflect the cultural ambience necessary to pursue scientific and technological development. They also affect the communication of science and technology, with some necessary right angle turns and discontinuities, and a more efficient application of previous knowledge to present problems. Deontological problems and scientific and technological policy-making are important here.

4. Recognition of indicators which reflect novel development at their intersections should help explain medieval discontinuities in thought and scientific and technological evolution.

5. Identification of the systems represented by certain indicators. This systems approach which works for a much simpler scientific and technological period would be helpful for validating procedures involving the history and philosophy of Arabic and Latin science and technology.

Not all of the possibilities have been outlined of an approach that would combine the history and philosophy of science and technology in an investigation of the relations of Arabic culture to that which succeeded it. Much of this is still in the drawing board stage. I should like, however, to discuss an example of the kind of indicator valuable to help delineate succeeding levels. I shall confine my example to medieval Arabic medicine for various reasons.

For my example I wish to explore, briefly, methods of inquiry into early medieval materia medica and pharmacology. Aside from the exact sciences, the most appropriate and interesting area in which one may follow an Arabic science is in the development of drugs and their theory. Superstition in the health field is perhaps more easily excluded with experience and time. Another reason is the abundance of manuscript materials in the Arabic, Greek, Indian, Mesopotamian, Egyptian, and other medieval and ancient languages. Then, there are the rich *termini technici* in this field which are subject to scientific etymological study. Further, development of drugs is strongly linked with the evolution of Arabic medicine, chemistry, botany, zoology, geology, law, trade and commerce, and other areas of vital interest. Finally, Arabic materia medica and pharmacology carried over into the early nineteenth century with a large proportion of the energy it displayed throughout the Arabic Golden Period—c. A.D. 850–1150.

THE EVOLUTION OF MODEL CONSTRUCTION

I shall first discuss literary models of texts on pharmacology.[3]

Every age in history from about 3400 B.C. on has brought forward its own written forms into which its knowledge was cast. These models are significant in that they reflect, in a considerable fashion, the quantity and quality of knowledge, for example, of pharmacology in the medieval Arabic period. In various ages the types of pharmacological writing have also not only been indicators of the contemporary state of knowledge but have also pointed to potential avenues of greater learning and investigation. Let us look at these in some detail.[4]

It is essential to remember that thousands of years of scientific activity preceded that of the Muslims. In the earliest scientific literature, that written on tablets in the cuneiform languages such as Sumerian, Akkadian, and Hittite, there are the list forms where knowledge was organized into a variety of series of related words. Lists gave names of trees, parts of trees, products of trees, wooden objects, reeds, objects made of reeds, types of vessels, ovens, clay objects, hides, minerals, metals, stones, names of plants, anatomical terms, pharmaceuticals, etc.[5] These lists reflect the status of the ancient type of synthesis and understanding.[6]

In Dioscorides' *Materia Medica* (first century B.C.) each drug is treated separately, with its origin, description and the pharmacological uses of the various morphological parts. It is divided into five major books: aromatics, oils, resins, and trees; animal products and sharp herbs; roots, juices and other herbs; drugs useful for poison therapy; vines, wines, minerals and stones. Galen (second century A.D.) wrote books on purgatives, simple drugs, compounded drugs, nutritive drugs, and theriacs.[7] The medical encyclopedia of Paulus of Aegina (fl. ca. 640) contains much pharmacology, particularly in the seventh book on simple and compound remedies. The simples are arranged alphabetically together with their properties and uses. The compound remedies fall into such categories as purgatives, salves, emmenagogues, antidotes, pastilles, powders, mouth salves, sweet drinks, collyria, plasters, oils, and aromata.[8]

The Muslims elaborated the Greek classification and originated major new types of pharmacological literature. These new expressions of pharmacological knowledge not only became more numerous and diversified but were more flexible literary media. Since this literature considered its subject from a great variety of new directions, there resulted new ways of looking at pharmacology, and new lines opened up for exploration and more detailed investigation.

Since Arabic writers were excellent organizers of knowledge, their purely pharmacological texts were carefully directed along many paths which seemed either more promising or more useful to the apothecary and medical practitioner. As a result, these treatises generally fall into more or less well delineated groups. Some of these major types of Arabic pharmacological literature are categorized here briefly.

1. Medical formularies. These may vary somewhat in content but they usually include chapters on the following kinds of compounded drugs: myrobalans, confections, electuaries, pills, aperients, pastilles, powders, syrups, lohochs and rubs, gargles, collyria, suppositories, pessaries, cataplasms, oils and lotions, oral medicines and dentifrices, and pomades.

This is, in fact, the actual table of contents of Sahlān ibn Kaysān (d. A.D. 1582) in his *Mukhtaṣar fī al-adwiya al-murakkaba al-mustaᶜmala fī akthar al-al-amrāḍ,*[9] "Compounded drugs used in most ailments."

2. Books on Poisons. This model is a carryover from earlier types, but in ibn al-Waḥshīya's *Kitāb al-sumūm* he included additional chapters on poisons lethal by sight, sound, and odor, in addition to others.[10]

3. Synonymatic Treatises. These are lists of simples, usually in alphabetic order, whose main purpose is to help the reader identify the drug in other languages. It may be remembered that the Muslims were world traders in their Golden Age and so had to command many Asian, African, and European tongues.

4. Tabular, Synoptic Texts. It was in the Muslim period that an information explosion resulted in books which were much too long to be used by practicing physicians. Abstracts, then, were made of some treatises while others, where feasible, were turned into tabular works which were more accessible to quick and systematic usage. One of these was ibn Biklārish's (fl. 1106) work on pharmacology, his *Kitāb al-Mustaᶜīnī.*[11] In the columns of each set of two facing pages the following information is noted for each drug: name, Galenic nature and grade, synonyms in Arabic, Persian, Syriac, Greek, Latin and Old Spanish, substitute drug, the preparation, therapeutic value and uses of the drug. The marginal gloss by the author has much other random information.

5. Lists of Materia Medica. These texts include therapeutic considerations and opinions of various writers regarding them, preparation of the drugs, and description. Most of these are based on the organization and on much of the contents of Dioscorides' famous book. Nevertheless, the Arabic works are much fuller both in the number of drugs discussed and in the length of their descriptions.

Probably better known than any other Arabic writer on pharmacology is ibn al-Baiṭār (13th century), who followed this definitely Greek literary form. Much of his wellknown compilatory work *Kitāb al-jāmiʿ fī mufradāt al-adwiya waʾl-aghdhiya,* "Book of Simples," was borrowed from al-Ghāfiqī (12th century).

6. Substitute Drugs. Greek texts in this field were much improved upon by Arabic writers such as Abū Bakr al-Rāzī, Māsarjawaih, and others.[12] Qualitatively and quantitatively the Arabic texts were much better.

7. Medical Specialty Works. These are rich in the descriptions and minutiae of drugs and remedies. Some of these are independent sections of large encyclopedias of medicine. An excellent example of a specialized book is *Ten Treatises on the Eye,* ascribed to Ḥunain ibn Isḥāq.[13] Among other matter, it contains discussions of drugs, their preparation, pharmacological properties, and other attributes. The Arabic text was derived mainly from the works of Galen, much of it still in Greek at that time.

In most of the books of al-Zahrāwī's *al-Taṣrīf,* the major concern is with the materia medica and their pharmacological activity, as shown by a recent publication.[14]

The above classification of drug texts is an artificial one designed to clarify the study of the contributions of Arabic writers in pharmacology. The categories referred to are not in all cases mutually exclusive. In regard to the works of superior physicians, there was no slavish imitation of their predecessors. Thus it was that the Arabic scientific literature in pharmacology outgrew more and more the relatively rigid forms of previous work. The individual Arabic scientist increasingly wrote in a literary form which suited him and his work. To the better minds of the early Islamic period this meant greater freedom both in writing and in scientific thinking.

One must not forget the influence of other events in society at this point of history. It was at the end of the Arab conquest (c. 750) that papermaking became known to Arabic writers and made publication more extensive and cheaper than use of expensive parchment and the rapidly disappearing papyrus would have permitted. Because of the resulting weakening of the oral method and the multiplication of treatises in writing, new methods were developed, making knowledge much more accessible to the student. This spread of learning may be considered as an indicator.

All of this aided Muslim development in science and its methodology. In a time when the movement of ideas had been at a relative standstill, the Muslims introduced a fluid new outlook and brought forward new textual models which led to a sense of fresh inquiry, so that Europe could take over this thoroughly examined body of knowledge with ease and endow its ripeness with a completely fresh approach of its own.

FACHLITERATUR AND BOTANONYMY

Another major methodology, which coincides with changes in the models of literary texts, is one linked with growth and change in the *Fachliteratur*. This literature involves study of botanical names, primarily etymological, or botanonymy.[15] It is, in a way, related to some of the texts discussed earlier.

Just as the model texts in pharmacology are on a certain qualitative level and yield an enlarged degree of understanding of how Arabic pharmacology progressed, so also the synonymatic texts and the etymology of drug names contribute to a greater appreciation of the work of medieval Arabic writers. One should remember that this type of study is not of continuous events but rather of "discontinuous history."

Let us examine in more detail the etymological study, particularly of names in materia medica. This should give a rough idea of the sources of medieval Muslim plant names and, as a result, perhaps throw light on the scientific origin of early medieval medicine and chemistry and suggest the relative importance of the various paths of transmission of knowledge in these two fields.

The evidence indicates that a number of botanical names came into Arabic as loan words or as translations from many ancient languages of Europe, Asia, and Africa. An example of a loan word is the Arabic *jirjīr* for "rocket," from Akkadian *gingira*, *gurgirū*, *egengir*, probably through the Syriac, *gargīrā*. The Arabic *basbāyij* for the "common polypody" is a loan word from the Persian *bas-pāyak* "many feet." The Syriac *sekā reglē* also has the same meaning, as does the Greek *polypódion* which is the origin of the English.

Because the meaning of a technical term frequently changes with time, I have found it valuable to check the usage of terms, particularly in medical, chemical and technological texts, over a number of centuries. Wherever possible I have consulted original texts in hieroglyphic Egyptian, Akkadian, Sumerian, Turkish, Persian, Sanskrit, Hebrew, Syriac, Aramaic, Arabic, and other languages for mutual comparison. My intent was to carry my study of the uses and names of the materia medica through the entire Arabic period in as great a diversity of texts as possible. I have also examined present-day uses, occurrences, and names of the drugs. Because etymological evidence is sometimes inconclusive, yielding insufficient data to decide the geographic or ethnic origin of the name of a botanical, it is then necessary to employ other checks. These include the investigation of the regions in which the botanicals were indigenous in medieval and other times; the number of species of a genus in various geographic areas; archeological remains of plants and their representations; fossils; ancient, medieval, and later agriculture; modern uses in the Near East, Asia, and North Africa; and the names presently used in India, Persia, Iraq, Egypt, and North Africa, both in the professions and in the bazaars.

Fortunately, because of the strong interest in language in the medieval Muslim world, there is extant a considerable number of manuscripts listing synonyms for Arabic drugs. These synonyms were given in languages ranging from India to Spain. Further, this interest is closely associated with the grammatical and lexicographical works of the time.

An important work in this area is al-Bīrūnī's remarkable text, *Kitāb al-ṣaidala fī al-ṭibb*, "Book on the Pharmacopoeia of Medicine." It gives synonyms for drugs in Syriac, Persian, Greek, Baluchi, Afghan, Sindi, Indian dialects, and other languages. Maimonides' book on drugs contains synonyms in Syriac, Sanskrit and Indian dialects, Persian, Arabic, Hebrew, Berber, and Old Spanish. An important text because of its North African origin, and therefore for its Berber synonyms, is an unknown author's *Tuḥfat al-aḥbāb fī māhīyat al-nabāt waʾl-aʿshāb*, "A Precious Gift to Friends Concerning the Attributes of Plants and Simples." This text has 462 entries arranged alphabetically. Abū Manṣūr Muwaffaq b. ʿAlī Harawī's (fl. 961–76) *Kitāb al-abnīya ʿan ḥaqāʾiq al-adwiya*, "Book on the Basis of the Properties of Drugs" has synonyms in Persian, Syriac, Sanskrit and Greek.

There are many other valuable texts but they cannot all be mentioned. In addition, works on botany, travel, agriculture, stones, zoology and other subjects are rich in linguistic material.[16]

BOTANONYMY: WORKING RESULTS

By means of an extended etymological inquiry the origins of many Arabic pharmacological names have been determined.

A few working results are given below:

1. Ar. *wajj*, *Acorus calamus* L., sweet flag or sweet reed.

Sum.	*GI.DUG*
	↓
Akk.	*qanū ṭābu*
Heb.	*qānĕh haṭṭōbh*
Gr.	*akoron asplēnion*
	↓
Mod. Ar.	*aikar, ighir, ikkur*
Hiero. Egypt	*kǎ*
	↓
Coptic	*kas*
Sans.	*vucha* or *vaca*

Guzerat	*vaz*
Deccan	*bache*
Malabar	*vazabu*
Concan	*vaicam*
Hindi	*gora vach*
	↓
Pers.	*vāj*
	↓
Ar.	*wajj*

2. Ar. *zaʿfarān, Crocus sativus* L., saffron.

Sum.	*HAR. SAG. SAR*
Akk.	*azupirānu*
	↓ (often confused with *kurkanū*)
Ar.	*zaʿfarān*
	↓
Jap.	*safuran*
Chin.	*safalan*
Sans.	*kumukuma, kunkuma*
	↓
Heb., Aram.	*karkōm*
	(saffron or turmeric)
Ar.	*kurkum* (confused)
Sans.	*kāvera* = saffron
	kāverī = turmeric

3. (a) Ar. *simsim, Sesamum orientale* L., sesame.

Akk.	*šamaššamu* →	Hiero. Eg.	*šimšmt*
Gr.	*sēsamon*	Coptic	*šemšem*
Heb.	*šumšum*		↓
		Ar.	*simsim*
Aram.	*sumsema*		

(b) Ar. *simsim, Sesamum indicum* L., sesame.

Hindi	*gingerli*
Mod. Ar.	*juljulān*
Kurd.	*kunjad*
Turk.	*kinjid*

In a study of al-Kindī's *Aqrābādhīn* (ninth century), it was found that 33 percent of the Arabic names of the materia medica mentioned came originally from older Mesopotamian languages, such as Sumerian and Akkadian, through Syriac, Aramaic, Ethiopic, Hebrew, Persian, and other intermediaries. There is also the possibility of an unbroken oral transmission, a factor which present-day authors tend to overlook because it is a cultural element very remote from the modern West. About 23 percent came originally from Greek sources, 18 percent from Persian, 13 percent from Indian, 5 percent from Arabic, and 3 percent from ancient Egyptian sources.[17] The remainder are of unknown origin. The Persian and Indian figures should, perhaps, be added together since it is difficult to separate them in the case of most drugs. In that event, the Persian-Indian and the Mesopotamian nomenclatural contributions are about equal. The Greek percentage comes third, hardly proving a "Greek miracle" in this area of knowledge.

In another "Medical Formulary," one by al-Samarqandī (early 13th century), four centuries after al-Kindī, the Persian-Indian simples account for 54 percent of the materia medica, the Mesopotamian for 20 percent, Greek 17 percent, pre-Islamic Arabic 6 percent, Egyptian 2 percent, and Chinese less than one percent.[18]

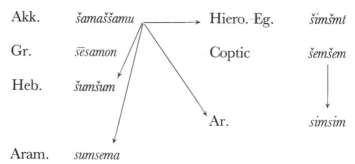

THE INTEGRATION OF METHODOLOGY AND HISTORY OF SCIENCE AND THE FUTURE

Various conclusions may be drawn from statistics such as these and others within the Arabic time period. In many cases they demonstrate the path of transmission of drugs and pharmacological knowledge to the Arabs. The growth of pharmacology with time is shown with the increase in the number of drugs from more distant parts of the world. Attempts to improve the quality of the materia medica and their therapeutic uses were made through continued theoretical development; the purity of drugs was also a constant challenge to the medieval workers who developed the relevant early chemical and physical procedures.

Nineteenth—and twentieth—century proponents of a Greek origin for modern science and medicine cannot meet this new objective evidence. Further, the results make obvious the excellent lexicographical and linguistic development in the Arabic period.

What has been discovered by using the literary models and botanonymic studies of Arabic times as indicators may be collated with similarly obtained data of the succeeding Latin period. A preliminary comparison shows that their influence and greatness display only minor differences.

From the results obtained to the present it appears that the use of indicators reflecting the integration of methodology and history of science may be a promising procedure. It will not only bring these two fields of study together after an increasing separation for too long a time, but will help explain the past in terms of the present and the future.

NOTES

[1] "Freedom is the recognition of necessity," according to Hegel.

[2] Specialized writings on arts, crafts, sciences and professions.

[3] From now on I define "pharmacology" with Webster as the science of drugs including materia medica, toxicology, and therapeutics. It does not, of course, encompass pharmacognosy, pharmacodynamics, and other newer studies as known in the modern sense.

[4] M. Levey, *The Medical Formulary of Aqrābādhīn of al-Kindī* (Madison, 1966), pp. 7–15.

[5] M. Levey, *Chemistry and Chemical Technology in Ancient Mesopotamia* (Amsterdam, 1959), chap. 1.

[6] M. Levey, *Transactions and Studies of the College of Physicians of Philadelphia* 30 (1963): p. 158.

[7] G.C. Anawati, *Drogues Médicaments* (in Arabic) (Cairo, 1959), pp. 117–18. For the texts in Greek and in Latin translation, cf. K.G. Kuehn, *Claudii Galeni opera omnia* (Leipzig, 1821–33). This title comprises the first twenty volumes of *Medicorum Graecorum opera quae exstant*, ed. by K.G. Kuehn. Volume 21 is an index.

[8] J. Berendes, '*Paulos*' *von Aegina Sieben Bücher* (Leiden, 1914), pp. 606 ff.

[9] P. Sbath and C.D. Averinos, *Deux Traités Médicaux* (Cairo, 1953).

[10] M. Levey, *The Book of Poisons of ibn al-Waḥshīyā* (Philadelphia, 1966).

[11] MSS Leiden 1339, Rabat 481, Naples 287, Madrid 5009. M. Levey and S. S. Souryal, "The Introduction to the *Kitāb al-Mustaᶜīnī* of ibn Biklārish." *Janus* 55 (1968): 134–66.

[12] M. Levey, *Substitutes According to Pythagoras, al-Rāzī, and Māsarjawaih* (in press); cf. M. Levey, *Medical History, VII*, 176–82 (1963).

[13] Max Meyerhof, ed. and trans., *The Book of the Ten Treatises on the Eye Ascribed to Ḥunain ibn Isḥāq* (Cairo, 1928).

[14] S.K. Hamarneh and G. Sonnedecker, *A Pharmaceutical View of Abulcasis al-Zahrāwī in Moorish Spain* (Leiden, 1963), pp. 77 ff.

[15] M. Levey, *The Medical Formulary of al-Samarqandī* (Philadelphia, 1967) pp. 23–28.

[16] For greater detail see M. Levey, *Early Arabic Pharmacology* (in press).

[17] M. Levey, *al-Kindī*, p. 20.

[18] M. Levey, *al-Samarqandī*, p. 27.

ARABIC AND THE CONCEPT OF BEING

FADLOU A. SHEHADI

The problem of expressing the Greek concept of being in Arabic did not escape classical Islamic writers. But the discussion of this problem as an instance of the general question of the influence of grammar on the formation of philosophical concepts is to be found among some recent writers on Islam, although unfortunately there is hardly anything approaching a sustained treatment from this perspective.

A few quotations from two recent writers will bring into focus those distinctive features of the Arabic language which produce philosophical problems and at the same time will provide our analysis with a point of departure.

In his useful book *Philosophical Terminology in Arabic and Persian,*[1] Soheil Afnan identifies the problem for the Arabic translator of Greek metaphysics in these words: "the translator can easily find himself helpless."[2] This is generalized to all Semitic languages which are said to be "still (!) unable to express the thought adequately."[3] Afnan attributes this to what he calls "the complete absence of the copula."[4]

Another writer, Professor Angus Graham, a linguist, in a stimulating article,[5] singles out another, but related feature of Arabic, the sharp separation of the existential and predicative functions, a feature notably lacking in classical Greek.[6]

These two features, the absence of the copula and the existential-predicative separation, are supposed to have stood in the way of expressing the Greek concept of being adequately or accurately. And what is meant by this, in the words of Afnan, is the failure to express "the precise concept of being as distinct from existence."[7] Professor Graham puts it this way: "because of the structure of the language, they (the Arabic translations of Aristotle) transform him at one stroke into a philosopher who talks sometimes about existence, sometimes about quiddity, *never about being*."[8]

Since the general topic of the concept of being in Arabic has so many facets and requires different specialities for its full and adequate treatment, my objective in the one brief attempt of this paper will have to be a very limited one. It is one sort of discussion fitting in with a number of others, dealing with one question among others.

I shall assume that the nature of the difficulty of expressing the Greek concept of being in Arabic can be stated in more stringent or in less stringent terms. Now, it is not altogether clear what degree of stringency the two writers quoted would subscribe to since their comments are rather brief, although the language used tends towards the more stringent. So I shall go ahead, insofar as I can, and discuss possible claims without worrying over whether these claims have sponsors, or who the sponsors are. I shall examine the above noted features of the Arabic and clarify the nature of the difficulty, in order to determine what bearing those features have on that difficulty, and what degree of stringency is justified in the characterization of the difficulty. I shall maintain that the language-type differences between Greek and Arabic do not warrant a stringent diagnosis of the difficulty for Arabic. Perhaps enough clarifications will come about to compensate for the rather negative tenor of this conclusion. And while our discussion of the case of Arabic can be related to the general question of the influence of grammar on the formation of philosophical concepts, this general question will not be dealt with here. However, our effort may be presented as a case study for the general question, and a rejection of a stringent thesis for Arabic may well echo a readiness to reject such a thesis on the more general issue.

THE FIRST FEATURE

Absence of Copula

Let us examine the first feature. This may be called "the complete absence of the copula," in which case one would be talking about the natural language, as a "surface" grammarian would describe it. What is in mind here is the fact that Arabic grammatical syntax does not require any word to 'link' subject and complement, because none is needed. The case of a sentence with a verb is obvious, for any language. For the nominal sentence, however, the connection between subject and complement *(mubtada*ʾ and *khabar)* is indicated by the convention of placing the two parts in the nominative case. No linking word is needed. But it is also possible to add certain words to a given nominal sentence and make the same predication, in the sense that the predicative construction is reestablished and the same complement is meant to apply to the same subject, although there may be a change of tense or emphasis. For example, to mention only some words in the natural language, the assertive particle *inna* which by itself may be translated as "indeed," "verily," "truly," when it is added to a nominal sentence, places the subject in the accusative case and the complement in the nominative. Its semantical function can be compared to the assertive or emphatic use of *esti* when the latter is not omitted and is suitably placed in the word order. *Kāna,* usually translated as "to be," is a verb, and can therefore have tense, but does not always. When it is the only verb in a sentence it can function either in a predicative construction (the incomplete *kāna)*, or in an absolute construction, and indicate occurrence or existence (the complete *kāna*). When it is used along with another verb it becomes auxiliary, and is no longer of interest to us here. Then there is a pronoun *huwa* (he, it; or *hiya* for the feminine) which in certain cases is grammatically required to intervene between subject and complement to prevent the latter from becoming a mere apposition. ʿ*Allāhu l-khāliq*' (God the creator) needs completion. '*Allāhu huwa l-khāliq*' is a complete setence, and it is the intervention of *huwa* that dispels the appositional relation and clearly establishes the predicative construction in a grammatically complete sentence.

These are some of the functions of *inna, kāna,* and *huwa*[9] in the natural language which made them obvious candidates for the office of copula, when Arabic logicians who had been exposed to Greek decided to introduce the copulative device into their logical writings. It is clear that the logicians introduced a use for certain words which was not allowed for by the grammarian's description of the natural language. I shall leave to a separate discussion the question of how to characterize the status of the copula in Arabic in the light of the controversy between grammarian and logician.[10]

Fortunately our discussion here does not depend on resolving that controversy. So suppose we were to stay within the obvious sense which the grammarian has in mind about the absence of the copula in Arabic. What consequence can this have for the problem before us?

Of course the problem before us is not whether one can produce an Arabic sound and let it stand for the Greek sound *to on*. Nor is it the question of how to say *to on* in Arabic, as when one asks: how would you say "interesting" or "establishment" in Arabic? Nor is it the simple morphological question of whether one can form a word from a certain verb root. The problem as I shall formulate it is this. Since Greek and Arabic belong to different family types with respect to 'to be,'—and this is the difference that concerns us—does Arabic have the necessary linguistic equipment for the formation of a philosophical term (or terms) which shall be like *to on,* in two respects? First, semantically, so that the Arabic vocabulary shall have the meaning or meanings of *to on;* second, and this is a logical-semantical feature, so that it shall stand for a higher level concept which could range over its constituents in a variety of specific ways, depending on whether it is thought to name a class, or a property common to all that in some sense is, or analogically to embrace a family of different concepts.[11] (I suppose even when the term "being" is dismissed as a logical mistake, in that the term suggests a common thread of meaning when none exists, one can half seriously speak of its futile attempt to range, or of a semantically vacuous or frustrated ranging.)

The question immediately before us is whether the presence of a copula in Greek is a necessary condition for the formation of *to on,* and consequently whether its absence in Arabic counts against the possibility of forming an equivalent term.

If we look at Greek, we find that the copulative function of *einai*, although present, is not highly developed for it is not syntactically necessary. Certainly it is not as developed as the 'to be' of the more modern Indo-European languages. But more importantly, one finds[12] that insofar as the uses of *einai* have bearing on the meanings of *to on* and *to einai*, it is primarily the *semantical*, not syntactical functions that are to the point. So if we are talking about the presence of the copula as a syntactical device, that is not a relevant condition, let alone its being a necessary condition.

Where there is a relevant grammatical characteristic of *einai*, it is morphological not syntactical. For example, Kahn takes the fact that *einai* has no aorist and no perfect, and the fact that all its tenses (present, imperfect, and future) are formed from the single present-durative stem which represents action as durative i.e., as a state which lasts or a process which develops in time—this durative aspect of *einai* is taken as possibly shedding some light on the classical contrast between being and becoming, in which being is the stable unchanging reality.[13] My interest here is not in the merits of this connection, but in noting that this single instance, where the grammar of *einai* is relevant, concerns morphology, not syntax, and the copula is a syntactical device.

But perhaps what is meant is not the presence or absence of a copula as a syntactical device as such, i.e., as purely syntactical, but the presence in Greek and the absence in Arabic of a privileged verb such as *einai* which besides its copulative function (developed or not) has important semantical functions as well. And here one may want somehow to attribute or connect the privilege of performing the semantical functions to the privileged syntactical status.

If one were to maintain this, all that one can maintain is that, if a language has a copulative 'to be,' the semantical functions are likely to attach themselves to that singular syntactical device. This does not imply that the presence of the copula is a necessary condition for the development of those semantical functions for either Arabic or Greek. So, if a language does not have a copulative term, this does not mean that the semantical functions cannot develop and be performed by words, one or more, that in the grammar of that language are not copulas.

Thus in Arabic the functions of indicating that something exists or happens or is located, and of saying that X is such and such, and that it is the case that such and such, and similar to–be–type functions, can be performed by a variety of words, not one of which needs to be a copula in order to perform those functions. When Arabic logicians seized upon such words for use as copulas they selected those which had already been performing to be–type functions other than that of syntactical linking. They proceeded to invest those words with one more function: to act as link between subject and complement in any proposition logically considered. But it was the assigning of the copulative function that historically followed their semantical functions, and it was the presence of these semantical functions that made them good candidates for the formation of the concept of being in Arabic.

Nonsingularity of To Be

What has been called the absence of the copula in Arabic needs to be described in terms of a wider situation with respect to to-be–type words and their functions. The striking difference between Arabic, on the one hand, and Greek and the other Indo-European languages, on the other, is that in these languages there are several functions, syntactical and semantical, which are performed by the verb 'to be.' These functions can of course be performed in these languages without 'to be,' but this verb is more often and more typically used to perform those functions, so that 'to be' may be given a special or singular status in the assignment of credit for their combined performance.

In Arabic there is no single privileged device that combines similar or corresponding functions. Rather, as we noted earlier, the burden of performing these functions is shared by a number of words, differing in grammatical type. Of these only *kāna* is ordinarily given a dictionary meaning of "to be." Let us call this situation the nonsingularity of 'to be' in Arabic, or the absence of a single and privileged to-be–type device.

Each one of the Arabic to-be–type words has yielded a candidate for an equivalent of the Greek, *to on,* in one or another or all its senses. The question now is what is the relevance of this nonsingularity of a to-be–type device in Arabic to the difficulty of expressing the concept of being as distinct from existence?

Let us first be clear about the ways in which being may be distinguished from existence. There are two sorts of ways. The first is one in which 'being' is in a logical sense a higher level concept than existence. (This is the logical feature of *to on.*) The concept of being, according to this distinction, ranges over a number of concepts of which existence may be one. This first way would be in evidence when someone was making comments about the logical status of the concept of being, or of the term "being." The second way in which 'being' can be distinguished from existence arises when some philosopher, as a metaphysician, asks the question: What is being? and proceeds to give his theory of being. One is here adopting one sense of "being" as the proper or primary sense (supplying the semantical aspect of *to on*), and it turns out that this is distinct from the meaning of existence. For example, the Greek rationalist tradition from Parmenides on (including Aristotle, of course) emphasized the sense of being, the really real, what truly is, as the proper object of knowledge, what can be truly known. This is the 'collusion' between Greek epistemology and Greek ontology, a collusion which indeed defines any rationalist tradition. In the course of a study of Greek thought one could then note that this meaning of being is different from the concept of existence, say, as it developed in the Middle Ages. This contrast between being as what can be truly known and existence is a contrast of two concepts, as it were, at the same logical level, a contrast between sibling concepts.

Professor Kahn, in the article to which I have already referred, shows in an interesting and convincing way how this fundamental sense of being in Greek philosophy—as what can be truly known and truly said—reflects the primarily veridical sense of *einai*, 'to be' as to be the case, to be truly so. This veridical sense is not developed in Arabic in the uses of any of the to-be-type devices, nor, for that matter, in the English 'to be.' Now although we have here the case of a linguistic fact helping to shed light on the meaning of a philosophical concept, it is a case that seems to cut across family types, and has Greek, on the one hand, pitted against Arabic and English on the other (although this will be qualified later). Furthermore, this is a sort of linguistic difference that would not justify a stringent form of the thesis about the influence of the linguistic features of Arabic or English on the formation of philosophic concepts in either language (the matter of family-type differences aside for the moment).

One could say that, since the Greek *einai* had such and such a predominant sense, a correspondingly predominant sense of being was likely to develop. It was less likely to develop in that sense in English or Arabic. But this is not the same as saying that one could not express in those two languages the concept of being as what can be truly known and as distinct from existence.

How one specifies the nature of the relation between 'being' and its logical constituents will determine how one conceives the relation between the two ways of distinguishing 'being' from existence. If 'being' is thought to be analogical, then the second way of distinguishing becomes reabsorbed into the total picture of the first. Existence is here different from 'being' as what is truly known, but both are ways of being; existence is still part of the parent concept of being (despite the logical generation gap). If on the other hand "being" is the name of a class or a common property and is distinct from existence, then existence is 'expelled' once and for all from the notion of being. The same could be said if 'being' were considered a mistake. There is no higher sense of being which could reinclude it. In other words, only if one takes the analogical view of being can one distinguish being from existence in the two ways, and still keep existence among the concepts over which 'being' ranges.

For our discussion at this point we need to take for our model the analogical view of the concept of being. (Or one could take the view that it is a mistake. What we will say applies to both views equally.) For we are confronted with the historical and linguistic fact of an *einai* with many functions from which developed a *to on* and *to einai* having more than one sense. And the question before us is whether the nonsingularity of any to-be–type device in Arabic stands in the way of expressing a concept of being which is distinguishable from existence in the first way we mentioned, namely, as a concept which could range over existence but would not be reduced to it.[14] Is the nonsingularity of a to-be–type device in Arabic much to the point? I see the answer in the negative.

The relevant condition fulfilled in Greek, or in any of the other Indo-European languages, is not that there is one and no other 'to be' or to-be–type device, but that whatever the device, it should have *different* functions. The logical condition for an analogical sense (or the condition presupposed in dismissing it as a mistake) is: having more than one different function, and for the semantical functions this is ambiguity. And it is sufficient for this condition to be fulfilled *at least once*. It is not necessary that it be fulfilled *only* once. And the crucial difference between Arabic, on the one hand, and the Indo-European languages (including Greek), on the other, is not that the condition is fulfilled in the latter family of languages but not fulfilled in Arabic. Rather, the difference is that in the Indo-European languages one privileged device, the verb 'to be,' has the big contract. The condition is fulfilled in that special way only once. In Arabic, on the other hand, the business is shared by a number of devices, each of which is or can be multifunctioning in the requisite sense, though none is specially anointed. Thus in Arabic there is a variety of to-be–type words and a corresponding variety of words for the concept of being, while in the Indo-European languages there is a central 'to be' from which the word for the concept of being derives. My claim has been that this difference is not to the point, and consequently anyone who wishes to support the thesis, at least in stringent form, that different grammar-types stand in the way, or prevent the formation of equivalent philosophical vocabulary, will have to bypass the cases of Greek and Arabic and look elsewhere, at least as far as the concept of being is concerned.

THE SECOND FEATURE: EXISTENTIAL PREDICATIVE SEPARATION

We must now consider whether there are *specific* and crucial differences in the functions of the Greek and Arabic devices.[15] Our new question no longer pertains to the number of functions, but to specific differences in those functions, and differences which reflect the different family types. We turn to the second feature of Arabic: the sharp separation between the predicative and the existential functions.

It is often said in contrasting Greek and English that the existential-predicative distinction marks the 'is' but not the '*esti*.' But what is meant primarily about the Arabic separation is that predication, in other than the cases of the nominal sentence, can be expressed by one set of words *(inna, kāna, huwa)*, while the usual way to indicate existence is with words formed from a different root, *w j d*. So unlike English, in the contrast with Greek, it is not a separation of functions for the same word, but an allotting of the different functions to different words. And this seems to be a more radical kind, that retains the distinction of linguistic family types. This, one might contend, makes the crucial difference since the Arabic separation yields terms for existence from the existential side, and terms for essence from the predicative side, with perhaps no promising linguistic resource for expressing the abstract 'being' which is not reducible to either essence or existence.[16]

Now it is true of other languages that one could perform the existential and predicative functions by resorting to a different vocabulary for each function. However, performing these functions with one term, say 'to be,' may be a more general practice in some languages than in others.

In Arabic, as we have maintained, each of the to-be–type words can perform (or was made to perform) both the predicative and the existential functions. Therefore, the sharp separation thesis cannot mean that in Arabic it would be impossible to indicate both functions by the same term. It would be accurate, however, to say that the separation by different vocabulary of those two functions is the more striking feature of Arabic, but then this is due to the nonsingularity of any of the to-be–type devices. In other words, as in many other languages, the functions of predicating and of indicating existence can be performed in Arabic in either of two ways: either by vocabulary deriving from different roots, or by some multifunctioning to-be–type device. What distinguishes Arabic is not that only the former takes place, but that the former is not overshadowed by some one dominating to-be–type word which combines the functions. Thus the second grammatical feature of our discussion, the existential-predicative separation, has to be stated in terms of the first feature, the nonsingularity of a 'to be.' Both are parts of the same picture.

The importance of underscoring such a link between the two features of Arabic is that this has a bearing on how one would state the thesis we are presently examining. For it would now be too stringent to say that such and such Arabic philosophers (e.g., al-Fārābī and Ibn Sīnā) could not escape making the ontological distinction between essence and existence because of the sharp separation—as we have explained it—of the predicative-existential functions.[17] There are possibilities in the language that could have been resorted to which fulfill the requisite logical condition for forming an abstract term for being.[18]

There remains one question of importance for our entire discussion, and especially relevant to the semantical feature of *to on*. How does one decide whether a given Arabic equivalent to *to on* is accurate or not, if, all previous considerations aside, it turns out that the meaning of this Arabic term is stipulated without regard to previous usage? The assumption of the view as we stated it, that the term for existence comes from the existential side and that for essence from the predicative side, seems to be that the meaning of the *to on* equivalent is ruled inaccurate on the basis of some ancestral linguistic fact such as etymology. But surely no one would say that the Arabic word for the telephone, *al-hātif*, is inaccurate on the grounds that it comes from the verb root *hatafa* which means to call loudly or shout, and one does not always shout when using the telephone. One would simply say that etymological affinity might be a useful guide for selecting a verb root from which to derive or coin a word, but that such ancestry is neither a necessary nor a sufficient condition for determining a stipulated meaning.

It would be instructive for us to examine briefly the Arabic translation of Aristotle's discussion of the senses of *to on* and *to einai* (*Metaphysics*, V, 7), and Ibn Rushd's commentary on it. In the Isḥāq translation of the *Metaphysics*, V, 7, what is said there to have the various senses is "*al-huwiyyah*" which could be said to be derived from the copula *huwa*. In the language of the separation-of-functions thesis one could say that this derives from the copulative-essence side. On the other hand, Ibn Rushd in his commentary prefers the term "*al-mawjūd*" for the various senses, and this, it would be said, comes from the existential side. Between Isḥāq the translator, and Ibn Rushd the philosopher-commentator we have two candidates for *to on*, reflecting the predicative-existential split.

However, it should be noted that regardless of their linguistic ancestry, each term, "*al-huwiyyah*" and "*al-mawjūd*," is proposed for *all* the senses distinguished by Aristotle (except for Ibn Rushd's once stated reservation that "*huwiyyah*" does not apply to the sense of 'It is true').[19] Here there is obvious stipulation, and one would in this case be begging the question if one were to judge the new use as inaccurate on the ground that its root or its previous meaning is such and such. If Ibn Rushd tells us that he uses "*al-mawjūd*" to mean . . . , and he then gives the four senses of Aristotle, one could reply: you have distorted Aristotle, because "*al-mawjūd*" means "what exists." He will answer, as in fact he does,[20] that "for the populace"—i.e., the prevalent or common meaning—"*al-mawjūd*" means such and such, and this is its meaning as etymologically derived ("*mushtāqq*"), but in philosophy it means... (and he would refer to the four senses of Aristotle). These are its meanings in the context of translation ("*ism manqūl*").[21]

That Ibn Rushd said this, and therefore was himself aware of the stipulative situation, fulfills one essential condition of stipulated meaning—namely, that the stipulator shall have intended the word to be used in such and such a sense. For even if Ibn Rushd used "*al-mawjūd*" for Aristotle's four senses, he might still have misunderstood Aristotle and thought that the Greek philosopher was speaking about different sorts of existence. We needed to know that Ibn Rushd himself was aware that he was departing from common usage.

This saves us from having to be in the position of engineering a way out for the stipulating Arabic translator or philosopher, when the matter depends not on *our* being aware of what it is to stipulate, but on its being historically the case that some Arabic translator or philosopher was himself aware of what he was doing.

NOTES

[1] Soheil Afnan, *Philosophical Terminology in Arabic and Persian* (Leiden: Brill, 1964).

[2] Ibid., p.29

[3] Ibid., p.30

[4] Ibid., p.29

[5] Angus Graham, "'Being' in Linguistics and Philosophy", *Foundations of Language* 1 (1965): 223–31

[6] Ibid., p.223

[7] Afnan, *Philosophical Terminology,* p.29.

[8] Graham, "Being," p.226; italics in the original.

[9] For a fuller discussion of these and other to-be-type words see this author's "Arabic and 'To Be'," in *The Verb 'Be' and Its Synonyms*, ed. John W.M. Verhaar, vol. 4, (Dordrecht: D. Reidel, 1969), pp. 112–25.

[10] "Logic Versus Grammar and the Arabic Language," read at the Fourth International Congress on Logic, Methodology, and Philosophy of Science, held in Bucharest, Roumania, 29 August–4 September 1971.

[11] The thesis about Arabic could take the following form: that the necessary conditions for expressing *to on* (with the two features) are not present in Arabic, and consequently one cannot express such a concept within the given structure of the language. Our contention is that such a thesis would be false, for the necessary conditions are present in Arabic, as we shall see.

[12] See the excellent article by Charles Kahn, "The Greek Verb 'To Be' and the Concept of Being," *Foundations of Language,* 2 (1966): 245–66.

[13] Kahn, "The Greek Verb," 254.

[14] This pertains to the logical feature of *to on.*

[15] This is relevant to the semantical aspect of *to on.*

[16] See Graham, " 'Being,' " pp.225, 227.

[17] "It is a misplaced compliment to credit al-Fārābī. . . and Ibn Sīnā. . . with the discovery of the ontological difference between essence and existence; it was impossible for an Arab [this must mean Arabic writer, for al-Fārābī was a Turk and Ibn Sīnā a Persian] to confuse them." Graham, " 'Being,' " p.227.

[18] Of words in the natural language *kāna* would be my choice in spite of the sense of becoming in one of its forms (*kawn*). See article by this author n. 9 above, pp.114–118.

[19] See his *Compendio de Metafisica*, ed. Carlos Quiroz-Rodriguez (Madrid, 1919), p.13.

[20] Ibid.

[21] We are not here necessarily endorsing either Isḥāq's or Ibn Rushd's translation of *to on*. Our preference would be for *kaynūnah*, but that is another matter.

THE ANALYSIS OF "SUBSTANCE" IN ṬŪSĪ'S *LOGIC* AND IN THE IBN SĪNIAN TRADITION

PARVIZ MOREWEDGE

INTRODUCTION

Ṭūsī's Text and the Methodology of our Inquiry

The aim of this paper is to clarify the salient features of a method by which Naṣīr al-Dīn Ṭūsī, a thirteenth century Iranian Muslim philosopher-scientist, presented an analytical exposition of the concept of "substance" *(jauhar)* in his fundamental text on logic.[1] Before we turn to the detailed analysis of this concept, let us note some of the striking features of this work.

The text bears the title of *Asās al-Iqtibās*, hereafter cited as *Asās*, which can be translated as "Principles of Inference" or "Foundations of Learning (Deduction)." Examination discloses the work to be a Persian version of Aristotle's logical works as well as of Porphyry's *Isagoge* [εἰσαγωγή] (Introduction). In agreement with Rescher we note that as yet no major study has appeared on this important Persian version of Aristotle's logic, although it is well known among western scholars that Aristotle's logical works with their Porphyrian introduction have been extensively translated and commented upon in Syriac and Arabic.[2]

The reader should be warned at the outset not to expect from this text any attempt on Ṭūsī's part to "Persianize" the logical vocabulary already present in both Greek and Arabic; Ṭūsī follows the Arabic terminology closely. Even in the titles for his nine books, he uses both the transliteration of the Greek term and the Arabic term. Accordingly, the first book carries the double title *Isāghūjī*, a transliteration of the Greek εἰσαγωγή, and its Arabic version, *Madkhal*, both meaning "introduction." The other eight books in the collection follow the order for logical texts adopted by medievalists (the standard name for each text is given here followed by Ṭūsī's Arabic usage): "Categories" *(Maqūlāt)*, "Hermeneutics" *(ʿIbārāt)*, "Prior Analytics" *(Qiyās)*, "Posterior Analytics" *(Burhān)*, "Topics" *(Jadal)*, "Sophistics" *(Mughāliṭah)*, "Rhetoric" *(Khiṭābah)*, and "Poetics" *(Shiʿr)*. Ṭūsī presents a detailed treatment of these topics in a text of approximately 600 pages, which, because of its size, the editor called a major work on logic in Islamic philosophy, second only to the *Manṭiq* of ibn Sīnā's *Shifāʾ*.[3] In comparing its size with ibn Sīnā's texts on logic *(manṭiq)* found in the two other encyclopedic texts, the *Dānish Nāma ʿAlāʾī* and *al-Ishārāt wa-l-Tanbīhāt*, we observe that it exceeds both in length.[4]

Extrinsic considerations alone point to the significance and the eminent position of this text in the corpus of logic in the peripatetic tradition of Islamic philosophy. But its deeper significance lies in the methodology to which Ṭūsī resorts in explaining "substance" and in its unusual display of his analytical ability, which enabled him to avoid difficulties inherent in some metaphysical approaches to this concept.

As the present inquiry concerns itself with the topic of substance, traditionally a part of metaphysics, but presented by Ṭūsī in a text on logic, we shall begin by examining some of the problems inherent in the Aristotelian notion of metaphysics. We shall then proceed to some parallel topics in the works of other Islamic philosophers who preceded Ṭūsī, in order to indicate that his work does not stand in isolation or show a break in the continuity of philosophical development in the Muslim tradition. The major part of this paper will consist of a systematic reconstruction of a philosophical scheme in which the notion of "substance," and the set of conceptual terms associated with it, can be formulated without the confusions which will be enumerated in the following sections of our introduction. We shall also turn to a few topics which appear in other works of Ṭūsī, in which he presents a view of substance which differs radically from the standard Aristotelian analysis of substance. Finally, we shall offer a few tentative conclusions about Ṭūsī's philosophy and voice a note of caution against the common practice of classifying philosophers by categories which, though pedagogically convenient, are not entirely accurate. Thus the usual estimates of Ṭūsī do not take account of his non-peripatetic works.

Metaphysics and its Subject Matter

Since metaphysics is a branch of theoretical inquiry, we shall note here Aristotle's list of the principal types inquiry and point out some of the difficulties which have a bearing upon our discussion. Aristotle divides inquiries into three general kinds: theoretical (θεωρητική), practical (πρακτική), and productive (ποιητική).[5] The differences among them are attributed to differences in their aims. Whereas it is the aim of theoretical inquiries to arrive at true statements regardless of any pragmatic utility they have, it is the aim of practical inquiries to attain to those truths which correspond with proper desires.[6] Productive inquiries are concerned with the production of useful objects.[7] In order to determine the distinction between metaphysics and natural science (or physics), it is necessary to subdivide the theoretical sciences into three groups: natural science or physics (φυσική), mathematics (μαθηματική), and metaphysics to which he refers by various terms.[8] Aristotle explains at some length the difference between natural science and mathematics. Whereas natural science investigates movable bodies in the actual world,[9] mathematics studies quantities, e.g., volume, surface, point and line, the relationships among quantities, and methodology.[10] For this reason the conceptual analysis of substance lies outside the domain of these disciplines.

Aristotle's renowned analysis of the scope of metaphysics is not without difficulties. The first problem, that he gives three different explanations of metaphysics without making their relationship clear, has been noted by scholars such as Ross, Owens, Merlan, and Jaeger and we shall not belabor it here.[11] Aristotle interprets metaphysics in three ways: first as "first philosophy" (ἡ πρώτη φιλοσοφία) which studies "being qua being" (τὸ ὄν ᾗ ὄν), next as an inquiry into principles and causes (ἀρχὰς καὶ αἰτιάς), and finally as theology (θεολογική) which investigates God (ὁ θεὸς) as a motionless (ἀκίνητος), everlasting (ἀΐδιος) entity.[12] The difficulty particularly relevant to our discussion is the following. If we assert that metaphysics studies substances, it is not clear which substance is meant, e.g., a conceptual specification of "being qua being", a cause for the composition of entities, or an elementary part of the universe derived from the divine being. For this reason Owens agrees with Jaeger's observation that there are at least two contradictory notions concerning the subject matter of primary philosophy; the first concerns a notion about a supersensible or immobile being, while the second describes a notion about a general concept of being which applies to particulars.[13] The former relates to the notion of metaphysics as theology, whereas the latter belongs to metaphysics as ontology.

A second difficulty with Aristotle's theory of metaphysics resides in the question of the emptiness of metaphysics. Obviously, no sense impression can be used to prove that the objects of metaphysics exist. Even if we grant that natural science is a legitimate study because it deals with physical bodies, which we take to exist, and concede further that mathematics is legitimate because its concepts are abstracted by definition from these sensible movables, there is still no guarantee that metaphysics is not empty, for its objects are not related to sensible movables either conceptually or by definition. Consequently, metaphysics cannot be introduced as the science which investigates purely abstract concepts, because it may be meaningless to speak about entities which are in no way related to sense experience. If one takes such an empiricist position, the assertion that metaphysics is based upon abstractions from physics and mathematics will be beset by difficulty. One cannot claim, without presenting further arguments, to have an experience of entities such as "causality" and "God," as the well-known controversies over such topics would seem to prove. In sum, it is not entirely evident that metaphysics contains subject matter such as substances. Perhaps, instead of assuming the existence of substance, we should employ logic and analysis to clarify the proper uses of the terms which designate substance in a philosophical system.

In addition to the difficulty with metaphysics, questions related to the subject matter of physics pose another serious problem in Aristotle's philosophy. Ross, for instance, points out, "It cannot be said that in practice the distinction between physics and metaphysics is maintained by Aristotle, and it may be noted that the bulk of the *Physica* is what we should call metaphysics. It is not an inductive inquiry into natural law, but an a priori analysis of material things and events that befall them."[14]

Further difficulty may be encountered in the attempt to interpret the Aristotelian theory of natural science in the light of contemporary views on philosophy of science, as is illustrated by some of the doctrines of Hempel, Carnap, and other contemporary philosophers. If we accept their view that empirical sciences are concerned with observational statements, then we are at a loss to find a basis for such statements in Aristotle's theory of scientific inquiry.[15] Although the philosopher clearly recognizes the distinction between what may be called "observational-epistemic" terms, such as "perception-sensation" (ἄισθησις), "experience" (ἐμπειρία), and "memory" (μνήμη), he does not extensively employ these terms in his discussions of science,[16] but relies heavily on two terms ἐπιστημή and νοῦς for the description and the premises of "scientific knowledge." Neither one of these terms is a satisfactory component upon which to base an observational statement. ἐπιστημή is the ability to deduce true statements or to generate valid arguments, a task that a computer can perform for simple languages.[17] Aristotle states that of the two, the more important term for scientific knowledge is νοῦς, supposedly an infallible ability which is able to grasp the first principles.[18]

If we read Aristotle in the light of contemporary views on conditions which characterize "observational statements," we are faced with the following specific problems. Requirements for observational statements, such as confirmation and testability, rule out incorrigible and at the same time infallible first person statements, like "I am in pain"; instead, these requirements apply to corrigible statements voiced by many persons, such as statements concerning the length of a rod based on the approximated measurements of several observers. According to Carnap's view, the idea of "observable" in an empirical science includes fallible cases of epistemic expriences, such as data received from measurements which have been approximated.[19] Measured by Carnapian criteria, Aristotle's notion of intuition cannot serve as an adequate basis for an empirical theory of science. It is beyond the scope of this paper to elaborate upon this point; we terminate this argument by pointing to the often overlooked passage in which Aristotle states that "intuition" enters as an outside element and calls it a "divine" element.[20]

Most problematical, for our purposes, is not the logical difficulty mentioned, but the obscurity spelled out below, which is probably not unrelated to the other problems embedded in his concept of metaphysics and natural science. Aristotle fails to make a sharp distinction between "being" and "substance." This obscurity poses such acute difficulties, particularly the problem of substance, that several scholars like Owens and Hope do not employ the term "substance" in their translations of Aristotle's works, preferring neutral terms, such as "primary being" and "entity."[21] As we shall have occasion to note subsequently, this complication does not exist in Ṭūsī's work or in the works of other Muslim philosophers, who define their terms sharply. Perhaps one might argue that such thinkers did not reject Aristotle's framework as much as they clarified and specified the ambiguity found in the Aristotelian texts.

Consequently, the nature of metaphysics, which is supposed to investigate substance as well as the meaning of the term "substance," is not clarified by Aristotle's inquiry into metaphysics. Inasmuch as his definition of natural science labors under difficulty, and his anti-Platonic views preclude any contribution from mathematics to the study of "substance," we must look to his logic for an answer. When we turn to Aristotle's logical works, we note that his concept of the categories which is discussed in *Categoriae* is absent from his metaphysical treatise. Consequently we are not in a position to make a definite connection between what may be called his logical and his metaphysical uses of the concept of substance as "οὐσία." Having acquainted ourselves with the major recognized problems and ambiguities related to the problem under consideration, let us leave the Aristotelian domain and investigate how some of these doctrines were received and modified by some of the significant predecessors of Ṭūsī in the Islamic cultural tradition.

Non-Aristotelian Features of Metaphysics in Islamic Philosophy

Ṭūsī's analytical treatment discussed in the next section should be seen against the background of some Aristotelian concepts and their modifications in Islamic philosophy. As has been observed by several writers, Islamic philosophers distinguished clearly between the meaning of the science of nature *(al-ᶜilm al-ṭabīᶜī)*, corresponding to the Greek φυσική, and metaphysics.[22] Like the Greeks, they embedded this distinction in the broader classification of a speculative or theoretical type of inquiry *(naẓarī)* and a practical kind of inquiry *(ᶜamalī)*.[23] However, more specific distinctions between the sub-classes of inquiries are to be found in the texts of various philosophers. By mentioning this distinction and attributing it to Aristotle, Fārābī definitely demonstrates his awareness of it.[24] Calling physics "the science of nature," he contrasts it with the science which comes after *(mā baᶜd)* nature, i.e., metaphysics.[25] Among Fārābī's well known works one finds a fourfold division of speculative inquiry into mathematics, the science of nature, metaphysics, and politics-civics.[26] In his most celebrated text on the subject, natural science is divided into eight parts and metaphysics into three parts. According to Fārābī, metaphysics investigates *(1)* the nature and characteristics of bodily existents, *(2)* the principles of demonstrations in particular sciences or metasciences, and *(3)* the nature of non-bodily existents.[27]

A more penetrating look at a newly edited text of Fārābī, a work on metaphysics of great significance, contains some points which are of particular import to this discussion.[28] In this work Fārābī explicitly distinguishes between "substance" *(jauhar)* and "being" *(maujūd)*.[29] He identifies substance with the Greek οὐσία and mentions that Aristotle, in his *Categoriae*, differentiates between "first substance" and "second substance."[30] His concept of substance, however, is obviously presented in a more detailed manner than Aristotle's. For example, he gives an analysis of one of the ordinary Arabic meanings of the term, "a precious entity," which does not appear in the Greek extended meaning of the term,[31] and states that the philosopher's applications of "substance" are derived from common usage—a theory for which we should look in vain in the works of Aristotle.[32] The care he takes in his analysis is notable, for instance, in the case of "being" *(wujūd)*, when he admits the lack of an Arabic term corresponding to the Persian, Greek, and Sogdian equivalents of this concept and mentions, moreover, that philosophers writing in Arabic eventually resort to *wujūd* as a substitute.[33] Accordingly, his distinction between words taken from common usage by philosophers to enrich the philosophical vocabulary and the difficult concepts for which philosophers have invented words or have postulated novel usages is quite clear.

Another example of the modification the Aristotelian doctrines related to metaphysics underwent is found in the works of ibn Sīnā. Even the medieval writer ibn Khaldūn regards ibn Sīnā's treatment of the science of nature as an original doctrine in which the philosopher departs from the Aristotelian philosophy.[34] Before turning to an examination of ibn Sīnā's analysis of "inquiry," we should take notice of an ambiguity in the translation of "science," for which two common meanings exist: *(1)* "science" as a general area of inquiry which includes the productive and practical disciplines as well as physics, mathematics, and metaphysics, and *(2)* "science" as natural science in terms of physics *(ṭabīʿiyyāt)*. To designate the first set of inquiries, which resembles Aristotle's general doctrine of intellectual virtue, ibn Sīnā uses three terms: *ʿilm, ḥikma,* and *dānish*. The last term is reserved for his Persian texts; as might be expected, either *ṭabīʿiyyāt* or *al-ʿilm al-ṭabīʿī* is employed in referring to the second category.[35]

Following Aristotle's general division of theoretical sciences, ibn Sīnā distinguishes among three kinds of speculative inquiries: physics *(tabīʿiyyāt)*, mathematics or syntax *(riyāḍiyāt, farhang)*, and metaphysics, variously designated, to which we shall attend next.[36]

The term *ilāhiyyāt* is regularly employed for metaphysics in most of ibn Sīnā's works.[37] However, in two texts, the Persian *Dānish Nāma-i ʿAlāī (Ilāhiyyāt)* and the Arabic *ʿUyūn al-Ḥikma*, a more specific formulation of metaphysics is presented. In the *Dānish Nāma* he uses *ʿilm-i barīn* for metaphysics, which is translated into Persian as first science or inquiry; it is distinct from natural science and mathematics. He states further that *ilāhiyyāt*, also termed *ʿilm-i rubūbiyya*, is a part *(para)* of yet another inquiry which he names *ʿilm-i barīn*, the latter being a higher and more general inquiry than the former.[38] Similarly, in the *ʿUyūn al-Ḥikma*, he mentions *al-falsafa al-awwaliyya* (first philosophy) and its part *(juzʾ) al-falsafa al-ilāhiyya*, also known as *al-rubūbiyya*, which is identical with the term used in his Persian text.[39] These data, as well as the arguments found in the *Dānish Nāma* and the metaphysical texts of *al-Shifāʾ*, *al-Najāt*, *al-Ishārāt wa-l-Tanbīhāt* lend support to the following lemmata. It is legitimate to say that in some of his writings, ibn Sīnā postulates that metaphysics proper investigates "being" *(wujūd, hastī)* and topics which are abstract entities, depending neither in their conception *(tawahhum)* nor in their definition *(ḥadd)* upon material bodies. A branch of this discipline is theology, which examines the Necessary Existent *(wājib al-wujūd)*.[40] This study follows logically the more abstract study of first philosophy proper, which includes the concept of substance. However, the more specific study is not a study of a substantial entity, for the Necessary Existent is not a substance. We may note then that some of the confusion observed in the Aristotelian system among the different senses of metaphysics has been avoided by ibn Sīnā.

In addition to this novel feature in the ibn Sīnian formulation, there is the suggestion of another new conception, which, however, is not supported by much evidence. In specifying mathematics, ibn Sīnā often refers to it as *riyāḍī*, as well as "an instructive science" *(taʿlīmī)*, "an intermediate inquiry" *(miyānagī)*, and as "syntax" *(farhang)*.[41] The last designation is rather significant, for it implies that mathematics is an inquiry of a structural and axiomatic kind and not a mere science dealing with quantities. Although Aristotle's works include investigations into music, astronomy, geometry, and arithmetic, ibn Sīnā's formulation of mathematical systems, as, for instance, in the *Shifāʾ*, is far more elaborate than any one of these studies.

With respect to the natural sciences, a division of speculative inquiry, we find ibn Sīnā's treatment to be as extensive and elaborate as its Aristotelian counterpart.[42] Undoubtedly, ibn Sīnā's formulation is more original and substantial than Aristotle's, because of his familiarity with post-Aristotelian science, a topic which we shall omit from this essay. It is evident that in physics, as well as in metaphysics, Islamic philosophers like ibn Sīnā arrived at a more systematic view of inquiry. Consequently, we may claim that an Islamic philosopher, such as Ṭūsī, could have held an analytically more precise doctrine of substance than Aristotle, especially if the modifications which his predecessors adopted on the Aristotelian system were relevant to his analysis of the subject.

Before turning to Ṭūsī's own work, we should note that we have omitted ibn Sīnā's analysis of being and its relationship to substance from this discussion because we have dealt with these points in terms of his celebrated "essence-existence" distinction in another paper.[43] One of the conclusions reached in that essay is relevant to the present discussion, namely that the essence-existence distinction is to be applied to a distinction between a method of analysis of concepts and an inquiry into the nature of actual existents. The logical analysis of substance, as will be pointed out subsequently, belongs to the former type of inquiry. As we claimed in the aforementioned essay that ibn Sīnā's distinction is significant from the point of view of methodology, we affirm in this study that the present subject of inquiry falls into the continuous tradition indicated in the previous arguments as well as in the aforementioned study.

A RECONSTRUCTION OF ṬŪSĪ'S ANALYSIS OF SUBSTANCE

While Ṭūsī follows the traditional grouping of the Peripatetics in the general format of his division of sciences, he demonstrates at the same time his originality in his detailed analysis of concepts related to substance. Let us take cognizance of the special features of his division of inquiries.

Ṭūsī's Remarks on Metaphysics and Related Disciplines

The two terms Ṭūsī uses in *Asās* in referring to metaphysics in the peripatetic sense are *ilāhī* and *falsafa-i awwalī*, terms commonly used by Muslim philosophers (*Asās*, pp. 404–405, *et passim*). In his well known work on *The Naṣirean Ethics*, he refers to metaphysics as *ilāhī*, but—following Fārābī's usage as well—notes that it is a science which is also called "that which studies *mā baᶜd al-ṭabīᶜiyya* (an Arabic transliteration of "metaphysics").[44]

Ṭūsī's debt to the Aristotelian doctrine as it was transmitted by the Arabic tradition also becomes apparent from a study of his vocabulary. For example, for every term he adopts for a branch of logic, he lists the Arabic word and a transliteration of the Greek term in the Arabic rather than the Persian version, although the text is written in Persian (*Asās*, pp. 34, 61, 186, 340, 515, 529, and 586). For instance, τοπικα is transliterated as *taubiqā*, in spite of the fact that its Persian transliteration, *tupikā* phonetically resembles the Greek term more closely.

Ṭūsī's recognition of Aristotle's importance is evident from his attempt to draw an important distinction between metaphysics and natural science. Of the many arguments he presents in this endeavor, he correctly attributes one to Aristotle, the doctrine that any science which is demonstrative, e.g., natural science, makes use of a middle term (τὸ μέσον) assumed by it but analyzed by another demonstrative science of a higher level.[45] Ṭūsī notes, moreover, that if two sciences investigate objects at different levels, then they must be different. Upon observing that there are many divers entities, he cites "body" and "eternal movement" as examples of entities whose existence is presupposed by natural science, but whose nature is analyzed by metaphysics. Thereupon he concludes that metaphysics must be different from natural science since the former studies entities which are presupposed by the latter.[46]

Ṭūsī observes great care in his delineation of the sciences. He explains in great detail, in a section corresponding to Aristotle's *Analytica Posteriora,* that each science has a subject matter, a set of presuppositions, and certain problems in need of solution *(Asās,* p. 393). He also cites some special cases, such as the notion of a body *(jism)*, drawing a distinction between a "natural body" *(jism-i ṭabīᶜī)* and "an instructional [representation of a] body" *(jism-i taᶜlīmī)* *(Asās,* p. 401). The former is the subject matter of natural science *(ᶜilm-i ṭabīᶜī)*, whereas the latter is the subject matter of the science of solids *(mujassamāt)*.

Ṭūsī affirms that logic *(manṭiq)* is definitely a science *(ᶜilm)* with a specific subject matter proper to it and that it investigates concepts of second intention, such as the universal, the particular, the essential *(dhātī)* and the accidental.[47] Concepts derived from first intentions are substance, accident *(ᶜaraḍ)* unity, plurality, and related concepts *(Asās,* p. 399). It follows that logic uses "substance," but does not itself define "substance" specifically. This distinction is of utmost importance to philosophical analysis, for Ṭūsī's various uses of the concept of substance in different contexts illuminate the meaning of this concept more adequately than do attempts which limit themselves to defining this term. In his logical text, however, Ṭūsī commits an apparent contradiction when he specifies substance. Nevertheless, a closer investigation of the relevant passages establishes clearly that in the aforementioned contexts he does not employ logic in the narrow sense in which logic is used to construct proofs about universal predictions and similar topics, but rather, makes use of analysis in dealing with metalogical problems, as for instance, when he employs the concept of substance in order to distinguish between particulars and universals, these latter being mental concepts of the second intention. Interestingly enough, because Ṭūsī is forced to introduce new refinements into the use of the concept, he gives us a family of features which characterize concepts (such as substance) as no categorical style of definition had done previously. The various philosophical theories of meaning and the numerous definitions which explain the reasons for the success of this method are well known and need not be reiterated in a paper which intends to do no more than to investigate Ṭūsī's theory.[48]

Notes on the Use of jauhar *(Substance)*

As has been pointed out, Fārābī uses *jauhar* for Aristotle's οὐσία, which is ordinarily translated as "substance." Parallels for such usage can be found in the works of many Muslim philosophers. For example, in his *Book of Definition* ibn Sīnā names the first ten categories, attributes them to Aristotle, and equates the first category with substance *(jauhar)*.[49] It appears that the term *jauhar* has been used uniformly in distinction to *wujūd* in the Arabic texts; in Persian texts *gauhar* is distinct from *hastī*, having been introduced by ibn Sīnā chiefly through the usage he establishes in the *Dānish Nāma ᶜAlāī*.[50] Throughout the *Asās*—as well as in his other texts—Ṭūsī resorts to the Arabic-Persian term *jauhar*, even though the text is written in Persian and *gauhar* is directly derived from Middle Persian. Yet Ṭūsī's usage is not unconventional, for inspection of the works of the post–ibn-Sīnian philosophers will reveal that ibn Sīnā's Persian vocabulary, in this respect, did not find acceptance with philosophers such as Suhrawardī and Kāshānī.[51]

Jauhar, as one might expect, was regarded as the first substance belonging to the ten categories *(maqūlāt)*. Since "being qua being" in Islamic peripatetic philosophy is held to be a general idea that includes even the concept of the categories, we shall focus our attention next on its analysis and proceed thereafter to more determinate theories, examining for each one the special uses of *jauhar*.

Being Qua Being

For Ṭūsī the most common, general, and determinable term is "being" in the Aristotelian sense of "τὸ ὄν ᾗ ὄν." To this concept in the ibn Sīnian sense of "*hastī*," we shall turn next. Ibn Sīnā uses two words to designate "being qua being," *hastī* and *wujūd*. The former, *hastī*, is a Persian term to which he refers in *Dānish Nāma: Ilāhiyyāt* as the most determinable concept in the language.[52] Reason *(khirad)* recognizes that it is without definition (since it has neither a genus nor a differentia) and description (since it is the most common notion).[53] Moreover, in this work ibn Sīnā identifies *anniyya* with *wujūd*. He clearly distinguishes *hastī* (being qua being), from *anniyya* and *wujūd* (existence).[54]

In his Arabic writings, however, ibn Sīnā uses the term *wujūd* to signify "being," as is illustrated in the celebrated passage in the first chapter of the *Ilāhiyyāt* of *al-Shifāʾ*, where he indicates that the primary ideas ("*maᶜnā*," which can be translated as "εἶδος") are *maujūd* ("existent"), *shāīʾ* ("thing"), and *ḍarūrī* ("necessary").[55] In this passage *maujūd* does not appear as *the* most primary concept, but as one of the three most primary concepts.

Ṭūsī seems to follow the ibn Sīnian doctrine which is expressed in *al-Shifā*ʾ more closely than that in the *Dānish Nāma*. Ṭūsī asserts that most philosophers agree that there are intelligibles which are more common (*ʿāmm*) than the ten categories. Among such intelligibles he mentions two classes: *(1)* the class of "existence" *(wujūd)*, "necessity" *(wujūb)*, and "contingency" *(imkān)*, and *(2)* that of entities which are related to the specification of some species, such as "unity" *(waḥdat)*, and "point" *(naughṭa)*.[56] In another passage, Ṭūsī observes a distinction among the ideas which are receptive to intelligences and minds. Those assigned to the first class are either absolutely intelligible *(maʿqul-i maḥḍ)* or they are sensible and receptive to the external and internal senses. Among the absolute intelligibles he lists "existence" *(wujūd)*, "necessity" *(wujūb)*, "contingency" *(imkān)*, and "impossibility" *(imtināʿ)*. As examples of entities to which the external senses are receptive, he mentions heat and cold, color, light and darkness. Corresponding to the internal senses he cites several feelings, such as happiness, sadness, satiety, and hunger. The criteria by which they are distinguished are these: whereas the first is of a universal nature, the second and third kinds possess particular natures. [*Asās*, 412]

Let us attempt to note two different ways in which Ṭūsī's doctrine can be stated and name them for purposes of clarification "epistemic-phenomenological" and "syntactical" explanations. From the first point of view, in the familiar Kantian language, "that there is a being" is a transcendental condition of experience. Since it is implicitly assumed that "nothing" does not denote anything, and that whatever we experience is a "something," we know necessarily that there is a being. The specific nature of this being, of course, depends on the peculiarity of sensations and other factors which are a posteriori to experience. In the syntactical way, the concept of "being" is handled quite simply without the traditional metaphysical importance attached to it.[57] Syntactically, the meaning of "being" can also be considered in the following way. Some words in the language can be arranged on different levels on the basis of the degree of determination they possess, which in turn depends partially upon whether or not a sign can be predicated of another sign and result in a well-formed expression. For example, "man" is more determinable than "Socrates"; consequently, "Socrates" is more determinate than "man" because "the man Socrates" [which reads "Socrates is a man"] is a significant expression in the language. "Animality" is more determinable than "humanity." (The cases of predicates with different numbers of places can easily be taken into account, as is illustrated in type-theoretical languages). Accordingly, the concept of *being* is explained as the designatum of a sign of the highest level in the language, which is predicated of a sign of any other level in the manner of a transcendental term, e.g., a number which is predicated of properties on different levels.[58]

It is legitimate to inquire whether we are reading modern themes into the philosophies of Ṭūsī and ibn Sīnā or whether these philosophers actually subscribed to a syntactical philosophy of being. The answer to this question is obviously in need of certain qualifications and clarifications, as these philosophers were not acquainted with the tools of contemporary symbolic logic, such as the theory of types. Nevertheless, from examples which both Ṭūsī and ibn Sīnā provide, it appears that each upholds a syntactical rather than epistemological sense of priority of "being" in the sense indicated. For instance, both make use of syntactical paradoxes to show that "substance" is not identical with "being"; e.g., if we substitute "substance" for "is" *(hast)* in the sentence "A substance is" we get "A substance substance," which is nonsensical.[59]

In sum, both Ṭūsī and ibn Sīnā attempt to present what might be termed a syntactical way of discussing "being." The so-called "necessity of being" would not be a difficult ontological problem for them. If a finite number of levels of predication alone explains our experience adequately, then there must be an upper boundary to the levels of predication. "Being" is that concept which is of the highest level. Ibn Sīnā considers it legitimate to combine "being" with modalities. Accordingly, he uses "being" with "actuality" in the following ways: "a Necessary Being is actual," "an impossible being is never actual," and "if the cause of a contingent being is actual, then the contingent being itself is actual." Employing such reasoning and certain premises about the nature of "goodness" of the "Necessary Being," he sets out to derive a proof for the existence of actual entities in this world.[60]

Categories

Apart from carrying many significant implications of a philosophical as well as an historical nature, the concept of "categories" is a useful tool in the exegesis of complex passages concerned with key terms, such as "substance."

Within a philosophical context there are two questions which may legitimately be asked of a philosopher who uses the apparatus of the categories. We could inquire whether he makes a distinction between logic and metaphysics and, if so, to which of these disciplines the theory of categories belongs, and, if to both, how the transformation is carried out from one to the other. A related question concerns a more acute problem since it touches on the very nature of the categorical investigation. The problem arises when the apparently simple, legitimate question is asked: what are the categories about? In the attempt to answer this question, what might prima facie be taken as two distinct possibilities present themselves: first, linguistic expressions, and second, the ultimate nature of entities in the nonlinguistic aspect of the world. In our present exposition we should note these problems but should also observe that these problems are of concern to us—not to the Islamic philosophers who, not being faced with them, cannot justly be accused of having evaded them. It is not surprising, therefore, that there is no clear-cut discussion of these points in Aristotelian works; ibn Sīnā assumes a position, and although Ṭūsī is aware of the problem, he merely follows ibn Sīnā's views on these controversial points after having offered minor arguments for the justification of his views.

Almost without exception Islamic philosophers followed a set of fixed Arabic equivalents for the original Greek terms. In the *Dānish Nāma* ibn Sīnā introduces Persian names for the categories which are not adopted by Kāshānī and other Persian writers after ibn Sīnā. In this text as well as elsewhere, Ṭūsī follows the Arabic version of ibn Sīnā's list given in his texts other than the *Dānish Nāma*. The list is presented below:[61]

English	*Greek*	*Arabic*	*Persian*	*Latin*
1. substance	οὐσία	jauhar	gauhar	substantia
2. quantity	πόσον	kammiyya	chandī	quantum
3. quality	ποιόν	kaifiyya	chigūnagī	quale
4. relation	πρός τι	iḍāfa	nisbat	ad aliquid
5. place	ποῦ	ᶜayn	kujāʾi	ubi
6. time	ποτέ	matā	kaīʾi	quando
7. posture	κεῖσθαι	waḍᶜ	nahād	poni
8. possession	ἔχειν	mulk	dāsht	habere
9. action	ποιεῖν	an yafᶜal	kinish	facere
10. passion	πάσχειν	an yanfaᶜil	bakunīdan	pati

Having discussed the terminology of individual categories, let us now turn to certain difficulties that arise in Ṭūsī's reformulation of Aristotle's original formulation. Even though Aristotle's philosophy, in which "substance" is the prime category, uses the notion of categories indirectly throughout its explanations, only in the *Categoriae* itself and in *Topica* 103b 21–25 do we find an explicit reference to a list. Moreover, the *Metaphysica* does not mention that the general notion of categories is an essential part of metaphysical analysis, even though some of its significant sections, notably Book Zeta, are devoted to the clarification of one of the most important categories, "substance." It should be noted that this difficulty may not be inherent in Aristotle's views but may be due to the incomplete or faulty transmission of his works. The attempt to find a connection between his metaphysical and his logical works is especially complicated because the entire order of what we take to be his *Metaphysica* is based upon nothing but tentative permises and fragmentary evidence, as indicated by attempts such as those of Jaeger to emend the text according to some reasonable order.[62]

In view of differences in terminology and emphasis in his *Categoriae* and *Metaphysica,* it is not surprising that several commentators express disagreement about the intention and the use of the doctrine of the categories and its place in Aristotle's philosophy.[63] For example, Moody, in his able exposition of Ockham's views on this topic, presents a comprehensive interpretation of Aristotle's *Categoriae* as part of his *Organon,* an idea implicitly supported by Bocheński.[64] Kneale and Kneale, on the other hand, consider the *Categoriae* as a metaphysical work.[65]

The doctrine of categories as Aristotle asserted it could not have been accepted by Neoplatonists (especially since it reduced genera and species to secondary substances), as has been noted by A.C. Lloyd and substantiated by the famous attack on this doctrine by Plotinus in *Enneads,* VI.[66] One of Plotinus' main objections was that the categories could not be interpreted in his own dualistic realms, viz., the realm of the sensible and the realm of the intelligible. Porphyry, in his specification of the nature of the categories, took Plotinus' objections into account by making the categories directly applicable to the sensible realm and applicable to the intelligible realm only by analogy.[67] The confusion about the meaning of the categories, however, remains in the Neoplatonic philosophies and has continued in contemporary discussions of Aristotle's philosophy.[68] In making historical notes on the topic of the categories, one should attempt to avoid the tendency of some modern philosophers like Anscombe and Ryle to interpret Aristotle's categories purely on the linguistic level and to criticize his linguistic shortcomings as well as those of other ancient and medieval philosophers.[69] But the results of the efforts of those who attempt to establish what can be said of the text of the *Categoriae* without reading into Aristotle's work any specific intention are often in disaccord. For example, Ackrill observes that Aristotle's categorical analysis is about things and suggests that in order to carry out his investigation, Aristotle has to pay attention to linguistic usage. Accordingly, the categories can be arrived at by means of two aspects: *(1)* the different kinds of questions that can be asked about substance, and (2) the various kinds of answers to a particular question which can be asked about any entity.[70]

In view of these diversities, we conclude that Aristotle's analysis of categories is by no means clear in its aims or in its actual results. When we turn to ibn Sīnā and Ṭūsī, the doctrine becomes more specific.[71] Ibn Sīnā asserts three times that the study of the categories belongs to logic—first in his momentous work on the *Categoriae* in the "Logic" of *al-Shifāʾ*, second in the "Metaphysica" of *al-Shifāʾ*, and finally in *al-Najāt*.[72] He adopts the Aristotelian category divisions, by passing, therefore, both Plotinus' rejection and the system of the four categories adopted by the Stoics. For the Stoics, Bocheński argues the theory that the categories belong to physics rather than logic.[73] The difference between the views of Aristotle and ibn Sīnā on this topic amounts to more than the mere specification of categories by the former as a part of philosophy and by the latter as a part of logic. One important distinction is that ibn Sīnā's metaphysical systems expressed in *al-Shifā᾽* and the *Dānish Nāma* are based explicitly on the doctrine of the categories, whereas Aristotle offers no explicit discussion of the categories in his *Metaphysica* or of lists as we know them from the Islamic philosophers.[74]

Ṭūsī, in *Asās* (pp. 34–35), demonstrates his awareness of the controversy about the nature of categories among his contemporaries. According to him they hold the view that the study of the categories does not belong to logic because neither the specification of the nature of universals nor the description of what exists, i.e., substances and accidents, belongs to logic. But he notes that definition, description, and deduction of the premises of deductions cannot be undertaken without consideration of the logical distinction among individual categories. He affirms the value of categorical analyses in stating that they can assist us in our discussion of cases in the actual world; moreover, such cases are employed only for pedagogical purposes to elucidate the logical relationship between individual categories.

Ṭūsī's discussion points to a significant problem concerning the use of syntactical categorical schemes in science. Even though categorical analyses may logically be independent of actual objects, nevertheless, the logical distinctions among the conceptual relationships of categorical terms illuminate our understanding of the domain with which science is concerned. Let us consider, for example, the problem of choosing a language for a physical theory. The problem lies essentially in choosing some primitive terms, a language, and a set of axioms, in the context of a Carnapian type of syntax.[75] Some considerations with which a scientist must deal are factors about the meaning of the categories of "space" and "time," e.g., the reversibility of the spatial realm and the irreversibility of temporal units, and the kinds of languages in which it is possible to express physical properties of the world, such as metric and topological languages. Such languages entail, obviously, a study in the logic of quantities, such as comparisons of cases of coordinate systems with a logic of relations expressing topological relations suited to the physical theory in question.

When a philosopher considers these factors, his analysis, to the extent that it is expressed in terms of the categories, does not go beyond concepts, for it does not take into account empirical facts, e.g., what the Muslims called properties and relations of sensible movables. Nevertheless, such an analysis results in alternative languages among which the scientist has to make a choice. In this sense then, a logical independence of categorical analysis from science does not imply that categories are irrelevant to science; it implies instead that the analysis of the categories is part of the theoretical aspect of a scientific inquiry.[76] In his syntactical analysis of the categories, Ṭūsī does not employ them as part of "science proper" but as a tool which is concerned with those languages science can use. He insists that the primary aim of logic is to clarify intelligible ideas, "*maᶜanā-yi ᶜaqlī*"; it is not a mere concern with linguistic expression for its own sake (*Asās*, p. 187). Ṭūsī notes that logic is a science of sciences, for its subject matter consists of the second intelligibles which are abstracted from the first intelligibles, such as substance, but are nonetheless useful for the derived sciences (*Asās*, p. 399). It follows then that philosophy concerns itself with concepts from which those general instances can be abstracted which serve as the theoretical framework of sciences. In this sense logic becomes an intermediate tool between philosophy and science. However, since Ṭūsī does not discuss this point clearly, it is unwarranted to present him in the garb of a twentieth century constructionalist in philosophy of science. From his discussion of the categories it has become evident that there is a difference between science and philosophy; even though their subject matters are logically independent, in the practical sense philosophical analysis can serve science through the medium of logic.

Ṭūsī's Concept of "Substance"

The notion of "substance" is generally associated with several problems of both an historical and a philosophical nature. Of course, "substance," derived from the Latin "*substantia*" was not used by Aristotle, who, it is thought, was the first philosopher to specify this concept by using "οὐσία" in *Categoriae* and "τί ἐστι" in *Topica* 103b 20-5 as the first of the categories. He discusses the meaning of "οὐσία" extensively in *Metaphysica*, especially in Book Zeta. Since the task of specifying the Aristotelian notion of substance is beyond the scope of this study, we offer the following notes upon which the subsequent discussion will be based.

(1) From the philosophical point of view, Aristotle's text on "substance" is prima facie confusing, as the following examples will demonstrate. *(a)* In *Categoriae* he presents the primary substance as consisting of individuals, and the secondary substance of species and genera; *(b)* he emphasizes in the *Metaphysica* the notion of concrete individuals as the primary case of being; *(c)* in the last chapter of *Metaphysica:* Zeta he attributes substantiality to what can be called a definition and a cause; and *(d)* in *Metaphysica:* Lambda he takes a nonsensible eternal God to be a "substance."[77]

(2) As far as terminology is concerned, it is questionable whether "οὐσία" can adequately be translated as "substance." In all probability, a clear presentation of Aristotle's views, as Owens has indicated, must "reconstruct" this notion under a "neutral" label, such as "entity."[78] To state, therefore, that "*jauhar*" means "οὐσία" does not contribute to an understanding of details of ibn Sīnā's or Ṭūsī's use of "*jauhar*."

(3) In taking the historical perspective, we note that the term "οὐσία"

underwent numerous diverse renderings in the Latin philosophical texts, and that we may not, therefore, take the liberty of regarding "οὐσία" as the equivalent of "substantia" merely on the basis of Boethius' use of these terms as equivalents in his commentary.[79]

These difficulties notwithstanding, we shall assume hypothetically the following theses: *(a)* Aristotle formulated two concepts of substance in the first of his categories—the first naming concrete individuals and the second species and genera; *(b)* although the primary existing entities were individual substances, we refer to their essences in defining them; and, finally *(c)* Aristotle was not explicit in the presentation of his views on substance, of what he called "οὐσία."

Let us now turn to ibn Sīnā's analysis of "substance." Here we notice a very clear separation of "substance" from "being," "essence," and "existence," a separation which we have discussed elsewhere.[80] Ibn Sīnā distinguishes explicitly between the concept of "the first substance" designating it as "*al-jauhar al-shakhṣī*,"[81] "*al-jauhar al-awwalī*,"[82] and that of "the second substance," which he designates as "*al-jauhar al-thānī*."[83] In his works this distinction becomes almost the cornerstone of an empiricistic view in the realm of his ontology.[84] For example, in the *Dānish Nāma* he relates the differences between the two substances to the difference between the conceptual analysis of an object and the empirical acquaintance with it. In discussing the nature of "substance," he draws a distinction between the "essence" *(ḥaqīqa)* of a substance *(jauhar)* and its existence *(wujūd)*. Asserting that there is a priori knowledge that an entity, such as an independent body, is a substance, he affirms that such knowledge is necessary and independent of observation. On the other hand, the question whether or not an instance of a secondary substance has been realized *(ḥāṣil)* cannot be answered a priori since such knowledge depends on observation of a subject *(mauḍūᶜ*, ὑποκείμενον).[85] For reasons like these, the distinction he makes between essence and existence is connected to the distinction between substances. The domain of the analysis of the secondary substances falls under syntactical inquiries, while propositions concerning existential facts about first substances can be justified only by an acquaintance with the material substratum, the subject matter of the first substance. Thus the difference between the two substances corresponds to the difference between an empirical inquiry, which illustrates a scientific kind of activity, and a conceptual inquiry, which is a philosophical activity.

Another point of interest in ibn Sīnā's analysis of substance is the fact that he makes a distinction between the first substance *(al-jauhar al-awwalī)*, a particular *(al-shakhṣ)*, the second substance *(al-jauhar al-thānī)*, a species *(nauᶜ)*, and the third substance *(al-jauhar al-thālith)*, a genus.[86]

Ṭūsī continues the ibn Sīnian doctrine, emphasizing, however, the syntactical aspect of the concept of the substance. For instance, in his first division of substance he establishes three categories: *(1)* individual particulars, which are first substances, *(2)* species, which are second substances, and *(3)* genera, which are third substances *(Asās*, p. 38). He accentuates also the differences between primary and other kinds of substances on the grounds of having previously drawn distinctions between a particular *(juzʾī)* and an universal *(kullī)*. Some of these salient points stressed by him in his presentation of the subject are enumerated below:

(1) In his attempt to provide a precise syntactical interpretation of the terms "universal" *(kullī)* and "particular" *(juzʾī)*, Ṭūsī points out that in any consideration of terms the range of what they can designate should be established. A particular term can designate exactly one entity in the actual domain, whereas a universal term designates, or can designate, more than one. His discussion of various kinds of proper names *(Asās*, p. 17) shows an awareness on his part of the possibility of reducing definite descriptions of terms to a combination of properties needed in specifying the term in question.

(2) Of significance is his notion that "universality" and "particularity" can be considered in the context of the predication of a sentence, rather than as semantical determinants of the interpretation of the sentence in question. For example, "humanity" is a universal with respect to its predication of individual but is a particular with respect to its relation to "animality."

In this context Ṭūsī's attempts to explicate universals and particulars can be clarified by pointing to their formulation in the contemporary language of determinables and determinates. Accordingly, if "an expression $\emptyset$ of a level *n* is predicated of an expression Ψ of a level *n-1* in a well-formed sentence," then "Ψ is a particular relative to $\emptyset$," and "$\emptyset$ is a universal relative to Ψ."

(3) A further distinction is drawn by him between the intensional aspect of universality *(kullī)* and the extensional feature of the sum of a class. This distinction is carefully couched in a language in which the accent falls on the explication of concepts rather than on references to existents. The only extension recognized by him is a sum *(majmūʿ)* of distinct parts *(juzʾiyyāt)*, and the only intension to which he refers is related to individuals by definition *(ḥadd)*. The existence of the extension (or the sum) depends upon the existence of the individuals, whereas the nonexistence of the case would not destroy the meaning of the intension (the concept).

(4) Whereas for some cases the extension (the sum) can be conceived, the totality of an intension may not be conceivable. For example, if there were only two human beings in the world, we could conceive the total extension of "humanity," although we might have some difficulty in conceptualizing the meaning of the concept of humanity, which is the intension of the term "humanity."

(5) While instances of an extended class are limited, the applicability of

the intension (concept) is unlimited. Even though the class as a whole cannot be a part of particular elements in the class, an intension is attributed to its members.

(6) The extension (the sum) does not exist in the particular individuals which comprise the extended sum, whereas the intension is attributed to every individual in the extended sum. For example, the set of all numbers is not a number, whereas "numerosity" is a feature of every particular number.

Another way of making this point is to assert that the conception of the extension is not presupposed in the conception of a particular, whereas the conception of the intension (the concept) is presupposed in the conception of the essence of a particular.

Ṭūsī follows ibn Sīnā and Fārābī in specifying the meaning of substance in the Aristotelian manner, as *(a)* not existing in a subject; *(b)* not having an opposite; *(c)* not admitting of degree; and *(d)* being the subject of contrary qualities in respect to its substratum [*Asās*, p. 37].[87] Nevertheless, in the actual exposition of the idea of substance we observe its syntactical presentation in terms of the exposition of the concepts of "universality" and "particularity." That Ṭūsī is less involved in an "ontological inquiry" than in a syntactical conceptual inquiry is indicated by the manner in which he relativizes such concepts as "being a substance" and "being a genus." In the sense that they are universals, universals exist only in the intelligence and in the understanding, but when they are instantiated in a particular *(Asās*, p. 29), they exist as actual entities. An entity "x" is a "genus" in relation to another entity "y," if "y" is a "species" with respect to "x." If "x" is a "species" with respect to some "y," then it is possible to consider "x" as a "genus" with respect to some "z," if "z" is of a lower level than "x." A "real" *(ḥaqīqī)* species is an entity which contains only particular existents under which nothing can be subsumed. That Ṭūsī's concept of this hierarchy of being is conceptual rather than ontological is apparent from the following example: Any given concept which is regarded as a genus may be transcended by another concept which is also considered a genus; however, we cannot conceive *(taṣawwar)* an idea *(maʿnā)* of infinitive levels. It follows, then, that there is such a concept as the highest genus, called "*jins al-ajnās*" (literally, the genus of genera), and that the same entity can actually be termed a species with respect to a higher level of predication, while it can be considered as a genus with respect to a lower level of predication. If we grouped entities in terms of species *(nauʿ)*, then the highest level conceivable would be the highest species *(nauʿ-i ʿālī)* [*Asās*, pp. 29–30].

Ṭūsī is well aware of the difference between talking about kinds of entities, such as "a body," and actual entities, which may include a set of specific bodies. For example, from the names he assigns to them, calling the former "*jism-i taʿlīmī*" and the latter "*jism-i ṭabīʿī*," we learn that a syntactical exposition of a bodily substance is distinguished from its naturalistic exposition, a task which belongs to science.

In sum, we note that Ṭūsī's analysis of substance is closely related to the distinction he upholds between science and metaphysics. It is possible to reconstruct his theory in two forms: either (1) by taking his distinction as the set of his premises for his proposition about substances, or (2) by considering his theory about substances as a premise from which to justify a distinction between science and philosophy. The arguments are sufficiently interrelated to permit either construction.

PROBLEMS IN EXTENDING OUR ANALYSIS TO SELECTED WORKS OF ISLAMIC PHILOSOPHY

So far our analysis has shown how an analytical and syntactical construction of the concept of substance both supports and illustrates the attempts of Muslims, like Ṭūsī and ibn Sīnā, to distinguish between philosophy and science. As has been illustrated, many texts corroborate our interpretation of the views of Ṭūsī and ibn Sīnā on this issue. In the light of the data cited, there might be a temptation to consider our exposition of "substance" as typical and representative of nearly all Islamic philosophical works on this subject. Among the works of virtually every Islamic philosopher, including ibn Sīnā and Ṭūsī, we find several texts with the following special features: the use of "substance" in the context of metaphysics, which Rescher calls "evaluative metaphysics," rather than in a context which places emphasis on the peripatetic traditional discussions of the categories.[88]

In such writings substances such as "the self" *(nafs,* ψυχή, *anima, jān)* and "intelligences" *(ʿaql,* νοῦς) are usually cited in support of doctrines which resemble what Rescher calls "the value of personhood." Even a cursory inspection of these texts leaves one with the impression that the concept of substance is used in a way which differs from our presentation.

Since an extensive illustration of this point is beyond the scope of this paper, we refer the reader to other studies in which he will find such an illustration as well as a discussion of several other issues associated with this topic.[89] But we shall offer some evidence in support of our thesis that the syntactical interpretation of substance should be restricted to the kinds of texts we have mentioned.

For instance, ibn Sīnā speaks of the "union" *(paiwand)* of persons with the Necessary Existent. It is obvious that such a relation cannot be applicable to substances, for the reason that the only kind of changes substances can undergo are generation and destruction, and for the additional reason that the Necessary Existent, according to ibn Sīnā's explicit assertion, is not a substance.[90]

Ibn Sīnā confronts us, then *(i)* with a doctrine which is definitely non-

Aristotelian, i.e., any "mystical union" of *psyche* with the "prime mover" would be nonsensical in Aristotle's system, while mystical union with the Necessary Existent is a cornerstone of ibn Sīnā's thesis, and *(ii)* with a complicated process of *paiwand* which no simple syntactical apparatus, such as the "particular-universal" distinction we have outlined, can express or explain adequately.[91]

The material we have quoted here stands by no means isolated in ibn Sīnā's works. For example, in *Maᶜrifat al-Nafs* we find a reference in which the soul is first described as belonging to the category of relation *(iḍāfa)* but is also viewed as a substance, *jauhar*, after the death of the body[92] and, upon reaching its ultimate state, is connected with the Divine Light.[93]

Similarly, in *al-Ishārāt wa-l-Tanbīhāt*, he points to the mystical intelligence as the only means by which we can relate to the Necessary Existent.[94] Consequently, it is highly questionable whether the syntactical view of substance described previously explains adequately the view of substance presented in ibn Sīnā's mystical writings.

When we consider the mystical works of Ṭūsī, we discover a similar situation. For example, in his *Auṣāf al-Ashrāf* and the *Aghāz wa Anjām*, Ṭūsī follows the point of view outlined by ibn Sīnā. In his analysis of *tauḥīd* (a mystical state denoting "unity") he claims that there is essentially no existent but the highest being, "God," and that which has emanated from God.[95]

The point here is that for the mystic there should be no differentiation between the phenomenon of the self and world. Thus, "the value of personhood" is explained in terms of the self's non-alienating union with the ultimate being—the world, which is essentially similar to ibn Sīnā's *paiwand* with the Necessary Existent. Ṭūsī points out that the aim of *ittiḥād* (unification) with God is to become one *(yagānagī)* with God.[96]

Higher than *ittiḥād* is the stage of *waḥdat* (unity), in which all differentiation between persons and the world is to disappear.[97] A similar doctrine of the "unity of being" *(waḥdat al-wujūd)*, in which the traditional substantial differentiations among entities are repudiated, is also advocated in another work of Ṭūsī. In *Aghāz wa Anjām*, Ṭūsī notes, for instance, that only through the annihilation (of the ego) of persons can we be led to an eternal mode of existence in God.[98]

Numerous discussions in this text deal with and support similar themes. For example, he considers the perfection of the mystic to be that stage in which there will be no essential *(dhātī)* difference between him and God. Such a depiction permits the union of the soul *(nafs)* with God in a process of self-realization, where God would be the last stage in the process of the soul's self-realization.[99]

It is not necessary to stress that this doctrine of *waḥdat al-wujūd* and the related themes to which we have pointed in the texts of Ṭūsī and ibn Sīnā are by no means as clear as we wish them to be. But a part of the noticeable confusion and complexity is specifically due to the fact that these doctrines deal with a process which cannot be explained by our traditional Aristotelian notion of substance. And this mystical tradition, it should be noted, cannot be overlooked or dismissed as theosophy or magic, if only for the reason that any objective inspection of the Islamic philosophy, not limited to what was available to the Latin and Hebraic translators, reveals a vast amount of material written about the themes of *waḥdat al-wujūd* and similar doctrines. So far we have pointed out a few examples in philosophy, but it is actually in the later medieval Persian poetry that such philosophical themes find their major expression, as the following few lines will illustrate:

(1) Rūmī:

Let me be emancipated from this soul *(nafs)* and this bodily element [lit. air]

Neither alive nor dead do I have a source of Grace *(faḍl)* but God.[100]

(2) Ḥāfiẓ:

I shall not cease to seek until my perfection is reached

When my life reaches the life [source] of life—when this life leaves the body.[101]

(3) Jāmī:

The entire world is but an image

It is but a ray of that Beauty.[102]

(4) Aṭṭār:

Let your self be annihilated, so that all the birds [mediums] of the way

Make way for you in the everlasting state in [His] Court.[103]

These are but a few of thousands of lines which one familiar with Persian literature might cite on the theme of "the unity of being" *(waḥdat al-wujūd)*. It is well known that one does not find in such poems a systematic exposition, that is, an attempt to produce a valid argument from well established premises about the truth of this doctrine, for treatments of such a nature belong to philosophy rather than to the realm of poetry. Nonetheless, the existence of such poems suggests that themes such as *waḥdat al-wujūd* which are related to a non-Aristotelian view of nature, stand not in isolation in the Islamic traditi-tradition; instead, they are essential aspects of the Islamic *Weltanschauung*, and, taken in such a context, help to clarify the philosophical doctrines which are part of the same tradition, e.g., the nature of the soul. One cannot dismiss the mystical texts of ibn Sīnā and Ṭūsī as "incidental" but should consider them as integral parts of their philosophy. The first consequence of such an acceptance would be greater caution in applying the definition of "substance" found in texts such as *Asās* to the "self" described in Ṭūsī's mystical works, in spite of the fact that Ṭūsī asserts in the *Asās* that the self is a substance. Having discussed this particular issue, let us note some of the possible results of our inquiry.

We close our paper with remarks of a philosophical as well as a methodological nature. Methodological distinctions, such as "analytic," "synthetic," and "essence-existence," should be judged not only in isolation by themselves or by their ontological meaning, but rather, by their use. Such distinctions may frequently be useful to the philosopher for the reason that they allow him to undertake a legitimate study in conceptual analysis without demanding that his work ultimately relate to the existents.

It appears that both Ṭūsī and ibn Sīnā made use of the two-fold meaning of "substance" in their works for the purposes we have indicated. To the methodological remarks already put forward, we should append that the analysis of "substance," like the analysis of other concepts, with which for lack of space we have not dealt here, should not be restricted to the works of Near Eastern philosophers written in the analytical, classical style of Greek philosophy. This is particularly true with regard to philosophers in the eastern part of the Islamic world, since almost every one of them wrote mystical texts containing ideas which were obviously harmonious with the rich *ṣūfī* tradition, especially in poetry, and were received at least in part by an audience familiar with their analytic writings. One problem upon which scholarly attention should focus is whether the analytical and mystical works are consistent in content. To complete an adequate inquiry on this topic, we should specify what we mean by these respective traditions and on what particular problem we have focused our attention, as has been illustrated elsewhere.[104] We should note that if the philosophers regarded their analyses not as descriptions of existents, but as analyses of concepts, then they would not be restricted to the construction of only one philosophical model.

A philosopher endowed with such freedom could develop an analytic of essences in the language of the mathematician, a set of physical substances in the scientific terminology, and a nonalienating doctrine of the unity of being for the mystic. But regardless of whether or not such a tentative hypothesis is correct, at least one recommendation should be made at this point. If we study the primary sources of Near Eastern philosophy, as we have attempted to do in the case of "substance," we may expose new trends and doctrines. These new insights may question, if not disprove, the old cliché that Near Eastern philosophy is a derivation of Greek philosophy and Islamic theology. For in addition to being part of the heritage of the world, Islamic philosophy and secular sciences may have messages and insights to offer which make them worthy of a study on their own terms.

It is our hope to have added to such insight through the data presented in this paper in support of the thesis that in Islamic philosophical texts, as for instance, in Ṭūsī's *Asās*, a distinction is drawn between "philosophy" and "science," a distinction which is corroborated by syntactical treatments of the important concept of "substance."

NOTES

[1] Ṭūsī, *Asās al-Iqtibās*, ed. M. Muddras-Raḍawi (Tehran, 1948) (hereafter cited as *Asās*). This text is mentioned in N. Rescher's *The Development of Arabic Logic* (Pittsburgh, 1964), p. 198, and in Carl Brockelmann, *Geschichte der arabischen Literatur*, 2 vols., 2nd ed. (Leiden, 1943–49); 3 suppl. vols. (Leiden, 1937–43). See 1, BK. 2, p. 673. Brockelmann mentions 59 texts of Ṭūsī, whereas Raḍawī lists 113 items, including minor letters, in addition to 21 works of doubtful authorship, Brockelmann, ibid., pp. 670–76; Raḍawi, pp. YJ–YH. *Khāwja Naṣīr* al-Dīn Ṭūsī Abū Jaʿfar Muḥammad ibn al-Ḥasan Abī Bakr (b. 18 Feb. 1201; d. 26 June 1274) is best known for his works on astronomy and ethics and a commentary on ibn Sīnā's *al-Ishārāt wa-l-Tanbīhāt*. The last work mentioned ed. S. Dunya in 4 vols. (Cairo, 1960). The most popular text of Ṭūsī, his *Akhlāq-i Nāṣirī*, has been translated into English as *The Nasirean Ethics*, by G.M. Wickens (London, 1964). See *Encyclopaedia of Islam*, 1st ed., vol. 4 (Leiden, 1913-42): 980-82; B.H. Siddīqī, "Naṣīr al-Dīn Ṭūsī", in *A History of Muslim Philosophy*, ed. M.M. Sharif, vol. 1 (Wiesbaden, 1963): 560–80; M. Madrisī, *Sarguzasht wa ʿaqāid-i Falsafiyya Khāwja Naṣīr al-Dīn Ṭūsī* (Tehran, 1954); S.H. Nasr, *Science and Civilization in Islam* (Cambridge, Mass., 1968), pp. 321–28.

[2] On the *Isagoge*, including Boethius' translation, see *Commentaria in Aristotelem Graeca*, ed. A. Busse 1, vol. 4, pt.1 (Berlin, 1887). For a discussion of Porphyry's *Isagoge* in Islam, see I. Madkour, *L'Organon d'Aristote dans le monde arabe* (Paris, 1934), pp. 70–75; A. Badawi, *La transmission de la philosophie au monde arabe* (Paris, 1968), pp. 105–106; M. Steinschneider, *Die Arabischen Ubersetzungen aus dem Griechischen* (Graz, 1960), pp. 75–78, 136–37; F.E. Peters, *Aristoteles Arabus* (Leiden, 1969), pp. 8–9; F.E. Peters, *Aristotle and the Arabs* (New York, 1968), pp. 79–87. On the controversy between ibn Sīnā's and Porphyry's views, see J. Finnegan, "Avicenna's Refutation of Porphyrius" in *Avicenna Commemoration Volume*, ed. V. Courtois (Calcutta, 1956), pp. 179–86. For two criticisms of Porphyry's views, see (1) E.A. Moody, *The Logic of William of Ockham* (1935; repr. New York, 1966), pp. 65–117; and (2) R.I.Aaron, *The Theory of Universals*, 2nd ed. (London, 1967), pp. 1–17. The remarks on the lack of studies on this text appear in Rescher's *The Development of Arabic Logic*, p. 198, where he translates the title as "The Bases of Learning in Logic,"

[3] *Asās*, p. yb. Of the nine books of *al-Manṭiq* of *al-Shifā'*, the following have been edited: (i) vol. 1, *The Isagoge*, ed. A.F. Ahwani (Cairo, 1959); (ii) vol. 2, *Categories* (*al-Maqūlāt*), ed. M. Khodeiri, A.F. Ahwani, G. Anawati, and S. Zayed (Cairo, 1959); (iii) vol. 4, *Syllogism* (*al-Qīyās*), ed. S. Zayed (Cairo, 1964); (iv) vol. 5, *Demonstration* (*al-Burhān*), ed. A. Afifi (Cairo, 1956); (v) vol. 6, *Dialectic* (*al-Jadal*), ed. A.F. Ahwani (Cairo, 1965); (vi) vol. 7, *Sophistic* (*al-Safsata*), ed. A.F. Ahwani, rev. ed. (Cairo, 1958); (vii) vol. VIII. *Rhetoric* (*al-Khiṭāba*), ed. M. Salem, rev. ed. (Cairo, 1954); and (viii) *Poetics* (*al-Shiʿr*), ed. A. Badawi (Cairo, 1966).

4 For Raḍawī's remark see *Asās*, p. yb. The notion of the categories is not developed in the *Manṭiq* of the other encyclopedic works of ibn Sīnā, such as *al-Najāt* (Cairo, 1938), *al-Ishārāt wa-l-Tanbīhāt*, and *Dānish Nāma-i ʿAlāʾī: Manṭiq*, ed. M. Moʿin and S.M. Mashkut (Tehran, 1951).

[5] Aristotle uses different terms for the heading of this general division which might confuse his simple triadic division. For example, in *Metaphysica*, 993b 19–20, he mentions that "philosophy [τὴν φιλοσοφίαν] is a knowledge (science) [ἐπιστήμην]" that seeks truths, and proceeds to divide these into the theoretical and the practical. Cf. 1026b 4–6. In *Metaphysica*, 1025b 25, Aristotle mentions that "all thoughts [πᾶσα διάνοια]" are either productive, practical, or theoretical, and then proceeds to say, in *Metaphysica*, 1026a 18–20, that "theoretical philosophies" [φιλοσοφίαι θεωρητικαί] are divided into mathematics, physics, and theology. A few lines later he names the third subdivision "first philosophy" [πρώτη φιλοσ-

σοφία]. In *Ethica Nicomachea*, 1139a 25–31, he refers to thinking [διάνοια] as being either practical theoretical or productive, and proceeds to classify "scientific knowledge" [ἐπιστήμη] as a "virtue" [ἀρετή]. Our choice of the neutral word "inquiry" is based on the wish to avoid the apparent confusion; it follows the method of using a neutral word for a multimeaning Aristotelian term initiated by J. Owens in his *The Doctrine of Being in Aristotelian Metaphysics* (Toronto, 1963), see pp. 315–65.

[6] *Ethica Nicomachea*, 1139a 25–31. Later in the same text, Aristotle notes that "practical wisdom [φρόνησις]" is "a truth-attaining quality, concerned with action in relation to things that are good and bad for human beings." Ibid., 1140b3–6.

[7] *Ethica Nicomachea*, 1140a 26. For Aristotle, a mark of practical inquiry and of art [τέχνη], the paradigm of productive inquiry, is their concern with variable states; theoretical inquiry deals with constant states.

[8] *Metaphysica*, 1026a18–22. See above n. 5.

[9] *Metaphysica*, 1061b28–30, 1064a15–18, and *Physica*, 193b23–25.

[10] *Physica*, 193b22–194b15.

[11] See, for instance, "The subject matter of metaphysics is stated differently by Aristotle in different places." W.D. Ross, *Aristotle's Metaphysics*, 2nd. ed. rev. (London, 1958), I: lxxix, and "Aristotle himself appears conscious of no inconsistency or contradiction in these various designations. Even when raising a question of what today seems to bring an antinomy to the fore, he writes as though unaware of any real difficulty. He does not seem in the least perturbed by what the modern commentators find embarrassing if not impossible." J. Owens, *The Doctrine of Being*; see p. Merlan, "Greek Philosophy from Plato to Plotinus," in *The Cambridge History of Later Greek and Early Medieval Philosophy* (London, 1967) pp. 51–52; W. Jaeger, *Aristotle: Fundamentals of the History of His Development*, trans. R. Robinson, 2nd ed. (London, 1960), pp. 217–219.

[12] See *Metaphysica*, 1026a24 for "metaphysics" as equated with "first philosophy"; 1003a 20–21, 1060b31 for the study of "being qua being"; 982a1–3, 982b9–10 for the study of "principles and causes"; 1026a18–22 for "theology" as a branch of "theoretical inquiry," and for several references to God, see 983a8, 1026a19–23, 1064b1–6, 1069a30. His "motionless" features are mentioned in 1071b1–5, 1073b3 5; "everlasting" in 1071b1–5, 1073b3–5, and finally "separated from sensible entities" in 1073b3–5.

[13] Owens, *The Doctrine of Being*, p. 36; Jaeger, Aristotle, pp. 222–28.

[14] Ross, *Aristotle's Metaphysics*, I: lxxix.

[15] R. Carnap, for instance, states "In the discussion on the methodology of science, it is customary and useful to divide the language of science into two parts, the observational language and the theoretical language. The observational language uses terms designating properties and relations for the description of observable things or events." "The Methodological Character of Theoretical Concepts," in *Minnesota Studies in the Philosophy of Science*, ed. H. Feigel and M. Scriven (Minneapolis, 1965), p. 38; see C.G. Hempel, *Aspects of Scientific Explanation* (New York, 1965), p. 177.

[16] In *Analytica Posteriora*, 100a3–5, he mentions that perception-sensation leads to memory from which experience is derived, cf. *Metaphysica*, 980a28.

[17] *Ethica Nicomachea*, 1139b15.

[18] *Analytica Posteriora*, 100b5-16

[19] R. Carnap, *Philosophical Foundations of Physics* (London, 1966), p. 225.

[20] *De Generatione Animalium*, 736b25–30.

[21] See Owens, *The Doctrine of Being*, pp. 316–28 (especially p. 317). Here Owens uniformly replaces what is traditionally translated as "substance" by the term "entity." As far as substance is concerned, he asserts that "substance" and "essence" seem to be the only translations of φύσις. Neither is satisfactory for a detailed study of Aristotle's "Being," (pp. 148–49). In the same passage, Owens objects to Cherniss' use of "reality" to explain

this term. The reference is to the latter's *Aristotle's Criticism of Plato and the Academy* (New York, 1962), p. 364. Hope systematically uses "primary being" for the usual translations of "substance," *Aristotle's Metaphysics*, trans. R. Hope (Ann Arbor, 1960).

[22] See N. Rescher, *The Development of Arabic Logic*, p. 47; G.E. von Grunebaum, *Islam*, 2nd ed. (London, 1964), p. 117; S.H. Nasr, *Science and Civilization in Islam*, p. 126. Nasr points to the proximity between the Islamic view of "physics" and the teaching of Aristotle in its basic outlines. In the case of natural science, the concept is common in Islamic philosophy, e.g., Ghazālī, *al-Munqidh min aḍ-Ḍalāl*, ed. and trans. F. Jabre (Beirut, 1959), p. 23; *Maqāṣid al-Falāsifa*, ed. S. Dunya (Cairo, 1961), p. 136. Apparently there is a clear relationship between "nature" in Arabic *(ṭabīʿa)* and φύσις: see L. Massignon, "Nature in Islamic Thought," in *The Mystic Vision*, ed. J. Campbell (Princeton, 1968), pp. 315–18.

[23] See *Dānish Nāma-i ʿAlāʾī, Ilāhiyyāt,* ed. M. Mo'in (Tehran, 1952), chap. 1; *al-Shifāʾ*, *al-Ilāhiyyāt*, ed. G.C. Anawati, Mohammed Yousef Mousa, Solayman Dunya, and Saʿid Zayed (Cairo, 1960), 1:3, *et passim*; *ʿUyūn al-Ḥikma*, ed. A. Badawi (Cairo, 1952), p. 16. A similar division also appears in the later philosophers. For example, Suhrawardī divides sciences into practical (*ʿamalī*) and theoretical (*naẓarī*) sciences, subdividing the latter into metaphysics (*ilāhī*), mathematics (*riyāḍī*), and physics (*ṭabīʿī*); see *Šihābaddīn Yaḥyā As-Suhrawardī*, *Opera Metaphysica*, ed. Henry Corbin, vol. 1 (Istanbul, 1945), p. 196.

[24] D.M. Dunlop's translation of an unpublished manuscript, "The Existence and Definition of Philosophy, from an Arabic Text Ascribed to al-Fārābī," *Iraq* 13 (1951): 76–94, in which Fārābī acknowledges Aristotle's division of theoretical philosophy into natural, mathematical, and divine philosophy; see Fārābī, *Falsafat Arisṭūṭālīs*, Arabic text, ed. Muhsin Mahdi (Beirut, 1961), where Fārābī contrasts Aristotle's notion of natural science with what he calls "the voluntary science" (p. 72) and comments on the nature of metaphysics to which he refers as *ilāhī* and *ḥikma* (wisdom) as well as other designations, such as "the wisdom" (see p. 77).

[25] Fārābī, *Fuṣūl al-Madanī*, Arabic text ed. and trans. D.M. Dunlop (London, 1961), p. 166.

[26] D.M. Dunlop, "al-Fārābī's Introductory Risālah on Logic," *Islamic Quarterly*, 3 (1957), 227.

[27] Fārābī, *Iḥṣāʾ al-ʿUlūm*, ed. O. Amine (Cairo, 1968), pp. 111–23.

[28] *Alfarabi's Book of Letters* (*Kitāb al-Ḥurūf*), *Commentary on Aristotle's Metaphysics*, ed. M. Mahdi (Beirut, 1969). The text is divided into three parts: Particles and Categories; The Origin of words, Philosophy, and Religion; and Interrogative Particles. For our purposes, the most important section of this work is the first part which is divided into eighteen chapters. Each chapter is devoted to a verbal as well as a philosophical concept important in metaphysics; it may extend beyond discussions found in the Greek version of any one text because of its precise references to the Arabic usage of the terms analyzed.

[29] Ibid., pp. 97–105 discusses *jauhar* and its main use in Arabic as well as in philosophy. See pp. 110–28 for a discussion of *maujūd* as a word constructed to convey the concept expressed in Greek, Persian, and Sogdian. The distinctions between the two concepts are very clear.

[30] Ibid., p. 102. He mentions that Aristotle's use of "first substance" concerns that which is not in a subject, while his use of "second substance" refers to universals.

[31] Ibid., pp. 97–98. Here Fārābī uses examples of sentences from ordinary Arabic to clarify the sense of *Jauhar*.

[32] Ibid., p. 102. In this passage, he is referring to the notion of "absolute substances" as well as the use of "substance" as an auxiliary to the thing in question.

[33] Ibid., p. 111 *et passim*.

[34] See Ibn Khaldūn, *The Muqaddimah*, trans. Franz Rosenthal, 2nd ed., vol. 3 (Princeton, 1967): 147–48, in which he mentions that in the "Physics" of *al-Shifāʾ*, Ibn Sīnā disagrees with Aristotle over many issues. Ibn Khaldūn himself describes four distinct steps in the

study of metaphysics so as to distinguish the study from physics, the subject of which is bodies and their motions, p. 152. See M. Mahdi, *Ibn Khaldūn's Philosophy of History* (Chicago, 1967), p. 76 for the fourfold division of theoretical sciences into logic, mathematics, physics, and metaphysics.

35 *ᶜilm* is used uniformly throughout most of his writings—even concurrently with other terms; e.g., *al-Shifā*ʾ, *al-Ilāhiyyāt* (*La Métaphysique*), ed. G.C. Anawati, Mohammad Yousef Moussa, Solayman Dunya, and Saᶜid Zayed, vol. 1 (Cairo, 1960): 4,5 *et passim. Ḥikma* usually means "wisdom" (σοφία), resembling the Persian term *khirād*; it is used extensively in ibn Sīnā's *ᶜUyūn al-Ḥikma*, ed. A. Badawi (Cairo, 1952), p. 17, *et passim*, and in the *Dānish Nāma-i ᶜAlāʾī, Ilāhiyyāt*, where *ᶜilm* and *ḥikma* appear together, pp. 1, 99, 100 *et passim. Dānish* is used only in Persian texts and is equivalent to the Arabic-Persian *ᶜilm* in ordinary usage and in poetry.

36 See *ᶜUyūn al-Ḥikma*, p. 17; *Al-Shifā*ʾ, *Ilāhiyyāt*, p. 4; *Dānish Nāma*, *Ilāhiyyāt*, pp. 1–3; *Najāt*, ed. M.S. Kurdi (Cairo, 1938), pp. 98, 198; *Fī Aqsām al-ᶜUlūm al-ᶜAqliyya* in *Tisᶜ Rasāʾil* (Cairo, 1908), p. 105; *Dānish Nāma-i Alāʾī, Ṭabīᶜiyyāt,* ed. S.M. Mishkāt (Tehran, 1952), p. 2.

37 *al-Shifā*ʾ, p. 3 *et passim.*

38 *Dānish Nāma*, *Ilāhiyyāt*, pp. 5, 8.

39 *ᶜUyūn al-Ḥikma*, p. 17.

40 Ibn Sīnā, *al-Ishārāt wa-l-Tanbīhāt*, ed. S. Dunya. We express this generalization not without some reservation; for example, in *al-Ishārāt wa-l-Tanbīhāt*, mystical experience rather than the "Necessary Existent" is emphasized and the political philosophy found in the *Shifā*ʾ (chap. 10) is absent from ibn Sīnā's other metaphysical texts.

41 For *taᶜlīmī*, see *al-Shifā*ʾ, p. 4, *Dānish Nāma*, *Ilāhiyyāt*, p. 3; for *farhang* see *Dānish Nāma passim.*

42 Ibn Sīnā's "physics" explicitly includes various sciences as subdisciplines, e.g., in his largest text, *al-Shifā*ʾ, "physics" comprises: (i) "physics proper" in four sections dealing with topics such as the nature of motion, the four elements, space and time; (ii) "The Heavens and the World" in ten chapters dealing with topics such as simple and composite bodies, the nature of the moon and the stars, and the problem of "infinity": (iii) "On Generation and Corruption," addressing itself to changes in the sublunary realm of bodies; (iv) "Action and Passion" in two sections, dealing with further changes in the class of elements, qualities such as coldness and heat, and the nature of sensible qualities; (v) "Metals and Meteorology" in two sections, discussing subjects such as mountains, water, temperature, metals, rainbows, and winds; (vi) the celebrated work on "The Soul" in five sections, including topics such as the definition of the soul, various faculties and kinds of souls, internal senses and the agent intellect; (vii) "the plants" in seven chapters, comprising the generation of plants, the principles of nutrition, distinctions among various kinds of plants, and the effect of temperature on plants; and (viii) "the animals" in nineteen chapters, observing distinctions among animals with respect to organs and internal elements, the various faculties of the animal genera, disease among animals, and differences of character among them.

For discussions of the various manuscripts of *al-Shifā*ʾ, see G.C. Anawati, *Muʾallafāt Ibn Sīnā*: *Essai de bibliographie avicennienne* (Cairo, 1950), pp. 29–79; Y. Mahdavi, *Bibliographie d'ibn Sīnā* (Tehran, 1954), pp. 125–74.

For editions of the "Physics," see the various publications directed by I. Madkour, particularly: (1) *Al-Shifā*ʾ: "Physics," 2. *The Heavens and the World*, 3. *Generation and Corruption*, 4. *Action and Passion*, rev. ed. text established Maḥmoud Qāssem (Cairo, 1969); (2) *al-Shifā*ʾ: "Physics," 5. *Mineralogy and Meteorology*; text established and ed. ᶜAbd el-Ḥalim Montasir, Saᶜid Zayed, ᶜAbdallah Ismaᶜil (Cairo, 1964), and, by the same authors, (3) *al-Shifā*ʾ "Physics," 7. *Plants* (*al-Nabāt*) (Cairo, 1965). Book. 6 of the "Physics," its *De Anima*, has been edited as *Avicenna's De Anima*, ed. F. Rahman (London, 1959), and Ibn Sīnā (*Avi-*

cenna): *Psychologie d'après son oeüvre Aš-Šifā'*, ed. and trans. Jan Bakoš, 2 vols. (Prague, 1956); *Fan-i Samā'-i Ṭabī'ī Az Kitāb-i Shifā'*, trans M. 'Ali Fūrūqī (Tehran, 1938), being a translation of the first Book of the "Physics" of *al-Shifā'* into Persian; ibn Sīnā, *Kitāb al-Shifā'*. Incomplete, 2 vols. (Tehran, 1886).

[43] P. Morewedge, "Philosophical Analysis and Ibn Sīnā's 'Essence-Existence' Distinction," *Journal of the American Oriental Society* 92 (1972), 425–35.

[44] N. Ṭūsī, *Akhlāq-i Nāṣirī*, ed. A. Tehrani (Tehran, 1967), pp. 14,45.

[45] The use of the expression "higher level" here implies that the objects of philosophy are more determinable than the objects of the science of an "inferior" level; thus, a study which investigates particular bodies on earth is considered as being on a "lower" level than the study which investigates the logical relationship between various aspects of the concept of a body, e.g., "dimension," "extension."

[46] For a more elaborate discussion of the distinction between "metaphysics" and "natural science" based on the general features of the former, see E.A. Moody, *The Logic of William of Ockham*, p. 118 *et passim*. E.A. Moody's discussion is based upon Ockham's view that metaphysics is not a discursive science. Aristotle makes some interesting remarks on this topic in *Analytica Posteriora*, 76b36 *et passim*.

[47] For a detailed theory of logic in medieval times as a theory of second intentions, see I.M. Bocheński, *A History of Formal Logic* (Notre Dame, 1966), pp. 154–56. Basically, the distinction is between entities of the first intention, which are outside of the soul, and entities of the second intention (*intentiones, ma'qūlāt)*, which are thought or conceptual entities. The latter constitute the subject matter of logic.

[48] Problems related to attempts of the ancient and medieval philosophers to use the concept of "real definitions" for analysis have been well criticized by contemporary philosophers. For example, see R. Robinson, *Definitions* (London, 1962), pp. 149–92. Presumably now no one would hold the view that the purpose of philosophizing is to define a concept such as "substance." An example of the application of the contemporary tools of analysis to classical philosophy is found in M. Lazerowitz, "Substratum," in M. Black, *Philosophical Analysis* (New Jersey, 1963), pp. 166–82. Contemporary discussions of this general problem in defining a concept by a single term are often expressed in reference to the presupposition of a picture theory of meaning in the doctrine of logical atomism. For a brief history of this issue, see J.O. Urmson, *Philosophical Analysis* (Oxford, 1963), especially pp. 130–62.

[49] Ibn Sīnā, *Livre des définitions*, ed. and trans. A.M. Goichon (Beirut, 1963), p. 23–25.

[50] Afnan claims that *gauhar* comes from the Middle Persian *gav* which means "to grow," *Philosophical Terminology in Arabic and Persian* (Leiden, 1964), p. 93. Ibn Sīnā makes extensive reference to "*gauhar*" and uses it interchangeably with "*jauhar*" in the *Dānish Nāma*, e.g., p. 11. The translation of "*gauhar*" as "*jauhar*" could not have started with ibn Sīnā because many philosophers prior to him made extensive use of "*jauhar*." For example, Kindī resorts to "*jauhar*" in his works, *Rasā'il al-Kindī al-Falsafīya*, ed. M. Abū Rīdah, 2 vols. (Cairo, 1950, 1953), pp. 10, 12, 14 *et passim*. Afnan points out that Ikhwān al-Ṣafā and Rāzī reportedly resorted to "*jauhar*" in their works. In Persian poetry, however, the use of "*gauhar*" is extensive as illustrated by poems of Jāmī and Ḥāfiẓ, *Divān-i Ḥāfiẓ*, ed. S.A. Anjūwi (Tehran, 1968), p. 87; *Divān-i Kāmil-i Jāmī*, ed. S.S. Gauharin (Tehran, 1964), pp. 5, 6, 17, 18, 23, 31–851, 853, *et passim*.

[51] Persian philosophers reverted apparently to the Arabic "*jauhar*" and ignored ibn Sīnā's attempt to popularize "*gauhar*." See S.Y. Suhrawardī, *Oeuvres Philosophiques et Mystiques*: vol. 2, *Oeuvres en Persan*; *Opera Metaphysica et Mystica*, vol. 3, ed. S.H. Nasr, (Tehran, 1970), pp. 6, 14, 31, 66 *et passim*. Afḍal ad-Dīn al-Kāshānī, *Muṣannafāt* vol.2 (Tehran, 1954): 591; in this text Kāshānī discusses the ten categories using the Arabic terms, omitting ibn Sīnā's Persian vocabulary presented in the *Dānish Nāma*.

[52] It corresponds to the first sense of *ens*, as Ockham states in *Summa totius logicae*,

I. c. xxxviii, clarifying it as "a concept which is common to all things and can be predicated of all things in the manner of quiddity, in the way that a transcendental term can be predicated in the manner of quiddity." *Ockham's Philosophical Writings*, ed. P. Boehner (New York, 1962), p. 90.

[53] *Dānish Nāma*, chap 3.

[54] Ibid., pp. 8–9.

[55] For a detailed analysis of this point, see P. Morewedge, "Philosophical Analysis and ibn Sīnā's 'Essence-Existence' Distinction," *Journal of the American Oriental Society* 92 (1972), 425–35.

[56] The notion of "common" (*ʿāmm*) is very confusing here. Obviously, Ṭūsī cannot mean that the concept of *a point* is presupposed in every experience in the sense that "being" (*hastī*) might be considered to be presupposed in every experience. His use of the concept of the *a point* may give us a clue that he is using *ʿāmm* as meaning simple, i.e., having no part, without being "a logical construction" out of other ideas (such as "uncle" can be explained in terms of "parent" and "brother"). In what may be called the "mystical cosmology" of a peculiar text attributed to ibn Sīnā, a point "*naughṭa*" has a special meaning. Here the author of the text states, "Know that the primary entity in the material universe is a point," elaborating on the theme that due to its simplicity, a point is the primary intelligible physical entity, presumably depicting the atom of fire. *Risāla dar ḥaqīqat wa kaifīyat-i silsila-i maujūdāt wa tasalsul-i asbāb wa musabbabāt*, ed. M. ʿAmid (Tehran, 1952), p. 17. However, there is no reason for us to assume that in the *Asās* Ṭūsī refers to this peculiar doctrine. The doctrine that "point" is primary is not new in Islamic philosophy. For an interesting discussion of the doctrine of the Pythagoreans on *point* as the beginning of dimensions, see W. K. C. Guthrie, *A History of Greek Philosophy*, 3 vols to date. (London, 1962), 1: 261.

[57] For examples of the metaphysical import attached to the concept of "being," note Heidegger's *Being and Time*, trans. J. Macquarrie and E. Robinson (New York, 1962). Here Heidegger cites the traditional features of "being" which resemble Ṭūsī's views, e.g., "indefinability" and "self-awareness" (p. 23). But Heidegger goes further in "investigating" being in terms of "*Dasein* (being-in-the-world)" and features such as "temporality" and "care." For Ṭūsī, as well as for ibn Sīnā, "being" does not pose any "philosophical problem"; it is merely the most determinable, the most indefinite concept, due mainly to the meaning of the term.

[58] For examples of type-theoretical languages, P. Andrews, *A Transfinite Type of Theory With Type Variations* (Amsterdam, 1965); A. A. Frankel and Y. Bar-Hillel, *Foundations of Set Theory* (Amsterdam, 1958), pp. 168–74; A. Church, "A Formation of the Simple Theory of Types," *Journal of Symbolic Logic*, 5 (1940): 56–68. In the context of "types" and "levels" of languages, "being" would be a sign of the highest level. For an interesting philosophical description of "determinables and determinates," see W. E. Johnson, *Logic* vol. 1 (reprinted New York, 1964): 173–75. According to this terminology, "being" is a supreme determinable. On the notion of "transcendental terms," note Moody's succinct explanation in *The Logic of William of Ockham*, pp. 45–46. Ṭūsī uses the term "being" in such a sense that it applies to both categorematic and syncategorematic terms.

[59] Several instances can be cited where both philosophers show an awareness of the differences between verbal and semantical relations. See *Dānish Nāma*, p. 37. Ṭūsī states that the intelligence (*ʿaql*) does not consider or necessarily presuppose a cause for "blackness" as a case of "color," or for "a triangle" as a case of "figure." Here there is a relationship between concepts as cases of "being." Ṭūsī observes, further, that when we note the existence (presence) of an actual patch of color or a triangular entity, we do seek its cause (or realization).

[60] See P. Morewedge, "Ibn Sīnā's Analysis of Metaphysical Concepts," *Philosophical Forum* (forthcoming).

[61] See N. Rescher, *Studies in Arabic Philosophy* (Pittsburgh, 1966), p. 50. Rescher's list includes *ayyu* for "quality," whereas the standard Arabic term is *kayfa*; Rescher also lists *kayfa* as "accident," whereas this term is usually rendered as *ᶜaraḍ*. Rescher's list is especially instructive, for it covers predicables (κατηγορούμενα) and special questions. See also A. Afnan, *Philosophical Terminology in Arabic and Persian* (Leiden, 1964). Afnan mentions an earlier Arabic list by ibn al-Muqaffaᶜ which differs from that of ibn Sīnā. Ibn Sīnā's list recurs throughout his works, e.g., *al-Najāt* (Cairo, 1938), p. 80. *al-Shifā'*: *al-Manṭiq*: *al-Maqūlāt*, ed. M. Khodeiri, G. Anawati, A. F. Ahwani, S. Zayed (Cairo, 1960), p. 93; *Dānish Nāma*, *Ilāhiyyāt*, pp. 29–31. *Kāshānī*, *Muṣannafāt*, 2: 591. In his Persian text, Kashānī uses the Arabic terminology; Ṭūsī does likewise in his *Asās* (pp. 34–59).

[62] Jaeger, *Aristotle*, pp. 167–227.

[63] D. J. Allan, *Aristotle*, rev. ed. (London, 1963), p. 111.

[64] Moody, p. 68, *et passim*. I. M. Bocheński, *A History of Formal Logic*, ed. and trans. I. Thomas (Notre Dame, 1961), p. 53. For Bocheński's discussion of different lists of the categories, see I. M. Bocheński, *Ancient Formal Logic* (Amsterdam, 1968), pp. 33–35; see C. Prantl, *Geschichte der Logik im Abendlande* vol. 1 (Leipzig, 1927): 207, n. 356.

[65] W. Kneale and M. Kneale, *The Development of Logic*, rev. ed. (London, 1962), p. 25.

[66] A.C. Lloyd, "Neoplatonic Logic and Aristotelian Logic," *Phronesis*, 1 (1955–56), 58–72; 2 (1957): 146–60. Plotinus, *The Enneads*, trans. S. McKenna, 2nd ed. rev. (London, 1956), p. 443.

[67] Lloyd, p. 65, 151; see *Enneads* VI. 1.

[68] *The Cambridge History of Later Greek and Early Medieval Philosophy*, ed. A. M. Armstrong (London, 1967), p. 79. W. D. Ross, *Aristotle* (New York, 1967), p. 27.

[69] G. E. M. Anscombe and P. T. Geach, *Three Philosophers* (London, 1961); Anscombe states for example, "Aristotle's intention was to find a complete list of fairly simple kinds of things, with significant logical differences between them, that might be said about a subject," p. 15. G. Ryle, "Categories," in *Logic and Language*, ed. A. Flew (New York, 1953), pp. 281–98. Ryle states, "In the main, Aristotle seems to content himself with taking ordinary language as his clue to the list of predicates, and so of types of predicates," p. 283.

[70] J. L. Ackrill, *Aristotle's Categories and De Interpretatione* (London, 1963), pp. 78–81.

[71] For translations into Arabic and various texts of the *Categoriae*, see F.E. Peters, *Aristoteles Arabus*, pp. 7–12; K. Georr, *Les Catégories d'Aristote dans leur versions syro-arabes* (Beyrouth, 1948).

[72] *al-Shifā'*: *al-Manṭiq*: *al-Maqūlāt*, pp. 4–5; *al-Shifā'*: *al-Ilāhiyyāt*, I, 93; *al-Najāt*, p. 208.

[73] The Stoics adopted four divisions of the categories and the concept of an "indefinite something" (τὸ τὶ). The four categories were (1) τὸ ὑποκείμενον (substratum-subject), (2) τὸ ποίον (quality), (3) τὸ πως ἔχον (state), and (4) τὸ πρός τί πως ἔχον (relation); τὸ τὶ represented the highest notion. See B. Mates, *Stoic Logic* (Berkeley, 1953), pp. 18–19; C. I. Khan, "Stoic Logic and Stoic Logos," *Archiv für Geschichte der Philosophie*, 51 (1969), 158–72; Bocheński, *Ancient Formal Logic*, p. 87.

[74] Ibn Sīnā lists the categories in the *Metaphysica of al-Shifā'*, p. 93, and in the *Metaphysica* of *Dānish Nāma*, pp. 28–31. For a discussion of the ibn Sīnian "categories," see I. Madkour's introd. to *al-Shifā'*: *al-Manṭiq*: *al-Maqūlāt*, pp. VII–XXVII.

[75] We are using "syntax" here in Carnap's sense of the term. See R. Carnap, *Symbolic Logic and Its Application*, p. 197–212.

[76] For an example of the constituents of "theoretical aspects," see R. Carnap, "The Methodological Character of Theoretical Concepts," in *Minnesota Studies in the Philosophy of Science*, ed. H. Feigel and M. Scriven, vol. 1 (Minneappolis, 1956): 38–78.

[77] See Jaeger, *Aristotle*, p. 46 for a nominalistic interpretation of Aristotle's doctrine of substance in the *Categoriae*. Jaeger questions seriously the composition of what we regard as Book Zeta. For a comprehensive defense of Aristotle's views expressed in this section, see

M. I. Woods, "Problems in Metaphysics Z," in *Aristotle*, ed. M.E. Moravcsik, pp. 215–38, and Allen, *Aristotle*, pp. 111–12.

[78] J. Owens, *The Doctrine of Being* pp. 137–54; Owens states, " 'Substance' and 'essence' seem the only two current translations of οὐσία. Neither is satisfactory for an express study of Aristotelian being." Ibid., pp. 148–49.

[79] Ibid., p. 143. In the attempt to present a consistent reconstruction of Aristotelian views, even a sympathetic interpreter like Moody notes a discrepancy in Aristotle's own usage and confusion regarding substance, *Logic of William of Ockham*, p. 137.

[80] P. Morewedge, "Philosophical Analysis and ibn Sīnā's 'Essence-Existence' Distinction," *Journal of the American Oriental Society*, 92 (1972), 425–35.

[81] Ibn Sīnā, *al-Shifā*ᵓ*: al-Manṭiq: al-Maqūlāt*, p. 96.

[82] Ibid., pp. 91, 95.

[83] Ibid.

[84] P. Morewedge, "Ibn Sīnā's Analysis of Metaphysical Concepts," *Philosophical Forum* (forthcoming).

[85] *Dānish Nāma*, p. 77.

[86] Ibn Sīnā, *al-Shifā*ᶜ: *al-Manṭiq*: *al-Maqūlāt*, pp. 95–111.

[87] These features, noted by Aristotle in the *Categoriae*, 4a5, *et passim*, were reiterated by Muslim philosophers, such as al-Fārābī, (e.g., *Kitāb al-Ḥurūf*, pp. 102–03), and ibn Sīnā: *Dānish Nāma*: *Ilāhiyyāt*, pp. 9–10; *Kitāb al-Ḥudūd*, p. 24; *al-Shifā*ᶜ : *al-Manṭiq*: *al-Maqūlāt*, p. 91, *et passim*; *al-Shifā*ᶜ : *Ilāhiyyāt*, I, 57, *et passim*.

[88] N. Rescher, "Evaluative Metaphysics," in *Metaphysics and Explanation* (Pittsburgh, 1964), p. 62.

[89] See, P. Morewedge, "Ibn Sīnā (Avicenna), Malcolm and the Ontological Argument," *The Monist*, 54, no. 2 (1970), 7234–49, where a nonsubstantial view of "the Necessary Existent" is described; "Ibn Sīnā's Concept of the Self," *The Philosophical Forum*, 2, no. 2 (Winter, 1969), for a discussion of logical problems encountered in any attempt to give a "substance" interpretation of ibn Sīnā's concept of "the self." See also "The Logic of Emanationism and Ṣūfism in ibn Sīnā," *JAOS* 91 : 4 (1971), 467–76 and 92:1 (1972), 1–18, where a distinction is made between a philosophical, a mystical, and religious interpretation of the relation between the "self" and "the ultimate being" with regard to ibn Sīnā's system.

[90] See P. Morewedge, "Ibn Sīnā's Concept of the Self"; *Dānish Nāma*, p. 102, for the view of "union"; ibid., p. 77, on the nonsubstantiality of "the Necessary Existent"; cf. *al-Shifā*ᵓ*: Ilāhiyyāt*, II, 354, for a privation of several properties from the Necessary Existent.

[91] *Dānish Nāma*: *Ilāhiyyāt*, p. 11; *al-Shifā*ᵓ: *al-Ṭabīᶜiyyāt*: *Kitāb al-Nafs*, p. 10.

[92] *Risāla fī Maᶜrifat al-Nafs wa Aḥwālihā*, in *Aḥwāl al-Nafs*, ed. A. F. Ahwani (Cairo, 1952), p. 186.

[93] Ibid., p. 183.

[94] *Al-Ishārāt wa-l-Tanbīhāt*, III, 53.

[95] *Auṣāf al-Ashrāf*, ed. H. Taqwā (Tehran, 1928), p. 65.

[96] Ibid., p. 66.

[97] Ibid., p. 67.

[98] Ṭūsī, *Aghāz wa-Anjām*, ed. I. Afshār (Tehran, 1957), p. 7.

[99] Ibid., p. 33.

[100] *Rūmī's Kulliyyāt-i Shams*, ed. B. Furauzānfar (Tehran, 1966), I, 31, poem 485.

[101] *Dīvān-i Ḥāfiẓ*, ed. S. A. Anjuwī (Tehran, 1968), p. 71.

[102] *Dīvān-i Kāmil-i Jāmī*, ed. H. Radi (Tehran, 1963), p. 100, poem 2026.

[103] *Aṭṭār's Manṭiq al-Ṭair*, ed. S. S. Gauharin (Tehran, 1964), p. 251, poem 4543.

[104] For a comparison of "the process" and "substance" theories of the self, see P. Morewedge, "Ibn Sīnā's Concept of the Self"; for a comparison of "a mystical," "a religious," and "a typically philosophical (Aristotelian)" depiction of the relationship between "man" and "God," see *id.*, "The Logic of Emanationism and Ṣūfism in ibn Sīnā."

THE ARABIC THEORY OF TEMPORAL MODAL SYLLOGISTIC

NICHOLAS RESCHER AND ARNOLD VANDER NAT

I. BACKGROUND REGARDING THE TREATISE AND ITS AUTHOR

Arabic manuscript codex OR 12405 of the British Museum contains a logical treatise entitled *Sharḥ Al-takmīl fī ʾl-manṭiq*, whose author is one Muḥammad ibn Fayḍ Allāh ibn Muḥammad Amīn al-Sharwānī.[1] Nothing further is independently known about him,[2] apart from what can be gleaned from this manuscript itself. The codex contains two treatises by this scholar, written in the author's own hand, in a somewhat cramped naskhī of twenty-three lines per folio. In addition to the text at issue (in folios 72–104), it contains also (in folios 1–70) his contemporary on the well-known tract *Al-Ḥāshiyah* (or *Al-Risālah) al-ṣughrā fī ʾl-manṭiq* of ʿAlī ibn Muḥammad al-Jurjāni al-Sayyid al-Sharīf (A.D. 1340–1413).[3] Al-Shirwānī is thus a late medieval Persian scholar of presumably the early fifteenth century who must be considered obscure in view of his nearly total absence from the manuscript tradition. One item of biographical information which can be gleaned from our text is that the author is the great-grandson of Al-Ṣadr al-Shirwānī Muḥammad Ṣādiq ibn Fayḍ Allāh ibn Muḥammad Amīn, also otherwise unknown.

Al-Shirwānī's treatise is of some interest because it enables us to confirm and extend in significant ways our information regarding the Arabic theory of temporal modal syllogistic as available from other sources.[4] This paper seeks to present the new light this source affords for our knowledge of Arabic logic. On the information now available it would seem that the theory of temporal modalities represents the most significant addition made by the medieval Arabic logicians to the body of logical material that they received from the Greeks. The entire subject has only begun to be studied in recent years, and until many more texts have been studied and analyzed our conclusions must remain provisional and tentative. Much work remains to be done before our feet can be set on firm ground. But already at this early juncture a claim can be entered with considerable assurance regarding the value and interest of such further work.

II. BASIC ELEMENTS OF THE ARABIC THEORY OF TEMPORAL MODALITIES: THE SIMPLE MODES

The theory of temporal modal syllogisms as presented in Arabic logical texts further qualifies the relation that the predicate bears to the subject in the four basic categorical propositions **A** ("All A is B"), **E** ("No A is B"), **I** ("Some A is B"), and **O** ("Some A is not B") in certain characteristic ways. For *simple* modal propositions two qualifications are added:

(1) a *modality* of one of the following four types
- i. ($\Box$): of necessity
- ii. ($\Diamond$): by a possibility
- iii. ($\forall$): in perpetuity
- iv. ($\exists$): in (some) actuality, or, sometimes

(2) a *temporality* qualifying the modality of one of the following four types
- i. (E): when the subject at issue exists; that is, during times of the existence of the subject.
- ii. (C): when the subject at issue exists and meets a certain condition as specified by the subject term of the proposition; that is, during times of the existence of the subject when it meets the condition stipulated by the subject term.
- iii. (T): when the subject at issue exists during a definite, specifiable time; that is, during a certain *specified* and determinate period of the existence of the subject (e.g., its youth).
- iv. (S): when the subject at issue exists during some indefinite, unspecifiable time; that is, during some *unspecified* and indeterminate period of the existence of the subject.

Note that the temporalities (T) and (S), being inherently time-restricted, do not allow of further qualification by the specifically temporal modalities $\forall$ and $\exists$.

In "order of strength" the four modalities are arranged as $\Box$, $\forall$, $\exists$, $\Diamond$, and may be termed necessity, perpetuity, actuality, and possibility, respectively. The order of strength of the temporalities E, C, T, S depends on their combination with modality. (Concerning these relative strengths see section VI below.) The four temporalities may be called the existential, the conditional, the temporal, and the spread temporality, respectively. Examples of categorical propositions displaying these temporalities are:

(E) All men are animals, as long as they exist.
(C) All writers move their fingers, as long as they write.
(T) All moons are eclipsed at the time when the earth is between it and the sun.
(S) All men breathe at some times.

In these examples modality has, for simplicity, been put aside.

The (simple) modal propositions arrived at by the full-scale use of this machinery are as shown in Table 1.

TABLE 1

STANDARD EXAMPLES OF SIMPLE MODES

(□E):	All men are rational of necessity (as long as they exist).[5]
(□C):	All writers move their fingers of necessity as long as they write.
(□T):	The moon is eclipsed of necessity at the time when the earth is between it and the sun.
(□S):	All men breathe of necessity at some times.
(∀E):	All men are rational perpetually (as long as they exist).
(∀C):	All writers move as long as they write.
(∃C):	All writers move while they are writing.
(T):	All writers move at the time they are writing.
(S):	All men breathe at certain times.
(∃E):	All men breathe (at some times).
(◇C):	All writers move with a possibility while they are writing.
(◇T):	The moon is eclipsed with a possibility at the time when the earth is between it and the sun.
(◇S):	All men breathe with a possibility at all times.
(◇E):	All writers move with a possibility (at some time).

By ringing the changes on the two factors of modality and temporality, fourteen theoretical combinations arise. Six of these, (□E), (□C), (∀E), (∀C), (∃E), and (◇E) are explicitly listed and discussed by al-Qazwīnī [ca. 1220–80], and he refers also to (□T), (□S), (∃C), and (◇C), though not giving them an explicit place in his inventory.[6] Al-Shirwānī explicitly recognizes all fourteen, and his presentation of them is summarized in Table 2. The more detailed analysis of these modal propositions is deferred until section VI below.

TABLE 2

SIMPLE MODES IN SHIRWĀNĪ

TYPE	NAME
I. Modes of Necessity	
□E	absolute necessary
□C	general conditional
□T	absolute temporal (#)
□S	absolute spread (#)
II. Modes of Perpetuality	
∀E	absolute perpetual
∀C	general conventional
III. Modes of Actuality	
∃E	general absolute
∃C	absolute temporary or absolute continuing (#)
T	temporal absolute (*)
S	spread absolute (*)
IV. Modes of Possibility	
◇E	general possible
◇C	possible continuing (#)
◇T	temporal possible (*)
◇S	spread possible or perpetual possible (*)

NOTE: An asterisk (*) marks those modes missing in Qazwīnī and (#) marks those which are recognized by Qazwīnī but not listed or discussed by him.

In an earlier publication,[7] the analysis of the Arabic temporal modalities was based on the *Risālah al-shamsiyyah*, the *Sun Epistle* of al-Qazwīnī al-Kātibī.[8] Al-Qazwīnī's treatment differs from that of al-Shirwānī in that in Qazwīnī the temporalities (S) and (T) never occur with simple but *only* with compound propositions and in that Qazwīnī's analysis does not include the mode (∃C). Presumably, Qazwīnī assimilated these simple modes under the temporality condition (E). (So with Ibn al-Assāl [ca. 1190–1250] who appears to assimilate the weak modes (∃C) and (◇C) and (◇T) with (∃E) and (◇E), interchanging ◇ and ◇ on the one hand and ∀ and ∃ on the other).[9] Apart from this difference, there is complete agreement between Qazwīnī and Shirwānī regarding the nature and nomenclature of simple modes. Shirwānī's treatment in effect extends Qazwīnī's on the side of temporal conditionalization.[10]

III. NEGATION AND CONVERSION FOR SIMPLE MODALITES

The rule of negation for simple modal propositions is as follows. Let the initial proposition to be negated take the form

(modality/temporality) P

Then its contradictory takes the form

(o-modality/temporality) ∼ P

Here the o-modality is the *modal opposite* of the initial modality (formed by interchanging □ and ◇ on the one hand and ∀ and ∃ on the other). Moreover, the initial categorical proposition P is replaced by its *contradictory* ∼ P, and the temporality remains unchanged.

It must be noted at this juncture that in analyzing the modal propositions of Shirwānī we are dealing with *modes of predication* (modality *de re)* rather than with strictly propositional modes (modality *de dicto)*: the issue is one of qualifying the relation of the predicate to the subject rather than qualifying an entire categorical proposition. For example, the modal proposition

(1) (∀E) (All men are animals)

is to be understood as

(2) All men are always animals

rather than as

(3) It is always true that all men are animals

The difference between (2) and (3) becomes more striking when we consider the modal proposition

(4) (∼ ∀E) (All men are animals)

If we view the qualifying mode here as operating on the categorical proposition "All men are animals" then (4) becomes

(5) It is sometimes true that some men are not animals

whereas Shirwānī would have (4) be understood as

(6) All men are not always (i.e., sometimes not) animals.

Thus, for example, with regard to the *absolute necessary* (□E) proposition and its contradictory, the *general possible* (◇E), the following situation obtains:

Original Proposition	*Contradictory*
(□E) (All A are B) = All A are (□E) B	Some A are (◇E) not B
(□E) (No A are B) = All A are (□E) not B	Some A are (◇E) B
(□E) (Some A are B) = Some A are (□E) B	All A are (◇E) not B
(□E) (Some A are not B) = Some A are (□E) not B	All A are (◇E) B

The results of applying the negation principles are set out in Table 3.

TABLE 3

Contradictories of Simple Modes

Original Proposition		Contradictory	
(□E) P	absolute necessary	(◇E) ~ P	general possible
(∀ E) P	absolute perpetual	(∃ E) ~ P	general possible
(∃ E) P	general absolute	(∀ E) ~ P	absolute perpetual
(◇E) P	general possible	(□E) ~ P	absolute necessary
(□C) P	general conditional	(◇C) ~ P	possible continuing
(∀ C) P	general conventional	(∃ C) ~ P	absolute continuing
(∃ C) P	absolute continuing	(∀ C) ~ P	general conventional
(◇C) P	possible continuing	(□C) ~ P	general conditional
(□T) P	absolute temporal	(◇T) ~ P	temporal possible
(T) P	temporal absolute	(T) ~ P	temporal absolute
(◇T) P	temporal possible	(□T) ~ P	absolute temporal
(□S) P	absolute spread	(◇S) ~ P	perpetual (spread) possible
(S) P	spread absolute	(∀ ∃) ~ P	absolute perpetual[11]
(◇S) P	perpetual (spread) possible	(□S) ~ P	absolute spread

The situation regarding conversion is more complex. The converse of a modal proposition (X)P is a modal proposition (Y)P° such that

(1) P° is a categorical converse (possibly by limitation) of P

(2) (Y)P° is the *strongest* modal proposition implied by (X)P.

In Table 7 below the relative strengths of modal propositions are indicated.

There seems to be no set procedure for obtaining converses other than the process of demonstration, either by *reductio* or by *supposition*. The results of such conversion demonstrations for the simple modal propositions are listed along with the results for compound modal propositions in Table 6 below. We illustrate the conversion procedure with the following examples.

1. $(\Diamond E)$ (All A is B) converts to $(\exists C)$ (Some B is A). Suppose not. Then, $(\forall C)$ (All B is not A), and this, together with the original, yields $(\forall E)$ (All A is not A). (For this first figure syllogism see Table 8 below.) But this conclusion is a contradiction.
2. $(\exists E)$ (All A is B) converts to $(\exists E)$ (Some B is A). Let us suppose that x is A, then x is B at some time, and hence some B is A at some time. (For a more explicit analysis of this argument, cf. section VI below.)

IV. THE COMPOUND MODES

Compound modes are formed from simple ones by conjoining to the simple modes a *restriction*. This restriction can take only one of the two forms:

1. $(\sim\forall E)$: with non-perpetuity
2. $(\sim\Box E)$: with non-necessity

However, the second form of restriction occurs only as a qualification of basic propositions whose temporality is existential, (E).

Taken by themselves, these restrictions qualify the relation of the predicate to the subject in exactly the same way as do the simple modes. For example:

$(\sim\forall E)$ (All A is B) $\equiv$ All A is non-perpetually B

$(\sim\Box E)$(All A is B) $\equiv$ All A is non-necessarily B

Moreover, letting P' be the *contrary* of P, we have the general equivalences:

$$(\sim\forall E)P \equiv (\exists E)P'$$

$$(\sim\Box E)P \equiv (\Diamond E)P'$$

Note thus the difference between $(\sim\forall E)P$ and $\sim(\forall E)P$, and between $(\sim\Box E)P$ and $\sim(\Box E)P$. (Our previous exegeses err in suggesting that it is the contradictory rather than the contrary that is at issue.)

The compound modes of categorical propositions are formed by qualifying the relation of the predicate to the subject by a simple mode-*cum*-restriction, so that in a compound mode there is a *twofold qualification* of the predication relation.

Thus, given a simple mode (X), we are to understand compound modal propositions as follows:

$(X \,\&\, \sim\forall E)$(All A is B) $\equiv$ All A is (X)B, and they are not-perpetually B
$\equiv$ All A is (X)B, and they are sometimes not B

$(X \,\&\, \sim\Box E)$(All A is not B) $\equiv$ All A is (X) not B, and they are not necessarily not B
$\equiv$ All A is (X) not B, and they are possibly B

The situation regarding the other categorical forms that are not displayed here is entirely analogous. Thus, for example, the general absolute ($\exists$E) can be compounded into the non-perpetual existential ($\exists$E & $\sim\forall$E) or the non-necessary existential ($\exists$E & $\sim\Box$E):

($\exists$E & $\sim\forall$E)(Some A is B) $\equiv$ Some A is sometimes B, and they are not always B
$\equiv$ Some A is sometimes B, and they are sometimes not B

($\exists$E & $\sim\Box$E)(Some A is B) $\equiv$ Some A is sometimes B, and they are not necessarily B
$\equiv$ Some A is sometimes B, and they are possibly not B

Some further examples of compound modal propositions are:

($\Box$C & $\sim\forall$E): All writers move of necessity as long as they write, but not perpetually.

($\Box$T & $\sim$AE) All moons are of necessity not eclipsed at the time of the quarter moon, but not perpetually.

($\Diamond$E & $\sim\Box$E): With a special possibility, all fires are cold.

Note here that an affirmative (negative) compound modal proposition is composed of an affirmative (negative) simple modal proposition and a negative (affirmative) general absolute or general possible.

The compound modes presented by Al-Shirwānī are set forth in Table 4. It does not appear that he considered this list to be exhaustive of all the obtainable compound modes. His considerations seem to have centered around those compound modes which were needed for conversion and—above all—for first syllogisms. (See Table 8 below.) For example, those compounds of possibility which are conspicuously absent in Table 4 are presumably missing because they *invariably* yield nonproductive syllogisms in the first figure.[12]

TABLE 4

COMPOUND MODES IN SHIRWĀNĪ

TYPE	NAME
I. Modes of Necessity	
□E & ∼∀E	non-perpetual necessary (*) (impossible combination)
□C & ∼∀E	special conditional
□T & ∼∀E	temporal
□S & ∼∀E	spread
II. Modes of Perpetuality	
∀E & ∼∀E	non-perpetual perpetual (*) (impossible combination)
∀C & ∼∀E	special conventional
III. Modes of Actuality	
∃E & ∼∀E	non-perpetual existential
∃E & ∼□E	non-necessary existential
∃C & ∼∀E	non-perpetual continuing (*)
T & ∼∀E	non-perpetual temporal absolute (*)
S & ∼∀E	non-perpetual spread absolute (*)
IV. Modes of Possibility	
◇E & ∼□E	special possible[14]
◇E & ∼∀E	non-necessary existential[15]

(*) Missing in Qazwīnī.

V. THE NEGATION AND CONVERSION OF THE COMPOUND MODES

The negation of a compound mode follows the negation of each of its component modes in the following way:

> Given an affirmative (negative) compound modal proposition, which is an affirmative (negative) simple modal proposition *conjoined* with a negative (affirmative) general absolute, or a negative (affirmative) general possible—its negation is the negation of the simple modal proposition *disjoined* with an affirmative (negative) absolute perpetual, or an affirmative (negative) absolute necessary.

For example,

$\sim(\forall C \;\&\; \sim\forall E)$ (All A is B) $\equiv$ Some A is not B while they are A, or they are perpetually B

$\sim(\Box S \;\&\; \sim\forall E)$ (All A is B) $\equiv$ Some A is not B possibly at all times, or they are perpetually B

Let us introduce some notation which will enable us to describe adequately the negation process for compound modes. Given a categorical proposition *P* let us define *P**, the pronominalization of *P*, as follows:

P	P*
All A is B	*they* (i.e., the A's at issue) are B
All A is not B	*they* (i.e., the A's at issue) are not B
Some A is B	*they* (i.e., the A's at issue) are B
Some A is not B	*they* (i.e., the A's at issue) are not B

We can now represent a compound mode $(X \;\&\; \sim\forall E)$, or $(X \;\&\; \sim\Box E)$ as follows:

$$(X \;\&\; \sim\forall E)P \equiv (X)P \;\&\; (\sim\forall E)P^*$$
$$(X \;\&\; \sim\Box E)P \equiv (X)P \;\&\; (\sim\Box E)P^*$$

and negation can be described as in Table 5.

TABLE 5

CONTRADICTORIES OF COMPOUND MODES

COMPOUND ORIGINAL	CONTRADICTORY
$(\Box E \;\&\; \sim\forall E)P$	$(\Diamond E) \sim P \vee (\forall E)P^*$
$(\Box C \;\&\; \sim\forall E)P$	$(\Diamond C) \sim P \vee (\forall E)P^*$
$(\Box T \;\&\; \sim\forall E)P$	$(\Diamond T) \sim P \vee (\forall E)P^*$
$(\Box S \;\&\; \sim\forall E)P$	$(\Diamond S) \sim P \vee (\forall E)P^*$
$(\forall E \;\&\; \sim\forall E)P$	$(\exists E) \sim P \vee (\forall E)P^*$
$(\forall C \;\&\; \sim\forall E)P$	$(\exists C) \sim P \vee (\forall E)P^*$
$(\exists C \;\&\; \sim\forall E)P$	$(\forall C) \sim P \vee (\forall E)P^*$
$(T \;\&\; \sim\forall E)P$	$(T) \sim P \vee (\forall E)P^*$
$(S \;\&\; \sim\forall E)P$	$(\forall E) \sim P \vee (\forall E)P^*$
$(\exists E \;\&\; \sim\forall E)P$	$(\forall E) \sim P \vee (\forall E)P^*$
$(\exists E \;\&\; \sim\Box E)P$	$(\forall E) \sim P \vee (\Box E)P^*$
$(\Diamond E \;\&\; \sim\forall E)P$	$(\Box E) \sim P \vee (\forall E)P^*$
$(\Diamond E \;\&\; \sim\Box E)P$	$(\Box E) \sim P \vee (\Box E)P^*$

The conversion process for compound modal propositions is essentially analogous to that for the simple modes. Given a compound mode $(X \,\&\, {\sim}Y)P$, its converse, if there is one, is a proposition $(Z)P^{\circ}$, where (Z) can be either simple or compound, such that

1. P° is the categorical converse of P
2. $(Z)P^{\circ}$ is the strongest modal proposition such that $(X\&{\sim}Y)$ P implies $(Z)P^{\circ}$

(For relative strengths of modal propositions, see section VI below.) Again, as for simple modes, the procedure for determining conversion is that of *demonstration*. Thus, for example, the special conventional converts to the non-perpetual absolute continuing, in the universal affirmative case:

> $(\forall C \,\&\, {\sim}AE)$ (All A is B) converts to $(\exists C \,\&\, {\sim}\forall E)$ (Some B is A). Otherwise, $(\forall C)$ (All B is not A) or $(\forall E)$ (they are A); so that $(\forall C)$ (All B is not A) or $(\forall E)$ (All B is A). But the first disjunct together with the original yields $(\forall C)$ (All A is not A), which is absurd, and the second disjunct together with the original simple mode yields (All B is B), which, with the original restriction $(\exists E)$ (All B is not B), in turn yields a pair of contradictories. (For these first figure syllogisms see Table 8 below.)

In Qazwīnī and Shirwānī there are three references to the "non-perpetual-about-some conventional": by Qazwīnī in *The Sun Epistle* †67/65 and †72/70, and by Shirwānī in the present text in Table 11 A (below) for the sixth mood **(AEE)** of the fourth figure.

In †67/65 Qazwīnī says that the universal negative general conditional and general conventional convert to the universal negative general conventional, and that the universal negative special conditional and special conventional convert to the *non-perpetual-about-some conventional*.

> The reason of this process in reference to the general conventional is that it is an *adherent* of both kinds of general propositions. The reason why the converted proposition is non-perpetual-about-some is because [if] it is not true that some B is with a general absolute C, [then] it is true by perpetuity that no B is C, and thus [this is] converted into perpetually no C is B. But the original proposition was [that no C is B as long as it is C but not perpetually, and so] that every C is B.

Now, the (partial) converse of $(\forall C \,\&\, {\sim}\forall E)$ (No C is B) that *adheres* to the generals is $(\forall C)$ (No B is C). Also, $(\forall E)$ (No C is B), which is All C is sometimes B, converts to Some B is sometimes C, which is $({\sim}\forall E)$ (Some B is not C). Thus the converse of $(\forall C \,\&\, {\sim}\forall E)$ (All C is not B) is $(\forall C)$ (All B is not C) & $({\sim}\forall E)$ (Some B is not C); and the latter is aptly called "the non-perpetual-about-some conventional." We note, thus, that (1) *only a universal negative* special proposition converts to a non-perpetual-about-some conventional;

and (2) the latter is a sort of halfway house between the universal negative specials and the particular negative specials—yet it is neither of them.

This interpretation is further verified by the fact that Shirwānī has the non-perpetual-about-some conventional as a conclusion for the mood **AEE-4,** where the syllogism does not yield a particular special proposition.

The conversion results for both simple and compound modes is given in Table 6. These results are not given by Shirwānī, but are taken from Qazwīnī, and Qazwīnī's account is supplemented by our own calculations. (In Table 6 we represent the *direct* converse of a universal negative proposition P, i.e., the converse *not* by limitation, as P°_{d}, and the converse of P by limitation as P°_{1}.)

TABLE 6

CONVERSION OF MODAL PROPOSITIONS ACCORDING TO CATEGORICAL FORM

	Original	**A, I** Converse	**E** Converse	**O** Converse
	(□E)P	(∃C)P°	(∀E)P°_{d}	—
	(∀E)P	(∃C)P°	(∀E)P°_{d}	—
	(□C)P	(∃C)P°	(∀C)P°_{d}	—
	(∀C)P	(∃C)P°	(∀C)P°_{d}	—
(c)	(∃C)P	(∃C)P°	—	—
(c)	(□T)P	(∃E)P°	—	—
(c)	(□S)P	(∃E)P°	—	—
(c)	(T)P	(∃E)P°	—	—
(c)	(S)P	(∃E)P°	—	—
	(∃E)P	(∃E)P°	—	—
	(◇X)P	— (*)	—	—
(c)	(□E & ∼∀E)P	(∃C & ∼∀E)P°	(∀E)P°_{d} & (∼∀E)P°_{1}(a)	—
(c)	(∀E & ∼∀E)P	(∃C & ∼∀E)P°	(∀E)P°_{d} & (∼∀E)P°_{1}	—
	(□C & ∼∀E)P	(∃C & ∼∀E)P°	(∀C)P°_{d} & (∼∀E)P°_{1} (#)	(∀C & ∼∀E)P°
	(∀C & ∼∀E)P	(∃C & ∼∀E)P°	(∀C)P°_{d} & (∼∀E)P°_{1}	(∀C & ∼∀E)P°
(c)	(∃C & ∼∀E)P	(∃C)P°	—	—
	(□T & ∼∀E)P	(∃E)P°	—	—
	(□S & ∼∀E)P	(∃E)P°	—	—
(c)	(T & ∼∀E)P	(∃E)P°	—	—
(c)	(S & ∼∀E)P	(∃E)P°	—	—
	(∃E & ∼∀E)P	(∃E)P°	—	—
	(∃E & ∼□E)P	(∃E)P°	—	—
	(◇E & ∼X)P	—	—	—

(c) Our own calculations.
(*) Not convertible in this categorical form.
(a) The non-perpetual-about-some perpetual, constructed in analogy with the non-perpetual-about-some conventional.
(#) The non-perpetual-about-some conventional.

VI. THE LOGICAL ANALYSIS OF MODAL PROPOSITIONS

We shall now attempt an analysis of the modal propositions considered thus far in terms of presentday symbolic notation. R_t is the basic operator for realization-at-time-*t*.[16] We shall make use of the following abbreviations:

$TQx = R_T(Qx)$	$\Box TQx = \Box R_T(Qx)$	$\Diamond TQx = \Diamond R_T(Qx)$
$SQx = R_S(Qx)$	$\Box SQx = \Box R_S(Qx)$	$\Diamond SQx = \Diamond R_S(Qx)$
$\exists Qx = (\exists t)R_t(Qx)$	$\exists\Box Qx = (\exists t)\Box R_t(Qx)$	$\exists\Diamond Qx = (\exists t)\Diamond R_t(Qx)$
$\forall Qx = (\forall t)R_t(Qx)$	$\forall\Box Qx = (\forall t)\Box R_t(Qx)$	$\forall\Diamond Qx = (\forall t)\Diamond R_t(Qx)$

In our symbolizations of modal propositions, *we shall systematically suppress the temporality condition (E)* relating to the existence of the subject.

Simple Modes of the A Proposition (All A is B)

TYPE	EXAMPLE	NAME
$(\Box E)$	$(\forall x)[\exists Ax \supset \forall\Box Bx]$	absolute necessary
$(\Box C)$	$(\forall x)[\exists Ax \supset \forall\Box(Ax \supset Bx)]$	general conditional
$(\Box T)$	$(\forall x)[\exists Ax \supset \Box TBx]$	absolute temporal
$(\Box S)$	$(\forall x)[\exists Ax \supset \Box SBx]$	absolute spread
$(\forall E)$	$(\forall x)[\exists Ax \supset \forall Bx]$	absolute perpetual
$(\forall C)$	$(\forall x)[\exists Ax \supset \forall(Ax \supset Bx)]$	general conventional
$(\exists C)$	$(\forall x)[\exists Ax \supset \exists(Ax \& Bx)]$	absolute continuing
(T)	$(\forall x)[\exists Ax \supset TBx]$	temporal absolute
(S)	$(\forall x)[\exists Ax \supset TBx]$	spread absolute
$(\exists E)$	$(\forall x)[\exists Ax \supset \exists Bx]$	general absolute
$(\Diamond C)$	$(\forall x)[\exists Ax \supset \exists\Diamond(Ax \& Bx)]$	possible continuing
$(\Diamond T)$	$(\forall x)[\exists Ax \supset \Diamond TBx]$	temporal possible
$(\Diamond E)$	$(\forall x)[\exists Ax \supset \exists\Diamond Bx]$	general possible
$(\Diamond S)$	$(\forall x)[\exists Ax \supset \Diamond SBx]$	perpetual possible

Compound Modes

$(\Box E \& \sim\forall E)$	$(\forall x)\{\exists Ax \supset [\forall\Box Bx \& \sim\forall Bx]\}$	non-perpetual necessary
$(\Box C \& \sim\forall E)$	$(\forall x)\{\exists Ax \supset [\forall\Box(Ax \supset Bx) \& \sim\forall Bx]\}$	special conditional
$(\Box T \& \sim\forall E)$	$(\forall x)\{\exists Ax \supset [\Box TBx \& \sim\forall Bx]\}$	temporal
$(\Box S \& \sim\forall E)$	$(\forall x)\{\exists Ax \supset [\Box SBx \& \sim\forall Bx]\}$	spread
$(\forall E \& \sim\forall E)$	$(\forall x)\{\exists Ax \supset [\forall Bx \& \sim\forall Bx]\}$	non-perpetual perpetual
$(\forall C \& \sim\forall E)$	$(\forall x)\{\exists Ax \supset [\forall(Ax \supset Bx) \& \sim\forall Bx]\}$	special conventional
$(\exists C \& \sim\forall E)$	$(\forall x)\{\exists Ax \supset [\exists(Ax \& Bx) \& \sim\forall Bx]\}$	non-perpetual continuing absolute

$(T \,\&\, \sim\forall E)$	$(\forall x)\{\exists Ax \supset [TBx \,\&\, \sim\forall Bx]\}$	non-perpetual temporal absolute
$(S \,\&\, \sim\forall E)$	$(\forall x)\{\exists Ax \supset [SBx \,\&\, \sim\forall Bx]\}$	non-perpetual spread absolute
$(\exists E \,\&\, \sim\forall E)$	$(\forall x)\{\exists Ax \supset [\exists Bx \,\&\, \sim\forall Bx]\}$	non-perpetual existential
$(\exists E \,\&\, \sim\Box E)$	$(\forall x)\{\exists Ax \supset [\exists Bx \,\&\, \sim\forall\Box Bx]\}$	non-necessary existential
$(\Diamond E \,\&\, \sim\Box E)$	$(\forall x)\{\exists Ax \supset [\exists\Diamond Bx \,\&\, \sim\forall\Box Bx]\}$	special possible

Concerning the symbolic rendition of modes, we take notice of only the following points. First, in adopting the symbolic machinery that we have, we assume here that all the usual quantificational and modal principles hold. Secondly, in the E-modes the existence condition has been suppressed; fully stated, $(\Box E)$ (All A is B), for example, would be $(\forall x)\ [(\exists t)\ R_t Ax \supset (\forall t)\ \Box R_t\ (Ex \supset Bx)]$. Thirdly, T and S modes are special time-instantiations, with regard to the existence of the subject, and accordingly, we use "T" and "S" as a time-constant.

Since the texts have very little to say about the implicational relations among modes, we must rely heavily on our symbolic interpretation of the modes to be able to say what relations hold. There is, in particular, a question concerning the relationship between the T-modes and the C-modes. As an example of the temporal absolute, (T), Shirwānī gives "All writers move at the time they are writing." Comparing this with the continuing absolute, $(\exists C)$, "All writers move while they are writing," we would conclude that Shirwānī holds that $\exists C \rightarrow T$. Table 7, then, presents the implicational relations among modes as we have calculated them. Note that the compound modes $(X \,\&\, \sim AE)$ and $(X \,\&\, \sim\Box E)$ both imply the simple mode (X).

TABLE 7

Relative Strengths of Modal Propositions

Simple Modes

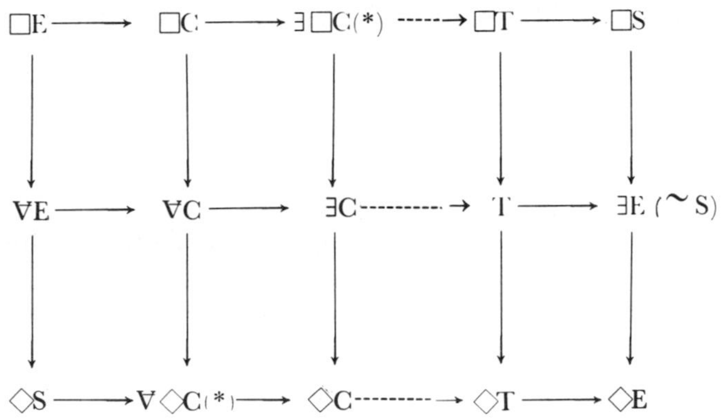

Compound Modes

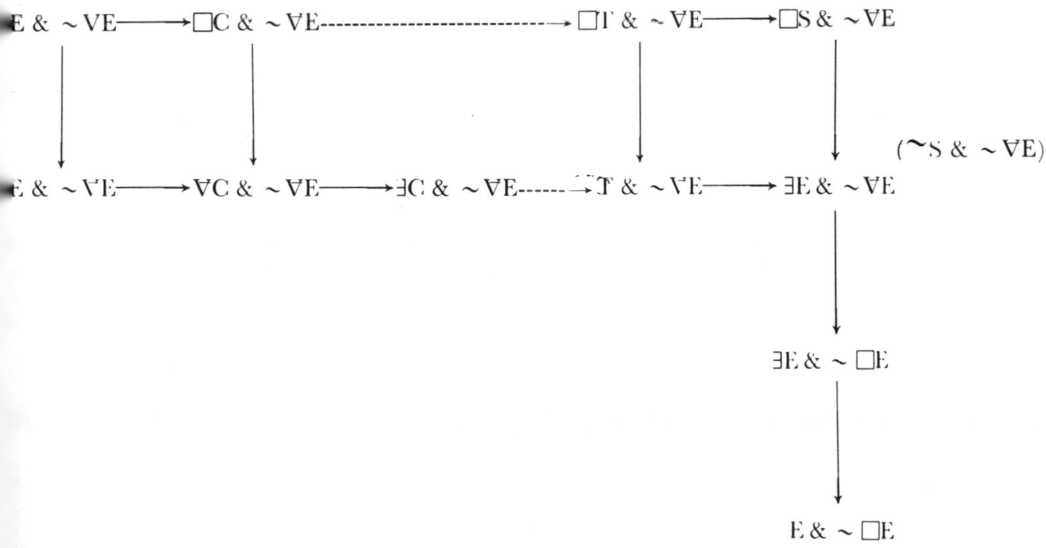

Missing in Shirwānī.

When we view modes in the light of the symbolic apparatus just presented, it becomes clear that we may distinguish five additional modes. In section VIII we will see that these five modes are necessary to describe adequately third figure syllogisms. We noted that the mode (T) is really a time-instantiation with respect to the temporality (E). In analogy we can also have a time-instantiation with respect to the temporality (C), thus giving rise to three new modes:

($\Box$TC) $(\forall x)[(Et)R_t Ax \; C \; \Box R_T(Ax \,\&\, Bx)]$

continuing absolute temporal

(TC) $(\forall x)[(Et)R_t Ax \; C \; R_T(Ax \,\&\, Bx)]$

continuing temporal absolute

($\Box$TC) $(\forall x)[(Et)R_t Ax \; C \; \Box \, R_T(Ax \,\&\, Bx)]$

continuing temporal possible

Also, since the temporality (S) is really the modality ($\exists$) combined with the temporality (E), we can, in analogy with the modes ($\Box$S) and ($\Diamond$S), distinguish the modes:

($\Box$SC) $(\forall x)[(Et)R_t Ax \supset (Et)\Box R_t(Ax \,\&\, Bx)]$

continuing absolute spread

($\Box$SC) $(\forall x)[(Et)R_t Ax \supset (At)\Diamond R_t(Ax \,\&\, Bx)]$

continuing perpetual possible

The compound modes that could be constructed out of the new modes are to be construed in analogy with the other compound, for example:

($\Box$TC & $\sim\forall$E) $(\forall x)\;\{(\exists t)R_t Ax \supset [\Box R_T(Ax \,\&\, Bx) \,\&\, \sim(\forall t)R_t Bx]\}$

To make the relation of the new modes to the other modes clearer, we present in Table 7A the relative strengths of the augmented number of simple modes. We shall in this table explicitly display the modalities ($\forall$) and ($\exists$) and the temporality (E) that are implicitly present in modes.

TABLE 7A

RELATIVE STRENGTHS OF MODAL PROPOSITIONS

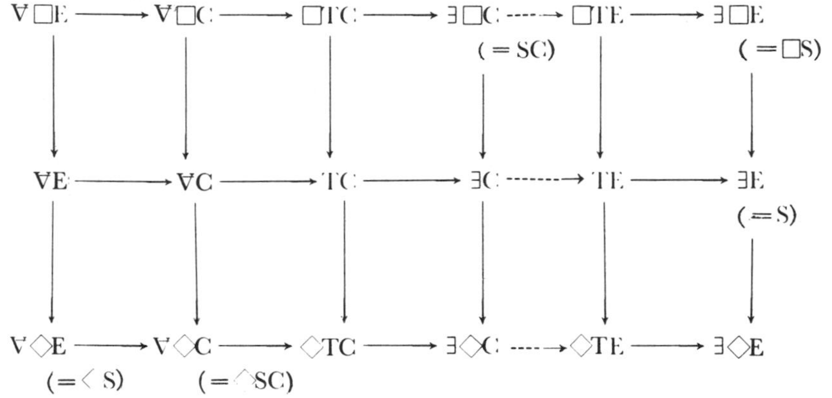

VII. FIRST FIGURE SYLLOGISMS

In "The Sun Epistle" *Al-Risālah al-shamsiyyah* († 81), al-Qazwīnī outlines the productive (i.e., valid) first figure modal syllogisms as follows:

> As to the first figure, its condition regarding modality is the actuality of the minor.[17] The conclusion here is the same as the major, if it [i.e., the major][18] is other than one of the two conditionals and the two conventionals; and otherwise [i.e., if the major *is* one of these four] it is like the minor when it is without the condition of the non-necessary or the non-perpetual, and the necessity which belongs specially [i.e., only] to the minor,[19] if the major is one of the two generals, and adding the non-perpetual to it if it is one of the two specials.

Shirwānī renders the last clause more clearly, and says:

> otherwise, it is like the minor, omitting the non-necessary, the non-perpetual, and the necessity special to it, if it was found in it, adding the non-perpetual of the major, if it was found in it.

Thus, the account for the first figure syllogisms is the following:

(1) The minor premise must be one of the seventeen actuals.[20]

(2) If the major is not one of (□C), (∀C), (□C & ∼∀E), and (∀C & ∼∀E), then the mode of the conclusion is that of the major.

(3) If the major is one of these four, then the mode of the conclusion is like that of the minor except that

   (a) the *restriction* of the conclusion is the same as the restriction of the major

   (b) the conclusion is necessitated if and only if both the minor and the major are.

(4) All other moods are nonproductive.

Shirwānī supplements this account by a table. Table 8 gives Shirwānī's table as he himself presents it (using, of course, the mode names, rather than our symbolic abbreviations). Note that the table deals only with condition (3). Concerning the first figure Shirwānī says that there are four valid categorical moods *(Barbara, Celarent, Darii,* and *Ferio)* and that each of these four, when mixed with modes, gives rise to 374 productive moods,[21] resulting from the seventeen actual minor modes times the twenty-two major modes—the fourteen simples and the eight standard compounds (□C & ∼∀E), (∀C & ∼∀E), (∃C & ∼∀E), (□T & ∼∀E), (□S & ∼∀E), (∃E & ∼∀E), (∃E & ∼ □E), and (◇E & ∼ □E).[22]

As far as we can determine the standard account given by both Qazwīnī and Shirwānī is correct except for moods containing the *continuing* modes (∃C), (∃C & ∼∀E), and (◇C) in the major. In these first figure moods, as far as can be ascertained by independent calculation, the conclusion is (∃E), (∃E & ∼∀E), and (◇E), respectively, for each of the seventeen minors.

TABLE 8(#)

	MAJOR / MINOR	□C	∀C	□C & ∼∀E	∀C & ∼∀E
1	□E	□E	∀E	□E & ∼∀E	∀E & ∼∀E
2	∀E	∀E	∀E	∀E & ∼∀E	∀E & ∼∀E
3	□C	□C	∀C	□C & ∼∀C	∀C & ∼∀E
4	□T	□T	T	□T & ∼∀E	T & ∼∀E(*)
5	□S	□S	S	□S & ∼∀E	S & ∼∀E(*)
6	∀C	∀C	∀C	∀C & ∼∀E	∀C & ∼∀E
7	∃C	∃C	∃C	∃C & ∼∀E	∃C & ∼∀E
8	T	T	T	T & ∼∀E	T & ∼∀E
9	S	S	S	S & ∼∀E	S & ∼∀E
10	□C & ∼∀E	□C	∀C	□C & ∼∀E	∀C & ∼∀E(*)
11	∀C & ∼∀E	∀C	∀C	∀C & ∼∀E	∀C & ∼∀E
12	□T & ∼∀E	□T	T	□T & ∼∀E	T & ∼∀E(*)
13	□S & ∼∀E	□S	S	□S & ∼∀E	S & ∼∀E(*)
14	∃E & ∼∀E	∃E	∃E	∃E & ∼∀E	∃E & ∼∀E
15	∃C & ∼∀E	∃C	∃C	∃C & ∼∀E	∃C & ∼∀E
16	∃E & ∼□E	∃E	∃E	∃E & ∼∀E	∃E & ∼∀E
17	∃E	∃E	∃E	∃E & ∼∀E	∃E & ∼∀E

(#) Displayed by Shirwānī.
(*) Proposed correction, in accordance with condition (3b), removing the necessity of the simple component mode.

The account of modal syllogisms in the first figure, duly corrected in the manner indicated, can be verified by means of the symbolic apparatus for modal propositions given above in section VI. It is intended to show by the following examples that the various claims regarding syllogistic results are in fact justified.

Example 1

major:	$(\Box E)$(All B are C)	1	$(\forall x)[\exists Bx \supset \forall \Box Cx]$	
minor:	$(\exists E \,\&\, \sim\forall E)$(All A are B)	2	$(\forall x)[\exists Ax \supset (\exists Bx \,\&\, \sim\forall Bx)]$	
conclusion:	$(\Box E)$(All A are C)	3	$\exists Ax$	
		4	$\exists Bx \,\&\, \sim\forall Bx$	2, 3
		5	$\exists Bx$	4
		6	$\forall \Box Cx$	1, 5
		7	$(\forall x)[\exists Ax \supset \forall \Box Cx]$	3-6

Example 2

major:	$(\Box C \,\&\, \sim\forall E)$(All B are C)	1	$(\forall x)[\exists Bx \supset (\forall \Box (Bx \supset Cx) \,\&\, \sim\forall Cx)]$	
minor:	$(\exists E)$(All A are B)	2	$(\forall x)[\exists Ax \supset \exists Bx]$	
conclusion:	$(\exists E \,\&\, \sim\forall E)$(All A are C)	3	$\exists Ax$	
		4	$\exists Bx$	2, 3
		5	$\forall \Box (Bx \supset Cx) \,\&\, \sim\forall Cx$	1, 4
		6	$\forall \Box (Bx \supset Cx)$	5
		7	$\exists Cx$	4, 6
		8	$\exists Cx \,\&\, \sim\forall Cx$	5, 7
		9	$(\forall x)[\exists Ax \supset (\exists Cx \,\&\, \sim\forall Cx)]$	3-8

Example 3

major:	$(\exists C)$(All B are C)	1	$(\forall x)[\exists Bx \supset \exists (Bx \,\&\, Cx)]$	
minor:	$(\forall C)$(All A are B)	2	$(\forall x)[\exists Ax \supset \forall (Ax \supset Bx)]$	
conclusion:	$(\exists E \,\&\, \sim\forall E)$(All A are C)	3	$\exists Ax$	
		4	$\forall (Ax \supset Bx)$	2, 3
		5	$\exists Bx$	3, 4
		6	$\exists (Bx \,\&\, Cx)$	1, 5
		7	$\exists Cx$	6
		8	$(\forall x)[\exists Ax \supset \exists Cx]$	3-7

Thus, for modal syllogisms in Shirwānī we have neither the Aristotelian rule of inference regarding modal syllogistics that the mode of the conclusion follows the mode of the major, since, as in Example 2, it sometimes follows the mode of the minor; nor the variant rule that it follows the minor, since, as in Example 1, it sometimes follows the major; nor the Theophrastean *(peiorem)* rule that it follows the mode of the weaker premise, since, as in

Example 1 it sometimes follows the mode of the stronger. Moreover, as in Example 3 the mode of the conclusion sometimes follows neither the mode of the major nor the minor. Note also that the restriction of the conclusion mode follows only the restriction of the major mode, as is illustrated in Examples 1 and 2. Note finally, as in Example 1, that when the major does not involve the temporality *(C)*, the Aristotelian rule that the conclusion follows the major *does* obtain. In general, however, the logical situation in the theory of temporalized modal syllogistic of the Arab logicians is far more subtle than in the Aristotelian tradition of their Greek precursors.

VIII. SECOND, THIRD, AND FOURTH FIGURE SYLLOGISMS

The first figure syllogisms were held to be self-evident, and the other syllogisms were to be demonstrated by reduction to the first figure by converting one or both premises, by interchanging the premises and converting the conclusion, or by *reductio ad impossibile*.

Concerning the second figure Shirwānī says that each of the four categorical moods *(Cesare, Camestres, Festino,* and *Baroco)*, when combined with modes, gives rise to 144 productive moods.[23] Shirwānī's account, in perfect accord with Qazwīnī,[24] is as follows.

There are two conditions for valid syllogisms in the second figure: (1) truth by perpetuity must pertain to the minor (so that the minor is □E or ∀E), or the major must be one of the convertible negative propositions (i.e., one of □E, ∀E, □C, ∀C, □C & ~∀E, and ∀C & ~∀E); (2) a possibility proposition may be used only when the other premise is necessary (and is, thus, □E, □C, or □C & ~∀E). If both these conditions are met, then: if either premise is perpetually true, then the conclusion is ∀E; if the major is a conditional or a conventional proposition, then the mode of the conclusion is like that of the minor except without restriction and without necessity. All remaining moods are nonproductive.

In Table 9 we reproduce Shirwānī's table for the second figure. This table concerns only the case when the major is a conditional or a conventional proposition. The remaining cases are as just described.

TABLE 9(*)

<table>
<tr><th colspan="2">MAJOR
MINOR</th><th>□C</th><th>□C & ~∀E</th><th>∀C</th><th>∀C & ~∀E</th></tr>
<tr><td>1</td><td>□C</td><td colspan="4" rowspan="4">∀C</td></tr>
<tr><td>2</td><td>∀C</td></tr>
<tr><td>3</td><td>□C & ~∀E</td></tr>
<tr><td>4</td><td>∀C & ~∀E</td></tr>
<tr><td>5</td><td>∃E</td><td colspan="4">∃E</td></tr>
<tr><td>6</td><td>∃C</td><td colspan="4">∃C</td></tr>
<tr><td>7</td><td>T</td><td colspan="4">T</td></tr>
<tr><td>8</td><td>S</td><td colspan="4">S</td></tr>
<tr><td>9</td><td>∃E & ~∀E</td><td colspan="4" rowspan="2">∃E</td></tr>
<tr><td>10</td><td>∃E & ~□E</td></tr>
<tr><td>11</td><td>∃C & ~∀E</td><td colspan="4">∃C</td></tr>
<tr><td>12</td><td>□T & ~∀E</td><td colspan="4" rowspan="2">T</td></tr>
<tr><td>13</td><td>□T</td></tr>
<tr><td>14</td><td>□S & ~∀E</td><td colspan="4" rowspan="2">S</td></tr>
<tr><td>15</td><td>□S</td></tr>
<tr><td>16</td><td>◇E</td><td colspan="2" rowspan="2">◇E</td><td colspan="2" rowspan="5">nonproductive</td></tr>
<tr><td>17</td><td>◇E & ~□E</td></tr>
<tr><td>18</td><td>◇C</td><td colspan="2">◇C</td></tr>
<tr><td>19</td><td>◇T</td><td colspan="2">◇T</td></tr>
<tr><td>20</td><td>◇S</td><td colspan="2">◇S</td></tr>
</table>

(*) Displayed by Shirwānī.

As regards the third figure, there are six valid categorical moods (*Darapti, Felapton, Datisi, Ferison, Disamis,* and *Bocardo*), each producing 374 valid modal moods. The account given by Shirwānī is the following.

The condition for syllogisms in the third figure is that the minor premiss be one of the actual propositions. When the major is a conditional or a conventional proposition, the mode of the conclusion is like the mode of the converse of the minor, removing the nonperpetual from it or adding it to it, according as the major is general or special. Otherwise, the mode of the conclusion is like that of the major. All other moods are nonproductive.

Table 10 is the table that Shirwānī presents for the third figure. And this table is correct in its entirety. The undisplayed cases, however, present some difficulty, in that the given account seems not to describe them adequately.[25] As far as can be ascertained by independent calculation, the given account is correct except (1) when the major is a *continuing* mode, the conclusion is like the major with (C) *weakened* to (E) in certain places, and (2) when the minor is true by perpetuity, the conclusion is like the major with (E) *strengthened* to (C) in certain places. Specifically, the situation is as follows:

When the major is □C, ∀C, □C & ~∀E, AC & ~∀E, the mode of the conclusion is like the mode of the converted minor removing the non-perpetual from it or adding it to it, according as the major is general or special. When the major is ∃C, ∃C & ~∀E the conclusion is like the major, with (C) weakened to (E) in all cases in which the modality (∀) does not pertain to the minor. When the major is ◇C, the conclusion is like the major with (C) weakened to (E) in all cases in which the modality (∀□) does not pertain to the minor.

Otherwise, when the major is not one of these seven, the following holds. When the minor is (□E), the conclusion is like the major, with (E) strengthened to (C) in all cases for which (∀) does not pertain to the major. When the minor is (∀E), the conclusion is like the major, with (E) strengthened to (C) in all cases for which (∀), (□), or (◇) do not pertain to the major. Otherwise (when the minor is neither (□E) nor (∀E),) the conclusion is like the major. (Note that we here have need of the new modes introduced in section VI.)

TABLE 10(*)

<table>
<tr><th colspan="2">MINOR \ MAJOR</th><th>□C</th><th>∀C</th><th>□C & ~∀E</th><th>∀C & ~∀E</th></tr>
<tr><td>1</td><td>□E</td><td colspan="2" rowspan="8">∃C</td><td colspan="2" rowspan="8">∃C & ~∀E</td></tr>
<tr><td>2</td><td>∀E</td></tr>
<tr><td>3</td><td>□C</td></tr>
<tr><td>4</td><td>□C & ~∀E</td></tr>
<tr><td>5</td><td>∀C</td></tr>
<tr><td>6</td><td>∀C & ~∀E</td></tr>
<tr><td>7</td><td>∃C & ~∀E</td></tr>
<tr><td>8</td><td>∃C</td></tr>
<tr><td>9</td><td>□T & ~∀E</td><td colspan="2">∃E(#)</td><td colspan="2">∃E & ~∀E(#)</td></tr>
<tr><td>10</td><td>□S & ~∀E</td><td colspan="2" rowspan="8">∃E</td><td colspan="2" rowspan="8">∃E & ~∀E</td></tr>
<tr><td>11</td><td>□T</td></tr>
<tr><td>12</td><td>□S</td></tr>
<tr><td>13</td><td>T</td></tr>
<tr><td>14</td><td>S</td></tr>
<tr><td>15</td><td>∃E & ~□E</td></tr>
<tr><td>16</td><td>∃E & ~∀E</td></tr>
<tr><td>17</td><td>∃E</td></tr>
</table>

(*) Displayed by Shirwānī.
(#) Here Shirwānī has (∃C) and (∃C & ~∀E).

Finally, as to the fourth figure, Shirwānī says that there are eight valid moods, five of which are categorically valid *(Bramantip, Dimaris, Camenes,* (*Fesapo,* and *Fresison)*, the other three (**AOO**, **OAO**, and **IEO**) being valid only when the negative premiss is one of the specials. Shirwānī, noting his departure from Qazwīnī, orders the moods as follows: (i) **AII**, (ii) **IAI**, (iii) **EAO**, (iv) **OAO**, (v) **EIO**, (vi) **AEE**, (vii) **AOO**, and (viii) **IEO**. The first, second, sixth, and eighth moods are reduced by interchanging the premises and converting the (resultant) conclusion; the third and the fifth by converting each of the premises; the seventh by converting the minor, resulting in a second figure syllogism; and the fourth by converting the major, resulting in a third figure syllogism.

The conditions for fourth figure syllogisms as given by Shirwānī are as follows. (1) Both premises must be actuals. (2) The negative propositions in the syllogism must be convertible. (3) In the sixth mood (**AEE**) the minor must be true by perpetuity (or else the major mode must be one of the six negative convertibles).[26] (4) In the seventh mood (**AOO**), the major mode must be one of the six negative convertibles. (5) In the eighth mood (**IEO**) the minor must be one of the two specials, and the major one of the negative convertibles.

The productive combinations in both the first and second moods (**AAI**, **IAI**) are 289. Their condition is that the premises be actual propositions. The mode of the conclusion is the converse of the minor, if the minor is $\Box$E or $\forall$E, or if both premises are in the six negative convertibles. Otherwise, the conclusion mode is ($\exists$E). All other cases are nonproductive. This situation is presented in table 11.

TABLE 11(*)

<table>
<tr><th>MINOR / MAJOR</th><th>□E</th><th>∀E</th><th>□C</th><th>∀C</th><th>□C & ∼∀E</th><th>∀C & ∼∀E</th><th>REMAINING ACTUALS</th></tr>
<tr><td>□E</td><td colspan="4" rowspan="6">∃C</td><td colspan="2" rowspan="2">(#)</td><td rowspan="9">∃E</td></tr>
<tr><td>∀E</td></tr>
<tr><td>□C</td><td colspan="2" rowspan="4">∃C & ∼∀E</td></tr>
<tr><td>∀C</td></tr>
<tr><td>□C & ∼∀E</td></tr>
<tr><td>∀C & ∼∀E</td></tr>
<tr><td>∃C</td><td colspan="2" rowspan="3"></td><td colspan="4" rowspan="2">∃C(**)</td></tr>
<tr><td>∃C & ∼∀E</td></tr>
<tr><td>remaining actuals</td><td colspan="4">∃E</td></tr>
</table>

(*) Not displayed, but only described by Shirwānī.
(#) Since the premises here are contradictory, the conclusion is problematic.
(**) Described by Shirwānī as (∃E).

The productive combinations in both the third and fifth moods (**EAO**, **EIO**) are 102. Their condition is the general condition that the premises be actual and that the negative premise be convertible. The moods are reduced to the first figure by converting each premiss. Thus, the conclusion is ∀E, if the major is ◇E or ∀E; otherwise, the mode of the conclusion is the same as the mode of the converted minor after removing the non-perpetual from it. All other cases are nonproductive. The situation is presented in table 11A.

TABLE 11A(*)

<table>
<tr><th colspan="2">MAJOR / MINOR</th><th>□E</th><th>∀E</th><th>□C</th><th>∀C</th><th>□C & ~∀E</th><th>∀C & ~∀E</th></tr>
<tr><td>1</td><td>□E</td><td colspan="2" rowspan="17">∀E</td><td colspan="4" rowspan="6">∃C</td></tr>
<tr><td>2</td><td>∀E [2]</td></tr>
<tr><td>3</td><td>□C</td></tr>
<tr><td>4</td><td>∀C</td></tr>
<tr><td>5</td><td>∀C & ~∀E</td></tr>
<tr><td>6</td><td>□C & ~∀E</td></tr>
<tr><td>7</td><td>∃C & ~∀E</td><td colspan="2">∃C</td><td colspan="2" rowspan="2">∃C(#)</td></tr>
<tr><td>8</td><td>∃C</td><td colspan="2">∃C(#)</td></tr>
<tr><td>9</td><td>□T & ~∀E</td><td colspan="4" rowspan="9">∃E</td></tr>
<tr><td>10</td><td>□S & ~∀E</td></tr>
<tr><td>11</td><td>□T</td></tr>
<tr><td>12</td><td>□S</td></tr>
<tr><td>13</td><td>T</td></tr>
<tr><td>14</td><td>S</td></tr>
<tr><td>15</td><td>∃E & ~□E</td></tr>
<tr><td>16</td><td>∃E & ~∀E</td></tr>
<tr><td>17</td><td>∃E</td></tr>
</table>

(*) Displayed by Shirwānī.
(#) Shirwānī has (∀C) here.

The productive combinations in the fourth mood (**OAO**) are 34. The condition for the fourth mood is the general condition that the premisses be actual and that the negative premise be convertible and, therefore, that the major be one of the specials. The conclusion is the same as in the third figure after converting the major. Since the major is a special proposition, the conclusion is thus the same as the converse of the minor. All other cases are non-productive. The situation is as displayed in Table 11B

TABLE 11B(*)

<table>
<tr><th colspan="2">MINOR \ MAJOR</th><th>□C & ∼∀E</th><th>∀C & ∼∀E</th></tr>
<tr><td>1</td><td>□E</td><td colspan="2" rowspan="8">∃C & ∼∀E</td></tr>
<tr><td>2</td><td>∀E</td></tr>
<tr><td>3</td><td>□C</td></tr>
<tr><td>4</td><td>∀C</td></tr>
<tr><td>5</td><td>□C & ∼∀E</td></tr>
<tr><td>6</td><td>∀C & ∼∀E</td></tr>
<tr><td>7</td><td>∃C & ∼∀E</td></tr>
<tr><td>8</td><td>∃C</td></tr>
<tr><td>9</td><td>□T</td><td colspan="2">∃E & ∼∀E(#)</td></tr>
<tr><td>10</td><td>□S</td><td colspan="2" rowspan="8">∃E & ∼∀E</td></tr>
<tr><td>11</td><td>□T & ∼∀E</td></tr>
<tr><td>12</td><td>□S & ∼∀E</td></tr>
<tr><td>13</td><td>T</td></tr>
<tr><td>14</td><td>S</td></tr>
<tr><td>15</td><td>∃E & ∼□E</td></tr>
<tr><td>16</td><td>∃E & ∼∀E</td></tr>
<tr><td>17</td><td>∃E</td></tr>
</table>

(*) Displayed by Shirwānī.
(#) Shirwānī has (∃E) here.

The productive combinations in the sixth mood (**AEE**) are 58. The condition for the sixth mood is the general condition that the negative premise (the minor) is one of the negative convertibles, and the particular condition that the minor is □E or ∀E, or that the major is a negative convertible. The conclusion mode is AE, if either premise is □E or ∀E; otherwise, the conclusion has the same mode as the converse of the minor. All other cases are nonproductive. The situation is as displayed in Table 11C.

TABLE 11C(*)

<table>
<tr><th colspan="2">MAJOR \ MINOR</th><th>□E</th><th>∀E</th><th>□C</th><th>∀C</th><th>□C & ~∀E</th><th>∀C & ~∀E</th></tr>
<tr><td>1</td><td>□E</td><td colspan="2" rowspan="17">∀E</td><td colspan="2" rowspan="2">∀E(#)</td><td colspan="2" rowspan="2">∀E</td></tr>
<tr><td>2</td><td>∀E</td></tr>
<tr><td>3</td><td>□C</td><td colspan="2" rowspan="4">∀C</td><td colspan="2" rowspan="4">The non-perpetual-about-some conventional</td></tr>
<tr><td>4</td><td>∀C</td></tr>
<tr><td>5</td><td>□C & ~∀E</td></tr>
<tr><td>6</td><td>∀C & ~∀E</td></tr>
<tr><td>7</td><td>□S & ~∀E</td><td colspan="4" rowspan="11">nonproductive</td></tr>
<tr><td>8</td><td>□T & ~∀E</td></tr>
<tr><td>9</td><td>□T</td></tr>
<tr><td>10</td><td>□S</td></tr>
<tr><td>11</td><td>T</td></tr>
<tr><td>12</td><td>S</td></tr>
<tr><td>13</td><td>∃C & ~∀E</td></tr>
<tr><td>14</td><td>∃C</td></tr>
<tr><td>15</td><td>∃E & ~∀E</td></tr>
<tr><td>16</td><td>∃E & ~□E</td></tr>
<tr><td>17</td><td>∃E</td></tr>
</table>

(*) Displayed by Shirwānī.
(#) Shirwānī has ∃C & ~∀E here.

The productive combinations in both the seventh and eighth moods (**AOO**, **IEO**) are 12. The condition for the seventh mood (**AOO**) is the particular condition that the major is one of the negative convertibles, and the general condition that the negative premise be convertible and, thus, that the minor premise is one of the specials. The mood is reduced to the second figure by converting the minor. All other cases are non-productive. The situation is displayed in Table 11D.

TABLE 11D(*)

<table>
<tr><th colspan="2">MINOR / MAJOR</th><th>□C & ∼∀E</th><th>∀C & ∼∀E</th></tr>
<tr><td>1</td><td>□E</td><td colspan="2" rowspan="2">∀E</td></tr>
<tr><td>2</td><td>∀E</td></tr>
<tr><td>3</td><td>□C</td><td colspan="2" rowspan="4">∀C</td></tr>
<tr><td>4</td><td>∀C</td></tr>
<tr><td>5</td><td>□C & ∼∀E</td></tr>
<tr><td>6</td><td>∀C & ∼∀E</td></tr>
</table>

(*) Displayed by Shirwānī.

The condition for the eighth mood (**IEO**) is the particular condition that the major be one of the negative convertibles and that the minor be one of the specials. The mood is reduced to the first figure by interchanging the premisses and converting the conclusion. All other cases are nonproductive. The situation is displayed in Table 11E.

TABLE 11E(*)

	MAJOR \ MINOR	□C & ∼∀E	∀C & ∼∀E
1	□E	∀C & ∼∀E(#)	
2	∀E		
3	□C	∀C & ∼∀E	
4	∀C		
5	□C & ∼∀E		
6	∀C & ∼∀E		

(*) Displayed by Shirwānī.
(#) Since the premises are contradictory here, the conclusion is problematic.

With the end of the fourth figure ends Shirwānī's account of temporal modal syllogisms, which, despite its occasional slips, reveals a detailed and sophisticated comprehension of temporal modal logic.

IX. CONCLUSION

We have come to the end of a long and somewhat complicated account, and a word of retrospective appraisal is in order. Clearly, the Arabic logicians of the Middle Ages were in possession of a complex theory of temporal modal syllogisms, which they elaborated in great and sophisticated detail. When one considers that all reasoning was conducted purely verbally, largely on the basis of somewhat vague examples, without any symbolic apparatus, and even without abbreviative devices, one cannot but admire the level of complexity and accuracy. The logical acumen of these medieval scholars was of a very high order indeed. But their successors were not able to maintain this standard. Sprenger remarks in his translation of the *Shamsiyyah* of Qazwīnī:

> [The paragraphs dealing with modalized inferences] are omitted in the translation because they contain details on modals which are of no interest. The last named four paragraphs are also omitted in most Arabic text books on Logic, and are not studied in Mohammedan Schools.[27]

When the logical tradition of Islam passed from the hands of the scholars into that of the schoolmasters, the standard of work went into a not surprising decline. The medievals had a firmer grasp.

NOTES

[1] During the academic year 1967/68, the senior author of this paper [N.R.] spent a sabbatical term in England with the support of a grant-in-aid from the American Philosophical Society to examine the Arabic logical manuscripts of several libraries, the British Museum in particular. This occasioned contact with the manuscript now at issue, and the assistance of the American Philosophical Society is herewith gratefully acknowledged. At this point the authors would also like to thank Mr. Zakaria Bashier for his help in translating and interpreting several passages of Shirwānī's text.

[2] He is nowhere mentioned in Brockelmann's *Geschichte der Arabischen Litteratur*.

[3] For this logician see N. Rescher, *The Development of Arabic Logic* (Pittsburgh, 1964), pp. 222–23.

[4] N. Rescher, *Temporal Modalities in Arabic Logic*, *Foundations of Language*, Supplementary Series, no. 2 (Dordrecht, 1966) is the basic publication, although the data presented there are extended and amplified in chapters 7–8 of *id.*, *Studies in Arabic Philosophy* (Pittsburgh, 1967). The materials with which the present paper deals make it possible not only to extend but also in important ways to correct the presentation of the theory given in these earlier discussions.

[5] The existence condition is usually unstated.

[6] It would seem that the six modes are considered by al-Qazwīnī to be the *standard* modes—modes, as he says, "into which it is usual to inquire."

[7] Rescher, *Temporal Modalities in Arabic Logic*.

[8] For this writer see *The Development of Arabic Logic*, pp. 203–204. Appendix I of Aloys Sprenger's *Dictionary of the Technical Terms Used in the Sciences of the Musulmans*, 2 (Calcutta, 1862), gives a text edition of this treatise, as well as an English translation of its nonmodal parts. (The latter are translated in *Temporal Modalities in Arabic Logic*).

[9] For Assāl's account of modal propositions see Rescher, *Studies in Arabic Philosophy*.

[10] Shirwānī seems to be following Qazwīnī's text quite closely. Besides the occurrence of amazing textual similarities between Shirwānī and Qazwīnī, Shirwānī explicitly refers to *The Sun Epistle* in his discussion of fourth figure moods.

[11] Note that the *logical structure* of the spread absolute and the general absolute appears to be the same. The difference between these two modes seems only to be that the spread absolute has connotations of *spreading* the attribution of the predicate, as in, for example, "all men breathe"—whereas the general absolute does not. On this matter see text section VI.

[12] In fact, when Shirwānī introduces the compound modes he specifically says that there are (only) *eight* of them, which he goes on to discuss, namely, ($\Box C$ & $\sim \forall E$), ($\forall C$ & $\sim \forall E$), ($\Box T$ & $\sim \forall E$), ($\Box S$ & $\sim \forall E$), ($\exists C$ & $\sim \forall E$), ($\exists E$ & $\sim \forall E$), ($\exists E$ & $\sim \Box E$), and ($\Box E$ & $\sim \Box E$). Later in the text, however, he mentions four additional modes. The matter seems to resolve itself if we consider the eight modes in question to be the *standard* modes "into which it is usual to inquire."

[13] Concerning this classification of modes, it should be mentioned that neither Qazwīnī nor Shirwānī presents a classification of modes as such. Rather, they refer to modes as follows. Propositions are either *actuals* or *possibles*. The actuals consist of the perpetuals, $\Box E$, $\forall E$; the conditionals, $\Box C$, $\Box C$ & $\sim \forall E$; the conventionals, $\forall C$, $\forall C$ & $\sim \forall E$; the continuing propositions, $\exists C$, $\exists C$ & $\sim \forall E$; the temporals, $\Box T$, T, $\Box S$, S, $\Box T$ & $\sim \forall E$, $\Box S$ & $\sim \forall E$· the existentials, $\exists E$ & $\sim \forall E$, $\exists E$ & $\sim \Box E$; and the general absolute, $\exists E$. The possibles are $\Diamond C$, $\Diamond T$, $\Diamond S$, $\Diamond E$, and $\Box E$ & $\sim \Box E$.

[14] Note here that ($\Diamond E$ & $\sim \Box E$) P-($\Diamond E$ & $\sim \Box E$) P', where P' is the contrary of P. Thus it is described in the text as "composed of two general possibles, one negative, the other positive."

[15] Note that ◇E & ~∀E is equivalent with ∃E & ~□E and is thus the nonnecessary existential all over again.

[16] For details regarding this operator see N. Rescher and A. Urquhart, *Temporal Logic* (New York and Vienna, 1971).

[17] In the earlier translation of †81, in *Temporal Modalities in Arabic Logic*, the first sentence was erroneously translated as "as to the first figure, its condition [obtains] in relation to the modality operative for the minor."

[18] In the earlier translation of †81, in *Temporal Modalities in Arabic Logic*, "than one of the two conditionals and the two conventionals" was interpreted as "if it (i.e., the minor) is other than...." In the light of Shirwānī's account, however, the present interpretation is clearly the correct one.

[19] In the earlier translation of †81, in *Temporal Modalities in Arabic Logic*, the phrase "and the necessity which belongs specially to the minor" was (erroneously) suppressed as a seeming corruption of the text.

[20] Note that there are twenty-two possible major, and minor, premises: fourteen simples and eight compounds, which divide into seventeen actuals and five possibles. Thus, for example, there are seventeen minor premises—the actuals—displayed in Table 8, since the possibles as minor are nonproductive.

[21] Note, thus, that when these 374 modal moods are combined with the four categorical moods there results a total of 1,496 productive syllogistic moods in the first figure alone.

[22] See note 12, section IV. Note also that the other four compounds never occur as premises in Shirwānī's account of the four figures, and that the eight standard compounds but for (∃C & ~∀E) are the only seven compounds discussed by Qazwīnī.

[23] The 2 perpetual minors times 17 actuals majors, plus the remaining 15 actual minors times the 6 negative convertible majors, plus the absolute necessary minor times the 5 possible majors, plus the absolute necessary major times the 5 possible minors, plus the 2 conditional majors times the 5 possible minors = 144 moods.

[24] And so it is with all four figures: Shirwānī is in perfect accord with Qazwīnī.

[25] For example, according to the text we are to have (∃E)P, (∀E)P', therefore, (∃E)P". Yet, it is clear that the following holds: (∀x) [∃Mx ⊃ ∃Px], (∃x) [∃Mx & ∀Sx], therefore, (∃x) [∃Sx & ∃ (Sx & Px)]. If our interpretation of modes is correct, the mood should thus be (∃E)P, (∀E)P', therefore, (∃C)P".

[26] This clause is missing in the text, but Qazwīnī's otherwise identical discussion contains the clause. Cf. Table 11A.

[27] A. Sprenger, *Dictionary of Technical Terms*, p. 25.

THE ETERNITY OF THE WORLD AND THE HEAVENLY BODIES IN POST-AVICENNAN PHILOSOPHY

Fazlur Rahman (1)

Aristotle claims to be the first philosopher to affirm that the world is ungenerated and incorruptible, i.e., eternal. That the series of movements is infinite—all movement and change implies potentiality which has to be realized by something already actual—that hence time which is the measure of movement is also infinite, is a fundamental Aristotelian thesis. Eternity is, therefore, implied in the very concepts of cause and movement. However, since in the actually constituted cosmos it is the highest celestial sphere that provides both movement and time and since the body of the heaven is incorruptible and ungenerated, it becomes the actual cause of the eternity of the world. In the Aristotelian doctrine of the eternity of the world, therefore, besides the logical implications of the concepts of cause and movement, the nature and constitution of the heavens play a central role. In the case of the celestial eternals, Aristotle asserts that they have no objective possibility but are necessary.[1]

Philoponus, in his *De Aeternitate Mundi Contra Proclum*, seeks to destroy both of these positions. He seeks to counter the argument from the eternity of movement and causation by, among other considerations, denying the possibility of infinity in the past. He also refutes specifically the eternity of the movement of the heavens, even if the eternity of the world soul is conceded, by a variety of arguments. From among these arguments one, which had a lasting tradition in Islamic philosophy, asserts that no body can have unlimited effects because the potentiality of all bodies is finite. Philoponus, therefore, believes in the creation of the world in time, including the celestial spheres which, he says, are a part of the world.[2]

In Islamic thought, a subtle but important change occurs in the emphasis on these two types of argument, viz., the one resting on the implications of the concepts of movement and cause and the other on the nature of the heavenly spheres. This change stems from Avicenna's doctrine of essence and existence, of the possible-in-itself and necessary-by-the-other on the one hand and the necessary-by-itself on the other. This doctrine itself emerges from the application of the Aristotelian concept of the potential and the actual within the context of the Neoplatonic emanationism, which alters the character both of Aristotelianism and Neoplatonism. The Neoplatonic emanation process occurs by a necessity which does not admit of possibility and, therefore, the eternal existents are not only eternal but necessary (although there is a difference between the timeless eternity of God and the temporal eternity of the heaven). According to Aristotle too, as we have seen, the possible and the necessary coalesce in the case of eternal existents like the heavens, and here Aristotle gives up the idea of a real or objective possibility, i.e. potentiality.

In Avicenna, however, every emanant from the first principle is infected with potentiality—including not only the heavenly spheres but the intelligences as well. In themselves they all deserve nonexistence and become existent only through God. Although, therefore, the world is eternal and the world process is in effect necessary, this necessity is borrowed. This principle of a borrowed and extraneous necessity tends to polarize God and the world and dislodges the heavens from an intermediate position of quasi-autonomy, which they occupied in Greek thought, into a position not intrinsically different from any other body in the world except that they exist eternally and cause the temporal world: for everything except God is intrinsically only a potential existent. That the motivation for this change is religious, without violating the demands of rational thought, is evidenced by the explicit statements of Avicenna himself to the effect that what religion really requires is this eternal dependence of the world upon God and not the temporal creation of the world "as is asserted by weak-minded theologians."[3]

Beyond this, Avicenna asserts that the body of the heavens is eternal and incorruptible and is moved by volition in a circle. He does not raise the question with regard to the body of the heavens as to how it can be eternal if it is afflicted by potentiality-in-itself. He raises this question with regard to the material bodies alone, as distinguished from the soul, and answers that the finitude of their existence arises from the combination of a particular form with a particular matter, while the soul, since it is simple, cannot suffer the finitude of existence. But in the case of the heavens, the matter of each is specific to its soul and, therefore, asserted to be inseparable from it. It is not clear, however, why the matter of a heaven should remain eternally united with its soul. The argument that the heavens have no contrary as opposed to sublunary bodies, which are subject to contraries, itself seems to beg the question, viz., why nonbeing, which is opposed to being, cannot occur to heavenly bodies.

Al-Ghazālī, in his refutation of the thesis of the eternity of the world, concentrates on the subject of eternity of movement and causation and regards infinity in the past as inconceivable. Since, then, al-Ghazālī regards both time and the world as created (he denies that there was time before creation), he naturally regards the heavenly bodies as created. Al-Ghazālī, therefore, does not deem it necessary to prove that all bodies are finite in their potentiality of existence and activity, as Philoponus had done. Indeed, al-Ghazālī, while treating questions of natural philosophy, denies causation and, therefore, any potentialities or objective possibilities in things—as a good Ashᶜarite.

Al-Ghazālī does not discuss the nature of time as such beyond his assertion that time is created and that this statement does not imply that there is a time before time.[4] In the Eastern Islamic philosophy after him, however, the nature of time assumes great importance with special reference to the problem of the eternity of the world. In these developments, al-Ghazālī's dictum that time is created, coupled with the assertion that there is no time before time, is reformulated in the sense of eternity of time and thus commits suicide, since this dictum is sufficient to prove the eternity of the world and the beginninglessness of time, and al-Ghazālī's further statement that "there was God without the world" is generally accepted in its "essential" sense but becomes irrelevant in its temporal sense. Thus we see that all post-Ghazalian philosophers, from Abuʾl-Barakāt to Mullā Ṣadrā, believe in the eternity of the world, whether they believe in the eternity of the heavens or not, whether they believe in creation or not. In this new setting, questions of the meaning of creation and the world-process and of whether the heavenly bodies possess infinitude of potentiality gain a fresh importance. In his *al-Mabāḥith al-Mashriqiya,* Fakhr al-Dīn al-Rāzī declares the problem of time to be insoluble and contents himself with stating different theories on the subject. In his commentary on Avicenna's *ᶜUyūn al-Ḥikma,* however, he gives credence to the view which is attributed to Plato, that time is a transcendent, self-subsistent substance. This substance, when it is related to eternal existents —like the intelligences (identified with angels)—is called *Sarmad* or timeless eternity (Greek *Aiōn*); when related to the world of change and movement as a whole it is called *Dahr* or eternity, and when the content of the world is related to it or, rather, when it is used as a referent to each of the emergents in the world of change, it is called *Zamān* or time. The world, as a whole, therefore constitutes eternity—which has been created by God timelessly.[5]

For al-Rāzī, therefore, time, transcending as it does the world-process, equally transcends the heavenly spheres and is not created by their circular movement. Indeed, he believes all bodies to be limited in their potentialities for effects and accuses the philosophers of inconsistency in their affirmation of the finitude of potentialities in the case of physical bodies but denial of finitude in the case of the body of the heavens.[6] Of course, once the *ontological* status of time is pushed beyond the world, it becomes immaterial whether all bodies or some bodies are limited or unlimited in their potentialities. The whole world, including the heavens, becomes ontologically subordinate to the reality of time and the assertion of the eternity of the world falls less heavily on the religious conscience, and eternity and creation become equivalent from this point of view.

This is what happens in the thought of Abūʾl-Barakāt al-Baghdādī. According to Abūʾl-Barakāt, the notion of time, although it arises in the mind initially from the phenomenon of movement, is, nevertheless, seen, on further examination to be independent of movement. The idea of duration, or persistence in time, is, in fact, found to be ontologically anterior to both movement and rest. It appears to envelop all existence, for existence cannot be imagined without time. It would therefore be truer to say that time is the measure of existence than to say that it is the measure of movement. We can, in fact, abstract from all movement in the world but cannot free ourselves from the notion of time. Further, not only is the world-process in time, but God, too, is in time. "Those people," says Abūʾl-Barakāt, "who have divested the existence of their Creator from time, say that He exists in Eternity. . . . These people have only changed the word 'time' but have not changed its concept and meaning. . . .When they are asked, 'What is Eternity?' they reply, 'it is lasting existence in which there is no movement (and change).' Now, 'lastingness' is a characteristic of duration and time. Thus, they have changed the word but the conceptual content is the same which can be related both to what moves and to what does not move." Abūʾl-Barakāt contends that time is indefinable because it is prior to everything except existence whose concomitant it is.[7]

God works in time, and the world-process depends on His direct and incessant creative activity. There are eternal existents like the intelligences and the heavens which are created by His eternally persistent will and there are transient existents which are created by His ever renewed will. "He wills and acts and acts and wills," "He creates and wills and wills and creates"—incessantly. Abūʾl-Barakāt criticizes philosophers for positing a series of emanants as intermediary agents for the world of change and movement. He castigates the function of the first intellect as source of multiplicity as a mere device forged by the philosophers to keep God immune from contamination with the process of change. If, he asks, the first intellect, while still being a simple intellect, can give rise to multiplicity, why cannot God do so?[8] That the motivation of Abūʾl-Barakāt is not merely philosophical but equally religious is shown by the fact that he regards God as directly answering prayers, as reliever from pain and deliverer from evil, etc. But he is also critical of theologians like al-Ghazālī who want to bring God directly into relation with the world but, in their anxiety to save God from change, take flight to the notion of an eternal, changeless will.[9]

God is, then, the creator of the world which is coextensive with Him. For creation as such does not necessarily imply time as does origination (*ḥudūth*). The world has, therefore, been timelessly created, although each particular unit in the world-process is originated by God in time conditional upon its antecedent. Certain parts of the world are eternal and never cease to be. The heavens are such existents, for their corruption is impossible. For proving the incorruptibility of the heavens, Abū ʾl-Barakāt uses the familiar argument that corruption comes about through change and change, being from one contrary to the other, cannot occur to the heavens since these have no contrary. The heavens, however, do not create anything since they themselves, like everything else in the world, are directly under the finger of God. Their eternal existence, therefore, is innocuous to religious sensitivity and is even quite compatible with it, for Islam does believe in angels—the eternal creations of God. Abū ʾl-Barakāt, in fact, states quite explicitly that the movers of the heavens are the angelic souls and he rejects the view that angels are necessarily free from contact with matter. He also insists that there exist many more stars than are visible to us and that each one of the stars is a living and ensouled body moving within its sphere round a fixed axis, without losing its fixed position within its sphere.[10]

Finally, two points should be borne in mind in connection with Abū ʾl-Barakāt's account. One is that it may be objected that if all existence is characterized by time, then time would be prior even to God's existence. Abū ʾl-Barakāt's answer is that time itself is not a self-subsistent existent (for otherwise another time will have to be postulated, in which time as an existent exists, and this would introduce an infinite regress): it merely is a concomitant of existence which it quantifies. But neither is time subjective, existing in the mind only. Just as volume or extension characterizes all bodies but does not exist apart from bodies, and is not a subjective existent, so does time behave vis-à-vis existence.[11] And just as body is both existentially and ontologically prior to volume, so is God prior to time and time is, in fact, His inseparable effect.[12]

The second important point is that a fundamental shift has begun to occur in the interrelationship between the terms "eternal *(qadīm)*" and "originated *(ḥādith)*" as applied to the world. We shall see later that Mullā Ṣadrā applies the term *ḥadīth* not only to the individual items in the world-process but to the world-process as a whole and the ability to do so he regards as his unique achievement in Islamic philosophy, i.e., the ability to say both that the world-process is eternal—beginningless and endless—and that it is *ḥādith* or originated. Mullā Ṣadrā's position seems to be facilitated by the doctrine of Abū ʾl-Barakāt. The first shift in this trend had been effected by Avicenna himself, as we have seen, when he introduced the notion of possibility *(imkān)* in his description of the world: the world is eternal but in itself it is only *mumkin*. In itself it only deserves nonexistence and its actual existence is, therefore, a genuine movement from possibility to actuality. But Avicenna, with his emanationism, could describe the relationship of God and the world only as cause and effect *(ʿilla* and *maʿlul)*. Abū ʾl-Barakāt, as we have seen, rejects al-Ghazālī and affirms the world to be an eternal process as does Avicenna. But, unlike Avicenna, he regards the world as a definite creative act of God—a *makhlūq*, rather than a necessary emanation-process; although creation *(khalq)* does not necessarily require the element of time, nevertheless it mediates between *qidam* and *ḥudūth*. Secondly, by attributing every *ḥādith* directly to the incessant creative will of God and bringing God into the flow of time, Abū ʾl-Barakāt removes the philosophic inhibition which creates the chasm, the unbridgeable hiatus between the *qadīm* and the *ḥādith*. If the world *as a whole* is still declared *qadīm* by Abū ʾl-Barakāt, it is not because the eternal cannot come into touch with the temporal but because the temporal series is beginningless since one cannot imagine a beginning for time. From Abū ʾl-Barakāt's proposition that the world is eternal but *makhlūq*, Mullā Ṣadrā will seek to arrive at the proposition that the world is eternal but *ḥādith*. But much ground still remains to be covered between the two propositions and it appears to me that the work of al-Suhrawardī al-Maqtūl is a necessary link between the two.

In the "Philosophy of Illumination" of Shihāb al-Dīn al-Suhrawardī, whose doctrine of being we have described elsewhere,[13] all Aristotelian categories are declared to be subjective and Avicenna's distinction between essence and existence in the objective world is equally rejected. Even possibility is considered by him to be neither real nor based on anything real. Aristotle could not have spoken of a real possibility in the sense of an objective potentiality of existence, for this would involve a vicious regress. We are, therefore, told that "the possibility of a thing precedes its existence (only) in the mind.'[14] and that possibility is a "mental perspective or abstraction *(iʿtibār dhihnī)*". In order to vindicate this stand, al-Suhrawardī assails the Aristotelian doctrine of matter and form and declares them both to be mere myths of the Peripatetics. For the dualism of matter and form al-Suhrawardi substitutes the dualism of darkness and light. Whereas matter is something positive, darkness is something totally negative: it is pure negation of being. One may say that the world of change and movement is an admixture of darkness and light but one must guard against attributing positive being to darkness. It would be truer to say that the world of change and movement has less of being than the transcendent world. Having gotten rid of all distinctions, al-Suhrawardī leads up to the only distinction he accepts in reality, viz., that between "more and less *(al-ashadd waʾl-anqas)*", which represents the core of his philosophy.[15]

Another line of thought developed to lead to the same thesis is his theory of knowledge. Self-awareness or self-manifestation *(ẓuhūr)* is the primordial form of knowledge. All indirect knowledge is characterized by nonbeing. When I know myself, this knowledge is nothing but my awareness that I am.

This is common to God and myself. In the ultimate analysis, however, the situation of self-awareness cannot be analyzed into two (or more) constituents, e.g., that I am and I am aware of myself. Being and awareness are not two things. Being itself means nothing but self-luminosity or self-manifestation. Being is, therefore, light. My self is, therefore, constituted by light just as the ultimate ego is. There is no differentia, no specific distinction that separates my ego from God's—except the category of "more and less" or "perfect and imperfect." Man is imperfect God or less of God, just as God is perfect man or more of man.[16]

The Peripatetics hold that when an accident, for example, black color, increases in intensity, a specifically new black color comes into existence: it is not the case that in intensification the previously existing black color remains and an additional black is adjoined to it. The essence of "black" itself changes. This doctrine is attacked by al-Suhrawardī and he declares that intensification of "black" or "hot" or "cold" does not bring into existence a new species of "black" or "hot" or "cold"; "more and less" implies no change in the essence which remains constant.[17] Secondly, the Peripatetics do not admit "more" or "less" in the case of substances but only in the case of accidents. Black becomes more black but a man does not become more of man nor an animal more of animal. This doctrine is also severely rejected by al-Suhrawardī. Substances admit of becoming more or less just as much as qualities do; cause, for example, being higher than its effects, must possess in a more perfect manner that which the effect possesses. But when a substance increases in strength and becomes more of itself, it does not become something different but remains selfsame.[18]

The upshot of this way of thinking is the establishment of pantheism. Reality, for al-Suhrawardī, shows no intrinsic differentiations; it is one single continuum punctuated only by "more and less," "more perfect and less perfect." But this difference does not bring about any intrinsic or essential change in the substance. The most perfect being is God, the light of lights—"the Light of the Heavens and the earth" as the Qurʾān calls Him. Light is essentially invisible and a ray of light is totally incorporeal in its essential nature. God is the most invisible and the most real. Light can, however, become accidentally visible when it comes to inhere in a substratum. Heavens and stars are such light. They are visible because they inhere in their substrata. Al-Suhrawardī classifies light-beings more or less on the same pattern as Muslim Peripatetics classify intelligences and heavenly souls. In al-Suhrawardī's language every higher light overwhelms the lower one and every lower one desires and loves the higher one. In Peripatetic language there is nothing corresponding to this sense of "overwhelming *(qahr)*" by the higher of the lower. Al-Suhrawardī also suggests that while the soul of the heaven desires the higher principle, the body of the heaven is moved through a kind of ecstatic rapture. After stating the view that the heavenly bodies move through a rational volition, he says that when a man tries hard and exerts himself to find truth, the truth suddenly dawns upon him like lightning.

> Thus, he continues, when you know that there is in you a pleasurable, bursting light, you can understand that heavens...are more deserving of spiritual pleasures and bursting lights. You will thus know that their movements are not merely [out of desire] for assimilation [to God] by way of bringing out their potential positions into actuality. For, if this had been the case, their circular movement would not have been on fixed poles. ... On the contrary, the heavenly bodies receive brilliant holy illuminations and thus motions arise from within them. These movements then lead to another illumination and thus illuminations lead to motions and motions to illuminations, (as the poet says):
>
> "When I recede into Absence, He appears,
> And when He appears, He renders me absent!"
> Sometimes, when you experience rapture, your body also moves.
> For the body is affected by the states of the soul,
> and the soul is affected by the states of the body."[19]

Of all the visible lights, the sun, the creator of the day, is most exalted and sublime and deserving of adoration.[20] Since time is beginningless, the world is eternal. No body, however, not even the heavenly body, is in itself eternal, since it is incapable of infinite acts. Nor is the heavenly soul capable of infinite activity, since, like our human souls, it is attached to a body. But *in fact* all heavenly bodies are eternal, for continuous powers flow into them from the separate Lights (the Intelligences). A body may in itself be finite and destructible—as the heavenly bodies are—but it may in fact last for ever, thanks to the continuous influx of powers from the separate Lights.[21]

If al-Suhrawardī had formulated a view of reality as a single, stable continuum, the task of Ṣadr al-Dīn al-Shīrāzī was to put that continuum into a ceaseless motion. For just as al-Suhrawardī had introduced the idea of "more and less" in the category of substance itself in addition to qualities, so now al-Shīrāzī (known as Mullā Ṣadrā) insists that it is not only quality and quantity, etc., that are subject to movement, but that movement occurs in the substance itself. Indeed, according to Ṣadrā, movement primarily occurs in the substance and only secondarily affects the rest of the categories. The result is substance-in-motion; or, rather, since substance, being liable to perpetual change and motion, is itself not stable, the result is a ceaseless flux and pure movement, without there being anything moving, and this continuous movement and change is the only stable reality or substance.

Mullā Ṣadrā is the first philosopher in Islam to establish a philosophy of flux, although he was followed in this by his disciples and commentators, particularly important among whom was al-Sabzawārī. The question about the historical sources of this doctrine of flux appears to me difficult to answer. The only theory within the Islamic tradition of philosophy that approaches flux would appear to be the atomism of Kalām. Atomism, however, denies the reality of movement absolutely and posits recreation every moment. Mullā Ṣadrā, on the other hand, bases his whole theory on the assertion that movement not only exists but is, in effect, the only reality in the world and his thought appears to operate within the terms of Aristotelianism, although through a radical modification of that doctrine.

It is also not easy to establish that Mullā Ṣadrā was inspired by Heracliteanism. Apart from the difficulty of seeing how the Heraclitean doctrine could have reached him, as has been pointed out just now, our philosopher works within the Peripatetic framework of ideas as they were expounded by Avicenna, particularly the dualism of form and matter. Mullā Ṣadrā, as we shall see, denies the identity of matter and asserts that with each particular form a different matter comes into existence. It also cannot be maintained that the *content* of Ṣadrā's doctrine is substantially identical with Heracliteanism. For Heraclitus, movement and change are fundamentally characterized by strife. The conflict of opposites is the essence of that teaching: hot becomes cold, cold hot; night changes into day, day into night; life gives place to death, death to life. To explain this ceaseless flow of reality, Heraclitus regards fire as the essential substance and asserts that fire generates everything and finally consumes everything: "everything is kindled in measure and extinguished in measure." In Mullā Ṣadrā, on the other hand, not only is the talk of a perpetual conflict and movement between opposites wholly absent, but it has no place whatever in his system. His movement is essentially unidirectional and irreversible: a movement backward, to use his terminology, from the more perfect to the less perfect is impossible. This shows that the essential movement of the world—the movement-in-substance *(ḥaraka fi'l-jawhar)*—as Mullā Ṣadra sees it, is evolutionary. Mullā Ṣadrā, no doubt, affirms that there are movements from hot to cold, etc., but all these movements are not "essential motions" but "accidental motions," according to him. Flux is also attributed to the physical world by Plato (e.g., in *Cratylus)* and Plotinus, and in the late Greco-Roman philosophy the constant change to which the human body is subject is a frequent semi-philosophic theme. Muslim philosophers like Avicenna used this as an argument to prove that the essence of man consists in an immaterial soul which is not subject to change.[22] These later Greek doctrines have no doubt influenced Ṣadrā's conception of body as something continuously in motion and he approvingly quotes Plotinus to this effect from the pseudo-Aristotelian *Theologia Aristotelis* (Ṣadrā, *al-Asfār al-Arbaʿa,* Tehran, 1958 (III, pp. 111–12).

Ṣadrā's doctrine is, nevertheless, not just a doctrine but a full-fledged *philosophy of change*—which is something different from the assertions of Plotinus and other philosophers of late antiquity. In these philosophies, again, change is simply identified with not-being and is restricted to the physical reality. In Ṣadrā, however, as in Heraclitus, change appears as the only permanent reality, and not only is the physical reality subject to it but everything in the world—except God, who is the author of change, and pure intellect, which is part of God.

In the light of the foregoing, it would appear more fruitful to regard the immediate antecedents of Mullā Ṣadrā as his sources of inspiration. We have seen above that Abū ʾl Barakāt regards the flow of continuous and ceaseless creativity on the part of God as the true reality of the world. Far from looking for some unchanging principle or substance as the source of world-change, Abū ʾl-Barakāt had drawn God Himself into the vortex of ceaseless change and had regarded Him as subject to time. To prove the creation of the world, he had not refrained from putting God in direct creative touch with the world and phrases like "He wills and creates and creates and wills" and "thinks and performs and performs and thinks," etc. abound in him. For this, al-Suhrawardī is, indeed, angry with Abū ʾl-Barakāt and empties the vials of his wrath upon him in most abusive words.[23] For al-Suhrawardī, in turn, creation is a word that has no meaning and no place whatever in the continuum of reality, which is characterized only by "more and less" or "more perfect and less Perfect." For Ṣadrā, the world-process is eternal but at the same time the term creation has a very real meaning. Nor is he prepared to accept a changing God with Abū ʾl-Barakāt. He, therefore, proposes to solve the problem of creation and eternity of the world by positing the principle of change in the very essence of the world and making movement the only permanent reality so far as the world is concerned—while keeping the evolutionary structure of the world as embodied in Aristotelianism. As a result, the world emerges as a dynamic process *in time*, which is a radical departure from Aristotle, and which gives to Ṣadrā's thought a close resemblance with evolutionary and dynamic doctrines. The most important factor which, however, differentiates his system from these doctrines is that his problem is primarily theological, viz., the relationship of a transcendent God with the world, whereas for modern dynamic doctrines God is generally immanent.

According to Ṣadrā, movement as ordinarily understood as occurring to a body—as an external accident—entails in the final analysis an essential change in the body as well. For if that which "supports" and is "the subject of" an accidental movement, e.g., in quality or quantity, were itself to remain stable and enduring, we could not be conscious of movement as something "passing," for in that case the stable element would retain the parts of movement also as stable entities. But if parts of movement were not "passing" but were to be retained in the stable substratum, then movement would cease to be movement. From this it follows that beneath this external, accidental movement, there is a fundamental, essential movement to which every substance is subject. Every substance is per se in movement, i.e., no substance endures through time. "It has been, therefore, shown that every body is something whose being [i.e., existence] is renewed constantly. . . . And hence the temporal origination *(ḥudūth)* of the physical world together with all physical substances and their accidents—be they elemental or celestial—has been established."[24]

Every matter-form complex contains the potentiality of the succeeding matter-form composite. Mullā Ṣadrā illustrates the succession of body in time with the example of the continuity of body in space. Just as a body extended in space is made up of continuous and successive parts, so do the potentially infinite successions in time constitute movement and extension in time. This continuity ensures both the difference and unity of a thing in time. Just as parts of an extension in space are essentially and existentially different from one another, so are the parts of movement in time different from one another: A thing is no longer the same in two successive moments. It is not only of the nature of matter to experience continuous change through different forms, but it is of the nature of bodily form itself to change continuously. An apparently stable substance is actually a series of changes or events. Indeed, since matter is only pure potentiality of existence and for change something actual is necessary, it is primarily the function of form to be subject to a ceaseless flow.

To the question whether there is any element or factor that endures through change, Mullā Ṣadrā gives a negative answer. His philosophy requires, and this is also his undoubted real position, that there is no factor that endures identically through change. Thus, he says that strictly speaking there is existentially no such thing as a substratum of change: "What has been said in the preceding section, that the substratum of change must identically persist, is true only if we mean by the substratum of change its substratum as an [abstracted] essence. . . or else if we mean by it the substratum of accidental changes like spatial movement, qualitative change, or growth."[25] Sometimes, however, Ṣadrā seems to admit that some substratum for change is necessary; but on such occasions he insists that the substratum can be constituted by a form-in-general and no particular form is necessary to constitute it.[26] When the question is asked: If the substance itself does not endure, then what is it that changes? Ṣadrā replies that in the case of this fundamental type of change—i.e., continuous replacement of substance—that which causes change and that which suffers change is identically the same; there is no difference in that which is potential and that which is actual.

When we conceive of the movement of nature, we must not conceive of it as a series of discrete movements but of a single moving continuum. When one instant-form is replaced by another, it is in the same manner as a black merges into another black, when black color intensifies. For, when black color intensifies, in a sense the same black color remains but acquires greater intensity, but in an existential sense a new species of black color comes into being for existentially it is not true that, in the intensified form, the previous color exists *plus* something additional; or rather, just as in the case of black color it is not true to say that there are two things, viz., color *plus* black, but simply black color, so in the case of the movement of nature, the posterior or the more perfect is not an aggregate of the anterior or the less perfect *plus* something additional. Man is not animal *plus* something additional, but something absolutely new, *sui generis*. Just as a genus loses itself entirely in species and has no independent existence, so does the anterior lose itself entirely in the posterior and when the posterior exists, the anterior totally loses its being and becomes unreal.[27]

Are words like "thing," "man," "horse," etc. empty illusions or do they have a genuine content? Ṣadrā's reply to this question exhibits a good deal of terminological confusion, although an overall view can be achieved once this terminological confusion is settled. At times, Ṣadrā affirms that things are existentially continuously changing while their essence persists; at other times, he asserts just the opposite and avers that the essence of things is in continuous flux but their existence remains the same.[28] It appears that Ṣadrā uses both these terms—essence and existence—in a double meaning in these contexts, and his commentator al-Sabzawārī is of real assistance on this point. The truth seems to be that when existence is said to be in flux, this means that the *existent* must change. But the existent is always *something*, i.e., something to which a description applies, that is to say, an *essence*. In this sense essence must change. That is why Ṣadrā says that when an intensified black comes into existence, a new species or essence comes into existence. "Existence," in this context, becomes an abstraction, and, in this sense, of course, all existence is the same.[29]

But there is a more fundamental dichotomy of existence and essence, i.e., that something exists, the fact of its existence on the one hand, and what exists, i.e., the essence, on the other. In this context, Ṣadrā unequivocally affirms the absolute primacy of existence over essence. The reality, that which flows, is existence and not essence; in fact, essence does not exist but is the result of a mental operation. On this point, Ṣadrā reproaches later Muslim philosophers who consider existence to be an abstraction, i.e., a concept shared by and abstracted from actual existents. Existence means the actual being of things-in-process. In this context our philosopher also accuses Avicenna and his followers of confounding essence with existence when they disallow the subjection of substance to movement by contending that if substance itself were to change, an ever new essence will emerge, but that there would be no substratum to support an ever-emergent essence. They ignore the fact that emergents are existents and not essences, and with regard to an emergent existent the question of a support is out of place.[30] The problem remains: if existence is in flux, how can the mind construct essences which are enduring? This problem, however, arises equally for a philosophy like Bergson's, according to which the human intellect carves out stable entities from the existential flux in order to manipulate nature. Heraclitus explained the apparent stability of nature by a "temporary balance" between opposite movements.

Words like "a thing," "man," "horse," etc., therefore, do have a meaning, but they do not refer directly to reality but to a mental construct which arises through abstraction *(bi-ḥasab al-taḥlīl al-ʿaqlī)*. These mental constructs, however, have a foundation in reality thanks to continuity in change and movement *(ḥarakat al-ittiṣāl)*:

> In the case of intensification of black it is correct to say there is an elemental original black which persists as a weak unity and there are blacks (i.e., actual black instant-existents), each one of which can be said to comprise the original black plus something additional–but only on the basis of a mental analysis.[31]
>
> This persistent existence is identically the continuously changing and shifting existence, and it is at the same time identical with each of its parts and instant-existences. . . . Therefore, if we say that it is one, we will be right, and if we say that it is many, we will be correct; if we assert that it persists from the beginning of the process till the end, we will be right and if we state that it emerges every instant, we will be speaking the truth. How astonishing is this existence and its renewal every moment. People are heedless of this fact while their being is such that they are emerging every instant.[32]

On the basis of this theory of nature, Mullā Ṣadrā solves the perennial problem of Islamic philosophy: the relationship of God and the world. The world-process is eternal—beginningless and endless—but there is nothing constant and stable, neither an earthly body nor a heavenly body. Permanence belongs to change only and it is this flux that is the true and lasting character of nature. On this basis the difficulty about the eternity and infinity of causation is not just solved but dissolved, i.e., this question can no longer be raised:

> It is said that since every originated existent must be preceded by another originated existent which is the cause of the former's origination, and so on, this would either involve a vicious regress or a vicious circularity or intro-

duction of change in the First Principle. . . . We say, however, that a thing will need an originating cause [only] if it is not of the nature of that thing to be originated. If, however, it is its very nature to emerge and be originated, it does not need a cause that will render it originated. . . .[33]

It seems to me that this argument for the self-emergence and self-origination of the content of the world-process renders God rather superfluous. For if a potentiality is self-realizing, it does not need a realizer from the outside. Ṣadrā, however, does not think so and he resolutely believes that he has established not only the flux of the world, but also the author of this flux, who has bestowed powers and potencies on nature of eternal self-renewal. He seeks to defend John Philoponus' thesis that since the potentiality of the world is limited, it must come to an end, against al-Suhrawardī who contends that although the native potentialities of bodies are finite, nevertheless, continuous powers from God flow into them. And yet Ṣadrā has totally transformed the very basis of Philoponus' theory. For Ṣadrā, the world is eternal but only as a process of endless flux, not as stable entities. God has created the world with just this nature, viz., as a ceaseless flow of self-emergents.[34]

In this theory, the heavenly bodies, together with their souls, share the flux-character of the rest of the world.[35] The nature of all bodies being this movement-in-being *(ḥaraka fīʾl-jawhar)*, the entire world is necessarily liable to constant origination and demise *(al-ḥudūth waʾl-duthūr)*. In this sense, therefore, there can be no talk of the eternity of the world, since nothing besides God has stable being. The pure transcendent intelligences (that ultimately move heaven) and the human mind, when it develops into pure intellect, are parts or functions of the Godhead and not independent beings. The dictum that time is the measure of movement is correct if by movement we mean the flux of being or movement-in-substance, since all other forms of movement, including the revolutions of the heavenly bodies, are themselves dependent upon this basic movement.

NOTES

1 Aristotle, *Physics,* iii, 4, 203b30.

2 Philoponus, *De Aeternitate Mundi,* ed. H. Rabe, p. 397, 14; ibid., pp. 336–37 for the finitude of bodily potentiality.

3 Avicenna, *Kitāb al-Najāt* (Cairo, 1938), p. 213, 10 ff.

4 See al-Ghazālī's *Tahāfut al-Falāsifa,* particularly the First Discussion, Second Proof.

5 Quoted by Ṣadr al-Dīn al-Shīrāzī (Mullā Ṣadrā) in his *al-Asfār al-Arbaʿa* (incomplete Tehran edition, 1958), III, pp. 145, 2 ff. The full text of al-Rāzī's commentary on Avicenna's *ʿUyūn al-Ḥikma* is not yet published. We have put al-Rāzī before Abūʾl-Barakat in our treatment because Abūʾl-Barakāt and al-Suhrawardī seem to be more directly logically prior to Mullā Ṣadrā on this issue, while al-Rāzī seems more directly connected to al-Ghazālī.

6 Ibid., III, p. 241, 3 ff.

[7] The contents of this paragraph are based on III, *Maqāla* i, *Kitāb al-Muʿtabar* of Abūʾl-Barakāt: *Faṣl* 8, pp. 35 ff. The quotations are from pp. 41–43 ff.

[8] Ibid., III, *Maqāla* ii, *Faṣl* 4, pp. 156 ff.

[9] Ibid., III, *Maqāla* i, pp. 33, 17 ff.

[10] Ibid., II, Part ii, *Faṣl* 5, pp. 135–38, *Faṣl* 7, pp. 141–44.

[11] Ibid., III, p. 40, 11 ff.

[12] Ibid., III, p. 40, 15 ff.

[13] See the Introduction to my *Selected Letters of Shaikh Aḥmad Sirhindi* (Karachi: Iqbal Academy, 1968), pp. 9–18.

[14] *Opera Metaphysica,* II *(Ḥikmat al-Ishrāq)*, ed. H. Corbin (Paris, 1952), p. 68, 13.

[15] *Opera Metaphysica,* I, ed. H. Corbin (Istanbul, 1945), pp. 293 ff. Cf. Introduction to my *Selected Letters,* pp. 9–18.

[16] *Opera Metaphysica,* I, pp. 115, 8 to 116, end.

[17] Ibid., I, p. 293, 13 ff.

[18] Ibid., I, p. 156, 17 to 157, 3; I, p. 301, 12 ff.

[19] Ibid, I (para 177), pp. 443, 4 to 444, 6.

[20] Ibid., II, p. 149 (para 159).

[21] Ibid., I, p. 444 (para. 178).

[22] See Van den Bergh, *Averroes' Tahafut al-Tahafut* E.J.W. Gibb Memorial, New Series, 19, (Oxford, 1954), II, p. 199, notes pp. 353.3 and 353.4 for materials on flux in the later Greek philosophy. Averroes rejects this argument, given by Avicenna, to prove the incorporeality of the soul, and asserts that "none of the ancients put forth this argument to prove the incorporeality of the soul" (Ibid., I, 354). It is obvious, however, that this argument is implicit in the Plotinian doctrine that if there were no soul, the physical world would perish.

What makes Ṣadrā's conception of movement essentially different from the said philosophies is that it is linked up with his metaphysical doctrine of the successive levels of being *(nashaʾāt)*. Every lower level of being, thanks to this movement-in-substance, is transformed into a higher level of being and is, therefore, irreversible. This doctrine of emergent levels of being is really the heart of Ṣadrā's spiritual-metaphysical system. At the same time, however, and in contradiction to this fundamental thesis, Ṣadrā also uses it to prove the ephemeral character of the existence of this world—in line with earlier philosophies.

[23] In *Opera Metaphysica,* I, pp. 435–39, al-Suhrawardī says, "Among those of the recent ones who occupy themselves with matters that are none of their concern and who wish to defend doctrines that they do not know. . . is a person known as Abūʾl-Barakāt, the pseudo-philosopher. He attributed to the Necessary Being infinite emergent wills in succession. He asserted that God does one thing and then wills another—so He does and wills and wills and does. By this argument he opposed everyone who had the slightest sense. [In doing so] he opposed the Jewish religion to which he earlier belonged, and the religion of Islam which he later embraced. He therefore, had neither reason nor faith—as the phrase goes! But he thought that these religions probably required nonsensical beliefs. . . ."

Al-Suhrawardī then goes on (p. 437, 13 ff.) to say that it became possible for a "dirty lunatic *(al-majnūn al-qadhīr)*" like Abūʾl-Barakāt to philosophize because the spiritual methodology and ethical standards which the ancient philosophers had constantly observed broke down at the hands of self-seeking latter-day intellectuals. In what appears to be a cryptic critique of the expansion of Islam, or, at any rate, of organized religions based on Revelation, into Persia and Persian Iraq, al-Suhrawardī declares: "A group (successfully) endeavored to destroy the foundations of knowledge in Babylon and Persia and other neighboring regions. They accomplished some excellent and important reforms, but destroyed what was still better for some reason that God had predetermined." It is important to note that al-Suhrawardī talks about the destruction of the ancient Persian wisdom and not of Greek philosophy.

[24] Ṣadrā, *al-Asfār al-Arbaᶜa* (the incomplete 1958 Tehran edition), III, p.62, 3–6.
[25] Ibid., p. 62, 6–9.
[26] Ibid., p. 87, 1 ff.; p. 136, 1–4.
[27] Ibid., *Faṣl* 24, p. 80 ff., particularly p. 81, 4 to 88, 1.
[28] E.g., compare ibid., p. 62, 6 ff. and p. 86, 2 ff., and n.1. of the commentator on the same page.
[29] Ibid., p. 84, 3 ff., etc., *passim* in this important *Faṣl*.
[30] Ibid., p. 83, 8 ff.; p. 85, 12 ff. The question of a "support" is out of place because it is of the very nature of emergents to change and with regard to that which pertains to the very nature of a thing the question "why" or "whence" cannot be asked, e.g., why fire is hot. This is the difference between *jaᶜl basīṭ* (simple causation) and *jaᶜl murakkab* (composite causation). For an illustration, see *ibid.,* p. 61, 11 ff.
[31] Ibid., p. 82, 12–15.
[32] Ibid., p. 84, 11–17.
[33] Ibid., p. 68, 3–7.
[34] Ibid., p. 164, 13 till the end of the section, p. 166. Mullā Ṣadrā claims there (p. 164, 13 ff.) that he is the first Muslim philosopher to have proved the origination of the world through the doctrine of flux. It should be pointed out that, as is apparent from the preceding quotation from Ṣadrā, he regards the world as having been *ab initio* created with this nature, viz., to change and move incessantly. This is his overall doctrine because he recurrently appeals to the doctrine of *jaᶜl basīṭ* in this context. This is his doctrine of the emerging and developing world which, as such, does not even require a creator at all, as we have pointed out. In passages like the one under reference in this note, where Ṣadrā is concerned to show the dependence of the world-process on God and the origination and ephemeral nature of the world, he asserts that at every new movement the world-process receives a new form from God, which ensures God's ceaseless creative impact on the world. In such a context God is obviously needed, but then the self-developing character of the world becomes doubtful.
[35] See particularly ibid., *Faṣl* 31, p. 118 ff., where Ṣadrā,—after quoting from Avicenna to the effect that although the movement of the heavenly body occurs by "passing through" different positions, it can, nevertheless, be regarded as "stable" because it is continuously emergent and that this is thanks to the continuous flow of images in the soul of the heaven, —declares, p. 121, 1: "This is tantamount to the affirmation of movement in the essential form [i.e., substance]...because images in the heaven are renewed by way of continuous *process (al-ittiṣāl al-tadrījī)* and this is exactly what is meant by movement in the essential form [or physical nature]." See also *Faṣl* 33, p. 128 ff., where objections to the doctrine, that all change and origination are ultimately traceable to the eternal revolution of the heaven, are raised. On p. 131, 1 ff., Ṣadrā contends that the movement of the heaven cannot be regarded as eternal since the heaven is subject to change in its very substance. Ṣadrā regards this movement as the real and primitive movement, and time as something subjective "existing only through mental analysis" (p. 146, 6 to 147, 14).

Notes to pages 350 to 382

THE GOD-WORLD RELATIONSHIP IN MULLĀ ṢADRĀ

Fazlur Rahman (2)

INTRODUCTORY REMARKS

For Mullā Ṣadrā, as for Avicenna and Aristotle, being or existence is the primary concept that the mind acquires; it is, therefore, self-evident and indefinable. It is the most general concept and is the condition for the application of all other concepts to reality. Like Avicenna and Aristotle, Mullā Ṣadrā also asserts that existence is not the highest genus since it is not constitutive of the essence of anything, for if existence were regarded as genus, existence or being would still be predicated of it. Having said this, Mullā Ṣadrā proceeds to establish a radical distinction between existence in the external world and existence as a general concept, as it exists in the mind. All external existence is a unique fact or, rather, a unique process—as we shall see—intrinsically incapable of being captured by the mind, while existence as a concept is abstract and general, and does not represent true existence but is a kind of indirect index *(ᶜunwān)* of it. Ṣadrā seeks to establish this disparateness between real existence which is the unique mode of every reality and existence as a concept in the mind by saying of those aspects of reality which are capable of being effectively captured by the mind that their essence remains stable despite change in the modes of their existence. Now, the very meaning or "nature" of existence is "to be in the external world"; therefore, if existence were to come into the mind, this would involve transformation of its very nature. It is, therefore, in the nature of the case, impossible that existence be properly conceived by the mind.[1]

This doctrine called "the primacy of existence over essence" is, as it stands, not Aristotle's but presupposes a development after Avicenna. Although Aristotle states that it is only after something exists that we can legitimately enquire as to *what* it is, i.e., as to its essence—otherwise, as in the case of a goat-stag (or a unicorn) all we can do is to give the meaning of the word[2] (and not an essence)—the doctrine that existence itself is the sole basic reality which necessarily escapes the mind in conceptualization is obviously not the Stagirite's doctrine. Avicenna, in his theory of essence and existence, held that in all the contingents—i.e., in everything else except God—an objective distinction exists between essence and existence, since their existence is not necessary and depends upon God, the necessary being. That is to say, derivative existence is the meaning of contingency and, therefore, every object in the created world has a duality—it is an essence that exists, unlike God who is pure existence and has no essence. According to Avicenna, therefore, the distinction between essence and existence in contingent beings is an objective and real distinction. This distinction was rejected by Averroes, who accused Avicenna of having introduced extrinsic theological distinctions into philosophy and violating the very definition of a substance as that which exists by itself. In the history of Islamic philosophy in the East, however, this doctrine continued to play a central role and Mullā Ṣadrā formulated his view at the end of a long development and controversy where Avicenna's ideas had undergone radical transformation.

It must be borne in mind that Avicenna's distinction between essence and existence was intended to operate only as explanatory of the metaphysics of contingency. Logically speaking, Avicenna had made it clear that existence does not behave as an ordinary predicate or accident; it does not go beyond the subject and is not additional to it but is constitutive of it. Whereas the existence of all accidents (like white, round, etc.), he declared in the *Taʿlīqāt*, presupposes and is attendant upon the subject, and these accidents exist "in" the subject, the existence of existence merely means the existence of the subject itself and no more.[3] In the further development of the Avicennan doctrine, however, existence came to be regarded as an attribute and thus arose the famous doctrine that existence, being a verbal noun *(al-maʿnā al-maṣdarī)*, was equivalent to an abstract idea *(al-mafhūm al-intizāʿī)* or a mere subjective thing *(shayʾ iʿtibārī)*. This view owes its rise particularly to the activity of al-Suhrawardī al-Maqtūl who subjected Avicenna's theory to severe criticism on the assumption that, according to Avicenna, existence is an attribute additional to an existing essence. Al-Suhrawardī's arguments can be summarized as follows:

> If existence were to exist in reality, it would be an existent and since every existent is something that has existence, so existence will have to have another existence and thus it will regress *ad infinitum*. Again, if existence were an attribute of the essence in external reality, then the latter would be recipient of the former; this would involve that essence exists before existence since it can receive something only after it exists itself. Thirdly, if both essence and existence are in the external world, then they have a relationship to each other. This relationship, therefore, must have existence also, and so on *ad infinitum*.[4]

On the basis of these criticisms, al-Suhrawardī declares that existence is a purely mental affair to which nothing corresponds in the external world which is made up of essences. These essences differ from one another by being more perfect or less perfect or prior or posterior but not by being necessary or contingent as Avicenna held, for necessity and contingency are themselves only mental phenomena having no counterpart in reality.[5]

This dictum has to be made more precise in order to get at its real meaning. It does not purport to be anything like a subjective idealism and to deny the existence of an external world. What it means is that there is an external world in which things are, and existence simply means the being of things in the external world: existence, therefore, does not mean any quality or attribute constitutive of the content of things but simply refers to the status of things and assigns a form to them, i.e., a formal characteristic, viz., that they have their being in the external world. This formal characteristic is itself attributed by the mind and is, therefore, *in a sense*, mental. Thus, this theory approximates to, although it is obviously not identical with Kantianism.[6]

CRITICISM OF PREDECESSORS

Although the peripatetic philosophers after al-Suhrawardī did not accept his doctrine of being in terms of more perfect and less perfect and maintained the Avicennan distinction between the necessary and the contingent, nevertheless, al-Suhrawardī's critique of existence and his doctrine that existence is a subjective phenomenon had a decisive influence on them. Existence, for them, becomes an abstract idea *(al-maᶜnā al-intizāᶜī)* which accompanies the conception of essences in the mind. The distinction between the necessary and the contingent, then, becomes subjective also. The necessary being is that whose very conception in the mind yields the idea of existence in the mind and the contingent being is that whose conception in the mind does not itself lead to the idea of existence unless such being is related, in the mind, to the necessary being. The idea of existence, thus, becomes an abstract concept and a "secondary intelligible" like other concepts to which nothing corresponds in reality. That this doctrine entails a shift from al-Suhrawardī—even though Mullā Ṣadrā does not admit such a shift and classes al-Suhrawardī and later philosophers in the same category from this point of view—seems to me to be obvious. For, whereas for al-Suhrawardī existence, although a mental factor, applies directly to reality, or rather makes the reality of the external world possible, the doctrine of the later philosophers smacks more of subjectivism in the sense that existence, according to them, applies to the essences *when they are presented to the mind*.

Mullā Ṣadrā, whose central activity in the development of his own doctrine consists in a relentless criticism of this subjective theory of being, cites Jalāl al-Dīn al-Dawwānī as an illustration:

> This general idea participated in by all beings, belongs to the secondary intelligibles and is not identical with (i.e., does not correspond to) anything in reality. The truth is that it applies to the necessary being by His very essence and applies to other beings insofar as these latter are [conceived to be] caused by the necessary being (i.e., insofar as they owe their existence to the necessary being). Thus, this attribute [of existence] is addi-

tional to both (i.e., the necessary as well as the contingent beings) insofar as they are in the mind, but the difference between them is that the source of the abstraction of this attribute in the case of the contingents is that these are caused by God (i.e., in reference to God) whereas in the case of the necessary being, the source of abstraction is the necessary being itself. Thus, the necessary being is such that when the mind regards it in itself, it is able to abstract the quality of absolute existence from it.[7]

According to Ṣadrā, this doctrine of the necessary being as the source of the abstraction of the concept of existence is by its very nature so subjective that it renders the transition from subjectivity to the real existence of God, as an individual who is pure existence, illegitimate. The reality of existence can only be intuited, not conceived. Ṣadrā, after quoting al-Dawwānī, comments, "It is, therefore, clear by their line of thinking that the self-identity of existence in the necessary being is an empty phrase since there is no real individual which is named by the word 'existence.' What they have described holds good only insofar as existence as a verbal noun is concerned and has no reference to real existence."[8]

Indeed, Ṣadrā firmly upholds Ibn Kammūna's objection to the proof of the unity of God advanced by those philosophers who believe in the subjectivity of existence to which nothing corresponds in reality. This proof states that the existence of the necessary being is original, unborrowed and, therefore, self-identical. In other words, the *concept* of existence is produced in the mind by such a being per se without reference to any other being. The statement of the objection is: since existence has no reality except in the mind, the quality of self-sufficiency in producing the concept of existence in the mind may be actually shared by more than one being each of which would then be a necessary being. Ibn Kammūna's fatal objection against these philosophers can be effectively answered only on the basis that existence is exemplified outside the mind by an individual *(fard)*, i.e., that existence exists as an individual. For if in that case self-identical existence were to be shared by more than one being, as Ibn Kammūna asserts, then these beings, while sharing this characteristic, would have to be distinguished through some other particularizing quality and hence each one of them would be composite, not simple—which would mean negation of a necessary being. This answer is not possible on the basis of existence being a subjective concept because in that case the concept is being caused in the mind by something that is by definition not existence; therefore, the unique relationship between the cause and the effect cannot be established and hence more than one being could cause the concept of pure (or self-identical) existence.[9]

The essence of Ṣadrā's recurrent criticism of his predecessors among the *Muta᾿akhkhirīn*—the "later philosophers"—is that having regarded existence as a mere concept in the mind, and as such as a secondary intelligible to which nothing corresponds in reality, they have barred their way to the affirmation of God as pure existence—i.e., existence as a unique *fard* or individual—which they also inevitably have to affirm. If God is pure existence, then how can existence be a pure concept? And, conversely, if existence signifies only a general abstract idea, how can it be applied to a real existent whose nature is nothing but existence? That is why Ṣadrā insists that those who have regarded existence as a mental category—particularly al-Suhrawardī and those who followed him in this doctrine—use the word "existence" of God as a "mere convention" *(mujarrad iṣṭilāḥ)* or else they are involved in a plain contradiction as is the case with al-Dawwāni's argument for the existence of God and His unity which became very famous and popular with the "latter-day philosophers." This argument stated in al-Dawwāni's commentary on al-Suhrawardī's *Hayākil al-Nūr* is as follows: Not all derivative names imply the actual existence of the root idea in the derivative thing. For instance, the noun *ḥaddād* (ironmonger) does not imply the existence of *ḥadīd* or iron in the ironmonger, but iron has a separate existence of its own. The noun *maujūd* or existent similarly does not mean that existents possess existence as a substance possesses an attribute; existence, in fact, has a unique, separate being of its own which is identical with God. "Existent," like "ironmonger," therefore, implies merely a relationship to another substance: ironmonger to iron and existent to existence. God is, therefore, pure self-identical existence, separate being, and all other existents are called existents not because they "have" existence but because they are related to God as original, pure existence.[10]

Ṣadrā has subjected this proof to a detailed criticism, the essential point of which is that since on al-Dawwānī's own admission existence is a subjective mental category, how can he know and assert that there is an actual individual—God—to which this category uniquely applies? The utmost that he can say is that since the analysis of the word "existence" has led us to posit a necessary, uncaused something, let us call him by the name "Pure Existence."[11] Ṣadrā then goes on to assert that from an abstract concept of existence, there can be no way to the affirmation of a real individual existence. The real existence cannot be known except by direct intuition *(mushāhada, ḥuḍūr)* and any attempt to capture it in the mind by any idea must by definition fail. In other words, this critique asserts that the idea of a necessary being, like the Cartesian idea of a perfect being, cannot prove the actual existence of such a being, that "necessary being," like "perfect being," cannot serve as the name of any individual existent but only as a general mental description and that a necessary or a perfect being in the mind as such can only exist in the mind.

DOCTRINE OF BEING

Ṣadrā, indeed, affirms, as we noted earlier, that "existence" as a mental phenomenon is a general idea but he insists that this general idea does not reveal the nature of existence which ever escapes the mind. Mental ideas can do justice to and fully understand *(iktināh)* only essences because essences are mental phenomena par excellence while their share of real existence is more than dubious. Essences, indeed, as we shall see, are limitations of existence and its negation. They are not real but mental *(umūr dhihnīya)* and hence the mind is naturally made for understanding them. Existence which, on the contrary, is the only thing real, must necessarily defy the mind. This is why, among all mental concepts, "existence" is the only one which is really systematically ambiguous. The term "systematically ambiguous" means that the idea or the concept applied to reality is *(a)* shared by *(mushtarak)* all the individuals under it yet *(b)* differs with each application in its meaning *(mushakkik)*.[12]

Essences can never be systematically ambiguous because each essence applies univocally to all its members; existence, on the other hand, although it applies to every existent, nevertheless, does not apply to all existents in the same sense. This doctrine should be distinguished from Aristotle's, who asserted that "existence" or "being" is analogical, because Aristotle's intention was to distinguish the existence of things which he calls "primary substances" from that of forms or essences which he describes as "secondary substances," although both these types of substances "are" or "exist" in some sense. Ṣadrā's doctrine is developed under the combined influence of Avicenna and al-Suhrawardī. Avicenna held that "existence," when it is applied to the necessary being, does not have the same meaning as when it is applied to contingents. The existence of the Necessary being is self-sufficient and uncaused, whereas the existence of the contingents is caused and borrowed. Borrowed existence, Avicenna tells us, enters into the very definition of the contingent and therefore changes the very meaning of existence when it refers to the contingent as distinguished from God.[13]

Al-Suhrawardī, as has been seen earlier, rejects the "objectivity" of existence and asserts that the objectively real are the essences or, rather, the essence of light *(māhīyat al-Nūr)*. This single essence of light is in its absoluteness pure light or the light of lights, which is God, but as it proceeds into the contingent realm it becomes differentiated by grades of less and less. Indeed, contingency *means* less perfect, just as necessity means perfect self-manifesting light. To the question: how, on the basis of a pure monism of light, can one explain the various grades of light, without assuming some second principle whereby pure light becomes differentiated, al-Suhrawardī replies that the purpose of the category of "more perfect and less perfect" is just to perform this function and that no second principle is needed, since the limitation of light is not a positive but a negative phenomenon. Ṣadrā, who rejects al-Suhrawardī's view about the subjectivity of existence, nevertheless takes over the essential doctrine of al-Suhrawardī and, substituting existence for the essence of light, asserts that the only reality is existence itself and that this reality is subject to the principle of the more perfect and less perfect. The most perfect existence is existence-in-itself and existence-by-itself and, as existence proceeds downward, it gives rise to the world of contingency.[14]

But the substitution of existence for the essence of light does produce fundamental differences which mark off Mullā Ṣadrā's doctrine from that of al-Suhrawardī. These differences flow from a strict application of the principle of systematic ambiguity. By denying the reality of existence the Shaikh al-Ishrāq had deprived himself of a genuine utilization of this principle: light, as an essence, must be equally and essentially shared by all beings since in an essence there can be no intrinsic differences, which must then be attributed to extrinsic factors. That is to say, on the principle of essence as reality, sharing of common characteristics will be ensured but the induction of intrinsic differences will be impossible. Indeed, the principle of "more perfect and less perfect" in a doctrine of essentialism must become more or less formal, because perfection and imperfection cannot be attributed to anything innate in any being and al-Suhrawardī himself affirms that between my being and the being of God, for example, there is no essential difference but only that between perfect and less perfect.[15] The principle of systematic ambiguity alone will do justice both to the sharing of a common nature on the one hand and the affirmation of intrinsic differences in all beings. Only existence gives us this principle, for while existence is common to all reality, its individual instances are all different from one another since every existent is an absolutely unique individual. Perfection and imperfection, more and less, are not mere words but constitute the very nature of beings or, as Avicenna held, enter into their definition.

It is, in fact, existence alone which is one and many, i.e., essentially one and essentially many. The unity given by essences is only the unity of abstraction and is produced only in the mind. The very nature of existence is that it is *ᶜainī*, real, not *dhihnī*, or mental. That existence is one in reality is assured by the fact that otherwise every existent would be out of all relation with others, which is manifestly absurd. But it is equally true that every existent is unique. Some people have believed that existence is one single individual reality, viz., God, and that the multiplicity of contingents arises from the fact that essences come into an existential relation with this one and only reality. This notion is also false since it cannot explain the individual, separate existence of beings which share a common essence. It is, indeed, difficult to conceive the existence of a principle which itself would act both as unifying and differentiating at the same time. Thus, Fakhr al-Dīn al-Rāzī said that either existence is one word for different realities *(ishtirāk lafẓī)*, or else entities denoted by it must equally share a single nature and cannot be differentiated. This difficulty arises from the fact that unity and difference are mutually exclusive in the mind, for the very nature of the rational mind is to exclude them from each other.

Conception is deception; for this reason, existence, when it becomes a concept in the mind, distorts the character of existential existence and plays tricks upon us. It is this conceptualizing nature of the mind which necessarily seeks to transform the existential fact of existence into an essence. Essence, as such, has no existence. Essence is universal, existence is particular and unique. Existence is necessary, essence is contingent and it is the contingency of the essence which, when related to existence, makes existence contingent in a sense. This is because essence is a limitation or negation of being. In reality, essence is something indefinite, indeterminate *(mubham)*, dark, and unreal; without existence it cannot be pointed to either intellectually or perceptually. Even when it is said to exist, its existence is only metaphorical and it merely serves to authenticate the idea of contingency. Essence is by its very nature something concealed and inward *(muḥtajib, bāṭin)* and as Ibn al-ʿArabī's famous dictum has it, "Essences never smell of real existence." Existence, on the other hand, is concrete, determinate, luminous, and real;[16] it serves to bring essences out of their indeterminacy and makes them distinguishable from each other.[17] Yet it is at the expense of existence that essences reveal themselves, for essences, as we have said, are the negation of existence. The more powerful the existence, the less room there is for essences, and, conversely, the more manifest the essences, the more existence goes into concealment.

When we leave reality and come to the realm of the mind, this story is reversed. There essences are named and known *(maʿlūmat al-asāmī)*—for mind is the proper home for essences, while existences there are unnamed and unknown *(majhūlat al-asāmī)*.[18] This is because essences are static, stable, and fixed whereas existences are a ceaseless flow, a perpetual movement. The mind, in order to be able to negotiate and regard the ceaseless flow of reality, cuts it into segments for its own use and thus renders them static. It is the same as if one mentally carves out a chunk of a continuous movement *(ḥaraka ittiṣālīya)* between one given point and another and a discontinuous piece of movement *(ḥaraka infiṣālīya)* results. Because of this operation of the mind, essences arise. The continuous movement of existence and its identity-in-difference, which is the result of movement-in-substance *(ḥaraka fīʾl jauhar)*, can only be *intuited* and not *conceived* by the mind. That is why the sages have said that perception of existence requires a higher mode of reason than the ordinary intellect.[19]

It follows from this discussion that, in the realm of the real, things are not composed of two elements, an essence and an existence. In the case of the contingent existent, existence is a mode which serves to facilitate for the mind the abstraction of a certain essence and, conversely, essence is a mode of the mind which serves to underline the contingency of the external existent, i.e., to underline the fact that the existent is an existent of *some sort,* limited and not absolute. To say that existence is an accident of the essence in reality is, therefore, wrong; it is only in the mind that this appears to be the case. Mullā Ṣadrā quotes Avicenna to the effect that existence cannot be regarded strictly speaking as an accident since, whereas accidents presuppose the existence of a substance and hence the existence of accidents is *in* and *for* the substance, this is obviously not the case with existence since the existence of existence is not *in* and *for* the substance but existence *of* the substance itself.[20] Nevertheless, Ṣadrā's doctrine is patently different from Avicenna's for, although Avicenna disallowed the treatment of existence as an accident *logically,* he did not deny the objective existence of essences and did not hold that essences are purely mental affairs. Ṣadrā's position has been made possible by al-Suhrawardī's critique of Avicenna's distinction between essence and existence in things. Whereas al-Suhrawardī declared existence to be a mental category "to which nothing corresponds in reality" and allowed objectivity only to light essences, Ṣadrā now reversed this position, allowing objectivity only to existence and making essences purely mental.

Finally, Mullā Ṣadrā criticizes the philosophers' notion of necessity and contingency. Peripatetics and particularly Neoplatonizing peripatetics, by taking their starting point not from existence but from essences and by regarding the latter as something independent of existence, arrived at a tripartite division of being—the necessary, the contingent and the impossible—by the following consideration. Every essence, when considered in itself, either requires existence or resists existence or is neutral both to existence and nonexistence. They are then said to be necessary, impossible or contingent. However, when these philosophers actually come to prove the existence of the necessary being, they realize their contradiction, for on their own showing the necessary being has no essence and thus the notion of an essence which requires its own existence is given up as absurd. They then assume a new position by saying that if an *existent,* when presented to the mind, yields the idea of existence by itself, it is necessary, but if, when presented to the mind, it does not show itself to be self-sufficient but requires a cause, it is possible and contingent. It is the same as when these philosophers, in order to explain the world of contingency, posit intermediary causes after God, like the intelligences and the soul, but then affirm, as a modifier to this doctrine of mediation, that all real existence comes directly from God to all existents and that the intermediaries are not real causes but only conditions for the existence-bestowing action of God. Ṣadrā, however, exonerates the philosophers by asserting that this is a method of *teaching* used by the philosophers, since they first affirm something which may not be quite true but which has the merit that it appeals to the mind of the student, but later they modify it. He then attributes the same pedagogical method to himself in his own teaching and asserts that whereas he initially accepts the philosophers' doctrine of contingency, he will then go on to evolve his own doctrine based on his view of existence.[21] Perhaps we cannot do better than follow his own words:

> The first (i.e., that which per se yields the idea of existence) then is the idea of necessary-by-itself, the Supreme Being and the Light of Lights in the language of *Ishrāq* [Illuminationist philosophy], the True Unity according to the [neo-]Pythagoreans and the Essence of Essences with the Sufis. The second (i.e., the contingent) is not impossible in itself—since we have now taken the *existent* [i.e., as opposed to essences] to be the field of division. We shall name it 'Contingent' whether it is an essence or an entity—although it must be remembered that the being-in-existence (*maujūdīya*) of essences is only by existence becoming conjoined to them, which makes them appear,[22] while the being-in-existence of particular existences is thanks to their flowing-forth from the Perfect Maker. . . or, rather, by the devolution of Existence through existential stages to which essences are related by way of being delineated, described or perfected by them and the Sustaining Maker is related by way of sustaining, descending, flashing forth. . . . Thus, that which makes possible the attribution of existence per se is the being of the Necessary Being by itself. . . while this is made possible, in the case of the contingent, by its becoming conjoined and united with existence—if by the contingent is meant essence—or by being related [with the Necessary Existence]—if by the contingent is meant a particular form of existence. . . Thus the contingency of essences—when existence is abstracted from them—means that they are neither necessarily existent nor nonexistent in themselves, while the contingency of particular existences means that they are per se related to something else [i.e., Necessary Existence]. . . their being is nothing else but this relationship and their entities are nothing else but flashes [of the Necessary Existence] and they have no self-subsistence of their own.[23]

The language of this passage gives the impression that essences are real in some sense since they are admitted to be contingents and are said to be conjoined and united with existence. Ṣadrā hastens to add, however, that these have no existence except in the mind, and that is why they are conceived "to their very core." In that case, however, it is difficult to see how they are "united" with external existence, except to say that external existences "effect" essences in the mind. For Ṣadrā, indeed, declares that, whereas for the Neoplatonists[24] essences are created by the Creator—i.e., by a simple creation *(jaʿl basīṭ)*—and for the Peripatetics essences are qualified by existence by the creator, i.e., by a composite creation *(jaʿl murakkab)*, according to his own doctrine, essences are not created, but conceived by the mind, and contingent existence is created by a simple creation.

GOD AND THE WORLD

On the basis of his doctrine of existence, Mullā Ṣadrā now proceeds to prove the existence of God. This proof rests on the undeniability of existence and involves the following steps:

1. Existence is the simple, unitary, self-identical reality. It is not in its nature a concept—for it defies all attempts at conceptualization but refers to particular existences *(afrād)*. Existences or, at least, some existence is therefore absolutely indubitable. Ṣadrā's commentator, Muḥammad Ḥusain-i-Ṭabāṭabaʾī, expounds this statement by saying that existence is something whose denial involves its affirmation. Thus, when a skeptic doubts everything in existence, still his statement "nothing exists" claims existential truth for itself. It is, therefore, obvious that the proposition "something is the case" is absolutely and undeniably true.[25]
2. Since *some* existence is indubitable, and since existence, as we have affirmed earlier, is systematically ambiguous—i.e., it applies to all its instances or *afrād* both commonly and differently—it follows that there must be an instance of existence which is absolutely perfect in all respects and constitutes the paradigm of existence. That is to say, such a being is existence itself, regarded in its absoluteness and perfection. This being is the necessary being.
3. This necessary being must be both logically and ontologically prior to all other grades of existence *(marātib al-wujūd)*. God, therefore, is really and perfectly His own proof. On Mullā Ṣadrā's own admission, this proof is essentially the same as that employed by al-Suhrawardī in the case of light of lights or absolute light and it is quite obvious, I think, that Ṣadrā profoundly depends here on his Ishrāqī predecessor, in spite of his criticism of al-Suhrawardī that the latter reduces existence to the status of a concept and deprives it of its primordial, existential nature.

Ṣadrā calls this proof the best proof for the existence of God because here God is proved by Himself, not through any other being as, for example, the peripatetics prove God through contingents. It is the proof of the "*Ṣiddīqs*," i.e., those who directly affirm God without the mediation of anything else. It is really this "proof" of God that every creature carries in its own being—a direct and immediate proclamation of its Creator writ clearly and unequivocally in its very nature as an existent. There are, indeed, many other proofs for God's existence: from contingency, from temporal origination and from movement; all these proofs have a certain validity but since they involve others than God as premises, they seek God, as it were, through not-God.

Ṣadrā singles out for criticism the Muslim peripatetics' proof from contingency. This proof essentially states that since no contingent can bring itself into being, a necessary being is needed ultimately who is self-existent and uncaused. That is to say, God is brought in here in order to put an end to an infinite regress of the chain of contingent causes. There is, however, nothing intrinsic in the series of contingents to compel us to believe that at some supposedly final point the contingent will have no other contingent cause but a necessary one, and therefore this whole argument comes to assume an air of artificiality. Some philosophers, therefore, have restated the argument from contingency and have attempted to avoid the use of the idea of an infinite regress. This new formulation, which was also supported by al-Suhrawardī, asserts that we can take the entire contingent series as a whole, i.e., as a unit and then maintain that this unit, since it cannot be caused by itself or by a part of it, must have an exterior cause, namely God. To refute this argument Ṣadrā once again invokes his doctrine of the identity of one and existence. The really one is commensurate with the really existent; there are, therefore, as many ones as there are real existents. The unity of the whole over and above the individual real existents is only a mental construct having no counterpart in reality, just as the *concept* of existence is only a mental construct while in reality there are only real existents. Hence, the pseudounity of the totality of contingents does not get rid of the multiplicity of individual contingents and their individual causes and, therefore, the argument from the contingent cannot escape the infinite regress and the invocation of God to terminate this regress.[26]

To revert to Ṣadrā's own proof, the two capital ideas in it are the reality of existences and the systematic ambiguity *(tashkīk)* of existence. As for the first idea, it has been expounded in the preceding account; *tashkīk*, however, needs some elaboration. To begin with, we have rendered the term *tashkīk* by "systematic ambiguity" rather than by "analogy" or equivocality. The term "analogy," indeed, has a certain orientation towards the yielding of some positive knowledge on the strength of a certain relationship, proportion, or resemblance between two things, one of which is said to be known more directly and the other to be known by being *analogical* with the first. It is true that in the development of the doctrine of analogy in the medieval West, the point received notice and also emphasis that analogy conceals as much as it reveals and that perhaps it is more like family faces than the peeling of an onion, which leaves no residue. Nevertheless, what Ṣadrā appears to say, certainly what seems to emerge in the later stage of his doctrine, is that the *tashkīk* of existence conceals from the intellect more than it reveals, i.e., that even though the word "existence" is applied really and not metaphorically to all cases of existence, nevertheless, each case is in a sense so unique that all of them intrinsically differ from one another. Thanks to the fact of "more perfect and less perfect" which is characteristic only of existence to the exclusion of all essences, existence is that whereby things are at the same time same and different *(mā bihiʾl-ittifāq huwa ʿain mā bihiʾl-ikhtilāf)*. An essence cannot be like this because, being "narrow" and exactly definable, it is absolutely uniform within its own range. That is why Ṣadrā insists that existence is *not* a concept.

Ṣadrā himself tells us that he had not always held the doctrine of the primacy of existence, that at an earlier time he had held the essentialist doctrine but later changed his view.[27] His biographers also tell us that at the beginning of his intellectual career Ṣadrā had defended monism *(waḥdat al-wujūd)*, but that later he discarded or modified it.[28] This appears to be borne out by the treatment of existence in the first part and the third part of the *Asfār* respectively. For in the first part, although he holds the doctrine of the systematic ambiguity of existence, he still emphatically proclaims the absolute unity of existence and refers to an earlier treatise composed by him to prove it, viz., the treatise *Ṭarḥ al-Kawnain,* i.e., "the foundation of the two realms."[29] Indeed, Ṣadrā, after quoting from Avicenna's *Taʿlīqāt* to the effect that the being of God and that of the contingents differ qualitatively from each other since the former is original and uncaused while the latter is dependent upon and borrowed from God, concludes that the only being is the being of God and other beings are not really beings at all but are pure relations, or "twinklings" of the same light.[30] This doctrine, which is clearly a transformation of Avicenna's view, is repeated several times and Ṣadrā even goes so far as to state: "*No one disputes* that the distinction between existence and essence is only in the mind and not in objective reality."[31] This is hardly a faithful representation of Avicenna! And here comes the most unequivocal declaration: "It must be borne in mind that our affirmation of different grades of existence and our compromises at the level of discussion and pedagogy *(al-baḥth waʾl-taʿlīm)* with the multiplicity of existence, does not go against what we are really intent upon proving presently—God willing—viz., the identity of all existence and existents in essence and reality."[32]

The truth is that Ṣadrā's purpose here is to show that the contingent existent is so wholly dependent upon God that even during its existence, it cannot be seen as anything in itself but only as a being related to God. This is what he understands to be the meaning of the contingent-in-itself *(mumkin biʾl-dhāt)* and he vigorously denies the philosophers' assertion that effects have two aspects, one in relation to their cause, i.e., God and the other in themselves. For Ṣadrā, a contingent has no aspect in itself and an effect is totally exhausted in being a pure relation to its cause.[33] Only God and nothing else exists, says Ṣadrā and "it was through this spiritual melody that the Prophet [Muḥammad]'s soul reportedly vibrated with an exalted extasy, and not through a sensual passion [for music], when he heard the poet Labīd's verse:

Beware! Everything except God is vain and false;
And every joy of life must inevitably end.

To affirm that contingents have no existence in themselves and that their existence is "borrowed" as Avicenna held is one thing, but to conclude from this that you can so abstract the existence of a contingent from its essence that it is identically God's existence, is quite another. This doctrine, which has its origin in certain forms of Sufism, is known as the doctrine of unity in multiplicity *(waḥda fīʾl-kathra)*. It is also clear that this assertion of simple unity in diversity is not compatible with the idea of *tashkīk* or systematic ambiguity of existence since this latter involves the proposition that existents, even though fundamentally the same or from the same source, cannot be identical.

At the same time, however, some of Ṣadrā's statements give evidence for the opposite trend of his mind. In the chapter where he seeks to prove that God's essence is nothing else but His existence, our philosopher endeavors to point out in what sense God's existence is different from that of other beings and, although he rejects the peripatetic view that God's existence is *essentially* different from that of other beings and affirms the doctrine of the "Persian and Khusrawnic sages" that existence differs in point of "more perfect and less perfect,"[34] he begins to take seriously the implications of his *tashkīk*-doctrine:

> We shall show in our discussion of *tashkīk* that difference in the grade of a single nature and distinctions among its concrete realizations are sometimes due to that nature itself. Thus it is thanks to the nature of existence itself that its concrete actualizations differ—in terms of priority and posteriority, necessity and contingency, substantiality and accidentality, perfection and imperfection—and not through any additional and extrinsic factor.[35]

Thus, as the implications of this second aspect of the doctrine of *tashkīk* —the aspect, that is, of difference—are fully realized in the consciousness of our philosopher, the idea of systematic ambiguity of existence comes to its complete fruition. In the third volume of the *Asfār*, the idea of unity-in-multiplicity *(waḥda fīʾl-kathra)* is amended into the doctrine of multiplicity-in-unity *(kathra fīʾl-waḥda)*. In the twelfth chapter of the first *Mawqif* of the first *Fann* of the third *Safar*, Ṣadrā attempts to prove the proposition: "That which has a simple nature is all things *(basīṭ al-ḥaqīqa kull al-ashyāʾ)*," and his great commentator al-Sabzawārī remarks with perfect justice that the import of this proposition is not that the many are one but that the one is many.[36] After proving that the absolutely simple nature of God comprehends all positive being because nothing can be excluded from it—since otherwise it will cease to be simple—Ṣadrā proceeds to establish that God cannot be predicated of any other form of existence. The gist of his argument is that in the case of all concrete species—i.e., all species that *exist* as opposed to their definitions in terms of concepts—it is impossible to predicate the more general of the more specific although such predication is perfectly possible if the species are taken not as concrete existents but as definitional notions. Thus, it is perfectly possible to add the notion "sentient" to the notion "a body capable of growth," thus obtain the definition of animal, and then predicate "body capable of growth" of animal and say "animal is a body capable of growth." But if you take "body capable of growth" as a concretely existing species, i.e., plant, you cannot predicate "plant" of "animal." Hence, God, who is the most simple and absolute but also the most concrete of all existents, can neither be predicated of any other concrete existent, nor can any concrete existent be predicated of Him.[37]

The upshot of this argument is that whereas it is legitimate to say in general that God is everything, it is illegitimate to assert conversely that everything is God. In this developed statement of Ṣadrā's position, his doctrine that all existence comes from God, that the contingent suffers from an absolute poverty of existence in itself *(imkān* or *faqr dhātī)* and that the contingent's existence, therefore, consists in coming into an existential relationship with God, remains unchanged. But the idea that you can so abstract existence from the contingent that you may simply identify it with God's existence and consequently declare that nothing exists except God, is no longer there. You cannot abstract existence from the contingent because in the contingent, although its existence comes from God and is, therefore, in a sense God's existence, existence has come to possess a new mode, a new nature and cannot, therefore, be simply identified with God as existence. For every level of existence, although it is fundamentally the same, is nevertheless *sui generis* and existence can be attributed to it only as a systematically ambiguous term.

NOTES

[1] *Al-Asfār,* I, 1, p. 37, line 16 ff. All references here are to the (incomplete) Tehran edition of 1958.

[2] Aristotle: *Analytica Posteriora,* B, 89b33.

[3] *Al-Asfār,* I, 1, p. 47, last line ff.

[4] Al-Suhrawardī, *Ḥikmat al-Ishrāq* (Paris, 1952), pp. 64–67; the arguments are reproduced by Ṣadrā, *Al-Asfār,* I, 1, p. 39 ff.

[5] Ibid., p. 25 ff; see also Fazlur Rahman: *Selected Letters of Shaikh Aḥmad Sirhindī* (Karachi: Iqbal Academy, 1968), p. 12.

[6] This is the doctrine, which probably develops from al-Suhrawardī's thought on "modes" or "statuses" of existence *(Ẓurūf al-wujūd)*. Thus, the "external world" is a *mode* of existence *(Ẓarf al-wujūd al-khārijī)*; another *mode* of existence is that in the mind *(Ẓarf dhihnī)*; while a third mode is that of *nafs al-amr* or existence-in-itself of a reality—for example, that two and two are four is neither in "the external world" nor yet in "the mind" but is true "in itself." Yet it is the mind which *recognizes* these things to be in one mode or another.

[7] *Al-Asfār,* III, 1, p. 53, last line ff.

[8] Ibid., p. 54, line 6 ff.

[9] Ibid., p. 58, line 3–p. 60, line 18.

[10] Ibid., p. 63, line 15–p. 68, line 12.

[11] Ibid., p. 73, line 5 ff.

[12] *Al-Asfār* I, 1, pp. 35–36; III, 1, p. 18, line 6–p. 21, end.

[13] Ibid., I, 1, p. 46, lines 9–15.

[14] Ibid., III, 1, p. 19, line 10-p. 23, line 3.

[15] Rahman, *Selected Letters,* p. 15, last paragraph.

[16] *Al-Asfār,* I, 1, p. 63, line 15–p. 64, 12; pp. 68–69; p. 87.

[17] Passages referred to in the preceding note. It is, however, at the expense of existence that essences appear; the more the essence is manifest, the more existence recedes: ibid., p. 69, line 8 ff.

[18] Ibid., I, 1, p. 49, line 10 ff; only essences are known to their core, ibid., p. 37, line 16; ibid., p. 56, lines 3–10; ibid., p. 61, lines 1–6.

[19] Ibid., I, 1, p. 87, lines 11–12; for the doctrine of "movement-in-substance" see Fazlur Rahman: "The Eternity of the World and the Heavenly Bodies in Post-Avicennan Philosophy" in the present volume.

[20] See n. 3 above.

[21] *Al-Asfār,* I, 1, p. 84, line 11–p. 85, line 12.

[22] The idea that "essences in the external world are united or conjoined with existence," which recurs in Ṣadrā's discussion of the relationship of essence and existence, is intended to mean that essences have *no reality in the external world independently of existence* and does not mean that essences are *something which then gets united* with existence. See our comments in the following paragraph.

[23] *Al-Asfār,* I, 1, p. 86, lines 2–19.

[24] Ibid., p. 81, lines 1–2 (also p. 10, lines 2–8). The Arabic term "*al-Ruwāqīyūn*" which we have translated as "Neoplatonists" strictly means "Stoics" but it is obvious that (Muslim) Neoplatonists are meant here.

[25] Ibid., III, 1, p. 14, note 3 on the text. Ṣadrā's proof is in III, 1, pp. 12–18.

[26] Ibid., III, 1, p. 30 ff.

[27] Ibid., I, 1, p. 49, line 1 ff.

[28] Ibid., I, 1, Introduction by M. Riḍā Muẓaffar, section on Ṣadrā's intellectual career.

[29] Ibid., I, 1, p. 47, line 11.

[30] Ibid., I, 1, p. 46, line 15–p. 47, line 8.

[31] Ibid., I, 1, p. 67, lines 3–4.

[32] Ibid., I, 1, p. 71, lines 7–9.

[33] Ibid., I, 1, p. 80, lines 4–6.

[34] Ibid., I, 1, p. 108, lines 15 ff.

[35] Ibid., I, 1, p. 120, line 19–p. 121, line 1.

[36] Ibid., III, 1, p. 110 ff; al-Sabzawārī's comment no. 2 in the same page; al-Sabzawārī has explained Ṣadrā's position on the subject in detail in *al-Asfār,* I, 1, p. 71, n. 1.

[37] Ibid., III, 1, p. 115, line 1 ff.

BIBLIOGRAPHICAL NOTES ON THE NAQSHBANDI TARIQAT

Hamid Algar

The evolution of the Ṣūfī ṭarīqats in the past five centuries of the Islamic era is one of the most neglected aspects of the intellectual and spiritual history of Islam. There is a general recognition of their importance as organs of social cohesiveness and some awareness of their role, in the nineteenth century, in resistance to European encroachment on the Muslim lands. It is, however, commonly assumed that the establishment and expansion of the great orders—whether universal or regional—was synonymous with the "decay of Sufism," with intellectual sterility and narrowness of the spirit, and that the tariqats somehow participated in what is regarded as the overall decline of Muslim culture. There is a vast mass of evidence contradicting these assumptions, and despite the summary judgments of certain orientalists,[1] the major Ṣūfī orders continue even in the contemporary Islamic world to be limpid channels of spiritual grace sustaining the devotional life of the community.

For the intellectual development of the Muslim world between the sixteenth and nineteenth Christian centuries the Naqshbandī ṭarīqat possesses an importance second to that of no other order. In India, Central Asia and the Ottoman Empire, it was the ṭarīqat to which many of the ulama were drawn, since it realized in a distinctive and coherent manner the essential unity of ṭarīqat and sharīʿat. Numerous important figures in the latter-day development of Islamic thought were associated with the order: Maulānā ʿAbd ar-Raḥmān Jāmī (d. 1492), Shaykh Aḥmad Fārūq Sirhindī (d. 1625), and a whole line of prominent scholars descending from his branch of the Naqshbandi order in India, including Shāh Walīyullāh of Delhi (d. 1763), Shaykh ʿAbd al-Ghanī an-Nābulusī (d. 1730) in Syria, and many others. The ṭarīqat has been, moreover, with the single exception of the Qādirīya, the most widespread of all the Ṣūfī orders, with its range extending from Bosnia to Sumatra, from Cairo to Kansu, and it has thus functioned as a means of securing the unity of the umma in an era of increasing political fragmentation. This becomes especially clear during the ḥajj, when Naqshbandī shaykhs from all over the Islamic realm gather around the outward pivot of the faith, the Kaʿba.

The Naqshbandīya—in common with most of the ṭarīqats—has received little attention from western scholars. Apart from cursory and partially erroneous mention made in such general works as J. P. Brown's *The Darvishes* (new ed., London, 1968) and O. Depont and X. Coppolani's *Les Confrèries Religieuses Musulmanes* (Algiers, 1897), only a few articles have been devoted to the subject: V. A. Gordlevskiy's "Bakhauddin Nakshbend Bukharskii," in *Sergeyu Fedorovichu Ol'denburgu* (Leningrad, 1934), pp. 147–69 (reprinted in Gordlevskiy, *Izbrannye Sochineniya* (Moscow, 1962), III, 369–86); a bibliographical note by Franz Babinger, "Zur Frühgeschichte des Naqschbendi-Ordens," *Der Islam,* XIII (1923), 105–07; and a series of studies and texts published by the late Marijan Molé: "Quelques traités naqshbandis," *Farhang-i Irān Zamīn,* VI (1336 solar/1957), 273–323; "Autour du Daré Mansour: l'apprentissage mystique de Baha al-Din Naqshband," *Revue des Etudes Islamiques,* 1958, pp. 35–66; and "Tarjuma-yi Ṭālibīn va Iḍāḥ-i Sālikīn," *Farhang-i Irān Zamīn,* VIII (1339 solar/1960), 72–132. Finally, mention may be made of the article "Nakşbend" by Tahsin Yazici in *Islam Ansiklopedisi,* IX (1964), 52–54.

In the year 1969–70, with the aid of a grant from the Social Science Research Council, I was able to undertake research on the Naqshbandī order in the libraries of Europe and the Islamic world and to collect a large amount of material on different aspects of the life of the tariqat and various stages of its history. I offer below a select bibliography of mostly manuscript sources for certain significant periods in Naqshbandi history.

Prehistory and origins of the order in Transoxania: The initiatory chain of the tariqat reaching back, with a number of variations, to the Prophet, is given in diagrammatic form in Muḥammad b. Ḥusayn Qazvīnī's *Silsilanāma-yi Khwājagān-i Naqshband* (ms. Lâleli, 1381). Biographies of the links in the chain immediately preceding the eponymous founder of the order, Bahā' al-Dīn Naqshband (d. 1389), of the founder himself, and of his most prominent disciples are contained in the most important source for the early life of the order, Fakhr al-Dīn ʿAlī Ṣafī's *Rashaḥāt-i ʿAyn al-Ḥayāt.* The best printing of this work is that which appeared at Tashkent in 1329/1911. The primary source for the life and dicta of Bahā' al-Dīn is Muḥammad b. Salāḥ Bukhārī's *Anīs at-Ṭālibīn wa ʿUddat as-Sālikīn* (ms. Malik library, Tehran, 4252). A shorter recension of the work, drawn up by the author himself, contains some material not found in the fuller version (ms. Bodleian, Pers. E 37). There is also a work entitled *Maqāmāt-i Ḥaḍrat-i Naqshband* by one Abūl-Ḥasan Muḥammad Bāqir b. Muḥammad ʿAlī that was printed in Bukhara in 1327/1909. It appears to be one section of a fifteenth-century work entitled *Dar bayān-i maqāmāt va aḥvāl-i ṭabaqāt va khwājagān (sic)* (ms. India Office, Ethé 636), supplemented with material drawn from other sources by an anonymous hand. One disciple of Bahāʾ al-Dīn, Khwāja Muḥammad Pārsā (d. 822/1419), wrote a number of works, most important being *Tuhfat as-Sālikīn* (most recently published at Delhi in 1960 by Aḥmad

Shāh Hiravī), *Faṣl al-Khiṭāb* (ms. Nafiz Paşa, 431) and *Risāla-yi Qudsīya* (ms. Bibliothèque Nationale, supplément persan 968, ff. 6b–32b). The dicta of Khwāja Pārsā in exposition of the philosophy of Ibn ʿArabī were arranged by Maulānā ʿAbd ar-Raḥmān Jāmī into a treatise entitled *Sukhanān-i Khwāja Pārsā* (contained in *Kullīyāt* of Jāmī, ms. Bibliothèque Nationale, supplément persan 822, ff. 533b–543b, margin). The distinctive devotional practices of the early order are described in the *Risāla-yi Unsīya* of Maulānā Yaʿqūb Charkhī (ms. ʿArif Ḥikmat, Medina, taṣawwuf 3/14). After Bahāʾ al-Dīn the most important figure in the early life of the order was Khwāja ʿUbaidullāh Aḥrār (d. 845/1441), who established it as the dominant ṭarīqat in Transoxania, a position it was never to lose thenceforth. His life is described by Mīr ʿAbd al-Avval in *Majālis-i Aḥrār* (ms. India Office, D.P. 890); the anonymous *Maqāmāt-i ʿUbaidullāh Aḥrār* (ms. Majlis Library, Tehran, 1112), and Abū ʿAbdullāh Samarqandī's *Mukhtaṣar al-Vilāya* (ms. Esad Ef., 1702). Aḥrār's chief work was the *Faqarāt* (ms. India Office Ethé 1929). Finally, mention may be made of the brief biographical accounts of the early Naqshbandīs in Jāmī's *Nafaḥāt al-Uns*.

Some use has been made of this material by Fuat Köprülü in *Türk Edebiyatinda Ilk Mutasavviflar* (2nd. ed., Ankara, 1966) and Hasan Lutfi Şuşud in *Islam Tasavvufunda Hacegan Hanedanī* (Istanbul, 1958).

Origins of the Naqshbandī order in Turkey: The ṭarīqat was brought to the Ottoman Empire in the fifteenth century by Mollā Abdullāh Ilāhī of Simav (d. 896/1490), who travelled to Transoxania and returned to Anatolia as a *khalīfa* of ʿUbaidullāh Aḥrār. His life and work have been studied by kasim Kufrali in "Mollā Ilāhī ve kendisinden sonraki Nakşbendiye muhiti," *Türk Dili ve Edebiyati Dergisi*, III (1948), 129–51. He was a prolific writer; so far, only his *Dīvān*, consisting of poems in both Persian and Turkish, has been published (by Ismail Hikmet Ertaylan, Istanbul, 1960). Of his other works, the following may be mentioned: *Meslek at-Ṭālibīn* (ms. Topkapi Sarayi, hazine 305); *Esrārnāme* (ms. Haci Mahmud Ef., 2740); and *Ẓād el-Muştākīn* (ms. Ibrahim Ef., 420). His successor at the first Naqshbandī *tekke* in Istanbul was Emir Buhari, whose life is briefly described by Abdürrezzaq el-Eyyūbī in *Hediyet ül-Esdikā* (ms. Esad Ef., 3622). The only work of Emir Buhari discovered so far is a commentary in Turkish on some lines of Maulānā Jalāl ad-Dīn's *Masnavī* (ms. Istanbul University, türkçe yazmalari 2320).

Shaykh Aḥmad Fārūq Sirhindī and the Mujaddidīya: The life and achievements of Sirhindī, "regenerator of the second millennium," have received more attention than any other aspect of Naqshbandī history. Considering the magnitude of his achievement within the context of Indian Islam, this is not surprising; but the radiation of his influence, through the branch of the Naqshbandī order he instituted, into Sumatra, Transoxania, Anatolia, and the Arab lands has not yet been studied, and indeed has barely been even noticed. An analysis of Sirhindī's importance for Indian Islam is given by Aziz Ahmad in "The Naqshbandi Reaction," *Studies in Islamic Culture in the Indian Environment* (Oxford, 1964), pp. 182–90, and by Fazlur Rahman in his lengthy introduction to *Selected Letters of Shaikh Ahmad Sirhindi* (Karachi, 1968). Sirhindī's major work is the *Maktūbāt,* of which the most important editions are those published at Newal Kishore in 1332/1913 and Amritsar in 1352/1933, the latter containing a marginal commentary on the text. Complete translations exist in Arabic (by Muḥammad Murād al-Makkī) and Ottoman Turkish (by Sadeddin Efendi Mustakimzāde). A new edition of the Persian text and Arabic translation is now being prepared by Sönmez Neşriyatï of Istanbul. The primary source for the life of Sirhindī is Muḥammad Hāshim Badakhshānī's *Zubdat al-Maqāmāt* (Cawnpore, 1308/1890).

The further development of the Mujaddidīya in India is in itself a broad subject that cannot be covered bibliographically here. I will mention only the name of Mīrzā Maẓhar Jān-i Jānān (d. 1780), a poet of importance for the evolution of Urdu verse (see ᶜAbd ar-Razzāq Qurayshī, *Mīrzā Maẓhar Jān-i Jānān aur ūnka Urdū Kalām* [Bombay, 1961], and who also changed Naqshbandī attitudes to Hinduism from the radical hostility of Sirhindī to a sympathetic regard for Hindus as "people of the book." His major work is *Kalimāt-i Ṭayyibāt,* printed at Delhi in 1309/1891, and his life has been described by Naᶜīmullāh Bahrāʾichī in *Maᶜlūmāt-i Maẓharīya* (Cawnpore, 1275/1858).

The westward expansion of the Mujaddidīya: the Mujaddidīya was taken westwards by Muḥammad Murād Bukhārī (d. 1729), a disciple of one of Sirhindī's sons, Khwāja Muḥammad Maᶜṣūm. After travels in the Ḥijāz, Syria and Anatolia, he established a *tekke* in the Çarşamba district of Istanbul on the shore of the Golden Horn that became the fountainhead of the Mujaddidīya in Turkey. He composed three treatises on the practices of the order: *Silsilat adh-Dhahab,* in Arabic (ms. Veliyüddin Ef., 1807); and two unnamed treatises, one in Turkish (ms. Hacï Mahmud Ef., 206) and the other in Arabic (ms. Esad Ef., 1419). In addition he has a collection of letters written to his fellow shaykhs and his disciples: *Maktūbāt* (ms. Esad Ef., 1419). His life has been described by Muhammed Mekki Efendi in *Manakïb-ï Hazret-i Şeyh Muhammed Murad* (ms. Şeyh Murad Buhari, 256), and by Muḥammad Khalīl al-Murādī in *Silk ad-Durar fī Aᶜyān al-Qarn ath-Thānī-ᶜAshar* (Bulaq, 1301/1883), IV, 121–29.

Among the most important representatives of the Mujaddidīya in the Ottoman Empire was Shaykh ᶜAbd al-Ghanī an-Nābulusī, who expounded the principles of the order in *Miftāḥ al-Maᶜīya fi ṭ-Ṭarīqat an-Naqshabandīya* (ms. Fatih, 2857).

Maulānā Khālid Baghdādī and the Khālidīya: There arose in the early nineteenth century a powerful branch of the Naqshbandī order which has become the predominant form of the tariqat in Turkey, the Arab lands, Iranian Kurdistan and the Northern Caucasus. It was founded by a shaykh of Kurdish origin, Maulānā Khālid (d. 1826), generally known as Baghdādī despite his birth near Sulaymānīya. His initiation into the Naqshbandī order took place at the hands of a celebrated Mujaddidī shaykh, Ghulām ᶜAlī Dihlavī (concerning whom see Shāh Raʾūf Aḥmad, *Durr al-Maᶜārif* [Delhi, n.d.]. From India he returned to Sulaymāniya but was obliged to leave first for Baghdad and then for Istanbul. He finally settled in Damascus and was buried in Ṣāliḥīya, in the proximity of Ibn ᶜArabī. His eventful and turbulent life is recounted by Ibrāhīm Faṣīḥ Efendi Ḥaydarīzādā in *al-Majd at-Tālid fi Manāqib Maulānā Khālid* (Istanbul, 1316/1898); Muḥammad Amīn b. Muḥammad Asᶜad al-ᶜAyntābī, *Adhwāq al-Khālidī wa Aṭwār an-Naqshabandī* (ms. Hacï Hüsnü Pasa, 778); and ᶜAbd al-Majīd al-Khānī, *al-Ḥadāʾiq al-Wardīya fi Ḥaqāʾiq an-Naqshabandīya* (Cairo, 1306/1889). His chief works are a collection of poetry in Arabic, Persian, and Gorani Kurdish *(Dīwān* [Būlāq, 1260/1844]; a treatise concerning the spiritual link—*rābiṭa*—between shaykh and aspirant in the Naqshbandī ṭarīqat *(Risālat ar-Rābiṭa,* Preussische Staatsbibliothek, ms. or. oct. 2762); and a collection of letters to his followers (Istanbul University, arapça yazmalarï 728). The life and work of Maulānā Khālid now form the subject of a dissertation being prepared at Tehran University by Maẓhar Naqshbandī, brother of a Naqshbandi shaykh from Kurdistan.

The Khālidī branch of the order has distinguished itself by great militancy and enthusiasm in defense of the sharīᶜa. It opposed, and continues to oppose, the secular order in Republican Turkey; and the Daghistānī offshoot of the Khālidīya, under the leadership of the celebrated Imam Shamyl (d. 1870), met the Russian invasion of Daghistān in the mid-nineteenth century with fierce and prolonged resistance. A considerable historiography has grown up around Imam Shamyl, but the only work that at all concerns itself with the Naqshbandī-Khālidī roots of his movement is N. A. Smirnov's *Myuridizm na Kavkaze* (Moscow, 1963).

Other nineteenth-century Naqshbandīs in Turkey: In addition to the rise of the Khālidīya, nineteenth-century Turkey also witnessed a continued flourishing of other branches of the order. Particular mention may be made of Şeyh Mehmed Nuri Şemsettin (d. 1866), shaykh at the Yahya Efendi *tekke* in Beşiktaş, whose *Miftāh ül-Kulūb* is one of the most widely read Sūfī works in present-day Turkey (most recent edition, Istanbul, 1969). His life is described in Mehmed Emin, *Zübdet el-Usul* (ms. Hacï Mahmud, 3202). Also deserving of attention in this period is Erzurumlu Ibrahim Hakkï (d. 1808), author of a vast compendium of religious and worldly knowledge entitled *Marifetnāme* (Istanbul, 1330/1912; reprinted 1970).

The foregoing is merely a selection of sources for certain periods of Naqshbandī history. I am now engaged in a comprehensive study of all aspects of the order, including its distinctive devotional practices and present status throughout the Islamic world. As a first step to the realization of this ambitious project, I am preparing a series of papers on the following subjects, using the sources listed above as well as many others:

1. Some notes on the Naqshbandī ṭarīqat in Bosnia, *Die Welt des Islams,* xiii (1972), 168–203.
2. The *dicta* of Khwāja ᶜAbd al-Khāliq Ghijduvanī on the foundations of the Naqshbandī path.
3. *Khatm-i Khwājagān:* a Naqshbandī litany.
4. *Dhikr-i Khafī:* the silent invocation of the Divine Name in the Naqshbandī order.
5. *Rābiṭa:* the spiritual link between aspirant and shaykh in the Naqshbandī order.
6. The Bakrī *isnād* of the Naqshbandī order: its historical and spiritual implications.
7. The Naqshbandī affiliations of Maulānā ᶜAbd ar-Raḥmān Jāmī.
8. Mollā Abdullāh Ilāhī and the introduction of the Naqshbandī order into the Ottoman Empire.
9. Shaykh Muḥammad Murād Bukhārī: an eighteenth-century Naqshbandī mystic.
10. Maulānā Khālid of Baghdad and the regeneration of the Naqshbandī order in the early nineteenth century.

NOTE

[1] See, for example, G.-C. Anawati and Louis Gardet, *Mystique Musulmane,* 2nd ed. (Paris, 1968), p. 73.

APPENDIX I: ISLAMIC THINKERS

The following is a brief list of the principal philosophers, scientists, and theologians referred to in the articles, in chronological order. Names of contributors, in whose articles each thinker is primarily dealt with, are added in parentheses. Names of thinkers are not given in full, but sufficiently for the purpose of identification.

MĀSHĀʾALLĀH (Latin Messahala). Astronomer and astrologer. ca.A.D. 740–815. Jewish. ʿIraq. (Pingree)

KINDĪ, Abū Yūsuf Yaʿqūb b.Isḥāq. Scientist and philosopher. d.ca. 870. Arab. ʿIraq. (Ivry)

RĀZĪ, Abū Bakr Muḥammad b.Zakariyyāʾ (Latin Rhazes). Physician and philosopher. 865–ca. 925. Persian. Iran. (Goodman, Iskandar)

FĀRĀBĪ, Abū Naṣr (Latin Alfarabius). Musicologist and philosopher. 870–950. Turkish. Turkestan, ʿIraq and Syria. (Mahdi)

IBN SĪNĀ, Abū ʿAlī (Latin Avicenna). Scientist, physician, and philosopher. 980–1037. Persian. Turkestan and Iran. (Madkour; Marmura, 1; Morewedge; Rahman, 1 and 2)

GHAZĀLĪ, Abū Ḥāmid (Latin Algazel). Theologian and mystic. 1058–1111. Persian. Iran and ʿIraq. (Marmura, 2. Rahman, 1)

ABU L-BARAKĀT al-Baghdādī. Philosopher. ca.1077–1165. Jewish, converted to Islam. ʿIraq. (Rahman, 1)

SUHRAWARDĪ, Shihāb ad-Dīn Yaḥyā, al-maqtūl ash-shahīd. Mystical philosopher. 1155–91. Persian. Iran and Syria. (Gardet; Rahman, 1 and 2)

IBN RUSHD, Abu l-Walīd (Latin Averroes). Jurist, scientist, physician, and philosopher. 1126–98. Arab Andalusia. (Butterworth)

RĀZĪ, Fahkr ad-Dīn. Theologian and commentator on Ibn Sīnā. 1149–1209. Persian. Iran and Turkestan. (Goodman)

ṬŪSĪ, Naṣīr ad-Dīn. Astronomer and philosopher. 1201–74. Persian. Iran and ʿIraq. (Morewedge)

SHIRWĀNĪ. Logician. ca.15th century. Persian. (Rescher and Nat)

MULLĀ ṢADRĀ, Ṣadr ad-Dīn Shīrāzī. Philosopher and theologian. 1571–1640. Persian. Iran. (Rahman 1 and 2)

NAQSHBANDĪ TARĪQA. Ṣūfī order. Founded by Bahāʾ ad-Dīn Naqshband (d.1389) in Bukhārā. Spread especially in Turkestan, India and the Ottoman empire. (Algar)

APPENDIX II: ARABIC GLOSSARY

Words listed are those which appear without a translation in any of the articles. Book titles are not included. The order is Latin alphabetical, ignoring the sign ᶜ for Arabic ᶜ*ayn*.

ᶜ*ajam*, foreigners, contrasted with Arabs
ᶜ*aql*, intellect
aṣl, pl.*uṣūl*, root; principle of a science
falsafa, philosophy
fanāʾ, passing away; obliteration of normal consciousness through absorption in thought of God
farᶜ, pl.*furūᶜ*, branch; detail of a science, contrasted with a principle
faylasūf, pl.*falāsifa*, philosopher
fiqh, Islamic law as a science
ḥadīth, conversation; oral and written Traditions of Islam
ḥakīm, wise man; scientist, philosopher
ḥikma, wisdom; science, philosophy
ᶜ*ilm*, pl.ᶜ*ulūm*, science, knowledge
ᶜ*irfānī*, gnostic
ishrāqī, illuminationist
istidlāl, proof by induction
kalām, Islamic theology
kitāb, book
mamlaka(t), kingdom, realm
mashshāᶜī, Peripatetic
mawjūd, existent
naẓar, vision; theoretical study
risāla, treatise
tafsīr, commentary
ṭarīqa, (*tariqat*), way; Ṣūfī order
ᶜ*ulūm*, see ᶜ*ilm*
umma, nation; community of Islam
uṣūl, see *aṣl*
wujūd, existence